GREAT TEACHERS

GREAT TEACHERS

How to Raise Student Learning in Latin America and the Caribbean

Barbara Bruns and Javier Luque

with

Soledad De Gregorio
David Evans
Marco Fernández
Martin Moreno
Jessica Rodriguez
Guillermo Toral
Noah Yarrow

© 2015 International Bank for Reconstruction and Development / The World Bank
1818 H Street NW, Washington DC 20433
Telephone: 202-473-1000; Internet: www.worldbank.org

Some rights reserved

This work is a product of the staff of The World Bank with external contributions. The findings, interpretations, and conclusions expressed in this work do not necessarily reflect the views of The World Bank, its Board of Executive Directors, or the governments they represent. The World Bank does not guarantee the accuracy of the data included in this work. The boundaries, colors, denominations, and other information shown on any map in this work do not imply any judgment on the part of The World Bank concerning the legal status of any territory or the endorsement or acceptance of such boundaries.

Nothing herein shall constitute or be considered to be a limitation upon or waiver of the privileges and immunities of The World Bank, all of which are specifically reserved.

RIGHTS AND PERMISSIONS

This work is available under the Creative Commons Attribution 3.0 IGO license (CC BY 3.0 IGO) http://creativecommons.org/licenses/by/3.0/igo. Under the Creative Commons Attribution license, you are free to copy, distribute, transmit, and adapt this work, including for commercial purposes, under the following conditions:

- **Attribution**—Please cite the work as follows: Bruns, Barbara, and Javier Luque. 2015. *Great Teachers: How to Raise Student Learning in Latin America and the Caribbean.* doi:10.1596/978-1-4648-0151-8. Washington, DC: World Bank. License: Creative Commons Attribution CC BY 3.0 IGO

- **Translations**—If you create a translation of this work, please add the following disclaimer along with the attribution: *This translation was not created by The World Bank and should not be considered an official World Bank translation. The World Bank shall not be liable for any content or error in this translation.*

- **Adaptations**—If you create an adaptation of this work, please add the following disclaimer along with the attribution: *This is an adaptation of an original work by The World Bank. Views and opinions expressed in the adaptation are the sole responsibility of the author or authors of the adaptation and are not endorsed by The World Bank.*

- **Third-party content**—The World Bank does not necessarily own each component of the content contained within the work. The World Bank therefore does not warrant that the use of any third-party-owned individual component or part contained in the work will not infringe on the rights of those third parties. The risk of claims resulting from such infringement rests solely with you. If you wish to re-use a component of the work, it is your responsibility to determine whether permission is needed for that re-use and to obtain permission from the copyright owner. Examples of components can include, but are not limited to, tables, figures, or images.

All queries on rights and licenses should be addressed to the Publishing and Knowledge Division, The World Bank, 1818 H Street NW, Washington, DC 20433, USA; fax: 202-522-2625; e-mail: pubrights@worldbank.org.

ISBN (paper): 978-1-4648-0151-8
ISBN (electronic): 978-1-4648-0152-5
DOI: 10.1596/978-1-4648-0151-8

Cover photo: Teacher at Escola de Amanha Thomas Jefferson, Rio de Janeiro, Brazil. © Barbara Bruns / World Bank. Used with permission. Further permission required for reuse.

Cover design: Vladimir Herrera / iGraphi.

Library of Congress Cataloging-in-Publication Data has been requested.

Latin American Development Forum Series

This series was created in 2003 to promote debate, disseminate information and analysis, and convey the excitement and complexity of the most topical issues in economic and social development in Latin America and the Caribbean. It is sponsored by the Inter-American Development Bank, the United Nations Economic Commission for Latin America and the Caribbean, and the World Bank, and represents the highest quality in each institution's research and activity output. Titles in the series have been selected for their relevance to the academic community, policy makers, researchers, and interested readers, and have been subjected to rigorous anonymous peer review prior to publication.

Advisory Committee Members

Alicia Bárcena Ibarra, Executive Secretary, Economic Commission for Latin America and the Caribbean, United Nations

Inés Bustillo, Director, Washington Office, Economic Commission for Latin America and the Caribbean, United Nations

Augusto de la Torre, Chief Economist, Latin America and the Caribbean Region, World Bank

Daniel Lederman, Deputy Chief Economist, Latin America and the Caribbean Region, World Bank

Santiago Levy, Vice President for Sectors and Knowledge, Inter-American Development Bank

Roberto Rigobon, President, Latin American and Caribbean Economic Association

José Juan Ruiz, Chief Economist and Manager of the Research Department, Inter-American Development Bank

Ernesto Talvi, Director, Brookings Global-CERES Economic and Social Policy in Latin America Initiative

Andrés Velasco, Cieplan, Chile

Titles in the Latin American Development Forum Series

Great Teachers: How to Raise Student Learning in Latin America and the Caribbean (2014) by Barbara Bruns and Javier Luque

Entrepreneurship in Latin America: A Step Up the Social Ladder? (2013) by Eduardo Lora and Francesca Castellani, editors

Emerging Issues in Financial Development: Lessons from Latin America (2013) by Tatiana Didier and Sergio L. Schmukler, editors

New Century, Old Disparities: Gaps in Ethnic and Gender Earnings in Latin America and the Caribbean (2012) by Hugo Ñopo

Does What You Export Matter? In Search of Empirical Guidance for Industrial Policies (2012) by Daniel Lederman and William F. Maloney

From Right to Reality: Incentives, Labor Markets, and the Challenge of Achieving Universal Social Protection in Latin America and the Caribbean (2012) by Helena Ribe, David Robalino, and Ian Walker

Breeding Latin American Tigers: Operational Principles for Rehabilitating Industrial Policies (2011) by Robert Devlin and Graciela Moguillansky

New Policies for Mandatory Defined Contribution Pensions: Industrial Organization Models and Investment Products (2010) by Gregorio Impavido, Esperanza Lasagabaster, and Manuel García-Huitrón

The Quality of Life in Latin American Cities: Markets and Perception (2010) by Eduardo Lora, Andrew Powell, Bernard M. S. van Praag, and Pablo Sanguinetti, editors

Discrimination in Latin America: An Economic Perspective (2010) by Hugo Ñopo, Alberto Chong, and Andrea Moro, editors

The Promise of Early Childhood Development in Latin America and the Caribbean (2010) by Emiliana Vegas and Lucrecia Santibáñez

Job Creation in Latin America and the Caribbean: Trends and Policy Challenges (2009) by Carmen Pagés, Gaëlle Pierre, and Stefano Scarpetta

China's and India's Challenge to Latin America: Opportunity or Threat? (2009) by Daniel Lederman, Marcelo Olarreaga, and Guillermo E. Perry, editors

Does the Investment Climate Matter? Microeconomic Foundations of Growth in Latin America (2009) by Pablo Fajnzylber, José Luis Guasch, and J. Humberto López, editors

Measuring Inequality of Opportunities in Latin America and the Caribbean (2009) by Ricardo de Paes Barros, Francisco H. G. Ferreira, José R. Molinas Vega, and Jaime Saavedra Chanduvi

The Impact of Private Sector Participation in Infrastructure: Lights, Shadows, and the Road Ahead (2008) by Luis Andres, Jose Luis Guasch, Thomas Haven, and Vivien Foster

Remittances and Development: Lessons from Latin America (2008) by Pablo Fajnzylber and J. Humberto López, editors

Fiscal Policy, Stabilization, and Growth: Prudence or Abstinence? (2007) by Guillermo Perry, Luis Servén, and Rodrigo Suescún, editors

Raising Student Learning in Latin America: Challenges for the 21st Century (2007) by Emiliana Vegas and Jenny Petrow

Investor Protection and Corporate Governance: Firm-level Evidence Across Latin America (2007) by Alberto Chong and Florencio López-de-Silanes, editors

Natural Resources: Neither Curse nor Destiny (2007) by Daniel Lederman and William F. Maloney, editors

The State of State Reform in Latin America (2006) by Eduardo Lora, editor

Emerging Capital Markets and Globalization: The Latin American Experience (2006) by Augusto de la Torre and Sergio L. Schmukler

Beyond Survival: Protecting Households from Health Shocks in Latin America (2006) by Cristian C. Baeza and Truman G. Packard

Beyond Reforms: Structural Dynamics and Macroeconomic Vulnerability (2005) by José Antonio Ocampo, editor

Privatization in Latin America: Myths and Reality (2005) by Alberto Chong and Florencio López-de-Silanes, editors

Keeping the Promise of Social Security in Latin America (2004) by Indermit S. Gill, Truman G. Packard, and Juan Yermo

Lessons from NAFTA: For Latin America and the Caribbean (2004) by Daniel Lederman, William F. Maloney, and Luis Servén

The Limits of Stabilization: Infrastructure, Public Deficits, and Growth in Latin America (2003) by William Easterly and Luis Servén, editors

Globalization and Development: A Latin American and Caribbean Perspective (2003) by José Antonio Ocampo and Juan Martin, editors

Is Geography Destiny? Lessons from Latin America (2003) by John Luke Gallup, Alejandro Gaviria, and Eduardo Lora

Contents

Foreword xvii
Acknowledgments xix
About the Authors and Contributors xxi
Abbreviations xxiii

Overview 1
    Why teachers matter 3
    LAC's teachers inside the classroom 11
    Recruiting better teachers 23
    Grooming great teachers 34
    Motivating teachers to perform 40
    Managing the politics of teacher reform 47
    Note 51
    References 51

Chapter 1: How Good Are Teachers in the Region? 55
    How are LAC education systems performing? 55
    What drives student learning? 66
    What makes teachers effective? 72
    Who are LAC's teachers? 74
    Conclusions 91
    Notes 92
    References 93

Chapter 2: Inside the Classroom in Latin America and the Caribbean 97
    LAC classroom observation sample 99
    Observation method and instrument 100

What are we learning from classroom observations in LAC?   105
Conclusions   132
Notes   136
References   136

Chapter 3: Recruiting Better Teachers   139

Raising the selectivity of teacher education   144
Raising the quality of teacher education   151
Raising hiring standards   156
Recruiting better teachers over the next decade   167
Conclusions   174
Notes   176
References   176

Chapter 4: Grooming Great Teachers   179

Teacher induction and probationary periods   179
Teacher evaluation   182
In-service training   196
Grooming teachers through school leadership   208
Challenge and promise of information technology   211
Conclusions   215
Notes   218
References   218

Chapter 5: Motivating Teachers to Perform   223

What motivates teachers?   224
Professional rewards   225
Accountability pressure   230
Financial incentives   237
Conclusions   276
Notes   282
References   283

Chapter 6: Managing the Politics of Teacher Reform   287

Education policies through the lens of teachers' interests   288
Sources of union power   297
Political dynamics of education reform: Four recent cases   307

Conclusions   323
Notes   326
References   328

Index   331

Boxes

1.1	Math and reading skills as measured on PISA	62
2.1	How the Stallings Classroom Snapshot works	101
2.2	Explaining learning improvements in Mexico, D.F.	109
2.3	Innovations in system monitoring: Digitized Stallings observations	133
3.1	How top education systems attract talented teachers	143
3.2	Pupil-teacher ratio and average class size	171
4.1	Raising teacher quality through rigorous induction in Rio de Janeiro	183
4.2	Measuring teacher quality with classroom observation instruments	185
4.3	Teacher evaluation in Singapore	192
4.4	Raising quality through teacher evaluation in Washington, DC	197
4.5	Colombia's Escuela Nueva	206
4.6	Rio de Janeiro's Educopedia	214
5.1	Fair comparisons of school performance: The design of Chile's Sistema Nacional de Evaluación del Desempeño (SNED)	272

Figures

O.1	Cognitive skills and long-term economic growth across regions, 1960–2000	4
O.2	PISA reading scores and income per capita for LAC countries, 2012	5
O.3	Comparative PISA math improvement, 2000–12	6
O.4	Comparative PISA math performance of prospective teachers and prospective engineers	8
O.5	Comparative math content knowledge of future math teachers, 2008	9
O.6	Average salaries for teachers relative to other professional workers, 2000 and 2010	10
O.7	Average time on instruction in LAC countries	13
O.8	Breakdown of teacher time off-task, by country	14
O.9	Teacher time off-task and student learning in LAC	16
O.10	Teacher time on instruction with the entire class engaged	17
O.11	Distribution of schools by average time spent on instruction	18
O.12	Range in teacher time on instruction within schools	20

O.13	Colombia and Honduras variation in instructional time within schools, 2011	22
O.14	Tertiary graduates who studied education	24
O.15	Raising the bar for teacher education programs in Peru, 2006–10	26
O.16	Impact of accreditation information on teacher education enrollments in Chile, 2007–10	27
O.17	Compulsory pre-service teaching practice in LAC countries	28
O.18	Chile's framework for good teaching	29
O.19	Teacher exit exam pass rate in El Salvador, 2001–12	30
O.20	Change in stock of teachers needed, assuming expanded coverage and efficient pupil-teacher ratios, 2010–25	33
O.21	Three broad classes of incentives motivate teachers	41
1.1	Increase in secondary school attainment in LAC, 1950–2010	56
1.2	Secondary enrollment growth relative to population growth, 1960–2010	57
1.3	Cognitive skills and economic growth across regions	58
1.4	Cognitive skills and growth across countries	59
1.5	PISA reading scores and income per capita for LAC countries, 2012	60
1.6	Comparative LAC region performance on 2012 PISA math test	61
1.7	Comparative learning achievement in Latin America	64
1.8	Comparative PISA math improvement, 2000–12	65
1.9	Impact on student test scores of a change of teacher	70
1.10	Long-term economic benefits of exposure to an effective teacher	71
1.11	Comparative PISA math performance of prospective teachers and engineers	75
1.12	University of São Paulo entrance exam scores, by field of study, 2004–09	76
1.13	Socioeconomic background of university students in Peru, by discipline, 2000	77
1.14	Teacher performance on sixth-grade reading and math in Peru	78
1.15	Math content knowledge of future secondary school teachers, 2008	79
1.16	Math pedagogy knowledge of future secondary school teachers, 2008	79
1.17	Math content knowledge of future primary school teachers, 2008	80
1.18	Math pedagogy knowledge of future primary school teachers, 2008	80
1.19	Long-term decline in returns to university-level teacher education in Sweden, 1968–2003	81
1.20	Teacher-wage distribution in Sweden compared with nonteachers, 2004	81
1.21	Career salary trajectories for teaching and alternative professions in Sweden, 2004	82
1.22	Evolution of teacher salaries in Peru, 1960–2010	83
1.23	Chance of being employed, by age, for teacher graduates compared with other graduates in LAC	84

1.24	LAC teacher salaries in relation to GDP per capita, circa 2010	85
1.25	Average salary for teachers relative to other professional workers, adjusted for hours worked, circa 2000 and 2010	86
1.26	Average monthly salary for teachers relative to other professional workers, 2000 and 2010	87
1.27	Wage-experience profiles for teachers and other professional workers in Peru, 2010	89
1.28	Wage distribution for teachers compared with other professional occupations in Panama, 2009	90
1.29	Wage distribution for teachers compared with other professions in Chile, 2000 and 2009	91
1.30	Wage distribution for teachers compared with other professions in Costa Rica, 2001 and 2009	92
2.1	Education results chain and reduced form education production function	98
B2.1.1	Excerpt from Stallings Classroom Snapshot coding grid: Time use, materials use, and level of student engagement	103
2.2	Average time on instruction in LAC countries	107
2.3	Breakdown of teacher time off-task, by country	109
2.4	Instructional time and student learning across LAC countries	113
2.5	Instructional time with high student engagement and student learning outcomes in LAC	115
2.6	Core pedagogical practices across LAC countries	116
2.7	Teacher time off-task and student learning in LAC countries	117
2.8	Teachers' use of learning materials	118
2.9	Teachers' use of ICT in Pernambuco and Rio de Janeiro, 2010–11	119
2.10	Share of total class time with students not engaged	120
2.11	Teacher time on instruction with the entire class engaged	121
2.12	Distribution of schools by average time spent on instruction	123
2.13	Average instructional time in different provinces of Honduras, 2011	124
2.14	Classroom dynamics with the introduction of bonus pay in Pernambuco, Brazil	125
2.15	Range in teacher time on instruction within schools	128
2.16	Variance in instructional time within schools in Colombia and Honduras, 2011	131
B2.3.1	Snapshot of instant results	134
3.1	Key steps in the recruitment of high-quality teachers	140
3.2	Teacher recruitment in Singapore	141
3.3	Percentage of tertiary graduates who studied education	142
3.4	Share of recent teacher graduates employed in teaching	142

3.5	Students admitted into teacher education programs in Peru, 2006–10	146
3.6	Students enrolled in ISPs in Peru, 1981–2012	146
3.7	Number of teacher training programs by accreditation status in Chile, 2013	150
3.8	Enrollment in teacher education programs by accreditation status in Chile, 2007–10	151
3.9	Rise in formal education of primary school teachers in Brazil, 1995–2010	152
3.10	Compulsory pre-service teaching practice, in a selection of Latin America and the Caribbean countries	154
3.11	Chile's framework for good teaching	157
3.12	Pass rate of teacher college exit exam in El Salvador, 2001–12	160
3.13	Teacher graduates' performance on Prueba Inicia exit exam in Chile, 2011	161
3.14	Elimination of temporary license teachers in New York City, 2000–05	163
3.15	Failure rate on LAST certification exam for new teachers in New York City, by poverty quartile of school's students, 2000–05	163
3.16	Projected change in the stock of teachers needed in LAC, 2010–25	168
3.17	Change in stock of teachers needed, assuming expanded coverage and efficient pupil-teacher ratios, 2010–25	172
4.1	Performance levels in Chile's teacher evaluation system	188
4.2	Sample performance benchmarks in Chile's teacher evaluation system	189
4.3	Change in teacher evaluation ratings in Chile, 2005–12	190
B4.3.1	Singapore's three professional tracks in education	192
4.4	Consequences of teacher evaluations in Chile	193
4.5	Test scores for students exposed to outstanding or competent teachers in Chile, 2004–08	196
B4.4.1	Change in Washington, DC's teacher quality since introduction of teacher evaluation	199
5.1	Three broad classes of incentives motivate teachers	224
5.2	Teacher absence rates in Chicago public schools after change in probation policy, 2004–08	232
B5.1.1	Construction of homogenous school groupings in Chile's SNED	272
6.1	Total public spending on education as percentage of GDP in selected Latin America and the Caribbean countries, 1990–2010	295

Tables

O.1	Use of class time in Rio de Janeiro schools, fifth grade, 2010	14
1.1	Average educational attainment of the adult population, 1950–2010	57
1.2	Share of students scoring at the top and bottom on PISA mathematics, 2012	63
1.3	Impact of teachers' relative effectiveness on student test scores	68

1.4	Average difference in third-grade math scores across different classrooms in the same school	69
2.1	LAC classroom observation sample	100
B2.1.1	Activities captured in Stallings Classroom Snapshot	102
2.2	Stallings good practice benchmarks for instructional time use	106
B2.2.1	Classroom dynamics and student learning outcomes at the classroom level, Mexico, D.F., 2011	110
B2.2.2	Classroom dynamics and other factors that explain student learning outcomes, Mexico, D.F., 2011	111
2.3	Instructional time use in Rio de Janeiro schools, fifth grade, 2010	112
2.4	Within-school and across-school variation in average teacher time on instruction	127
3.1	Level and length of pre-service training in Latin America and the Caribbean countries	153
3.2	Post-training tests for teachers	158
3.3	Projected change in the stock of teachers needed from 2010 to 2025, because of demographic trends, assuming constant enrollment ratios and pupil-teacher ratios	169
3.4	Potential changes in teacher salaries possible with efficient pupil-teacher ratios, 2025	173
4.1	Induction programs for new OECS teachers	180
4.2	Roles of teacher evaluation	184
4.3	Rigorous evaluation evidence on the impact of teacher training	201
5.1	Career path reforms	240
5.2	Financial rewards under Chile's AVDI program, 2013	254
5.3	Teacher results under Chile's AVDI program, 2013	255
5.4	Bonus pay	260
B5.1.1	Six components of the SNED index and their respective weights	273
6.1	Characteristics of teachers' unions in Latin America and the Caribbean	298

Foreword

Over much of the past decade, countries in Latin America and the Caribbean saw unprecedented social progress. Almost 80 million people have been lifted out of poverty, more than 50 million have entered the ranks of the middle class, primary school coverage has become almost universal, and average years of schooling has been converging towards that of countries in the Organisation for Economic Co-operation and Development (OECD). While the region has benefitted from progressive social assistance policies such as conditional cash transfers, the principal driver of rising incomes has been economic growth, translating into poverty reduction and, more broadly, shared prosperity.

But the economic slowdown of the last few years has cast doubts on the sustainability of the prior decade's progress and revived old fears of low growth. The current deceleration in Latin America and the Caribbean (LAC) is arguably linked to external factors, including slower growth in China and its effects on export prices, as well as an expected increase in global interest rates. However, the solution cannot be to wait for the external environment to shift. The region must develop its own strategies for more diversified production, higher-value exports, and sustainable long-term growth.

Building human capital, the key ingredient for higher productivity and faster innovation, is thus a central challenge for the region. While education coverage in LAC has expanded rapidly, it is student learning—not years of schooling completed—that produces most of the economic benefits from investments in education. The troubling fact in this respect is that students in LAC remain more than two years behind their OECD counterparts in math, reading and critical thinking skills—and even further behind East Asian countries, including Vietnam.

But the positive message of this book is that countries across the LAC region are confronting this challenge and putting education quality at the center of the political agenda. With elegant simplicity, this book argues that the quality of education is conditioned by the quality of our teachers. It calls for a new focus on recruiting the most talented young people into teaching, raising the effectiveness of teachers already in service, and providing incentives that can motivate teachers to deliver their best effort in every classroom, every day, to every child.

Great Teachers: How to Raise Student Learning in Latin America and the Caribbean is the latest title in our Latin American Development Forum series, which since 2003 has brought research depth to the region's most pressing economic and social issues. In preparation for this study, the team built the largest globally comparable database on teacher practice in the classroom ever assembled, with observations of more than 15,000 different teachers in seven different LAC countries. The eye-opening results are an example of the World Bank Group putting innovative research at the service of development policy. More broadly, *Great Teachers* distills the latest evaluation evidence and practical experience with teacher policy reforms from both within and outside the region. It offers policy makers in Latin America and the Caribbean an invaluable support in achieving the faster education progress its next generation of students deserves.

Jorge Familiar
Vice President
Latin America and the Caribbean Region
The World Bank

Claudia Costin
Senior Global Practice Director for Education
The World Bank

Hasan Tuluy
Vice President (former)
Latin America and the Caribbean Region
The World Bank

Augusto de la Torre
Chief Economist
Latin America and the Caribbean Region
The World Bank

Acknowledgments

This study, part of the Latin America and the Caribbean Regional Studies program of the World Bank, is the work of a team managed by Barbara Bruns and Javier Luque. The study originated in a suggestion from Chingboon Lee that the wave of innovative teacher policy reforms sweeping across Latin America and the Caribbean in the first decade of the 2000s deserved to be researched and the findings shared with policy makers in other regions. Our ability to pursue this work through rigorous impact evaluations of innovative programs, beginning in Brazil, was thanks to Makhtar Diop's conviction that true knowledge generation was worth the time and money required to sustain such research. With additional generous support from the Netherlands Government through the Bank-Netherlands Partnership Program and the Spanish government through the Spanish Impact Evaluation Fund and Spanish Fund for Latin America and the Caribbean, our team began evaluating bonus pay and other programs aimed at rewarding teacher quality and looking into classrooms to understand whether and how incentives change teachers' practice. We owe a deep debt to Professor Jane Stallings for sharing the classroom observation instrument she developed and for guiding and encouraging our work.

This work is dedicated to the education leaders who were willing to partner with us in classroom observation research, despite initial resistance from schools and teachers and no guarantee that the findings would be useful. In Brazil, these include Maria Helena Castro in São Paulo; Danilo Cabral, Nilton Mota, and Margarethe Zaponi in Pernambuco; Vanessa Guimarães and Ana Lúcia Almieida Gazzola in Minas Gerais; Claudia Costin and Helena Bomeny in Rio municipality; Wilson Risolia in Rio state; and Mauricio Holanda and Maria Isolde Coelho in Ceara. We are equally grateful to Maria Fernanda Campo Saavedra and Humberto Diez Villela in Colombia; Andrew Holnes and Ronald Thwaites in Jamaica; Marlon Escoto in Honduras; German Cervantes in Mexico's D.F.; Josefina Pimental and Carlos Amarante Beret in the Dominican Republic; and Jaime Saavedra and Patricia Salas in Peru.

We also thank the many World Bank colleagues and other experts who have contributed ideas and guidance. Jorge Familiar, Hasan Tuluy, Augusto de la Torre, Keith Hansen, Daniel Lederman, Frederico Ferreira, Tito Cordella, Reema Nayar, Elizabeth King, Harry Patrinos, and Claudia Costin were champions of this work at every stage. Emiliana Vegas, Lucrecia Santibáñez, Halsey Rogers, Luis Benveniste, Miguel Székely, Jere Behrman, Norbert Schady, Rick Hanushek, Margaret Raymond, Jane Hannaway, Tom Kane, Felipe Barrera-Osorio, Fernando Reimers, Doug Lemov, Vicky Colbert, Claudio de Moura Castro, Cesar Callegari, Guiomar Namo de Mello, Rose Neubauer, Patrick McEwan, Alejandro Ganimian, Viviane Senna, Denis Mizne, Simon Schwartzman, Paula Louzano, Tomas Recart, Santiago Cueto, Guillermo Perry, José Joaquín Brunner, Violeta Arancibia, Gregory Elacqua, Daniel Hernández, Claudio Ferraz, Vitor Pereira, Teca Pontual, and Tamar Atinc provided invaluable suggestions and peer review feedback. Mark Ingebretsen, Vladimir Herrera, Marize Santos, and Anna Musakova provided superb support for the final publication.

Our classroom observation data could not have been collected without the incredible training, field management, and analytical talents of Audrey Moore and her team at FHI 360; Alexandre Rands and Andre Magalhaes at Datametrica; colleagues Madalena dos Santos, Leandro Costa, Tassia Cruz, Érica Amorim, Cristian Aedo, Ines Kudo, Isy Faingold, Cynthia Hobbs, Martha Laverde, Martha Hernandez, Luciana Rodrigues, and Jessica Rodriguez; and government counterparts Jurema Holperin, Mirela de Carvalho, Daniela Ribeiro, Vania Machado, Adriano Giglio, Verónica Villarán, Giuliana Espinosa, Martín Garro, Mauricio Perfetti, Humberto Diez, Elia del Cid, Denise Cáceres, Rafaela Ramirez, Vitor Sanchez, Grace McLean, and Jean Hastings. Finally, over the four years it took to build our classroom observation database and write this book, all of its core contributors moved on to other jobs. We are therefore especially grateful to Soledad De Gregorio, who contributed at every stage and saw the work through to completion.

About the Authors and Contributors

Barbara Bruns is lead economist in the Education Global Practice at the World Bank. She is lead author of the book *Achieving World Class Education in Brazil: The Next Agenda* (2011) with David Evans and Javier Luque and co-author of *Making Schools Work: New Evidence on Accountability Reforms* (2011) with Deon Filmer and Harry Patrinos. She was the first manager of the $14 million Strategic Impact Evaluation Fund at the World Bank and co-authored the World Bank/International Monetary Fund's *Global Monitoring Report* for 2005, 2006, and 2007. She also served on the Education Task Force appointed by the UN Secretary-General in 2003, co-authored the book *Achieving Universal Primary Education by 2015: A Chance for Every Child* (2003), and headed the Secretariat of the global Education For All–Fast Track Initiative (EFA–FTI) from 2002 to 2004. She holds degrees from the London School of Economics and the University of Chicago.

Javier Luque is a senior education specialist and focal point for the Central American region at the Inter-American Development Bank (IADB). Before joining the IADB, Luque was a senior education economist in the Latin American and Caribbean region of the World Bank, where he co-authored *Achieving World Class Education in Brazil: The Next Agenda* (2011) with Barbara Bruns and David Evans. Prior to joining the World Bank, Luque worked in the Central Reserve Bank and the Ministry of Economy and Finance in Peru and at the International Monetary Fund. He has taught at the undergraduate and graduate level at the Pontifical Catholic University of Peru (PUCP), Pacific University, University of Rochester, and the Universidad Nacional Mayor de San Marcos. He graduated with a BA in economics from PUCP and holds an MA and PhD in economics from the University of Rochester.

Soledad De Gregorio is a consultant in the Latin America and the Caribbean region of the World Bank. She has several years of experience developing programs with disadvantaged communities in Chile. She holds an MA in public policy from the

University of California at Los Angeles and is pursuing a doctorate in public policy and administration at the University of Southern California.

David Evans is a senior economist in the Office of the Chief Economist for the Africa region of the World Bank and previously worked as senior economist in the Latin America and the Caribbean Region of the World Bank. He has designed and implemented impact evaluations in education, early child development, health, and social protection in Brazil, The Gambia, Kenya, Mexico, Nigeria, Sierra Leone, and Tanzania. He holds a PhD in economics from Harvard University.

Marco Fernández is a professor at the Monterrey Institute of Technology in Mexico and former consultant in the Latin America and the Caribbean region of the World Bank. Prior to that, he was an adviser to the secretary of education in Mexico and a deputy director in the Office of the Presidency. He holds a PhD in political science from Duke University.

Martin Moreno is a consultant for the World Bank who has worked extensively in the Latin America and the Caribbean region. He holds an MA and is working toward a PhD in sociology and demography from Pennsylvania State University.

Jessica Rodriguez is a deputy director of policy and planning at the Washington, DC, Office of the State Superintendent of Education. She previously was a consultant in the Latin America and the Caribbean region of the World Bank. She holds degrees from Stanford University and the University of Chicago.

Guillermo Toral is a consultant in the Latin America and the Caribbean region of the World Bank. He holds an MPhil in political science from the University of Oxford and is pursuing a PhD in political science at the Massachusetts Institute of Technology.

Noah Yarrow is an education specialist in the Middle East and North Africa region at the World Bank and has worked in the Latin America and the Caribbean region. Previously a classroom teacher, he holds degrees in development management and education from the London School of Economics and Pace University.

Abbreviations

ADOFEP	Agremiación de Docentes y Funcionarios de la Educación Paraguaya
AEP	Asignacion de Excelencia Pedagogica
ALI	Aligning Learning Incentive
AMET	Asociación del Magisterio de Enseñanza Técnica
ANDE	Asociación Nacional de Educadores
APSE	Asociación de Profesores de Segunda Enseñanza
AVDI	Asignación Variable por Desempeño Individual
BVP	Beca Vocación de Profesor
CAMYP	Unión Argentina de Maestros y Profesores
CEA	Confederación de Educadores Argentinos
CEID	Centro de Estudios e Investigaciones Docentes
CENAPAFAS	Central Nacional de Asociaciones de Padres de Familia
CLASS	Classroom Assessment Scoring System
CM	Carrera Magisterial
CNA	Chilean National Accreditation Commission
CNB/DNCB	Currículo Nacional Básico
CNTE	Confederação Nacional dos Trabalhadores em Educação
CODICEN	Consejo Directivo Central
COLPROSUMAH	Colegio Profesional para la Superación Magisterial de Honduras
COLYPRO	Colegio de Licenciados y Profesores en Letras, Ciencias y Artes
CONAIE	Confederación de Nacionalidades Indígenas del Ecuador
CONEACES	Consejo de Evaluación, Acreditación y Certificación de la Calidad de la Educación Superior No Universitaria
CONEAU	Consejo de Evaluación, Acreditación y Certificación de la Calidad de la Educación Superior Universitaria

COPEMH	Colegio de Profesores de Educación Media de Honduras
CPM	Ley de Carrera Pública Magisterial
CRUCH	Consejo de Rectores de las Universidades de Chile
CTERA	Confederación de Trabajadores de la Educación de la República Argentina
ECAP	Evaluación de las Competencias Académicas y Pedagógicas
ECh	Enseña Chile
ENAHO	Encuesta Nacional de Hogares
ENLACES	standardized student achievement test, Mexico
EPD	Estatuto de Profesionalización Docente
FEC	Fondo de Estímulo de la Calidad
FECI	Federación de Educadores de Capital e Interior
FECODE	Federación Colombiana de Educadores
FENAPES	Federación Nacional de Profesores de Enseñanza Secundaria
FEP	Federación de Educadores de Paraguay
FOMH	Federación de Organizaciones Magisteriales de Honduras
FREPASO	Frente por un País Solidario (political party)
FUM-TEP	Federación Uruguaya de Magisterio-Trabajadores de la Enseñanza
FUNDEF	Fundo Nacional Para o Desenvolvimento do Ensino Fundamental
FUTE	Frente Unionista de los Trabajadores de Educación del Ecuador
GEC	Gobiernos Escolares Ciudadanos
GER	gross enrollment ratio
ICETEX	Instituto Colombiano de Crédito Educativo y Estudios Técnicos en el Exterior
ICFES	Instituto Colombiano para la Evaluación de la Educación
ICT	information and communication technology
IDEB	Indice de Desenvolvimento da Educacao Basica
IMPACT	teacher evaluation model, Washington, DC
INEE	National Institute for Educational Evaluation
INEP	Ministry of Education, Brazil
ISP	Institutos Superiores Pedagógicos
JTA	Jamaica Teachers' Association
LAC	Latin America and the Caribbean
LAST	Liberal Arts and Sciences Teacher
LLECE	Laboratorio Latinoamericano de la Calidad de la Educación
LRM	Ley de Reforma Magisterial
MBE	Marco de la Buena Enseñanza
MECESUP	Mejoramiento de la Calidad y la Equidad en la Educación Superior
MET	Measures of Effective Teaching Project
MPD	Movimiento Popular Democrático
NIE	National Institute of Education
OECD	Organisation for Economic Co-operation and Development

OECS	Organization of Eastern Caribbean States
OLPC	one laptop per child
OTEP	Organización de Trabajadores de la Educación del Paraguay
PAIC	Programa de Alfabetizacao na Idade Certa
PIBID	Programa Institucional de Bolsa de Iniciação à Docência
PISA	Program for International Student Assessment
PNP	People's National Party
PPP	purchasing power parity
PRI	Institutional Revolutionary Party, Mexico
PRICPHMA	Primer Colegio Profesional Hondureño de Maestros
PROHECO	Programa Hondureño de Educación Comunitaria
PSP	Planes de Superación Profesional
PSU	Prueba de Selección Universitaria
PT	Partido dos Trabalhadores [Worker's Party, Brazil]
PTR	pupil-teacher ratio
RDD	regression discontinuity design
SADOP	Sindicato Argentino de Docentes Privados
SAT	Sistema de Aprendizaje Tutorial
SBM	school-based management
SD	standard deviations
SEC	Sindicato de Trabajadores de la Educación Costarricense
Sedeba	Sindicato de Educadores de Buenos Aires
SER	Sistema Nacional de Evaluación y Rendición de Cuentas
SERCE	Second Regional, Comparative and Explanatory Study
SIDESP	Sindicato de Docentes de Educación Superior del Perú
SIMCE	Sistema de Medición de la Calidad de la Educación
SINEACE	Sistema Nacional de Evaluación, Acreditación y Certificación de la Calidad Educativa
SNED	Sistema Nacional de Evaluación de Desempeño
SNTE	Sindicato Nacional de Trabajadores de la Educación
SUTEP	Sindicato Único de Trabajadores en la Educación del Perú
TALIS	Teaching and Learning International Survey
TEDS-Math	Teacher Education and Development Study in Mathematics
TFA	Teach For All
TIMMS	Trends in International Mathematics and Science Study
UDA	Union de Docentes Argentinos
UNAE	Universidad Nacional de Educación
UNE	Unión Nacional de Educadores
UNESCO	United Nations Educational, Scientific, and Cultural Organization
UPC	universal primary education completion
USAID	U.S. Agency for International Development
USP	University of São Paulo

Overview

Over 7 million teachers file into classrooms across Latin America and the Caribbean each day. These women and men represent 4 percent of the region's overall labor force and over 20 percent of its technical and professional workers. Their salaries absorb close to 4 percent of the region's gross domestic product (GDP). Their working conditions vary widely—from mud-walled, one-room rural schools to world-class facilities—but Latin America's teachers share one important commonality: they are increasingly recognized as the critical actors in the region's efforts to improve education quality and results.

While the importance of good teaching may be intuitively obvious, over the past decade education research has begun to quantify the high economic stakes around teacher quality. In a world where the goals of national education systems are being transformed, from a focus on the transmission of facts and memorization to a focus on student competencies—for critical thinking, problem solving, and lifelong learning—the demands on teachers are more complex than ever. Governments across the world have put teacher quality and teacher performance under increasing scrutiny. The Latin America and the Caribbean (LAC) region is no exception to these trends; indeed, in some key areas of teacher policy, the region is at the vanguard of global reform experience.

In this context, this study aims to do the following:

- Benchmark the current performance of LAC's teachers and identify key issues.
- Share emerging evidence on important reforms of teacher policy being implemented in LAC countries.
- Analyze the political "room for maneuver" for further reform in LAC.

We focus on teachers in basic education (preschool, primary, and secondary education) because the quantitative and qualitative challenges of producing effective teachers at these levels differ in key ways from university-level education, which has been addressed in other recent World Bank publications (Rodríguez, Dahlman, and Salmi 2008; Salmi 2009). We also focus on public education systems. Notwithstanding growing basic education enrollments in private schools in many countries in the region, national and subnational governments deliver the bulk of basic education services and remain the guardians of education quality and the architects of education policy.

Chapter 1 analyzes global and regional evidence on the importance of education results for economic growth and competitiveness and the importance of teacher quality for education results. It profiles LAC's teachers and how their characteristics have changed in recent decades. Chapter 2 provides a first-ever insight into how the region's teachers perform inside the classroom, drawing on new research conducted for this report in over 15,000 classrooms in 7 LAC countries.

Chapters 3, 4, and 5 focus on three leading areas of teacher policy reform in LAC today: chapter 3 analyzes policies to *recruit* better teachers; chapter 4 looks at programs to *groom* teachers and improve their skills once they are in service; and chapter 5 reviews strategies to *motivate* teachers to perform their best throughout their career.

Chapter 6 analyzes the prominent role of teachers' unions in the region and recent national experience with major education reforms. This chapter, like those that precede it, tries to distill the growing body of evidence from within and outside the region that can guide the design of effective programs and sustainable reforms.

Six overarching messages emerge from this study:

- The low average quality of LAC teachers is the binding constraint on the region's education progress, and consequently on the contribution of national education spending to poverty reduction and shared prosperity.
- Teacher quality in the region is compromised by weak mastery of academic content as well as ineffective classroom practice: teachers in the countries studied spend 65 percent or less of class time on instruction (compared with a good practice benchmark of 85 percent), which implies the *loss of one full day of instruction per week*; they make limited use of available learning materials, especially information and communication technology (ICT); and they do a poor job of keeping students engaged.
- No teaching force in the region today (except possibly Cuba's) can be considered of high quality against global comparators, but several countries have made progress over the past decade in raising teacher quality and student learning results, most notably Chile.
- There are three fundamental steps to a high-quality teaching force—recruiting, grooming, and motivating better teachers—and substantial reform experience across and outside of LAC in all three areas can guide the design of better policies.
- Over the next decade, the declining size of the school-aged population in about half of the countries in the region, notably the southern cone, could

make it substantially easier to raise teacher quality; in the other half of the region, especially Central America, the need for more teachers will complicate the challenge.
- The deepest challenge in raising teacher quality is not fiscal or technical, but political, because teachers' unions in every country in Latin America are large and politically active stakeholders; however, a growing number of successful reform cases is yielding lessons that can aid other countries.

Why teachers matter

LAC education performance. Over the last 50 years, Latin American and Caribbean countries have achieved a mass expansion of education coverage that took a century or more to accomplish in many Organisation for Economic Co-operation and Development (OECD) countries. From a starting point of less than 10 percent of all children completing secondary school in 1960, today most LAC countries have achieved universal primary school completion and high rates of secondary schooling. Only Guatemala and Haiti stand in sharp contrast to the regional progress. While the average LAC worker's four years of schooling in 1960 was little more than half the level of workers in OECD countries, today the LAC average is converging on the OECD's average of 12 years. There has been a significant and rapid accumulation of human capital in Latin America over the past half century.

But recent research has deepened the understanding of how human capital contributes to economic growth; it has established convincingly that what counts is not how many years of schooling students complete, but what they actually learn. It may seem intuitively obvious that a year of schooling in Mali will not equal one in Singapore, but only recently have researchers been able to quantify this. A country whose average performance on international tests is one standard deviation (SD) higher than another's (roughly the 100-point difference between Mexico and Germany on the 2012 Program for International Student Assessment [PISA] exam) will enjoy approximately a 2-percentage-point-higher annual long-term GDP growth. This relationship holds across countries at all income levels, across regions, and across countries within regions (Hanushek and Woessmann 2012, figure O.1). Differences in countries' average level of cognitive skills are consistently and fairly strongly correlated with long-term rates of economic growth. It is quality—in terms of increased student learning—that produces the economic benefits from investing in education. The region's increasing participation in international and regional tests provides direct evidence of how well its students are learning, and four important conclusions emerge.

First, relative to its level of economic development, the LAC underperforms badly. As seen in figure O.1, LAC countries' average learning performance on all international tests over the past 40 years is lower than that of every other region except Sub-Saharan Africa. Of the 65 countries participating in the 2012 PISA test, all eight

FIGURE O.1: Cognitive skills and long-term economic growth across regions, 1960–2000

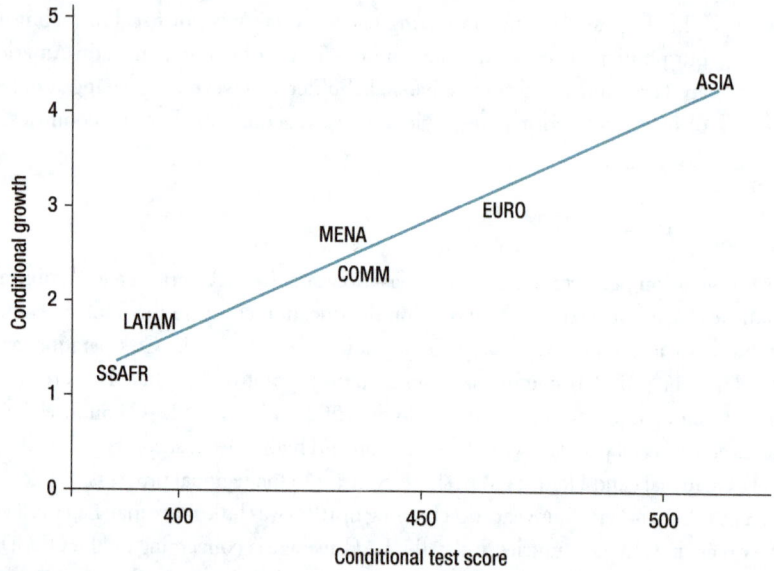

Source: Hanushek, Peterson, and Woessmann 2012, 2.
Note: This graph compares the average annual rate of growth (in percent) of real gross domestic product (GDP) per capita in 1960–2000 (adjusted for the initial level of GDP per capita in 1960) with average scores on international student achievement tests over this period. Region codes: Asia (ASIA), Commonwealth OECD members (COMM), Europe (EURO), Latin America (LATAM), Middle East and North Africa (MENA), Sub-Saharan Africa (SSAFR).

participating LAC countries scored below the average for their level of per capita income (figure O.2). The nearly 100-point difference between the OECD average math score (494) and the average for participating LAC countries (397) represents a disparity in skills equivalent to over two full years of math education. The gap with Shanghai, whose students averaged 613, is more than five years' difference in math skills. Given that a larger share of all 15 year olds have already dropped out of school in LAC countries than in the OECD or East Asia, the true gap in skills is even worse. All available evidence is that the average literacy and numeracy skills of youths in LAC badly trail those of other middle-income countries.

Second, the range in performance *within* the region is substantial. Among the LAC countries participating in PISA, the gap in skills between the top performer (Chile) and the lowest (Peru) is as large as the gap between Chile and Sweden in math and Chile and the United States in reading. Regional tests show that LAC countries that do not participate in PISA are even further behind: countries such as Honduras, República Bolivariana de Venezuela, and Bolivia are very far off track in terms of the amount of globally relevant learning a year of schooling produces.

FIGURE O.2: PISA reading scores and income per capita for LAC countries, 2012

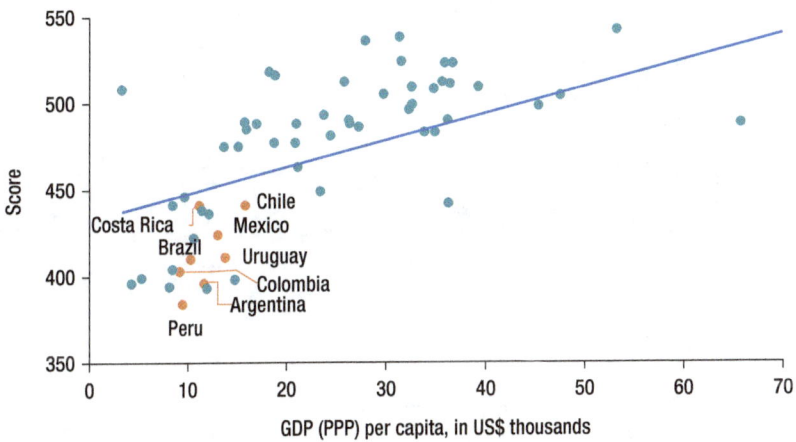

Sources: OECD 2013 and World Bank.
Note: GDP = gross domestic product; LAC = Latin America and the Caribbean; PISA = Program for International Student Assessment. GDP per capita is adjusted for purchasing power parity (PPP), in 2005 constant prices.

The third broad conclusion is encouraging: some LAC countries are making sustained progress in closing the gap with OECD countries. Between 2000 and 2012, Chile, Brazil, and Peru registered some of the biggest improvements in the entire PISA sample: more than twice the annual rate of improvement seen in the United States or the Republic of Korea (Hanushek, Peterson, and Woessmann 2012).[1] While the LAC region as a whole faces a large challenge, there is also the encouraging prospect of relevant lessons from within the region.

But the final conclusion, reinforced by the 2012 PISA results, is that there is no room for complacency. As figure O.3 shows, LAC's top improvers as well as other countries in the region all made far less progress than in prior rounds of PISA. This suggests that while other countries in the region may have something to learn from the policies adopted in Chile, Brazil, and Peru over the past decade, those countries also need to do more.

Teacher quality drives learning. If the economic benefits from education investments hinge on their effectiveness in producing student learning, the critical question becomes, what drives learning? Students' family background (parent education, socioeconomic status, and conditions at home such as access to books) remains the largest overall predictor of learning outcomes. A growing body of research confirms the importance of policies to protect children's nutrition, health, cognitive, and socioemotional development in the earliest years of life. But research over the past decade has also built new evidence that once children get to school, no single factor is as critical as the quality of teachers.

FIGURE O.3: Comparative PISA math improvement, 2000–12

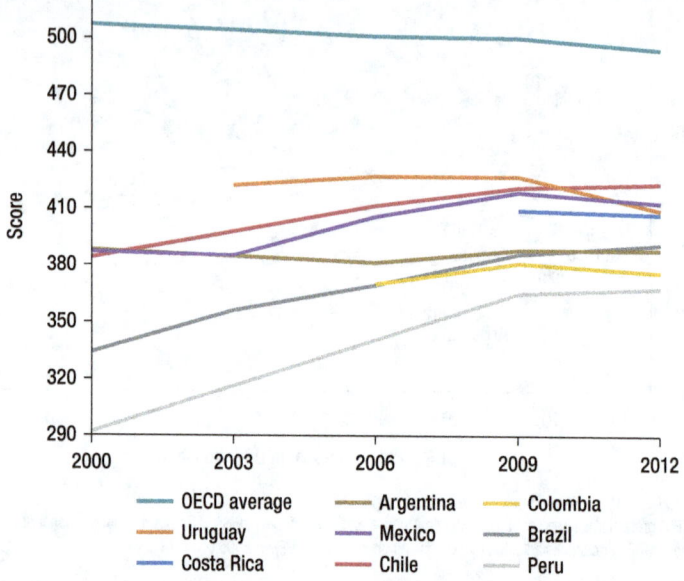

Source: OECD 2013.
Note: OECD = Organisation for Economic Co-operation and Development; PISA = Program for International Student Assessment.

Increasingly abundant student test data, especially in the United States, which allow researchers to measure the "value added" of individual teachers over the course of a single school year has generated eye-opening evidence of widely varying teacher effectiveness, even within the same school and same grade. Students with a weak teacher may master 50 percent or less of the curriculum for that grade; students with a good teacher get an average gain of one year; and students with great teachers advance 1.5 grade levels or more (Hanushek and Rivkin 2010; Rockoff 2004). The most recent research shows that exposure to even a single highly effective teacher raises a student's college participation rates and subsequent income (Chetty, Friedman, and Rockoff, forthcoming). A series of great or bad teachers over several years compounds these effects and can lead to unbridgeable gaps in student learning levels. No other attribute of schools comes close to this impact on student achievement.

This evidence has intensified the focus of policy makers and researchers on how to identify effective teachers. No one disputes that a comprehensive definition of teacher quality must encompass many different teacher characteristics and performance dimensions. But teachers' ability to ensure that their students learn is the sine qua non for students and nations to reap education's economic and social benefits.

Who are LAC's teachers?

What do we know about the characteristics and performance of teachers in Latin America? Available data paint a distressing picture.

Mostly female, with relatively low socioeconomic status. About 75 percent of Latin America's teachers are female, but this ranges from a low of 62 percent in Mexico to 82 percent in Uruguay, Brazil, and Chile. Teachers are also poorer than the overall pool of university students. University entrance data show that students majoring in education are of lower socioeconomic status and are more likely to be first-generation university students than entrants in other fields; the data point to a pool of students whose lives may have afforded them limited experience with other professions and, consequently, more limited academic aspirations. The teaching force in most of Latin America is also aging. In Peru, Panama, and Uruguay, the average teacher is more than 40 years old; the youngest corps in the region, in Honduras and Nicaragua, average 35 years of age.

High levels of formal education, but weak cognitive skills. Teachers' formal education has continued to rise across the LAC region. In 1995, only 19 percent of Brazilian primary teachers had university degrees; in 2010, 62 percent did. In all ten LAC countries for which comparable household survey data are available, the formal educational level of teachers today is higher than for all other professional and technical workers and considerably higher than for office workers.

The increase in formal education, however, is undercut by evidence that the individuals entering teaching in Latin America are academically weaker than the overall pool of higher education students. Fifteen-year-old students who identify themselves as interested in a teaching career have much lower PISA math scores than students interested in engineering in every country in the region, and score below the national average in every country except Uruguay (figure O.4).

Data from university entrance exams paint a similar picture. Students applying to teacher education programs average 505 on the Chilean university entrance exam (Prueba de Selección Universitaria, or PSU); the average for law is 660; engineering, 700; and medicine, 745. At the University of São Paulo, students applying for law and engineering programs score 36 percent higher than teacher education applicants, and medical school applicants score 50 percent higher.

There are few direct studies of how much Latin American teachers know about the subjects they teach, but those available show a disturbing disconnect between teachers' formal credentials and their cognitive skills. Fully 84 percent of sixth-grade teachers in Peru scored below level 2 on a 2006 test where level 3 meant mastery of sixth-grade math skills. On tests of teacher content mastery in Colombia, Ecuador, and Chile, fewer than 3 percent of teachers have scored in the range considered excellent.

On the one international study that directly compares teachers' mastery of math, Chile was the sole LAC country to participate. The study tested the math skills of teacher education students. Chile's future secondary school math teachers scored the lowest of the participating countries and its future primary school teachers were

FIGURE O.4: Comparative PISA math performance of prospective teachers and prospective engineers

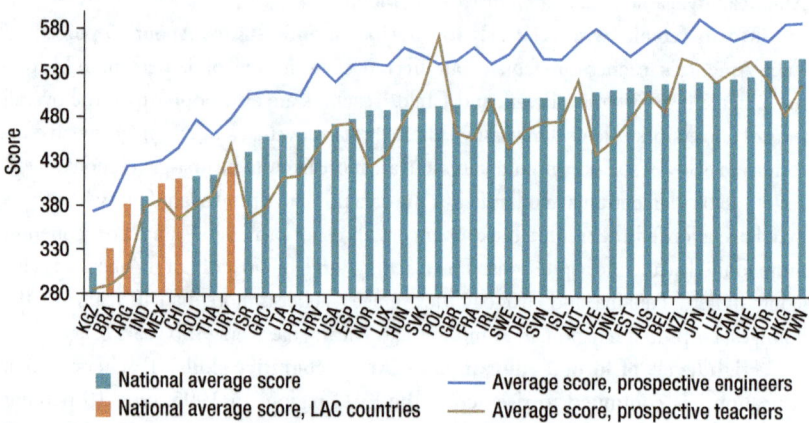

Source: OECD, PISA, 2000–06. Data are from PISA 2006, except for Brazil (from PISA 2000).
Note: LAC = Latin America and the Caribbean; PISA = Program for International Student Assessment. Country acronyms are ISO 3166 standard.

second lowest (figure O.5). Most of the countries in the study were high-income, high-achieving countries. Yet Chile's future secondary school teachers had weaker math skills than teachers from Botswana and the Philippines. Among future primary school teachers, only those from Georgia performed worse. Given that Chile is the LAC region's highest performer on international tests, these data point to deep issues for other countries in the region in raising the expertise of their teachers.

Relatively low salaries. What explains relatively weak students pursuing high levels of formal education to become teachers? What are the incentives to enter teaching today in LAC? Figure O.6 compares salaries for teachers to those of all other professional workers in all 10 of the countries for which comparable household survey data are available controlling for age, gender, urban or rural location, and employment experience. On a monthly basis, teachers' salaries in 2010 were between 10 and 50 percent lower than salaries for other "equivalent" professional workers and have been throughout the 2000s.

Teachers, however, work significantly fewer hours, reporting 30 to 40 hours per week on average, compared with 40 to 50 hours per week for other professional, technical, and office workers. Adjusted for working hours, teachers' relative position is different. In three countries (Mexico, Honduras, and El Salvador) teachers earn 20 to 30 percent more than comparable professional and technical workers; in three others they are on par (Costa Rica, Uruguay, and Chile); and in four countries they earn 10 to 25 percent less (Peru, Panama, Brazil, and Nicaragua).

FIGURE O.5: Comparative math content knowledge of future math teachers, 2008

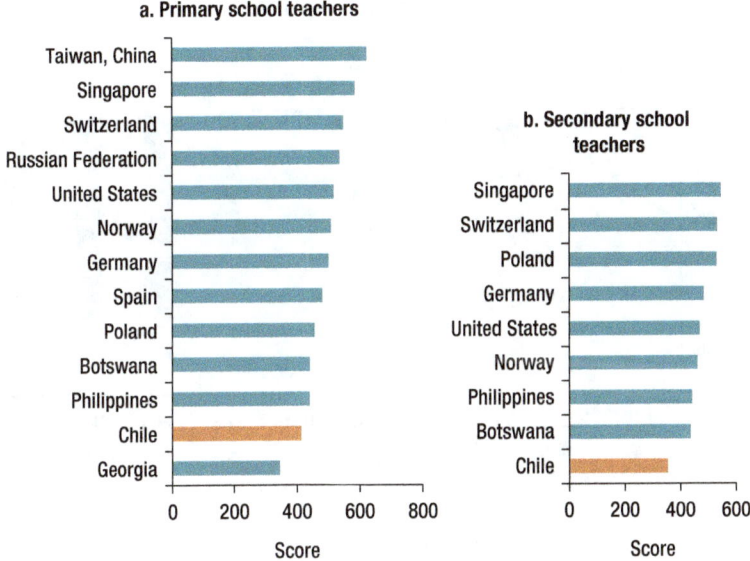

Source: TEDS-M 2008 (database).

Flat salary trajectory. Underlying these differences in average salaries, however, is a much flatter lifetime career trajectory for teachers than for other professional, technical, and office workers. Teachers' entering salaries in LAC are on par with other professional and technical workers in many countries but diverge significantly thereafter. Teachers' salaries rise very slowly, while other workers reap salary gains as their experience increases. There is also little wage differentiation in education compared with other sectors: irrespective of individual skills, talent, and experience, landing a job in teaching guarantees a salary within a relatively narrow band, with little risk of a very low or declining wage but little chance of a high one.

Research by Hernani-Limarino (2005) suggests that in Latin America and the Caribbean, individuals who tend to be less productive earn relatively more as teachers and those with attributes that make them highly productive tend to earn relatively less. This echoes research by Hoxby and Leigh (2004) for the United States that finds that talented women have been driven out of teaching over the past several decades by the "push" of a highly compressed wage scale, which is unattractive to more ambitious individuals. It is not only in the United States and Latin America that the average cognitive ability of university students getting teaching degrees has declined and higher-ability individuals have left the profession at a higher rate. Researchers in

FIGURE O.6: Average salaries for teachers relative to other professional workers, 2000 and 2010

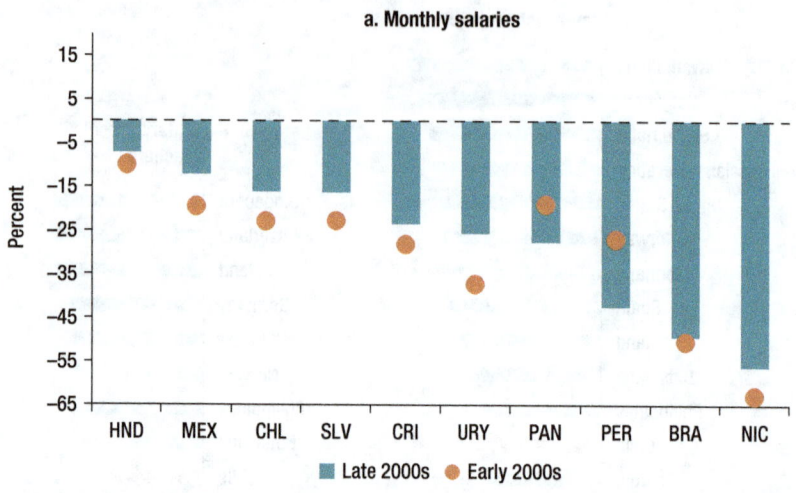

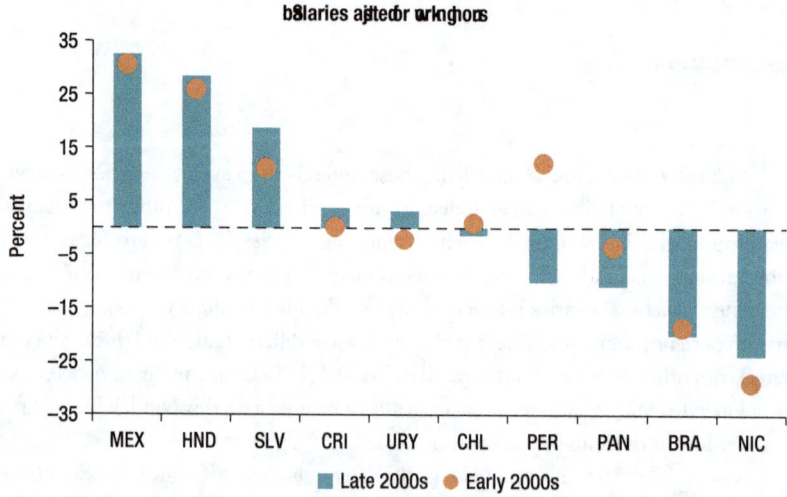

Source: World Bank analysis of household survey and labor market data for 10 Latin America and the Caribbean countries.
Note: All values control for age, education, gender, and urban or rural location and are adjusted for inflation. Teacher income is income from teaching only, but can reflect multiple teaching jobs. Country abbreviations are ISO 3166 standard.

Sweden have documented similar trends (Corcoran, Evans, and Schwab 2004; Eide, Goldhaber, and Brewer 2004; Hoxby and Leigh 2004; Fredriksson and Ockert 2007).

Job stability. As Mizala and Ñopo (2011) have observed, many nonpecuniary or "intrinsic" attributes of the teaching profession compensate for its relatively weak salary incentives in the eyes of prospective teachers. These include the mission of helping children and the satisfactions of professional mastery and collegial interaction. Teaching also offers long vacations, relatively generous health and pension benefits, and a "family-friendly" short official working day. Perhaps the most powerful attraction is high job security. Labor market data show that for women in particular, teaching offers stable employment; women who have graduated from teacher education over the past 40 years are significantly more likely to have been employed and stayed employed than women with other degrees.

Excess supply. Tertiary-level teacher education programs have proliferated in LAC over the past 15 years. The costs of establishing such programs are low and have attracted a large number of private providers into the field. From the demand side, the low or nonexistent academic standards for entry to these programs make them attractive to a rapidly expanding pool of secondary school graduates. Virtually all countries in the region report difficulty finding sufficient teachers for specialty subjects such as secondary school math and science or for bilingual schools in rural areas. But the broader picture in many parts of the region today is substantial excess production of teacher graduates of generally low academic quality. Recent data for Peru, Chile, Costa Rica, Panama, and Uruguay suggest that 40 to 50 percent of graduates from teacher training schools will not find work as teachers.

Available evidence suggests that Latin America is not attracting the high-caliber individuals it needs to build world-class education systems. Virtually all countries in the region appear trapped in a low-level equilibrium of low standards for entry into teaching, low-quality candidates, relatively low and undifferentiated salaries, low professionalism in the classroom, and poor education results. Moving to a new equilibrium will be difficult. No Latin American school system today, except possibly Cuba's, is very close to high standards, high academic talent, high or at least adequate compensation, and high professional autonomy that characterize the world's most effective education systems, such as those found in Finland; Singapore; Shanghai, China; Korea; Switzerland; the Netherlands; and Canada.

LAC's teachers inside the classroom

The magic of education—the transformation of schooling inputs into learning outcomes—happens in the classroom. Every element of an education system's expenditure, from curriculum design through school construction, book procurement, and teacher salaries, comes together at the moment when a teacher interacts with students in the classroom. How intensively this instructional time is used is a core determinant of the productivity of education spending.

Research conducted for this study provides a first-ever look inside LAC's classrooms to examine how teachers use class time and other available resources to support their students' learning. Over 15,000 classrooms in more than 3,000 schools in seven different countries were observed between 2009 and 2013: the largest-scale international study of this kind ever mounted. Through unannounced visits to national (or state) representative samples of schools, trained observers used a standardized research protocol called the "Stallings Classroom Snapshot" to generate internationally comparable data on four variables:

- Teachers' use of instructional time
- Teachers' use of materials, including computers and other ICT
- Teachers' core pedagogical practices
- Teachers' ability to keep students engaged

The method was originally developed in the United States, so LAC results may also be benchmarked against data from U.S. school systems collected over several decades by researchers Stallings and Knight (2003). Evidence from the observations in LAC supports five main conclusions.

Low use of instructional time contributes to low student learning in LAC. No school system in LAC studied, either at the national or state level, comes close to the Stallings good practice benchmark of 85 percent of total class time used for instruction. The highest averages recorded—65 percent for the national sample in Colombia, and 64 percent for Brazil and Honduras—are a full 20 percentage points below what Stallings's research suggested a well-run classroom achieves (figure O.7). Since Stallings measures are statistically representative of the functioning of the school system as a whole, this implies that 20 percent of potential instructional time is being lost across Latin America compared with the good practice goal. *This is the equivalent of one less day of instruction per week.*

Most of the time lost to instruction is used on classroom management activities, such as taking attendance, cleaning the blackboard, grading homework, or distributing papers, which absorb between 24 percent and 39 percent of total class time: well above the 15 percent benchmark. Teacher training programs in many OECD countries impart techniques for managing classroom transitions and administrative processes as efficiently as possible, with the mantra that "instructional time is a school's most expensive resource." Classroom teachers in Latin America appear to operate with little of this pressure.

The Stallings benchmarks also assume that teachers spend the entire class session either teaching or managing the classroom, but in every LAC country studied teachers spend at least 9 percent of time engaged in neither of these, which is considered teacher time completely "off-task" (figure O.8). The highest shares are 13 percent in Peru, 12 percent in Honduras, and 11 percent in Jamaica. In some systems, teachers are physically absent from the room as much as 6 to 11 percent of total class time.

FIGURE O.7: Average time on instruction in LAC countries

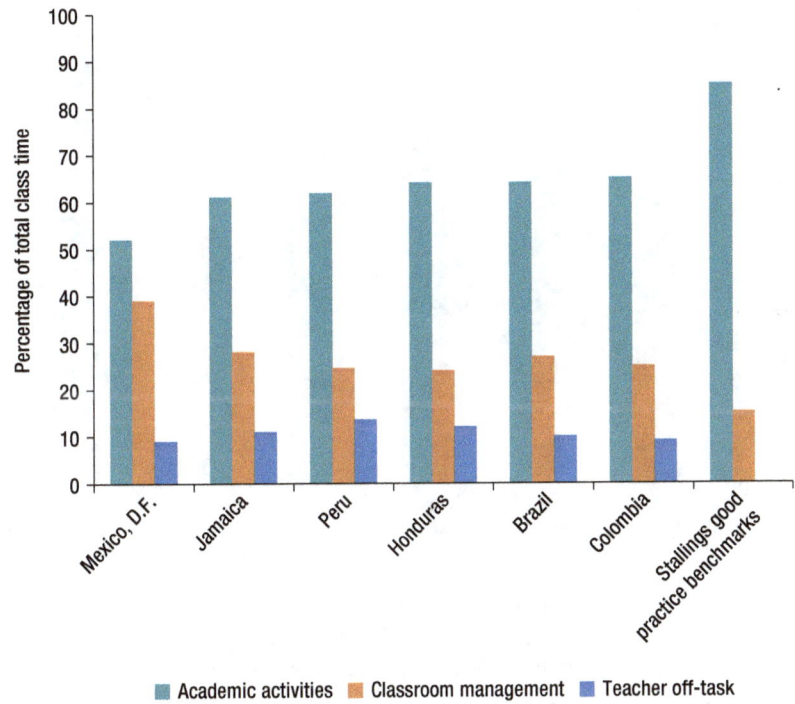

Source: World Bank classroom observation database.
Note: Values for Brazil in this and subsequent figures are pooled data from Pernambuco, Minas Gerais, and the municipality of Rio de Janeiro. Results for the Dominican Republic and Rio de Janeiro state are not included because the samples were pilots. D.F. = Distrito Federal; LAC = Latin America and the Caribbean.

In others, as much as 6 to 8 percent of the time teachers are engaged in social interaction with someone at the classroom door or simply not interacting with the class. Ten percent of total instructional time off-task equals 20 lost days in a 200-day school year. In these countries, half of the lost days of instruction are because teachers are physically absent from the classroom, arriving late to class, leaving early, or conducting other school business during class time.

In Brazil, Honduras, Mexico's Distrito Federal (D.F.), and Colombia, student test data permit correlation of teachers' use of time with learning results at the school level. Table O.1 shows a characteristic result: a very different pattern of time use between the highest- and lowest-performing schools in Rio de Janeiro (on a combined index of student test scores and student pass rates called the Index of Basic Education Development [IDEB]). Top schools averaged 70 percent of class time on instruction and 27 percent of time on classroom management. Teachers were off-task only 3 percent of the time and were never absent from the classroom. In the lowest-performing schools, only

OVERVIEW   13

FIGURE O.8: Breakdown of teacher time off-task, by country

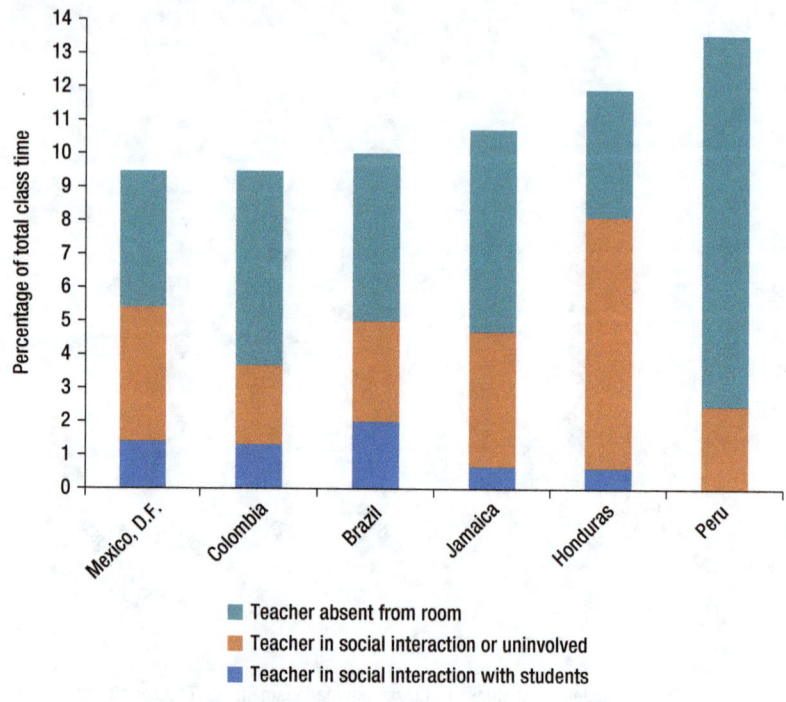

Source: World Bank classroom observation database.
Note: D.F. = Distrito Federal.

TABLE O.1: Use of class time in Rio de Janeiro schools, fifth grade, 2010

	Use of class time			
	Time on instruction	Classroom organization	Teacher off-task	Teacher out of classroom, within off-task
Rio de Janeiro municipality	58%	37%	6%	1%
Top 10% of schools on IDEB	70%	27%	3%	0%
Bottom 10% of schools on IDEB	54%	39%	7%	3%
Difference	0.16	−0.13	−0.03	−0.03
	[0,09]*	[0,09]*	[0,02]	[0,01]**

Source: World Bank classroom observation database.
Note: IDEB = Index of Basic Education Development. Robust standard errors in brackets: * statistically significant at 10 percent level, ** statistically significant at 5 percent level.

54 percent of time was spent on instruction, 39 percent was absorbed in classroom management, and teachers were off-task 7 percent and physically absent 3 percent of the time. These data mean that students in Rio de Janeiro's high-performing schools receive *an average of 32 more days of instruction* over the 200-day school year than their counterparts in low-performing schools. Observation data cannot establish causality, but gaps of this magnitude in opportunities to learn could clearly contribute to gaps in test scores and pass rates.

Schools at the top and bottom ends of the performance distribution in terms of student learning almost always show large, statistically significant differences in instructional time. In Honduras, the top 10 percent of schools on the national assessment averaged 68 percent of time on instruction, while the schools in the bottom 10 percent averaged 46 percent. In Mexico, D.F., the 10 percent of schools with the highest test scores averaged 62 percent of time on instruction compared with 51 percent of time on instruction in the 10 percent of schools with the lowest scores. Across the full distribution, positive correlations hold in all four countries, across all tested grades and subjects, with relatively few exceptions: students have higher learning outcomes in schools where teachers devote more time to academic activities.

When test scores are correlated with teachers' ability to keep students engaged in what they are teaching, the results can be even stronger. Teachers who successfully involve the entire class in the task at hand have better control of the class, fewer problems with discipline, and more time to impact student learning and afford a larger share of their students the opportunity to learn.

Strongest of all was the negative correlation between teachers' time off-task and student achievement. As discussed earlier, approximately 10 percent of the time LAC teachers are neither teaching nor managing the classroom. This pattern has clear consequences for student learning (figure O.9).

Although broad patterns are apparent, the correlations are statistically weaker than might be expected. A major explanation is that student test score data are analyzed at the school level and represent the average score for several different classrooms of students (for example, three or four different fourth-grade math classes) in a given school, while the observation data are for only one of those classrooms. Given large variation in classroom dynamics from one teacher to another, even in the same school—as discussed later in this section—comparing school-level average learning outcomes with the dynamics of a single classroom injected a large degree of random variation into the correlations.

Teachers rely heavily on the blackboard and make little use of ICT. A second finding of the research is that many learning materials available in LAC classrooms are not used intensively by teachers. Descriptive data collected by the observers shows that most schools in the region today offer students a reasonably enriched learning environment. Students are widely equipped with workbooks, writing materials, and textbooks. A fast-growing share of schools have visible ICT in the classroom: from televisions to digital whiteboards, LCD projectors, and

FIGURE O.9: Teacher time off-task and student learning in LAC

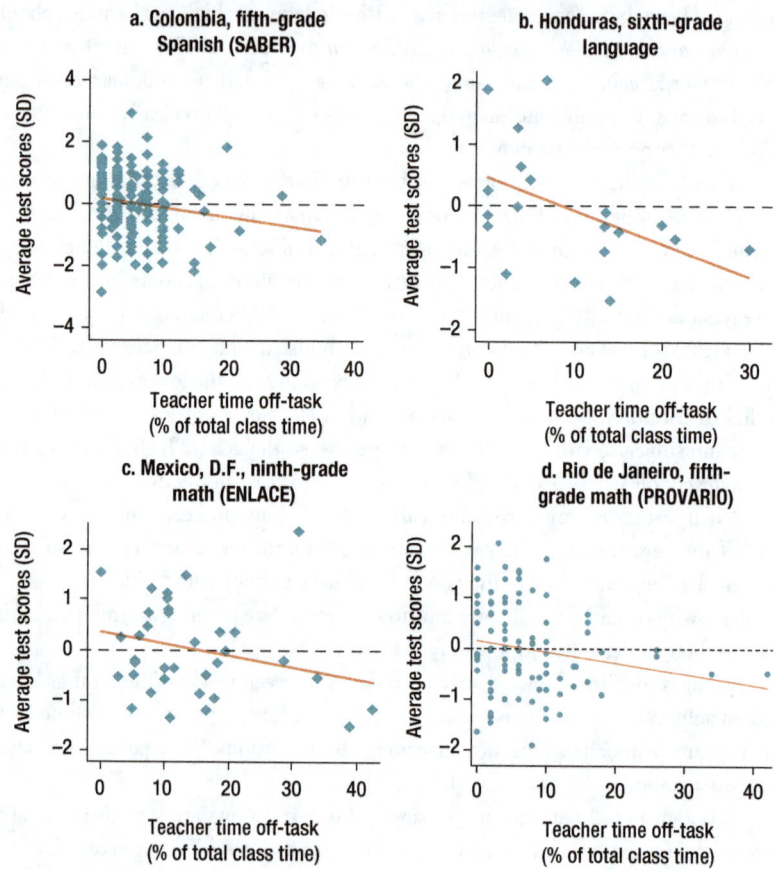

Source: World Bank classroom observation database.
Note: ENLACE = National Assessment of Academic Achievement in Schools; PROVARIO = standardized test, Brazil; SABER = standardized test, Colombia; SD = standard deviation.

laptops. In this sample, both Peru and Honduras had introduced One Laptop Per Child (OLPC) initiatives.

But teacher practice continues to rely heavily on a single, very traditional learning aid: the blackboard. For about one-third of all time spent on teaching activities, teachers use the blackboard and nothing else. Between 14 and 24 percent of the time, teachers use no learning materials. Teachers use available classroom-level ICT only 2 percent of the time. In Honduras and Peru—the countries with the largest investments in one-to-one computing in this sample—the share of total class time spent using these materials was in fact the lowest, 1 percent in Peru (in 2011) and less than 1 percent in Honduras (in 2011).

Students are unengaged. LAC's teachers have great difficulty keeping their students engaged in learning. In no system studied do teachers on average keep the entire class engaged in learning more than 25 percent of class time (figure O.10). More than half of all class time, in all countries, up to five students are tuned out. Between one-fifth and one-quarter of total class time, in all countries, a large group of students (six or more) is visibly not involved in the activity the teacher is leading. With an average class size of 25 across our sample, six students represent a significant share and can disrupt the work of other students. Observers in every country saw classrooms that were badly out of control, even with the teacher present and aware of being observed.

Given high repetition rates, LAC's teachers often face classes that span different ages and learning levels. Well-trained teachers, however, learn to handle such classes and with well-designed lesson plans keep all students engaged much more than 20 percent of the time. One of the clearest findings of this research is that poor student learning results can be directly linked to the failure of teachers to keep students engaged in learning. Important challenges for both pre-service and in-service teacher training programs in LAC are to ensure that teachers recognize the importance of drawing all students into the learning process; are equipped with a range of teaching strategies to achieve this; and arrive at school each day prepared to use these strategies, and every minute of class time, effectively.

Average classroom practice varies tremendously across schools. A fourth finding is the wide variation in average classroom practice across schools. In every system, there are many schools where the average share of class time used for instruction exceeds the Stallings 85 percent benchmark and others where instructional time is disastrously low: below 20 percent of total class time. Imagine attending a school where four days per week there is no instruction (figure O.11).

FIGURE O.10: Teacher time on instruction with the entire class engaged

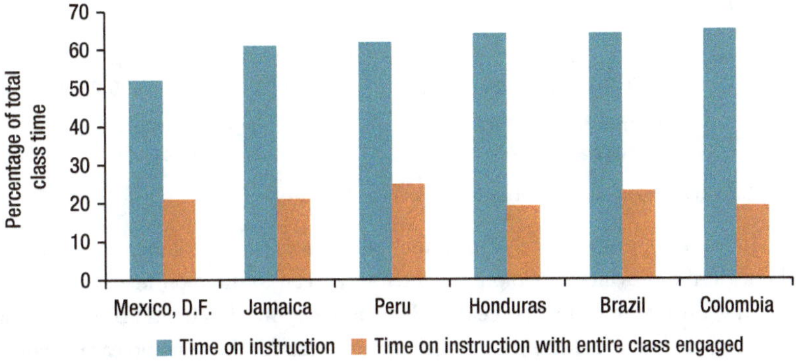

Source: World Bank classroom observation database.
Note: D.F. = Distrito Federal.

FIGURE O.11: Distribution of schools by average time spent on instruction

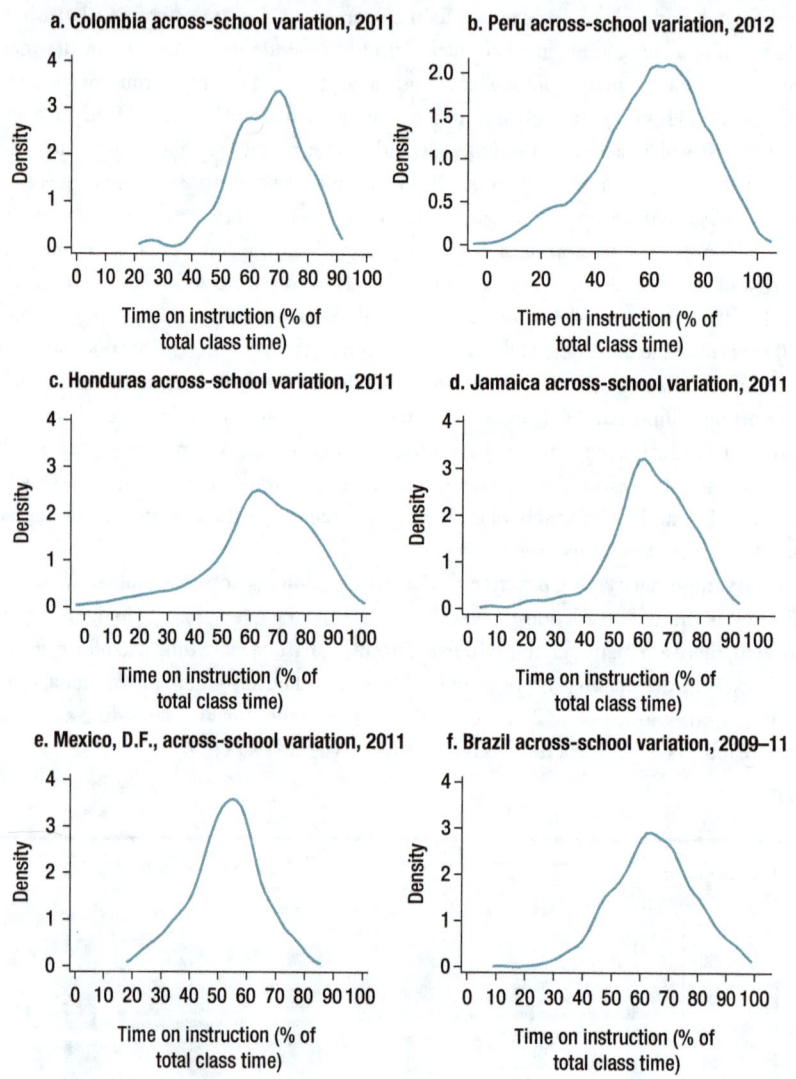

Source: World Bank classroom observation database.

In some countries, there were distinct differences across regions; in Honduras, schools in the province of Colón averaged 33 percent of time on instruction while those in Copán averaged 83 percent. In Pernambuco, Brazil, schools observed in late 2009 that went on to achieve their performance targets for the year and earn a school-level bonus averaged 63 percent of time on instruction compared to 54 percent in schools that failed to gain the bonus.

What is evident from this dispersion is that *school systems are not focused on the issue of instructional time.* Within a given national or subnational education system, schools operate in the same institutional and policy environment. They share the same policies for the selection of school directors, curriculum, teacher standards, preparation, and student assignment rules. Yet this research shows that these policies are playing out at the school level in widely different ways. And these differences have important consequences for students. In Honduran schools, 64 percent of time is spent on instruction, on average, across the system. But the top 20 percent of schools (in terms of instructional time use) average 85 percent: they achieve the Stallings benchmark. Schools in the bottom quintile average 37 percent. This 48 percentage-point difference means that students in top quintile schools receive an average of 96 more days of instruction than students in bottom schools *each year*. The consequences for students spending several years in a school that consistently delivers much less instruction are cumulative and highly unfair.

Average classroom practice varies tremendously within schools. The fifth and most surprising finding is the degree of variation in teacher practice *inside* schools. The difference in instructional time use between the best (highest time on teaching) and worst teacher in a single school is typically about two-thirds as large as the variation across the whole school system, a truly staggering range.

Virtually every country showed evidence of extreme and inexplicable variations in teachers' use of instructional across different classrooms in the same school. In Mexico, D.F., a school at the 25th percentile of the overall distribution of schools (ranked by average time on instruction) averaged 60 percent of time on instruction, but the best teacher spent 80 percent of time on learning activities and the lowest-performing teacher only 30 percent—a 50 percentage point difference from one classroom to another in the same school (figure O.12). At the 75th percentile of the distribution, a school averaged only 46 percent of time on instruction across all classrooms, but its best teacher also spent 80 percent of time on instruction – equaling the top teacher in the other school. The difference? In another classroom, observers recorded zero time on instruction: an 80 percentage point difference in the use of time across two classrooms in the same school on the same day. In Jamaica, in both the 25th and 75th percentile schools, the best-performing teachers spent 90 percent of class time on instruction—higher than the Stallings benchmark. But in the first school, the worst classroom used 44 percent of time (a 56 percentage point differential) while in the other, observers saw a class with zero time on task. A difference of 90 percentage points in the use of class time between two teachers in the same school on the same day is truly striking and in some sense unfathomable.

In Colombia, a school at the 75th percentile of the distribution, which averaged only 58 percent of time on instruction, had one teacher whose performance (90 percent of time on instruction) actually exceeded that of the best teacher in the school at the

FIGURE O.12: Range in teacher time on instruction within schools

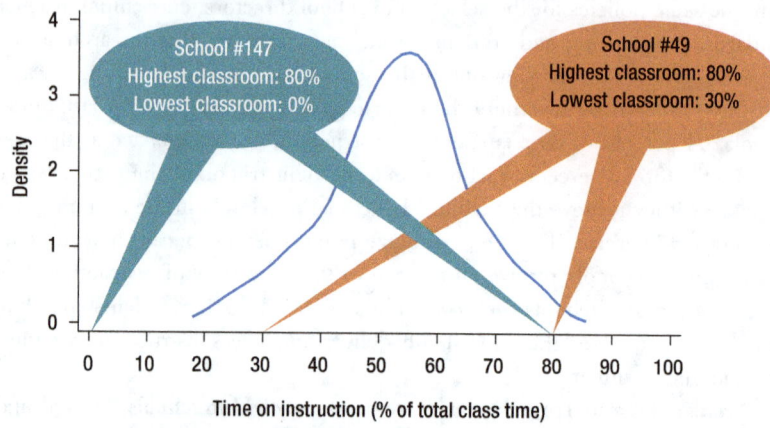

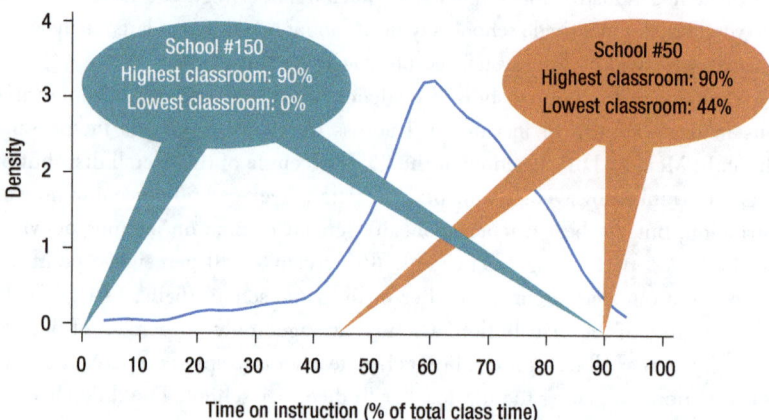

(continued on next page)

25th percentile. In Minas Gerais, Brazil, inside both a better-performing school at the 25th percentile and a school at the 75th percentile of the distribution there was a gap of 60 percentage points between the best and worst-performing teachers. Looking across these data as a whole, the most powerful conclusion is that even schools with extremely low average time on task have individual teachers doing an excellent job of using class time for instruction.

Figure O.13 analyzes these patterns further. In Colombia, for example, the average time on instruction nationally is 65 percent. Schools in the top quintile of the

FIGURE O.12: Range in teacher time on instruction within schools *(continued)*

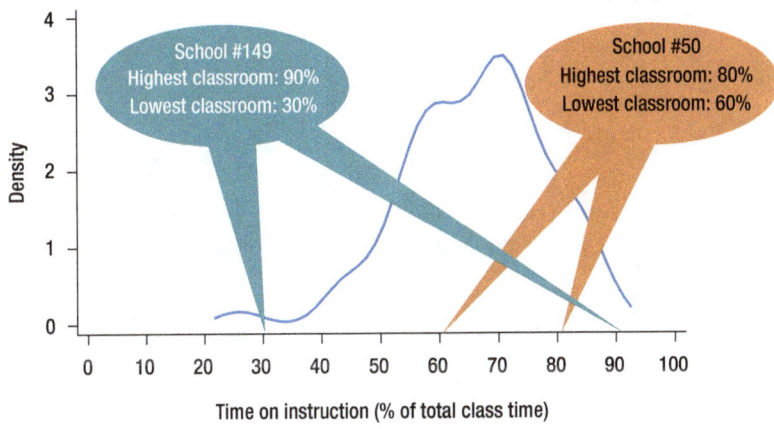

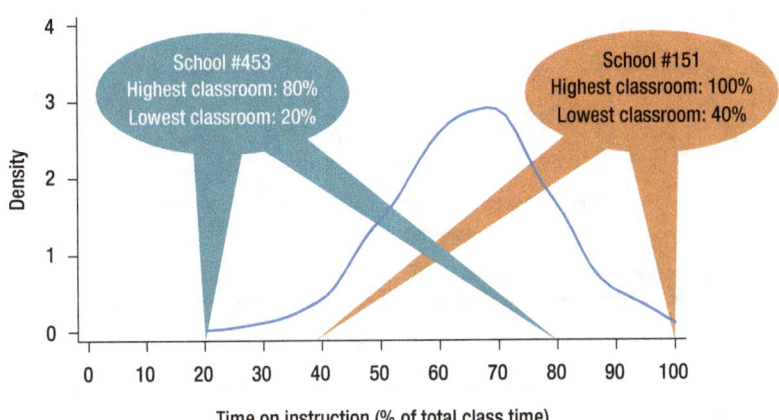

Source: World Bank classroom observation database.

performance distribution (of time use) average 82 percent, while schools in the bottom quintile average 49 percent: a 33 percentage point differential. But an even greater range exists between the best- and worst-performing teachers *inside* these schools. For schools in the lowest quintile, the best teachers in each school average 78 percent of time for instruction—not far from the Stallings benchmark—while the worst teachers average 18 percent. This 60 percentage point difference in time on task across different classrooms within these schools dwarfs the difference observed across quintiles of schools.

FIGURE O.13: Colombia and Honduras variation in instructional time within schools, 2011

Percentage of class time spent on instruction

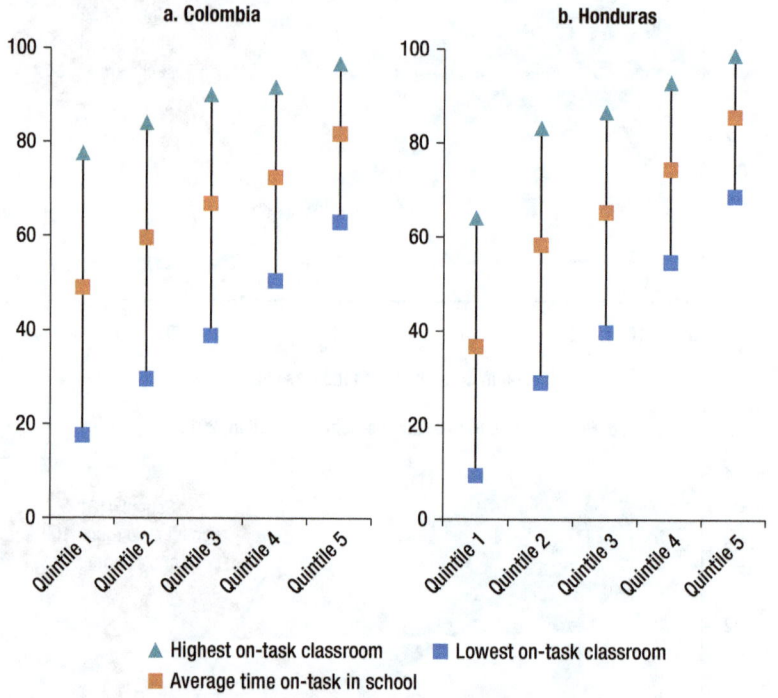

Source: World Bank classroom observation database.
Note: Quintiles refer to the distribution of schools ranked from highest to lowest average time on instruction.

In the 20 percent of schools with the highest average use of time, the gaps in time use between the best- and worst-performing teachers in each school is much smaller. Top teachers in these Colombian schools spend an impressive 97 percent of total class time on instruction, but even the least efficient teachers in these schools achieve 63 percent of time on instruction: a 34 percentage-point difference that is roughly half the size of the within-school gap in the bottom quintile of schools. What truly distinguishes top schools is consistency: good schools have less variation from classroom to classroom in one very basic parameter of teacher performance: the share of class time used for instruction. Whether the country has relatively high across-school variation (such as Honduras, Jamaica, or Brazil) or low (Mexico, D.F. and Colombia), the top quintile of the distribution is characterized by more consistent teacher performance across different classrooms.

The implications of these data are profound. First, school systems clearly are not focused on the issue of instructional time. In some sense, this is understandable. No LAC school system today collects standardized data on classroom dynamics; it is understandable that large differences can persist in the absence of any detection system.

But variations in classroom practice *within* a school are another matter. Direct observation of all the classrooms within a single school is not only technically feasible but also an implicit responsibility of school directors. There is clearly large scope for directors to promote more exchange of practice within their schools. The costs of identifying the most effective teachers within a school and ensuring that other teachers observe and learn from these examples are tiny compared to the costs of traditional teacher training programs, which require bringing large numbers of teachers off-site and hiring trainers.

Raising the average quality of teacher practice *across* schools is the responsibility of system managers. Many different approaches can be imagined: feeding back comparative classroom observation data to schools as an input to their development planning; initiating new forms of teacher training based on videotaped examples of good and weak teacher practice; and including assessments of teachers' classroom practice—whether by video or trained observers—in teacher performance evaluations. Policy makers in the seven countries involved in this program have taken the results as a stimulus to action along several of these lines. Our research created a baseline picture of what LAC students encounter inside the classroom today. It also provides a basis for tracking how ongoing and new reforms in these countries succeed in reshaping that reality.

Recruiting better teachers

There are three core challenges in raising teacher quality: recruiting, grooming, and motivating better teachers. Of these, recruiting—raising the caliber of teachers at the point of recruitment—is likely to be the most complicated for LAC countries, because it depends on raising the selectivity of teaching as a profession. Global research on high-performing education systems consistently points to the ability to attract top talent into teaching as a critical underlying factor that takes education systems from "good to great" (Barber and Mourshed 2007). But attracting highly talented individuals into teaching requires aligning a complex and interrelated set of factors that can be difficult and slow to change, including salaries and the salary structure, the prestige of the profession, the selectivity of entry into teacher education, and the quality of that education.

Raising selectivity. Our analysis suggests that salary increases may be necessary in some countries to make or keep teachers' average salaries—and the structure of teachers' salary incentives—competitive. But salary increases will raise quality only if they are accompanied by policies to raise the selectivity of teacher education programs. This is a crucial issue in the LAC region that gets far too little attention. In Singapore and Finland, only 20 percent of secondary school students who apply to teacher education programs are accepted, and all come from the top third of students. In LAC, there is virtually no winnowing of teacher candidates at the point of entry into teacher education, and academic standards are lower than in other professional fields. As a result, the share of tertiary education students in Latin America enrolled in teacher training is much higher than in many OECD countries, and many LAC countries are currently producing an excess of teacher graduates (figure O.14). In Peru, only 50 percent of teacher graduates find jobs as classroom teachers; in Costa Rica, only 54 percent. Chile's Ministry of Education in 2013 estimated that as many as half of all students graduated from teacher education programs in recent years are currently employed in retail.

Since teacher education is often subsidized by the public sector, producing an excess of teachers diverts resources from other, more productive investments in student learning. In countries where students finance teacher education with personal resources or loans, the overproduction of graduates from a four- or five-year program of study that does not lead to relevant employment can be even more problematic and may generate social unrest. Most fundamentally, a lack of selectivity undermines the prestige of the profession and makes teacher education less attractive for top students.

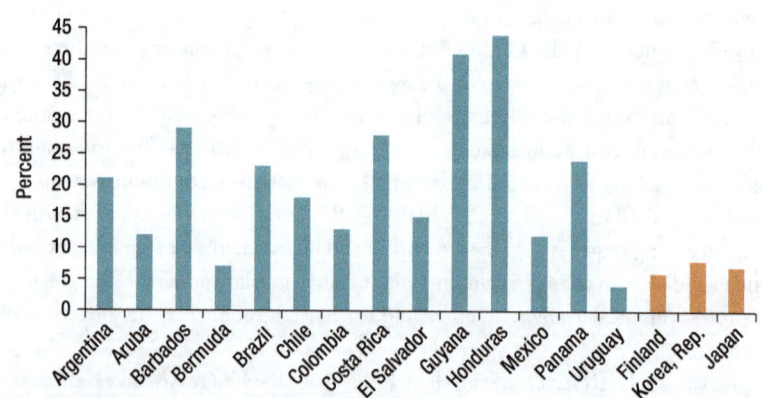

FIGURE O.14: Tertiary graduates who studied education

Source: UIS.Stat (UNESCO Institute for Statistics database).
Note: Data are for most recent available year between 2009 and 2012.

The selectivity and status of the teaching profession are not immutable qualities of an education system. Finland made raising teacher selectivity a cornerstone of an education reform strategy adopted in the 1970s. Over several decades, it transformed its labor market for teachers from one where a large number of teacher training institutions of variable quality produced an excessive number of teachers to one where a much smaller number of high-quality institutions produce just enough high-talent teachers, all of whom find teaching positions and enjoy high social prestige.

Global experience points to three key levers for making teacher recruitment more selective:

- Raising standards for entry into teacher education
- Raising the quality of teacher education schools
- Raising hiring standards for new teachers

Raising entry standards for teacher education. The principle of university autonomy in Latin America legally prevents most ministries of education from directly controlling admissions standards for pre-service teacher training. A few prestigious universities are selective, but in most countries the majority of new teachers are produced by low-quality private providers and nonuniversity teacher training institutes subject to weak quality assurance.

Four main strategies are being pursued by education ministries in the region to address these issues: (a) closing low-quality schools under direct control of the ministry (typically nonuniversity teacher education institutions); (b) establishing a national teacher university directly controlled by the ministry, such as Singapore's National Institute for Education; (c) creating special scholarships for top students; and (d) raising accreditation standards for autonomous tertiary institutions, forcing closure or adaptation.

Peru tackled the oversupply of low-quality teachers from nonuniversity teacher training schools (Institutos Superiores Pedagógicos [ISP]) in 2006 with the introduction of a national bar for admissions. Requiring candidates to achieve a minimum competency score on cognitive tests, a writing test, and an interview had a dramatic effect on ISP enrollments; they dropped from 11,000 to 389 in a single year (figure O.15). A number of regional institutes were suddenly threatened with closure, raising concerns about potential teacher shortages in bilingual and rural communities. In 2012, the ministry returned control over admissions to the institutions, but with annual enrollment caps set by the ministry.

Ecuador has been similarly aggressive in trying to raise the quality of teacher education. It closed 14 low-quality teacher preparation institutions in 2012 and is creating a high-level pedagogic university dependent on the Ministry of Education, the Universidad Nacional de Educación (UNAE). Researchers have identified a "tight coupling" between the Ministry of Education and the institutions where teachers are

FIGURE O.15: Raising the bar for teacher education programs in Peru, 2006–10

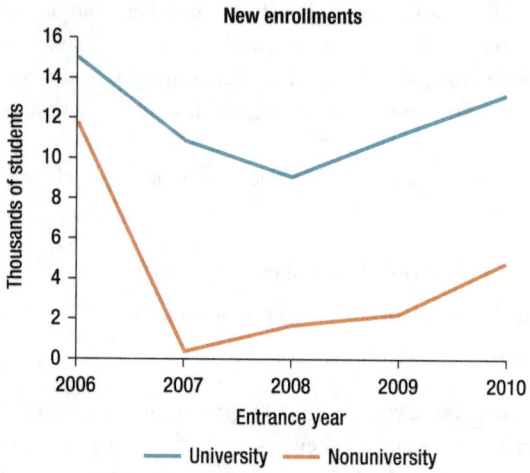

Source: World Bank construction using data from Peru's Ministry of Education.

educated as a factor in the educational success of countries as different as Singapore and Cuba (Carnoy 2007). "Tight coupling" ensures the coordination of teacher education with national education policy goals, such as higher selectivity at entry and stronger emphasis on math instruction, critical thinking, and twenty-first-century information technology skills. The UNAE will prepare teachers for a new national curriculum currently being designed in consultation with national and international stakeholders and experts. Another central idea is that the UNAE will become the link between national policy makers and other teacher training institutions, seeding the latter over time with highly qualified faculty trained at the UNAE.

A third strategy, which offers shorter-term impact, is the use of targeted incentives to attract top secondary school graduates into teaching. In Singapore; Finland; Hong Kong SAR, China; and Scotland, teacher training is open only to select candidates, but these students receive free tuition plus a salary or stipend while they are in training (Garland 2008). Colombia and Chile have recently launched similar programs. Chile's program, called the Beca Vocación de Profesor (BVP), in 2010 began offering full tuition for students who score 600 or higher on the university entrance examination (PSU), and agree to study education and work as a full-time teacher for at least three years in public or subsidized schools after graduating. About 3,500 students per year have qualified for the BVP since 2010, a relatively small share of the 130,000 students in teacher education in Chile. But researchers have confirmed the BVP's success in attracting students with a stronger academic profile. Feedback from top universities is that the new students are stimulating higher academic performance from their classmates as well.

The fourth and most important tool is the accreditation and review process. Developing the institutional capacity for a national higher education accreditation system is complex and takes time. Chile's experience, however, shows that accreditation information can exert important influence on student enrollment choices (figure O.16). When mandatory accreditation reviews of teacher education programs began in 2006, 80 percent of the country's 940 teaching programs received either no accreditation or the lowest category. Even without direct action to close low-quality institutions, in the space of a few years, the teacher training market shifted massively from 77 percent of enrollments in nonaccredited programs to 70 percent of enrollments in accredited programs. Proposed legislation goes further, requiring that all teachers hired into public (or publicly subsidized) schools must have graduated from accredited programs.

Raising the quality of teacher education. The academic quality of students entering teacher training is weak, but the quality of those programs is also dismally low. Qualitative accounts of pre-service training in Latin America generally describe it as failing to provide sufficient content mastery and student-centered pedagogy, being isolated from the school system and education policy making, and including practical exposure to work in schools only toward the end of the degree and sometimes not at all (UNESCO 2012).

While global research suggests that pre-service training programs focused on the work teachers will actually face in classrooms lead to more effective first-year teachers and higher learning for their students (Boyd et al. 2009), most Latin

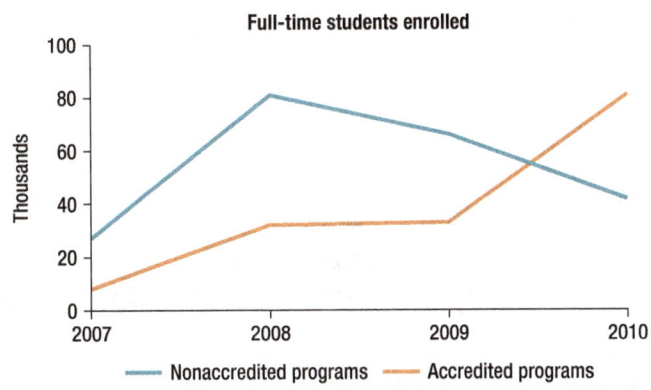

FIGURE O.16: Impact of accreditation information on teacher education enrollments in Chile, 2007–10

Source: World Bank construction using enrollment data from Chile's Ministry of Education.

American and Caribbean countries do not set a minimum standard for practice teaching and leave it to institutions to define. As a result, while in high-performing Cuba 72 percent of a teacher education program is spent doing practice in schools (i.e., more than 5,600 hours over 5 years), national thresholds in other countries require far less (figure O.17).

University autonomy prevents directly mandating changes in the content of teacher education, but several ministries of education in the region are creatively using competitive funding programs to stimulate such reforms. Chile in 2013 launched a new line of competitive funding to support a "rethink" of teacher education. Its ministry is open to proposals for major change, including shortening the number of years required, radically changing curriculum content, and increasing the time spent working in classrooms. The only requirement is that proposals be grounded in global research evidence. Peru's competitive fund for tertiary education (Fondo de Estímulo de la Calidad) also has a specific line of support to improve the quality of teacher training institutions.

Raising hiring standards. The low quality of teacher education programs makes it important that public education systems screen effectively at the point of hiring. Three main policy instruments can ensure this: (a) national teacher standards, (b) preemployment tests of teachers' skills and competencies, and (c) alternative certification.

National teacher standards, articulating "what a teacher should know and be able to do," are an important step in the development of a more professional

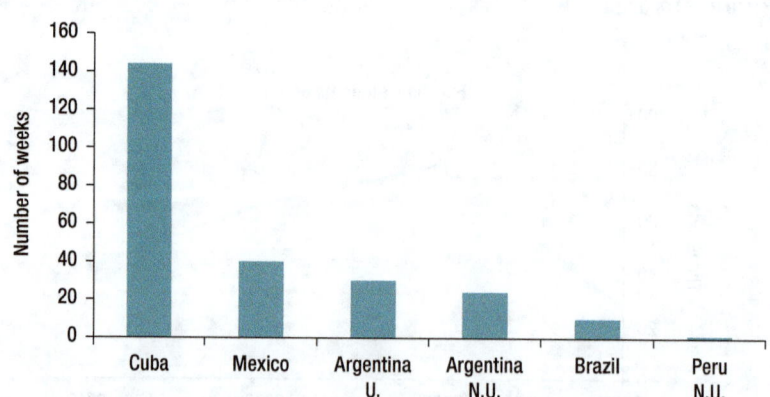

FIGURE O.17: Compulsory pre-service teaching practice in LAC countries

Source: Franco 2012.
Notes: N.U. = nonuniversity programs; U. = university-level programs. Figures assume 40 program hours per week and 40 weeks per year.

teaching corps. Over the past twenty years, most OECD countries have put serious effort into developing standards for teachers. Relatively few LAC countries have done so.

The exception is Chile, which adopted national teacher standards (Marco para la Buena Enseñanza) in 2003, after three years of joint work by a national commission and the teachers' union. Chile's framework remains a best-practice example for the region (figure O.18). It has guided the design of other key policies, including Chile's teacher evaluation system and teacher exit exam, the Prueba Inicia. National teaching standards take time and effort to develop, but formally establishing high standards for teachers lays the foundation for education quality.

A second tool is certification exams or competency tests to screen teacher candidates. Recent research from Mexico provides the strongest evidence to date on the importance of clear competency standards for teachers (Estrada 2013). By exploiting geographic variations in the pace at which different Mexican states began to implement a 2008 federal mandate that all new civil service teachers be hired on the basis of national competency tests, Estrada was able to compare the impact of "test-hired" new teachers with new teachers hired through the traditional method—state-level committees in which the teachers' union has a dominant voice. His results are striking. In a sample of small rural schools that gained only one new teacher in 2011, students who received a test-hired teacher scored .66 SD higher in

FIGURE O.18: Chile's framework for good teaching

Preparation
- Knows content and curriculum
- Knows the students
- Dominates the didactics
- Organizes objectives and contents coherently
- Uses coherent evaluation strategies

Learning environment
- Creates an environment of acceptance, equity, confidence, and respect
- Manifests high expectations about all students' learning and development possibilities
- Uses classroom norms
- Organized work environment and physical setting

Professional responsibilities
- Reflects systematically on teaching
- Maintains professional and team relationships with colleagues
- Takes on responsibility in orienting students
- Favors collaboration with parents and guardians
- Knows updated information about the profession, the education system, and current policies

Instruction for all students
- Communicates learning objectives
- Uses challenging, coherent, and significant teaching strategies
- Treats class content with conceptual thoroughness and ensures its comprehensibility for all students
- Optimizes use of time
- Promotes thinking
- Evaluates and monitors student learning

Source: Adapted from Chile, Ministerio de Educación 2008.

math and .78 SD higher in language than students who received a new traditionally hired teacher. These effects are huge, and demonstrate that even in a relatively short period, better-qualiified teachers can dramatically impact students' opportunity to learn. Colombia and El Salvador have also introduced mandatory exams that teacher graduates must pass to be hired by the public sector. In El Salvador there has been clear progress in raising the share of teacher graduates who pass the exam (Evaluación de las Competencias Académicas y Pedagógicas [ECAP]) since it was introduced in 2001 (figure O.19). An important further step will be research, similar to that in Mexico, on how the flow of better-prepared teachers into the school system affects student learning results.

In Colombia, the exam for graduating teachers established under the 2002 reform law also set a higher bar, yet there is limited evidence on its impact to date. The share of teachers hired under the new system remains relatively small, and there is unfortunately little evidence on their effectiveness.

Introducing mandatory certification exams that set a higher bar for teacher quality typically requires a transitional period. When New York state established a more stringent teacher certification exam in 1998, a high share of new teacher graduates could not pass it. The state permitted a five-year window for school districts to hire "temporary license" teachers who had not passed the exam. The new standards hit hardest in high-poverty urban school districts such as New York City, where temporary license teachers accounted for 63 percent of new hires in the poorest quartile of schools. To meet the 2003 deadline for eliminating such hiring, the city was forced to pursue aggressive strategies to attract higher-quality teachers. By 2005, it succeeded in eliminating the hiring of uncertified teachers, sharply narrowed the gap in teacher qualifications between high- and low-poverty schools, and saw large improvements in student performance in high-poverty schools (Boyd et al. 2008).

FIGURE O.19:  Teacher exit exam pass rate in El Salvador, 2001–12

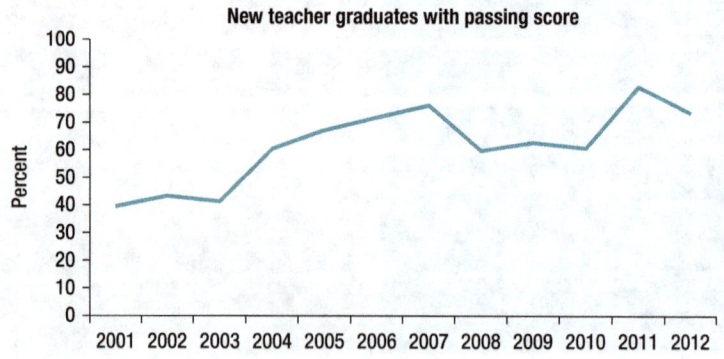

Source: Picardo 2012.

While mandatory certification exams are the most powerful instrument for raising teacher standards, nonbinding "exit exams" upon completion of teacher education programs can also support better hiring choices, monitor the quality of graduates over time, and expose quality differences across teacher training schools. Chile's 2008 Inicia test and the national teaching exam being developed in Brazil (Prova Nacional de Concurso para o Ingresso na Carreira Docente) are examples. Making such examinations voluntary has a downside, however; in Chile, only 40 percent of graduates, on average, opt to take the Inicia test, and of these, 70 percent fail to achieve the threshold score. Ministry concerns that the 60 percent of teacher graduates who refuse to take the exam are even less prepared to meet national teacher standards sparked a legislative proposal to make the exam mandatory.

A third strategy for raising the quality of new teachers is to bypass low-quality education schools entirely and recruit teachers trained in other disciplines, a practice known as alternative certification. This was key to New York City's rapid progress in raising teacher quality and is widely used in other U.S. urban school districts that have difficulty attracting teachers to work with disadvantaged populations. Rigorous U.S. studies have generally concluded that students of teachers with alternative certification, most notably those from the Teach For America program, do as well or better than students of regularly recruited teachers.

Most countries in LAC have not pursued alternative certification on any scale, although it is permitted in Colombia and proposed in Chile and Mexico. Since 2007, however, several LAC countries have launched national branches of Teach For All, modeled on Teach For America. In Chile, Peru, Mexico, Colombia, Argentina, and Brazil, Teach For All programs have recruited top university graduates from other disciplines willing to commit to two years of teaching in highly disadvantaged schools.

A randomized evaluation of the program in Chile, Enseña Chile, is currently underway, with first results expected in 2016. A 2010 study documented that the programs in Argentina, Peru, and Chile have succeeded in attracting high-talent university graduates and that students of Enseña Chile teachers had higher learning outcomes than those of comparable traditional teachers. Students of Enseña teachers also had better socioemotional competencies, including higher self-esteem and self-efficacy. The Enseña teachers had more positive attitudes about their students' ability to learn and higher expectations for them (Alfonso, Santiago, and Bassi 2010). Although the LAC programs currently operate on a small scale, they appear to be a useful tool, especially for raising of teacher quality in disadvantaged urban or rural schools and for hard-to-fill disciplines, such as secondary school math and science.

Raising teacher selectivity over the next decade. All LAC countries face the challenge of recruiting better teachers, but it will play out in different countries against very different demographic backdrops. Over half of the region—including all of its largest countries—will see student population fall by as much as 31 percent, while other countries, especially the Dominican Republic and those in Central America, will face continued growth in student numbers. The United Nations Educational, Scientific, and Cultural Organization (UNESCO) projects that with no change from 2010 in enrollment ratios or pupil-teacher ratios, the region would need 8 percent fewer teachers by 2025.

Since not all countries in the region have achieved universal schooling coverage, especially at the secondary level and preschool, the demand for teachers also depends on assumptions about how quickly these countries will expand coverage. To project a scenario of maximum potential demand for new teachers, we assumed that all countries in the region reach 100 percent primary education enrollment, 90 percent secondary enrollment, and 90 percent preschool enrollment of children ages four to six by the year 2025, even if this implies rates of schooling expansion far above countries' past trends.

Under this highly ambitious scenario of schooling expansion, the region would still need a smaller overall stock of preschool, primary, and secondary teachers in 2025, assuming that current pupil-teacher ratios in every country remain stable. The total stock of teachers would fall from 7.35 million in 2010 to about 6.61 million in 2025. While some countries would need to increase teacher numbers to support the expansion of coverage, others would see only modest changes or large declines. A net decline in teacher numbers implies an opportunity for countries to pay a smaller stock of teachers higher average salaries, which could help raise the attractiveness of the profession. But the salary increment would be relatively small, and even this potential "fiscal space" would materialize only if current pupil-teacher ratios did not decrease.

However, the tendency for school systems with a declining student population is to let the pupil-teacher ratio decline. It requires active management to reduce the teaching force pari passu with demographic decline, thus maintaining a stable pupil-teacher ratio. Both teachers' unions (which wish to protect job stability) and parents (who believe that a smaller class size is better for their children) resist this. The falling pupil-teacher ratios already observed in LAC countries with declining student populations indicate that this pattern has already taken hold.

The contrast with East Asian countries is sharp. Singapore, Korea, China, and Japan consciously maintain relatively high pupil-teacher ratios to free up resources for higher teacher salaries, a longer school day, and cost-effective non-salary investments. Teacher salaries in these countries are relatively high on average and are differentiated by competency and performance, which attracts more talented individuals.

To explore the implications of a similar trade-off in LAC, we projected the same ambitious trends in enrollment, but with active management of pupil-teacher ratios, to reach target levels of 18 to 1 in preschool education and 20 to 1 for primary and secondary education by 2025. While some countries would need to hire more teachers to meet the projected goals of close to universal coverage and lower pupil-teacher ratios than they currently enjoy, the overall size of the teaching force in LAC would decline by 11 percent (figure O.20).

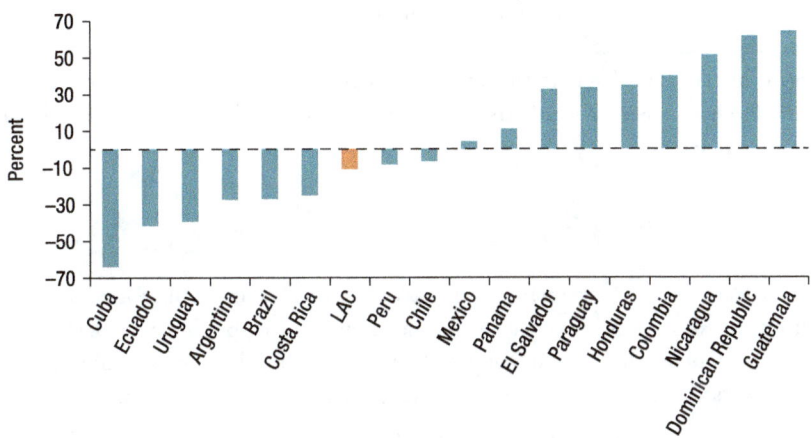

FIGURE O.20: Change in stock of teachers needed, assuming expanded coverage and efficient pupil-teacher ratios, 2010–25

Source: World Bank projections with data from UNESCO 2009, UIS.Stat (UNESCO Institute for Statistics database), and World Bank population data.
Note: LAC = Latin America and the Caribbean. Projections assume that all countries reach target gross enrollment ratios of 100 percent for primary and 90 percent for preschool and secondary education by 2025, and pupil-teacher ratios of 18 to 1 for preschool education and 20 to 1 for primary and secondary education by 2025.

For several of the larger countries in the region, policies to manage the pupil-teacher ratio combined with demographic trends would permit significant increases in teacher salaries. In Brazil, for example, this scenario results in a 27 percent decline in the number of teachers, from 2.9 million to 2.1 million, by 2025. But it would allow for a 36 percent real increase in average teacher salaries and move teachers' relative salaries from the 76th percentile of the wage distribution to the 85th percentile, compared to the 90th percentile for other professional workers.

In the coming decade, several countries will have a unique opportunity to raise teacher quality through higher salaries, stronger incentives, and higher nonsalary spending. There would be no increase needed in overall education budgets if school systems carefully manage teacher numbers in favor of teacher quality. Since these assumptions are based on constant real spending per student, countries that have declining student populations and raise education spending as a share of GDP would have even more resources per teacher to finance a move to higher quality.

This heterogeneity will create diverse challenges for teacher policy. Projected declines in the student population in half of the region—including its largest countries—will make it easier for school systems to finance higher teacher quality, but will pose the political challenge of pruning low performers out of the force to make room for higher-quality new recruits. With declines in some cases of 20 percent or more in the size of the teaching force by 2025, managing both teacher exits and selective recruitment with a strategic focus on quality is critical. In countries where increased need for teachers is projected over the next decade, the major challenge is the financial burden of raising education spending to support the recruitment of new teachers at higher standards. For these countries, efficient class size is a critical policy choice.

Grooming great teachers

Once teachers have been hired, it is the task of a school system to make them as effective as possible. This involves assessing, managing, and supporting individual teachers' development of their craft and building a professional community of teachers, both within schools and across the school system. Four essential tasks are

- *Induction*: support for teachers' development during their critical first five years of teaching
- *Evaluation*: systems for regular assessment of individual teachers' strengths and weaknesses
- *Professional development*: effective training to remedy teachers' identified weaknesses and leverage the skills of top performers
- *Management*: matching teacher assignments to schools' and students' needs, and building effective schools through shared practice and professional interaction

Teacher induction. A consistent finding of education research is that new teachers face a steep learning curve in their first three to five years on the job (Boyd et al. 2009; Chingos and Peterson 2010; Hanushek and Rivkin 2010). During this window, school systems have an important opportunity to support and maximize the development of new teachers and to identify those who should be counseled out of the profession. Because teachers are typically hired into civil service positions, which make dismissal on performance grounds difficult once they are confirmed, there is a high payoff to avoiding recruitment mistakes. Both of these goals are served by a well-organized induction program and the effective use of probationary periods.

In the LAC region, very few countries outside of the English-speaking Caribbean countries have formal induction programs for entering teachers. Belize's program, which over the course of a teacher's first year includes tutoring, observation in the classroom, mentoring support, action-research projects, and assessments, has a particularly impressive design.

Effective induction goes hand in hand with consequential probationary periods. Most OECD countries use probationary periods. Some school systems in the

United States have extended these to three years or more to allow more time to assess teachers' performance and growth potential before making a final contract decision. But in Latin America and the Caribbean, probationary periods with consequences are rare. Only two of seven countries reviewed recently (Colombia and the Dominican Republic) have consequential probationary periods that include a comprehensive assessment of new teachers (Vaillant and Rossel 2006). A 2013 program introduced in Rio de Janeiro municipality presents a promising model: new teacher candidates are given an intensive training course in effective classroom dynamics—which draws on the municipality's Stallings results—and are subsequently observed teaching and evaluated before their recruitment is confirmed.

Teacher evaluation. Top education systems invest heavily in the evaluation of teacher performance. Teacher evaluation plays two critical roles: improving teachers' quality and holding them accountable. Singapore, Japan, Korea, and China's Shanghai all have effective systems for assessing their teachers' performance and progress. The experience in Latin America to date is much more limited. While Mexico (in the 1990s) and Colombia in 2002 introduced the region's first teacher evaluation systems, implementation issues have undermined their impact and Mexico's system is currently being redesigned (Vegas and Umansky 2005; Ome 2012). Chile's 2003 system remains the region's best practice example to date. Ecuador began implementing teacher performance evaluations in 2007, and Peru is currently designing a comprehensive system similar to Chile's. Elsewhere in the region, countries have some elements in place, but they are less comprehensive and systematic.

Putting in place a sound system of teacher evaluation is expensive and institutionally challenging, but it can make other important education system functions more efficient. Teacher performance information can make in-service training investments more relevant, help target them better, and even reduce overall training costs. It creates the information base needed for individual performance incentives and accountability measures. It provides teachers with individualized feedback that might not be as forthcoming or insightful from their direct supervisors and peers and increases teachers' motivation to pursue training or professional improvement. If these benefits are captured, the net costs of a good teacher evaluation system may be small.

Growing global experience with teacher evaluation points to four key features of successful systems. First, they are grounded in teacher standards: a clear articulation of the competencies and behaviors that good teachers are expected to have and demonstrate. Second, they measure performance comprehensively. A three-year research program in the United States concluded that a reliable judgment about an individual teacher's performance requires multiple measures, including classroom observation (ideally multiple times) and student and peer feedback. In combination, these measures can produce assessments of teachers' effectiveness that are well correlated with their students' value-added learning gains (Kane and Staiger 2012). Chile's teacher evaluation system is a good example of comprehensive evaluation. It combines an observation of teachers' classroom practice (through a videotaped class), a sample lesson plan, a self-assessment, a peer interview, and an assessment by the school director and pedagogical supervisor.

Third, good evaluation systems use instruments that have technical validity and protect the integrity of evaluation processes. The implementation of Chile's system is contracted through competitive bidding to an independent education research group that conducts ongoing research to improve the robustness of the system. The evaluation team is responsible for assuring the quality and consistency of implementation. For example, it provides extensive training to the supervisors who evaluate the videos of teachers' classroom practice and the teachers who conduct peer interviews.

Fourth, good systems ensure that evaluation results have consequences for teachers: both positive and negative. Most OECD countries use their evaluation systems as a platform for performance incentives: identifying and rewarding top performers. In Chile and Ecuador, teachers who receive outstanding evaluations are eligible for bonus pay. Evaluation systems also provide the soundest basis for long-term grooming of individual teachers' potential and the fairest basis for promotions. Rather than promoting teachers on the basis of seniority alone—as most LAC countries currently do—teachers can be promoted on the basis of recognized competence. A salary structure aligned with evaluated performance creates the right incentives for current teachers and makes the profession more attractive to talented candidates in the future.

Effective teacher evaluation systems strengthen accountability. They allow school system managers to identify teachers in need of improvement and create strong incentives for these teachers to pursue the training offered and apply it to their work. In Chile, Ecuador, and Colombia, and under new proposals in Peru and Mexico, teachers who receive poor evaluations are offered training and required to be reevaluated.

Finally, teacher evaluation gives school systems data to deal with consistently poor performers forthrightly and transparently. In Chile, Ecuador, and Colombia, and under new proposals in Peru and Mexico, teachers who receive successive evaluations in the lowest performance categories are dismissed from service. An education system's capacity to identify its least-effective teachers is a powerful tool for raising schooling quality. Research suggests that systematically targeting the lowest 5 percent of teachers annually for "de-selection" can produce large gains in student learning over time (Hanushek 2011; Chetty, Friedman, and Rockoff, forthcoming.).

A rigorous evaluation of the impacts of the Washington, DC, teacher evaluation system, which is considered a best-practice model in the United States, concluded that the system has produced an impressive improvement in overall teacher quality in just the first three years of implementation. Researchers documented four main mechanisms: voluntary attrition of teachers with low performance ratings increased by over 50 percent; low-rated teachers who decided to stay in the system achieved big improvements in performance; a higher share of top teachers stayed in the system (rather than transferring to other school districts); and teachers at the threshold for bonuses made big improvements (Dee and Wyckoff 2013). Since the teacher evaluation system was introduced, not only teacher quality has improved, but student learning gains have been the largest of any urban district in the United States.

Teacher professional development. When the costs of teacher time are included, in-service training is a major element of education spending in LAC. In Brazil and Mexico, many teachers participate in more than one month of training annually. Yet evidence on the cost-effectiveness of training is almost nonexistent. The global evidence base is also limited. The most common conclusion of metastudies is that the relevance of training content, the intensity and duration of the course, and the quality of the delivery are key: observations that abstract from the central question of how to design relevant program content.

A review of the academic literature and different training approaches that figure prominently in the "improving" education systems identified by Mourshed, Chijioke, and Barber (2010) suggests that four broad strategies for teacher training are most relevant for LAC countries:

- *Scripted approaches*: training to prepare teachers in low-capacity environments to use specific teaching strategies and accompanying materials in the delivery of a well-defined daily curriculum
- *Content mastery*: training focused on filling gaps or deepening teachers' expertise in the subjects they teach and how to teach them effectively
- *Classroom management*: training focused on improving teachers' classroom effectiveness through lesson planning, efficient use of class time, strategies for keeping students engaged, and more effective teaching techniques
- *Peer collaboration*: school-based or cross-school opportunities for small groups of teachers to observe and learn from each other's practice and collaborate on curriculum development, student assessment strategies, research, and other activities that contribute to system quality and teachers' professional development

Scripted training programs are relevant for many LAC countries, and perhaps especially for early grade literacy instruction and math skills. Honduras' SAT (Sistema de Aprendizaje Tutorial) scripted training program for middle school teachers in rural areas has produced higher learning results at lower per-student costs (McEwan et al., forthcoming). Scripted approaches have also been used successfully in Colombia's Escuela Nueva to support teachers in multigrade schools and in the Brazilian states of Ceará and Minas Gerais to train early-grade reading teachers. By providing teachers with comprehensive support in the use of teacher guides, lesson plans, classroom reading books, and reading assessments to be applied at regular intervals, Ceará has seen significant improvements in reading and math results (Carnoy and Costa, 2014). The federal Ministry of Education is now supporting national scale-up of this approach.

Given the weak content mastery of many teachers in LAC, training in this area is also clearly relevant. Unfortunately, there is no rigorous evaluation evidence of successful LAC programs. Useful training in the U.S. context, however, has focused on the specific math content knowledge required for effective teaching at different levels (Thames and Ball 2010).

Improving teachers' classroom practice emerged as a clear issue from the classroom observations conducted for this report, including teachers' ability to use class time and materials effectively and to keep students engaged. It is encouraging that a number of LAC school systems are developing courses focused on classroom management techniques that can improve student engagement and learning performance, drawing on the work of U.S. educator Doug Lemov (Lemov 2010, Lemov et al., 2012). In several cases, governments are planning rigorous evaluations, with random assignment of teachers to different training options and careful measurement of both subsequent classroom practice (through classroom observations) and impacts on student learning. These experiences could contribute enormously to the evidence base to guide effective training investments not only in LAC but also globally.

Peer collaboration—as practiced in Finland, Ontario (Canada), and under Japan's "Lesson Study" method—is integral to the development of greater professionalism among LAC's teachers and to the informal exchange of practice at the school level that is the most cost-effective strategy for improving school results. There is an incipient trend in this direction in several LAC countries. For example, in Ecuador training needs are identified at the school level, and colleagues receive training together (Ecuador, Ministerio de Educación 2012). Under Peru's teacher mentoring program, external coaches work with all of the teachers in a school as a team, providing real-time feedback and advice grounded in the coaches' observation and understanding of the school's context and specific challenges. Under Rio de Janeiro municipality's Gente and Ginásio Carioca experimental programs, the school day has been extended to free up time for teacher collaboration and team teaching. All of these represent very new approaches for the LAC region and have yet to be evaluated. But the emphasis placed on looking inside schools and classrooms to identify the issues where teachers most need support is promising.

Designing and delivering capacity-building programs of the caliber and scale required in most countries will not be easy. As Carnoy (2007) has observed, "weak coupling" between education ministries and university education departments makes the latter ill-prepared to respond to ministries' needs. Increasingly, ministries (and secretariats in Brazil) are creating in-service teacher training institutes to take direct control of the content and delivery of teacher professional development. While it is too early to evaluate these institutes' effectiveness, there is a visible shift toward professional development programs that directly address identified issues. Using teacher evaluation data to determine training priorities; exploiting partnerships with nongovernmental organizations, think tanks, and other providers operating outside of university education departments; and investing in rigorous evaluation of at least the most important training initiatives will help make investments in this area more cost-effective, which is essential for faster progress in raising the caliber of the current stock of teachers.

Teacher deployment and management. Grooming teachers so they develop their full potential and contribute to the professional growth of their colleagues is a direct responsibility of school leaders. Global research shows that school directors have a large impact on teacher quality, both by screening and selecting high-talent teachers for their schools and by engendering a school climate of peer collaboration, supportive feedback, and collaboration that makes those teachers even better (Loeb, Kalogrides, and Béteille 2012). High-performing education systems such as Singapore and Ontario (Canada) pay close attention to how school directors are selected, trained, and developed, placing special emphasis on their ability to gauge and develop the quality of their teachers (Schwartz and Mehta 2014; Tucker 2011; Barber and Mourshed 2007).

Despite increasing awareness of the pivotal role of principals, empirical evidence on how to build their skills and effectiveness is sparse. Most LAC countries are just beginning to develop systems for the selection, training, and coaching of school leaders.

Chile provides a good example of an incremental strategy for raising the quality of school leaders. Just as with teacher policy, the Ministry of Education started by defining standards. The "Framework for Good School Leadership" (Marco para la Buena Dirección), developed in 2004, established criteria for the training and assessment of principals in the areas of leadership, curriculum management, resource management, and organizational environment management and established a competitive process for principal selection (Chile, Ministerio de Educación 2005; Concha Albornoz 2007). A 2011 law strengthened the selection process and increased principals' autonomy and accountability. Principals may dismiss up to 5 percent of their schools' teachers each year on performance grounds and must sign performance agreements with the local governments that hire them. The government also introduced the Program for the Training of Excellent Principals (Programa de Formación de Directores de Excelencia) in 2011, which has provided leadership training to more than 1,600 of the country's 7,000 principals. The program subsidizes fees and subsistence costs for graduate programs (master's degrees, diplomas, and courses) and externships focused on school leadership. Programs are selected through a public call for proposals: in 2013, applicants could choose among 29 programs from 15 institutions, mostly in Chile but also in Canada and England.

While Chile's approach allows for diversity in the training offered to principals, several OECD countries have chosen to develop in-house principal training. Australia's 2010 Institute for Teaching and School Leadership develops standards, accreditation, *and* training for teachers and school leaders (OECD 2012). Principals are also trained in-house in Singapore, where young teachers are evaluated for leadership potential early in their careers and follow a specialized leadership track. This approach was adopted recently by Jamaica, whose National Center for Educational Leadership is charged with training and certifying aspiring and existing principals.

Once principals are selected and trained, ongoing support during the early years is important. A study of New York City schools found that effective support for principals on the job, particularly in the first few years, has a significant positive effect on school performance as measured by student exam scores and student absenteeism (Clark, Martorell, and Rockoff 2009). Leading countries such as Singapore ensure that experienced principals mentor new ones in a systematic manner.

Motivating teachers to perform

Major progress in raising the quality of teachers in Latin America will require attracting high-caliber candidates, continuously and systematically weeding out the lowest performers, and motivating individuals to keep refining their skills and working their hardest over a long career. These three processes characterize the labor market for high-status professions in all countries. In countries with high-performing education systems, they operate in teaching as well.

Research confirms that individuals are attracted to the teaching profession and inspired to high performance for a variety of reasons. Vegas and Umansky (2005) set out a comprehensive framework of incentives that may be collapsed into three broad categories: (a) professional rewards, including intrinsic satisfaction, recognition and prestige, professional growth, intellectual mastery, and pleasant working conditions; (b) accountability pressure; and (c) financial incentives (figure O.21).

While it seems intuitively obvious that all three types of incentives are important, there is a deep asymmetry in the research base. Very little research exists on specific policies or programs to raise the professional rewards for teachers, and none in Latin America. There is more research on reforms to strengthen accountability pressures on teachers—especially through school-based management—but little evidence on key questions such as the impact of policies that reduce teachers' job stability or improve school directors' capacity to evaluate and manage teacher performance. The greatest research attention by far has been focused on financial incentives, especially bonus pay. But this research bias should not be taken to mean that financial incentives are the most important. If anything, cross-country studies suggest that professional incentives are a very powerful element in high-performing education systems. In Finland and Canada, for example, the professional rewards for teachers are very strong and accountability pressures and financial rewards are relatively weak.

It is also likely that these three types of incentives are complementary: they have extra impact if well aligned and undercut each other if not. Case studies of the world's highest-performing school systems show positive incentives in all three areas, although their relative strength can vary.

Professional rewards. There is virtually no experimental evidence on the impact of alternative strategies for raising the professional rewards to teaching, but cross-country studies show that high-performing school systems offer their teachers abundant opportunities for continued *mastery and professional growth* and that outstanding teachers receive substantial *recognition and prestige*. Compared with most of Latin America, countries with high-performing education systems invest more resources in teacher

FIGURE O.21: Three broad classes of incentives motivate teachers

Professional rewards:
- Intrinsic motivation
- Recognition and prestige
- Mastery and professional growth
- Well-equipped, congenial working conditions

Financial incentives:
- Salary differentials
- Pensions and benifits
- Bonus pay

Accountability pressure:
- Job stability
- Client feedback
- Managerial feedback

Center: Attracting and motivating effective teachers

Source: Adapted from Vegas and Umansky 2005.

professional development—Singapore's 100 hours annually of paid professional development for every teacher is a leading example—but most important is the quality of those investments. Courses are developed by university practitioners in close collaboration with ministries of education; are grounded in research evidence; and focus on specific issues in effective delivery of the curriculum, the classroom practice of highly effective teachers, and lessons from education systems elsewhere in the world. High-performing systems also support teachers' professional growth by promoting constant interaction and peer collaboration among teachers. Finland's teachers spend only 60 percent as much time as the OECD average in the classroom teaching; the rest of their time they work jointly on new curriculum content, learning materials, and ways of assessing students' progress. Peru's teacher mentoring program and Rio de Janeiro municipality's Ginásio Experimental Carioca programs are promising new examples in the LAC region of efforts to promote teachers' professional mastery through peer collaboration.

High-performing education systems also give substantial *recognition and prestige* to excellent teachers. They have systems to evaluate individual teachers' potential and performance and grant the best teachers special status as master teachers or leaders in specific curriculum areas, such as math. In contrast, teachers in Latin America are rarely observed or evaluated closely. Whether their performance is outstanding or deeply deficient, teachers in most systems advance equally through the ranks on the basis of seniority.

Accountability pressure. High teacher absence rates across the LAC region and classroom observations showing that teachers are often poorly prepared to use class time effectively are evidence that the pressures teachers feel to perform accountably are generally weak. Strategies for strengthening accountability include actions to *reduce or eliminate teachers' job stability, increase managerial oversight*, and *empower clients (parents and students)* to monitor or evaluate teachers. There is little research evidence to date on any of these strategies except client empowerment: "strong" forms of school-based management, in which parents and community members had a voice in the hiring and firing of school personnel and were given training and encouragement to exercise that power, have been shown in some contexts to reduce teacher absence and raise student learning results (Bruns, Filmer, and Patrinos 2011).

In terms of job stability, legislation in Chile, Peru, Ecuador, Colombia, and Mexico has created a path out of the profession for teachers with persistently unsatisfactory performance. While potentially very important, the number of teachers dismissed to date in these countries has been tiny. This contrasts with the practice in Singapore, where all teachers are evaluated regularly and the lowest 5 percent of performers are regularly counseled out of the profession, and in Washington, DC, in which 33 percent of the teaching force was either dismissed or left voluntarily in the first four years after its teacher evaluation system was introduced. Radical upgrading of the teaching profession in Latin America will require much more aggressive action to weed out the lowest-performing teachers on a continuous basis.

In terms of managerial oversight, the role of school directors in managing teacher performance in LAC has generally been weak. Research in the United States has documented what many LAC education leaders observe: high-performing schools achieve success through skilled management of the teaching force. These schools' principals attract good teachers, weed out ineffective teachers, and deploy and develop new teachers more effectively than principals at other schools. Effective principals have the capacity to observe teachers in the classroom, give them formative feedback, and manage their "exit" from the school if necessary. Effective principals support teachers' development and hold them accountable for performance (Branch, Hanushek, and Rivkin 2013; Boyd et al. 2008; Loeb, Kalogrides, and Béteille 2012).

Recent efforts in Chile, Jamaica, Brazil, Peru, and Ecuador to raise the standards for school directors and train and empower these directors to be accountable for instructional quality and teacher development are important initiatives. But Colombia's experience—where directors found it difficult to give teachers critical feedback—suggests that relying only on school directors for teacher performance evaluation can be problematic. Instead, teacher evaluation needs to be a systemwide function supported by expert external observers and guided by common standards, evaluation processes, and rubrics, both for fairness and for systemwide learning. The goals are to generate actionable, formative feedback to teachers across the system and to weed out the lowest performers on a continuous basis so the average quality of the teaching force keeps rising over time.

Financial incentives. Cross-country research suggests that the financial rewards for teaching must meet a threshold level of parity with other professions to attract high talent. As chapter 1 shows, average salaries and the pay trajectory for teachers in some LAC countries are currently below this threshold.

Across-the-board salary increases—which are politically popular and easy to implement—have the potential to shift the overall teacher supply curve outward. But these are inefficient. For the same fiscal expenditure, school systems can achieve higher quality by raising average salaries through a pay scale differentiated by performance. This avoids overcompensating weak performers, can keep overall pension liabilities lower, and creates stronger incentives for the most talented individuals.

The two main strategies for differentiated financial rewards are *career path reforms* and *bonus pay*. Career path reforms typically make permanent promotions contingent on teachers' skills and performance rather than on seniority and expand salary differentials across different grades. The number of LAC countries that have implemented career path reforms is small but growing. Although it is difficult to evaluate such reforms rigorously, since they are almost always implemented systemwide, by analogy with other occupations it is likely that career path reforms have more powerful selection effects than does bonus pay on who goes into teaching. Career path reforms signal a permanent and cumulative structure of rewards for high performance, have attractive pension implications, and are reaped by individual teachers.

Key lessons that can be drawn from the experience with career path reforms in LAC to date are as follows:

- Choosing valid measures of teacher quality and calibrating them appropriately are crucial steps. Global research suggests that comprehensive teacher evaluations are the soundest basis for promotion decisions. An example consistent with global best practice is Peru's 2012 teacher career law, which establishes teachers' knowledge and skills, rather than seniority, as the basis for promotions. Ministry proposals for implementing the law call for comprehensive evaluations of teacher quality, including expert observations of teachers' practice in the classroom; and "360-degree" feedback from peers, students, parents, and school directors—all consistent with the best global evidence.
- For school systems introducing competency-based promotion and pay for the first time, relying on a well-designed test of subject matter mastery and pedagogical knowledge alone, as in Ecuador, may be a practical first step. To be legitimate, tests should measure what teachers *know* in terms of content, what they *understand* about child development and learning styles, and what they are *able to do* to tailor pedagogical strategies for the delivery of content

at different grade levels. Tests must also be benchmarked appropriately; if promotions are gained too easily, as in the early years of Mexico's Carrera Magisterial, or are too inaccessible, incentive strength erodes. Finally, the most recent career path reforms in LAC do not base teacher promotions on student test scores. This appears sensible, given the technical complexity of value-added learning measures and the risks of perverse incentives.

- Who evaluates is important. Although ministries of education should closely control the design and implementation of teacher promotion policies, contracting external agencies to design and administer teacher evaluations increases their legitimacy. For classroom observations, using well-trained external experts, developing clear and consistent evaluation standards and instruments, and providing teachers with detailed individualized feedback are important.

- The steepness of the salary trajectory affects incentive strength, but there is little evidence as yet to guide reform design. Recent reforms expand the number of promotion levels and decompress the band between top and initial salaries. But across the new programs, these dimensions vary: three different promotion levels are proposed in some systems and eight levels in others. Top-level salaries are 100 percent higher than those at starting level in some systems and almost 300 percent higher in others. As most of these reforms are quite new, there is an important opportunity to research their differential impacts on the recruitment of new teachers over time.

- Strategies for managing the long-term fiscal implications of career path reforms are important. Although the permanence of promotions and base pay increases is central to its strength as an incentive, it runs the risk of locking in high compensation for teachers who are promoted but subsequently fail to keep up their skills. Ecuador's reform guards against this by requiring that teachers achieve either further promotion or recertification at the same level every four years, or face a downgrade of level and salary. This is the first case in the region of an "up or out" strategy built into a career path reform. It is an interesting design that deserves evaluation.

- Careful implementation planning of reforms as complex as these is important. The credibility of several programs—Mexico's original Carrera Magisterial, Peru's 2008 Carrera Pública Magisterial reform, and programs in Colombia and São Paulo—has been undermined by problems that might have been foreseen and managed differently.

- Incentive power hangs on the belief that the program will be sustained under consistent rules of the game. Whenever teachers perceive that the criteria for entry into a new career track are likely to change, soften, or be disbanded, the incentives to acquire new knowledge and apply it to their work erode. Career path reforms that truly signal substantially higher long-term financial rewards for talented teachers probably offer the clearest path to the recruitment of higher-caliber teacher candidates and more effective teaching. Policy makers across the region would gain from careful research on the new wave of career path reforms in LAC.

Bonus pay is the other major instrument for raising the financial rewards for teaching. Bonus pay programs are proliferating in LAC, especially in Brazil. They are politically and technically easier to implement than career path reforms and do not have long-term fiscal or pension implications. Bonus programs typically offer a one-time reward for teachers (or schools) for specific results achieved during the prior school year. There is no evidence yet on the impact of bonus pay programs on the critical long-term question of teacher selection: are bonus pay programs a sufficiently strong financial incentive to attract higher-caliber candidates into teaching? But the experience to date provides some evidence of short-term impacts on teacher and school performance and lessons for program design:

- Bonus pay programs can work in developing country contexts. Although the number of cases remains small, bonus pay programs in developing country settings have produced more consistently positive results than in developed countries (especially the United States) to date. The only two rigorously evaluated cases of bonus pay programs operating at scale (Chile's Sistema Nacional de Evaluación de Desempeño [SNED] and the school bonus in Pernambuco, Brazil) are both from Latin America, and both have demonstrated positive results on student learning and grade attainment. Measured impacts across all developing country programs to date are generally in the range of 0.1 to 0.3 SD improvements in test scores, which are significant-sized effects for education interventions. A reasonable hypothesis is that bonus pay incentives—which focus schools on student learning results—can be productive in systems where other accountability pressures and teacher professionalism are weak.

- Matching incentive design to context is crucial. Much of the experimental evidence to date is from studies that tested alternative bonus designs—group versus individual incentives; teacher versus student incentives; "gain" versus "loss" bonus awards—and it is striking how much the impact of alternative bonus designs can vary within a single context. The optimal bonus size is another design issue on which there is as yet little practical guidance from research; some of the largest reported impacts in the literature are from bonuses that represented a very small increment of teachers' monthly pay, while significantly larger bonuses—averaging one to two months' salary—are becoming common in Brazil. The research base today is far short of providing a guide to the most productive bonus pay designs for a given context. But it suggests that if a given program's impact appears to be weak, there probably exists a productive alternative design.

- Designing the performance measure(s) to be rewarded is a key challenge. Basing bonus pay on student test scores alone has been problematic in several U.S. settings because of documented cheating and broader concerns that it focuses teachers too narrowly on test preparation and specific subjects and makes them unwilling to teach at-risk students. No LAC country to date has introduced bonus pay based on test scores alone, and this strategy appears wise. The composite indicator used in Brazil, which is a product of test scores and pass rates, is an interesting model for countries to consider. It discourages automatic promotion of children who are not learning and the reverse strategy of holding children back or encouraging dropout to boost test scores.

- Programs may have heterogeneous impacts on different types of schools. In both of the bonus programs operating at scale, significant heterogeneity has been observed. In Chile's SNED program, about one-third of schools appear consistently "out of the money" in the bonuses granted every two years, despite the serious efforts made to ensure that schools compete only against similar schools (Contreras and Rau 2012). In the case of Pernambuco, Brazil, the bonus has produced stronger improvements in small schools, where teachers can collaborate and monitor each other more easily than in larger schools. Improvements have also been larger for academically weak and low-income students, suggesting that the bonus has stimulated schools and teachers to focus more effort on these students (Ferraz and Bruns, forthcoming). Research evidence of this type can provide useful guidance for program design.

- Students are a key partner in the production of learning results. The innovative design of the ALI (Aligning Learning Incentives) experiment in Mexico generated powerful evidence that school systems can gain by finding ways to make students feel more invested in their learning progress (Behrman et al., forthcoming). This is consistent with evidence that student learning performance on international tests is higher for countries with high-stakes examinations for students at the end of secondary school, which create strong incentives for student effort (Woessmann 2012).

- Our understanding of the mechanisms through which bonus pay improves student outcomes is still weak. The logic of incentive pay is to stimulate teacher behaviors that help raise student learning: either increased teacher effort or more effective effort. However, relatively few evaluations have documented changes in teachers' classroom practice that plausibly explain observed increases in student learning. Research on teachers' classroom practice is becoming more feasible, with the declining costs of installing video cameras in samples of classrooms and increasing use of standardized methods for coding and analyzing teacher-student interaction. Systematic inclusion of such analysis in impact evaluations of pay-for-performance programs will not only illuminate how such programs work but also generate evidence and examples of effective teaching that can more broadly benefit these school systems.

Ultimately, cross-country studies suggest that no education system achieves high teacher quality without aligning all three types of incentives: professional rewards, accountability pressures, and financial rewards. But these studies also suggest that the particular combinations that are most efficient are highly context-specific. Finland, Singapore, and Ontario (Canada), for example, have all built strong professional rewards for teaching, but accountability pressures are much stronger in Singapore than in Finland or Canada. And none follows a textbook approach on financial incentives: Finland has achieved a sharp upgrading of teacher quality over the past 20 years with little increase in teachers' relative salaries. Singapore keeps salaries for entering teachers on par with other professions and offers bonuses for high performance, but has an overall career ladder that is much flatter than in other professions. Ontario pays competitive salaries, but the core of its strategy is team-based professional development at the school level supported by outside experts but not otherwise incentivized. These examples suggest that there are multiple roads to the goal: a balanced set of incentives sufficient to attract talented teacher candidates, establish accountability for results, and motivate continued professional growth and pursuit of excellence.

Managing the politics of teacher reform

Teachers are not only key actors in the production of education results but also the most powerful stakeholders in the process of education reform. No other education actor is as highly organized, visible, and politically influential (Grindle 2004). Because of their unique autonomy behind the closed door of the classroom, teachers also have profound power over the extent to which new policies can be implemented successfully. By global standards, teachers' unions in Latin America and the Caribbean have been considered especially powerful. They have a history of effective use of direct electoral influence and disruptive actions in the streets to block reforms perceived as a threat to their interests.

Like all organized workers, teachers' unions exist to defend the rights they legitimately earn through negotiations and to oppose policy changes that threaten those rights. Teachers and their representatives are entirely justified in pursuing these goals, and teachers' unions throughout history have been a progressive force in achieving equal pay and fair treatment for women and minority members. But it is also true that the goals of teachers' organizations are not congruent with the goals of education policy makers or the interests of education beneficiaries—including students, parents, and employers who need skilled workers.

Viewed through the lens of teachers' legitimate interests, a number of education policies that governments adopt in pursuit of education quality pose threats to teachers' benefits (elimination of job stability and reduction or loss of other benefits); to teachers' working conditions (curriculum reforms, student testing, and teacher evaluation systems); or to union structure and power (decentralization, school choice, higher standards for teachers at entry, alternative certification, and pay linked to individual skills or performance). Relatively few education policies—higher spending on education, bonus pay at the school level, and lower pupil-teacher ratios—are positively aligned with unions' interests. Unions' ability to challenge policies depends on their structure (i.e., share of teachers unionized), their capacity for collective action, and the effectiveness of their political strategies. The latter include strikes and protests, government capture, legal strategies, and union-sponsored research and policy analysis to influence education debate. All of these strategies have been deployed effectively by unions in Latin America and the Caribbean in national debates over education reform during the past several decades.

But recent reform experiences in Mexico, Peru, and Ecuador suggest that the balance of power between governments and teachers' unions in the region may be shifting. In an age where mass media afford political leaders a direct channel of communication with even the most remote and rural of their citizens, one of the long-time sources of union power—the ability to mobilize their members for large-scale grassroots political campaigning—may be of diminishing utility. In a region where democracy has taken hold in most countries, mass media have become increasingly vociferous in exposing government failure and political corruption. This feeds public demand for more accountable and effective government and resonates particularly strongly in education, which touches every family's hopes and aspirations for its children. Increasingly, political leaders in LAC appear to be calculating that popular support for education reform is a stronger bet for their political future than the traditional quid pro quo of electoral support from teachers' unions in exchange for education policies that do not threaten their interests.

While there is substantial heterogeneity across the region in union power, government reform priorities, and the dynamics of the reform process, the most recent reform experiences support several cautious observations:

- Political leaders can build effective proreform alliances of business leaders and civil society through communications campaigns that paint a compelling picture of the current failures of the education system and the importance of better education for economic competitiveness. Successfully uniting two sides of the stakeholder triangle (civil society and government) in dialogue with the third (organized teachers) can create political space for the adoption of reforms, including three that challenge union interests (individual teacher performance evaluation, pay differentiated by performance, and loss of job stability).

- Reform momentum is greatest if launched at the start of an administration. In most cases, the process is contentious and unions have a strong interest in dragging it out. If leaders move quickly, they capitalize on their point of maximum political leverage and establish education as a top priority. As they begin to govern, administrations are inevitably forced to spend time on a wide range of other issues and suffer some political reversals; this diffuses messages and erodes leverage.

- Hard data on education system results are a crucial political tool. Especially powerful are data on student learning outcomes, results that are internationally benchmarked (such as PISA, TIMMS [Trends in International Mathematics and Science Study], SERCE [Second Regional Comparative and Explanatory Study], and LLECE [Latin American Laboratory for Assessment of the Quality of Education]) and data on teachers' performance on competency tests. Political leaders' use of these to build the case for reform has been a factor in all successful strategies to date. Of all international tests, the OECD's PISA seems to resonate most strongly with the business community and civil society groups. This is likely because the comparator countries are those that LAC countries aspire to join, and because it is easy to interpret the results, for 15-year-old youths, as a barometer of labor force quality and economic competitiveness.

- Reform strategies based on confrontation with unions may succeed in securing the legislative adoption of major reforms, but not necessarily their implementation. In many countries, the political space for negotiating major reforms with teachers' unions does not exist. In three recent cases (Mexico, Peru, and Ecuador) confrontation politics has produced the legislative or constitutional adoption of teacher policy reforms that global evidence suggests are needed for education quality: student testing, teacher performance evaluation, teacher hiring and promotions linked to skills and performance rather than seniority, and dismissal of teachers with consistently poor performance. There may be no political alternative to confrontation strategies in many contexts; in Mexico's case, a high-profile government effort to design reforms with the union foundered when the union could not deliver members' adherence with the agreements. But confrontation strategies imply a major trade-off: they make it impossible to gain input from teachers that could genuinely improve a reform's design and smooth its implementation.

- Sequencing reforms can ease adoption and improve implementation. The region's experience suggests a political logic to a certain sequence of education reforms. The first step is student testing, with transparent dissemination of results, both nationally and to individual schools; this is the anchor that makes it possible to guide overall education policy and to introduce performance-based reforms. A second step in several cases has been the adoption of school-based bonus pay, which establishes the concept of pay for performance and focuses schools on student learning progress, but has typically faced less union resistance than individual bonus pay. A third step is individual teacher evaluation on a voluntary basis, with the carrot of attractive financial rewards for teachers who take the risk of being evaluated and perform well. Unions have typically opposed this, but making programs voluntary can avoid confrontation. This sequence of reforms was implemented in Chile between 1995 and 2004, more recently by São Paulo state, and (proposed) in Rio de Janeiro state.

All of the available evidence suggests that the quality of teachers in Latin America and the Caribbean is the binding constraint on the region's progress toward world-class education systems. Low standards for entry into teaching; low-quality candidates; salaries, promotions, and job tenure delinked from performance; and weak school leadership have produced low professionalism in the classroom and poor education results. Moving to a new equilibrium will be difficult and will require recruiting, grooming, and motivating a new breed of teacher.

Raising the stakes further are the sweeping transformations occurring in global education. The traditional goals of national education systems and the traditional paradigm of teacher-student interaction made teachers the linchpin in the transmission of discrete bodies of knowledge to students in the classroom. The new paradigm is that teachers are not the only or even the major source of information and knowledge available to students. A core role of teachers today is to equip students to seek, analyze, and effectively use vast amounts of information that are readily available elsewhere. Teachers must also develop students' competencies in the broad range of areas valued in an integrated global economy: critical thinking; problem solving; ability to work collaboratively in diverse environments; adaptation to change; and the capacity to master new knowledge, skills, and changing employment demands across their lifetimes. No teacher preparation programs in LAC—or indeed in most OECD countries—are fully prepared to produce this profile of teacher today, let alone the profiles that may be needed over the next decade. But virtually all OECD countries are responding to these challenges by raising their expectations, and standards, for teachers.

Countries across Latin America and the Caribbean are also responding. Virtually all aspects of teacher policy are under review and reform in different LAC countries, and in some areas the region is in the vanguard of global policy experience. By drawing together in one volume the key teacher policy reforms being undertaken in the region today and the best available evidence on their impact, this book hopes to stimulate and support the faster progress that is needed.

Note

[1] Because Peru did not participate in the 2003 and 2006 rounds of PISA, researchers excluded it from the analysis of countries registering the most significant sustained progress between 1990 and 2006.

References

Alfonso, M., A. Santiago, and M. Bassi. 2010. "Estimating the Impact of Placing Top University Graduates in Vulnerable Schools in Chile." Technical Note IDB-TN-230, Inter-American Development Bank, Washington, DC.
Barber, M., and M. Mourshed. 2007. *How the World's Best-Performing School Systems Come Out on Top*. London: McKinsey. http://mckinseyonsociety.com/downloads/reports/Education/Worlds_School_Systems_Final.pdf.
Behrman, J., S. Parker, P. Todd, and K. Wolpin. Forthcoming. "Aligning Learning Incentives of Students and Teachers: Results from a Social Experiment in Mexican High Schools." *Journal of Political Economy*.
Boyd, D., P. Grossman, H. Lankford, S. Loeb, and J. Wyckoff. 2008. "Who Leaves? Teacher Attrition and Student Achievement." Working Paper 14022, National Bureau of Economic Research, Cambridge, MA.
———. 2009. "Teacher Preparation and Student Achievement." *Educational Evaluation and Policy Analysis* 31 (4): 416–40.
Branch, G., E. Hanushek, and S. Rivkin. 2013. "School Leaders Matter." *Education Next* 13 (2): 62–69.
Bruns, B., D. Filmer, and H. A. Patrinos. 2011. *Making Schools Work: New Evidence on Accountability Reforms*. Washington, DC: World Bank.
Carnoy, M. 2007. *Cuba's Academic Advantage: Why Students in Cuba Do Better in School*. Palo Alto, CA: Stanford University Press.
Carnoy, M., and L. Costa. 2014. "The Effectiveness of an Early Grades Literacy Intervention on the Cognitive Achievement of Brazilian Students." Paper presented at the Conference of Brazilian Econometric Society Conference, Foz do Iguaçu, Brazil.
Chetty, R., J. N. Friedman, and J. E. Rockoff. Forthcoming. "Measuring the Impacts of Teachers II: Teacher Value-Added and Student Outcomes in Adulthood." *American Economic Review*.
Chile, Ministerio de Educación. 2005. *Marco para la Buena Dirección*. Santiago: Ministerio de Educación. http://www.mineduc.cl/usuarios/convivencia_escolar/doc/201103070155490.MINEDUC.Marco_para_la_Buena_Direccion.pdf.
———. 2008. "Marco para la Buena Enseñanza." *Docente más*. Santiago (accessed July 24, 2012). http://www.docentemas.cl/docs/MBE2008.pdf.
Chingos, M., and P. E. Peterson. 2010. "Do School Districts Get What They Pay for? Predicting Teacher Effectiveness by College Selectivity, Experience, Etc." Harvard University Program on Education Policy and Governance Working Paper 10-08, Harvard University, Cambridge, MA.
Clark, D., P. Martorell, and J. Rockoff. 2009. "School Principals and School Performance." CALDER Working Paper 38, National Center for Analysis of Longitudinal Data in Education Research, Urban Institute, Washington, DC.
Concha Albornoz, C. 2007. "Claves para la formación de directivos de instituciones escolares." *Revista Electrónica Iberoamericana sobre Calidad, Eficacia y Cambio en Educación* 5 (5): 133–38.

Contreras, D., and T. Rau. 2012. "Tournament Incentives for Teachers: Evidence from a Scaled-up Intervention in Chile." *Economic Development and Cultural Change* 91 (1): 219–46.

Corcoran, S. P., W. N. Evans, and R. M. Schwab. 2004. "Women, the Labor Market, and the Declining Relative Quality of Teachers." *Journal of Policy Analysis and Management* 23 (3): 449–70.

Dee, T., and J. Wyckoff. 2013. "Incentives, Selection and Teacher Performance: Evidence from IMPACT." Working Paper 19529, National Bureau of Economic Research, Cambridge, MA.

Ecuador, Ministerio de Educación. 2012. *Sistema Integral de Desarrollo Profesional Educativo*. Quito (accessed September 7, 2012). http://sime.educacion.gob.ec/Modulo/SIPROFE/index.php?mp=9_0.

Eide, E. G., D. Goldhaber, and D. Brewer. 2004. "The Teacher Labour Market and Teacher Quality." *Oxford Review of Economic Policy* 20 (2): 230–44.

Estrada, R. 2013. "Rules rather than Discretion: Teacher Hiring and Rent Extraction." Manuscript. Paris School of Economics, Paris, France.

Ferraz, C., and B. Bruns. Forthcoming. "Paying Teachers to Perform: The Impact of Bonus Pay in Pernambuco, Brazil." Manuscript, World Bank, Washington, DC.

Franco, M. 2012. "Pre-Service Training in Latin America and the Caribbean: A Background Study for the World Bank LAC Study on Teachers." Manuscript, World Bank, Washington, DC.

Fredriksson, P., and B. Ockert. 2007. "The Supply of Skills to the Teacher Profession." Manuscript, Uppsala University, Uppsala, Sweden.

Garland, S. 2008. "Reform School." Daily Beast, December 17. http://www.thedailybeast.com/newsweek/2008/12/17/reform-school.html.

Grindle, M. S. 2004. *Despite the Odds: The Contentious Politics of Education Reform*. Princeton, NJ: Princeton University Press.

Hanushek, E. A. 2011. "The Economic Value of Higher Teacher Quality." *Economics of Education Review* 30: 466–79.

Hanushek, E., P. Peterson, and L. Woessmann. 2012. "Achievement Growth: International and U.S. State Trends in Student Performance." Harvard's Program on Education Policy and Governance/Education Next, Harvard Kennedy School, Cambridge, MA.

Hanushek, E., and S. Rivkin. 2010. "Generalizations about Using Value-Added Measures of Teacher Quality." *American Economic Review* 100 (2): 267–71.

Hanushek, E. A., and L. Woessmann. 2012. "Schooling, Educational Achievement, and the Latin American Growth Puzzle." *Journal of Development Economics* 99 (2): 497–512.

Hernani-Limarino, W. 2005. "Are Teachers Well Paid in Latin America and the Caribbean? Relative Wage and Structure of Returns of Teachers." In *Incentives to Improve Teaching: Lessons from Latin America*, edited by E. Vegas. Washington, DC: World Bank.

Hoxby, C. M., and A. Leigh. 2004. "Pulled Away or Pushed Out? Explaining the Decline of Teacher Aptitude in the United States." *American Economic Review* 94 (2): 236–40.

Kane, T. J., and D. O. Staiger. 2012. *Gathering Feedback for Teaching: Combining High-Quality Observations with Student Surveys and Achievement Gains*. Seattle, WA: Measures of Effective Teaching Project, Bill & Melinda Gates Foundation.

Lemov, D. 2010. *Teach Like a Champion*. San Francisco: Jossey-Bass.

Lemov, D. 2011. *Aula Nota 10*. São Paulo: Fundacao Lemann and Editora Safra.

Lemov, D., Woolway, E., and Yezzi, K. 2012. *Practice Perfect*. San Francisco: Jossey-Bass.

Loeb, S., D. Kalogrides, and T. Béteille. 2012. "Effective Schools: Teacher Hiring, Assignment, Development, and Retention." *Education Finance and Policy* 7 (3): 269–304.

McEwan, P. J., E. Murphy-Graham, D. Torres Irribarra, C. Aguilar, and R. Rápalo. Forthcoming. "Improving Middle School Quality in Poor Countries: Evidence from the Honduran Sistema de Aprendizaje Tutorial." *Educational Evaluation and Policy Analysis*. doi:10.3102/0162373714527786.

Mizala, A., and H. Ñopo. 2011. "Teachers' Salaries in Latin America: How Much Are They (Under or Over) Paid?" IZA Discussion Paper 5947, Institute for the Study of Labor, Bonn.

Moursched, M., C. Chijioke, and M. Barber. 2010. *How the World's Most Improved School Systems Keep Getting Better*. London: McKinsey and Company. http://mckinseyonsociety.com/downloads/reports/Education/How-the-Worlds-Most-Improved-School-Systems-Keep-Getting-Better_Download-version_Final.pdf.

OECD (Organisation for Economic Co-operation and Development). 2012. *Preparing Teachers and Developing School Leaders for the 21st Century: Lessons from Around the World*. Paris: OECD.

———. 2013. *PISA 2012 Results: What Students Know and Can Do—Student Performance in Mathematics, Reading and Science*. Vol. 1. Paris: OECD Publishing. doi :10.1787/19963777.

Ome, A. 2012. "The Effects of Meritocracy for Teachers in Colombia." Manuscript, Centro de Investigación Económica y Social, Fedesarrollo, Bogota.

Picardo, J. O. 2012. "La formación de docentes en América Latina y El Caribe: Caso El Salvador." Manuscript, San Salvador.

Rockoff, J. E. 2004. "The Impact of Individual Teachers on Student Achievement: Evidence from Panel Data." *American Economic Review* 94 (2): 247–52.

Rodríguez, A., C. J. Dahlman, and J. Salmi. 2008. *Knowledge and Innovation for Competitiveness in Brazil*. Washington, DC: World Bank.

Salmi, J. 2009. *The Challenge of Establishing World-Class Universities*. Washington, DC: World Bank.

Schwartz, J., and J. Mehta. 2014. "Ontario: Harnessing the Skills of Tomorrow." In *Lessons from PISA for Korea, Strong Performers and Successful Reformers in Education*, edited by OECD. Paris: OECD. http://dx.doi.org/10.1787/9789264190672-en.

Stallings, J., and S. Knight. 2003. "Using the Stallings Observation System to Investigate Time on Task in Four Countries." Unpublished paper for the International Time on Task (ITOT) Project, World Bank, Washington, DC.

TEDS-M (Teacher Education and Development Study in Mathematics [database]) 2008. International Association for the Evaluation of Educational Achievement, Amsterdam. http://www.iea.nl/teds-m.html.

Thames, M. H., and D. L. Ball. 2010. "What Math Knowledge Does Teaching Require?" *Teaching Children Mathematics* 17 (4): 220–29.

Tucker, M., ed. 2011. *Surpassing Shanghai: An Agenda for American Education Built on the World's Leading Systems*. Cambridge, MA: Harvard Education Press.

UNESCO (United Nations Educational, Scientific, and Cultural Organization). 2012. *Antecedentes y Criterios para la Elaboración de Políticas Docentes en América Latina y el Caribe*. Santiago: UNESCO.

UIS.Stat (UNESCO Institute for Statistics [database]). http://data.uis.unesco.org/.

Vaillant, D., and C. Rossel. 2006. *Maestros de escuelas básicas en América Latina: Hacia una radiografía de la profesión*. Santiago: Programa de Promoción de la Reforma Educativa en América Latina y el Caribe (PREAL). http://www.oei.es/docentes/publicaciones/maestros_escuela_basicas_en_america_latina_preal.pdf.

Vegas, E., and I. Umansky. 2005. "Improving Teaching and Learning through Effective Incentives." In *Incentives to Improve Teaching: Lessons from Latin America*, edited by E. Vegas, 21–62. Washington, DC: World Bank.

Woessmann, L. 2012. "Peering over the Hedge: How Do the Neighbours Do It?" *CESifo Forum* 13 (3): 16–20.

1
How Good Are Teachers in the Region?

What do we know about the quality of teachers in Latin America and the Caribbean? How important is teacher quality? What makes good teachers? This chapter reviews the available global and regional evidence on these questions. It starts with what we know about education system performance in Latin America and the Caribbean (LAC).

How are LAC education systems performing?

Over the last 50 years, Latin American and Caribbean countries have achieved a mass expansion of education coverage that has played out over two centuries in most Organisation for Economic Co-operation and Development (OECD) countries. From a starting point of about 10 percent of all children completing secondary school in 1960, today virtually all countries in the region have achieved universal primary school coverage and close to universal primary school completion, as well as high rates of secondary schooling (figure 1.1). Only Guatemala and Haiti stand in sharp contrast to the regional progress (Annex 1.1, table 1.4).[1]

Moreover, schooling coverage expanded in the face of rapid population growth. The school-age population across the region more than doubled between 1960 and 2010, and in countries such as Paraguay, Honduras, and Nicaragua it quintupled (figure 1.2). The number of children enrolled in primary and secondary education in Latin America and the Caribbean grew from 53 million to 127 million between 1970 and 2010, and the number of teachers quintupled, from 1.3 million to 7.4 million.

This chapter was coauthored with Martin Moreno.

FIGURE 1.1: Increase in secondary school attainment in LAC, 1950–2010

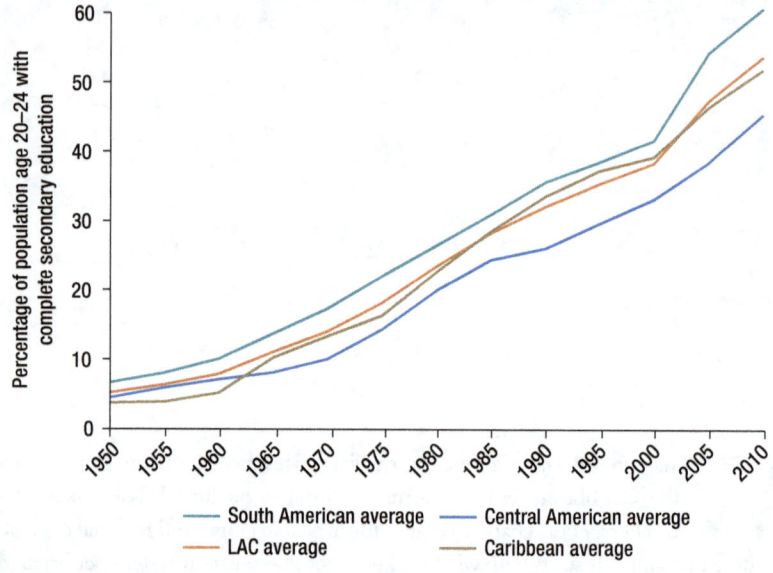

Source: Barro and Lee 2012.
Note: LAC = Latin America and the Caribbean. The sample is Latin America and Caribbean countries with education data for the whole period. Mexico and Central America are grouped together.

This achievement raised the average educational level of Latin America's labor force dramatically. While the average worker in 1960 had completed only 4 years of schooling, the region today is converging on the OECD average of 12 years. But schooling attainment remains relatively low in Central American countries, and other developing regions have moved even faster to expand education over the same period. East Asian countries today exceed the average educational attainment of the OECD (table 1.1).

Recent research has deepened the understanding of how human capital contributes to economic growth. It has established convincingly that what counts is not how many years of schooling students attain, but what they actually learn. It may seem intuitively obvious that a year of schooling in Mali will not equal one in Singapore, but not until recently have researchers been able to quantify the impact of this difference on economic growth.

An influential study by Hanushek and Woessman (2012) created a database of internationally comparable test scores from more than 50 countries over a 40-year period and demonstrates the correlation between countries' average student learning performance and their long-term economic growth. A country whose average test performance has been 1 standard deviation higher than another, roughly the 100-point difference between Mexico and Germany on the OECD's 2012

FIGURE 1.2: Secondary enrollment growth relative to population growth, 1960–2010

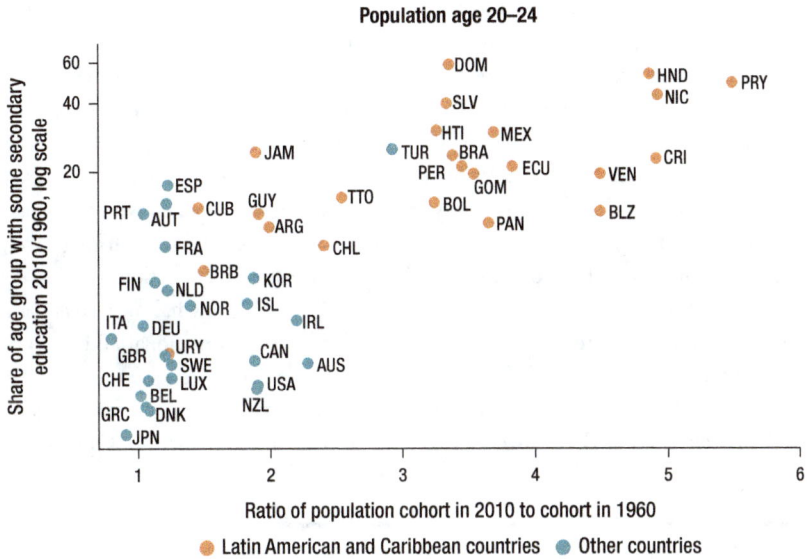

Source: Barro and Lee 2012.
Note: Three-letter country codes are ISO 3166 standard.

TABLE 1.1: Average educational attainment of the adult population, 1950–2010

	Years of schooling completed					
	1960	1970	1980	1990	2000	2010
Caribbean average	4.3	6.1	7.5	8.9	9.3	10.3
Central American average	3.8	4.5	6.2	7.4	8.2	9.6
South American average	4.5	5.9	7.2	8.3	8.9	10.5
LAC average	4.3	5.5	6.9	8.2	8.8	10.2
East Asian average	5.3	7.3	8.6	9.9	10.8	12.3
OECD average	7.7	9.0	10.1	10.8	11.3	12.1

Source: Barro and Lee 2012.
Note: LAC = Latin America and the Caribbean; OECD = Organisation for Economic Co-operation and Development. Based on average years of schooling completed for the population age 20 to 24. The sample is Latin America and Caribbean countries with education data for the whole period. The OECD average is calculated for 33 countries with education data for whole period. The East Asian average is calculated for four countries and two special administrative regions with education data for the whole period. Full table in Annex 1.1.

Program for International Student Assessment (PISA) exam, will enjoy approximately 2 percentage points higher annual long-term gross domestic product (GDP) growth. This relationship holds across high-income countries, low-income countries, and across regions (figures 1.3 and 1.4).

Hanushek and Woessmann's work has shown that the quantity of education, measured as average years of schooling of the labor force, is correlated with long-term economic growth in analyses that neglect education quality. But this association falls close to zero once a measure of education quality, such as average test scores on internationally benchmarked tests, is introduced. Differences in countries' average level of cognitive skills are consistently and fairly strongly correlated with long-term rates of economic growth. It is quality—in terms of increased student learning—they argue, that produces the economic benefits from investing in education.

If student learning results are what count for economic growth, how well is Latin America doing? The region's increasing participation in international and regional tests provides direct evidence. Four important conclusions emerge.

First, relative to its level of economic development, the region as a whole underperforms badly. The LAC region trails the average performance of OECD and

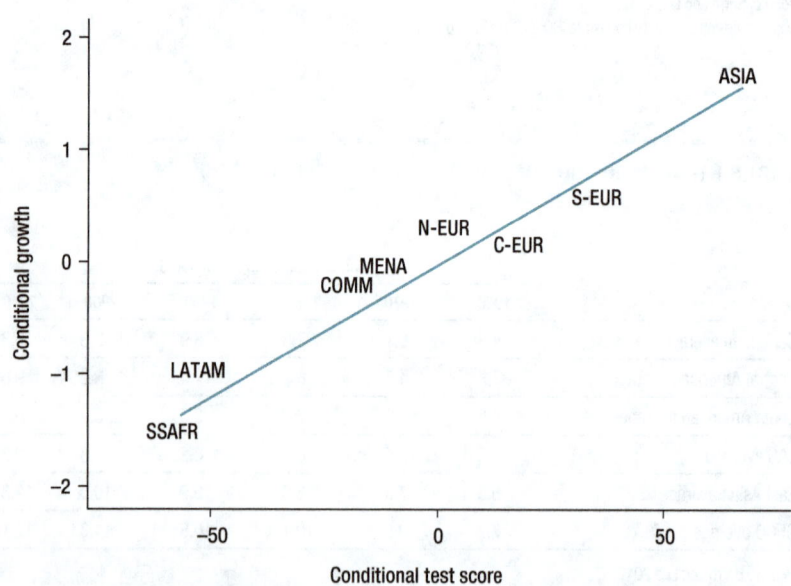

FIGURE 1.3: Cognitive skills and economic growth across regions

Source: Hanushek and Woessmann 2012.
Note: coefficient = .023, se (standard error) = .001, t = 17.7. Region codes: East Asia and India (ASIA), Central Europe (C-EUR), Commonwealth OECD members (COMM), Latin America (LATAM), Middle East and North Africa (MENA), Northern Europe (N-EUR), Southern Europe (S-EUR), Sub-Saharan Africa (SSAFR).

FIGURE 1.4: Cognitive skills and growth across countries

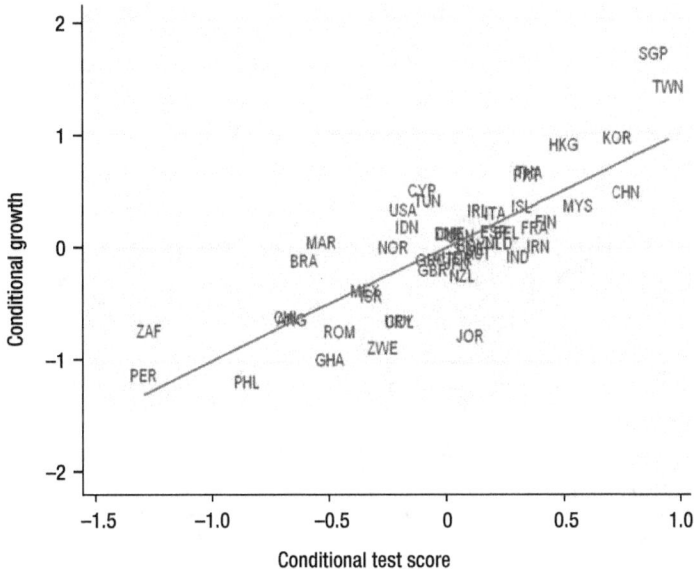

Source: Hanushek and Woessmann 2007.
Note: coefficient = .02305259, se (standard error) = .00130272, t = 17.7. Three-letter country codes are ISO 3166 standard.

East Asian countries by large margins. In figure 1.3, the LAC region's average learning performance on all international tests over the past 40 years is lower than in every other region except Sub-Saharan Africa.[2] In figure 1.4, the average test scores for all of the LAC countries for which long-term learning data exists fall well below East Asian countries and below several Middle Eastern countries. As Hanushek and Woessman report, the lower learning performance of LAC countries is correlated with their slower per capita income growth over the past 40 years.

Of the 65 countries participating in the 2012 OECD PISA test, all eight participating LAC countries scored below the average for their level of per capita income, as shown in figure 1.5. LAC countries defined the bottom end of the performance band for middle-income countries (figure 1.6). The 100-point difference between the OECD average math score on the 2012 PISA exam (494) and the average score of the eight participating LAC countries (397) represents a disparity in skills of more than two full years of math education.[3] The average score for students in Shanghai, China, (613) suggests math proficiency five years beyond the average student in LAC. Given that a larger share of all 15 year olds have already dropped out of school in LAC countries than in the OECD or East Asia, the true gap in average skills is even worse. All available evidence is that the literacy, numeracy, and critical reasoning skills of youths in LAC badly trail those of other middle-income countries.

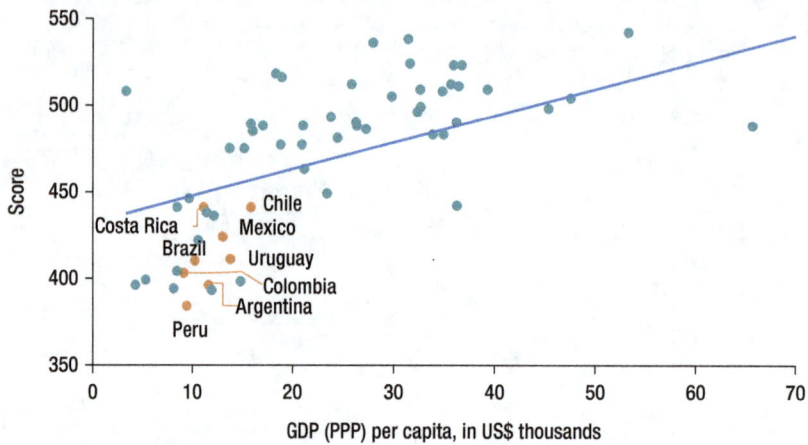

FIGURE 1.5: PISA reading scores and income per capita for LAC countries, 2012

Source: OECD/PISA and World Bank.
Note: GDP = gross domestic product; LAC = Latin America and the Caribbean; PISA = Program for International Student Assessment. GDP per capita adjusted for purchasing power parity, in 2005 constant prices.

The low average scores for participating LAC countries on the PISA test do not fully drive home how badly the region lags behind some of its economic competitors. Box 1.1 gives examples of questions that 15-year-old students scoring at level 2 or below cannot answer correctly. While less than 10 percent of students in Shanghai, China; Singapore; and the Republic of Korea scored below level 2 in mathematics on PISA, 74 percent of students in Peru and Colombia did. And at the top of the distribution, while 55 percent of Shanghai's students scored in the two highest performance bands in math (levels 5 and 6), along with 40 percent of students in Singapore and 31 percent in Korea, less than 1 percent of students in Mexico, Costa Rica, Brazil, Colombia, and Peru did. Only in Chile (1.6 percent of students) and Uruguay (1.4 percent) did the share exceed 1 percent (table 1.2).

Hanushek and Woessmann's research analyzes the contributions of both ends of the performance spectrum to labor productivity and economic growth. They conclude that achieving "learning for all"—ensuring that the broad base of the population has a core set of basic literacy and numeracy skills—is fundamental for the diffusion of knowledge and innovation that sustains economic growth. But they also find that having a critical mass of students at the top of the distribution seems to exert separate important effects on economic growth (Hanushek and Woessmann 2007).

Second, there is a substantial gap in performance within Latin American and the Caribbean. Among the LAC countries participating in PISA 2012, the gap between the top performer (Chile) and the lowest (Peru) was 55 points in math, 57 points

FIGURE 1.6: Comparative LAC region performance on 2012 PISA math test

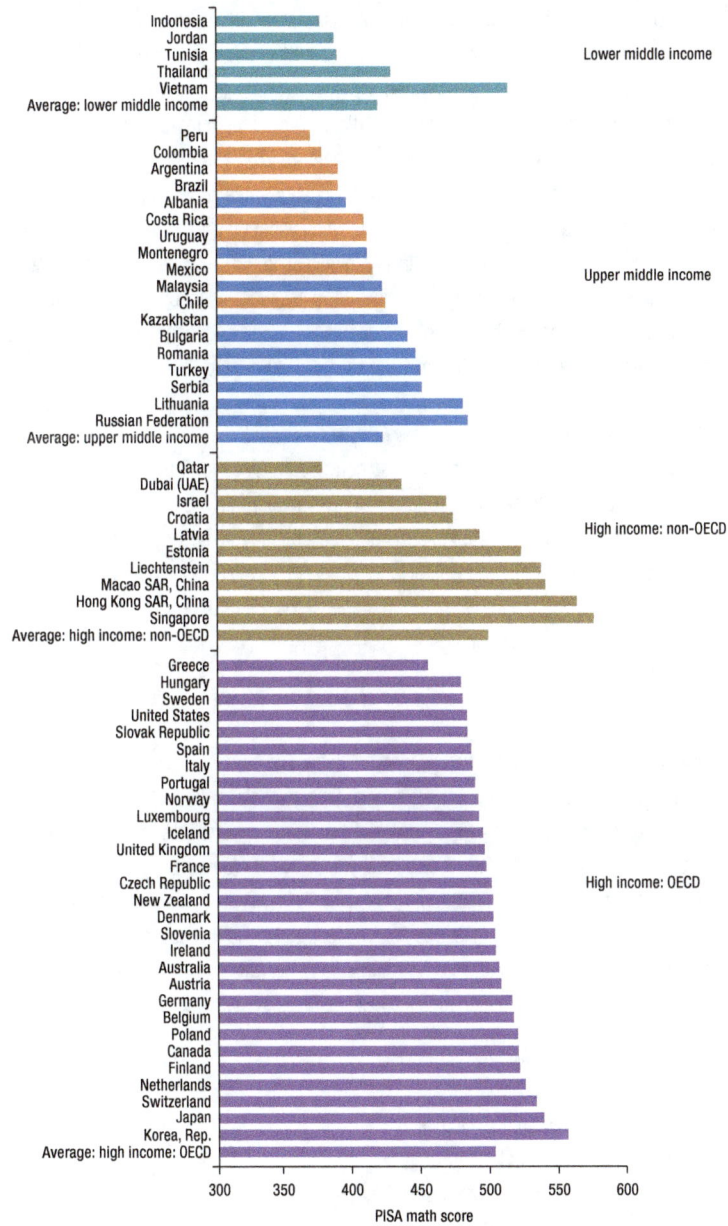

Source: OECD 2013b.
Note: LAC = Latin America and the Caribbean; OECD = Organisation for Economic Co-operation and Development; PISA = Program for International Student Assessment.

BOX 1.1 *Math and reading skills as measured on PISA*

On the 2012 Program for International Student Assessment (PISA), students who could not answer questions at the lowest levels of difficulty (level 1 and below) scored roughly 360, on average. Level 1 questions are designed to measure students' ability to understand simple texts and carry out routine math calculations. Typical math tasks include performing basic arithmetic problems; ordering a set of numbers; reading and reporting a value from a table or graph; and computing basic currency exchange rates. In reading, students are given a short text and asked to answer basic questions about it.

The questions below correspond to level 1 difficulty. In 2009, 95 percent of students in Shanghai answered this mathematics question correctly, while only 30 percent of Brazilian students did. Approximately 90 percent of students in Finland and Singapore answered the reading question correctly; only 35 percent of students in Peru did.

Mathematics question

Mei-Ling from Singapore was preparing to go to South Africa for 3 months as an exchange student. She needed to change some Singapore dollars (SGD) into South African rand (ZAR). Mei-Ling found out that the exchange rate between Singapore dollars and South African rand was SGD 1.00 = ZAR 4.20. Mei-Ling changed 3,000 Singapore dollars into South African rand at this exchange rate. How much money in South African rand did Mei-Ling get?
Correct answer: ZAR 12,000

Reading question

Do our teeth become cleaner and cleaner the longer and harder we brush them? British researchers say no. They have actually tried out many different alternatives, and ended up with the perfect way to brush your teeth. A two minute brush, without brushing too hard, gives the best result. If you brush hard, you harm your tooth enamel and your gums without loosening food remnants or plaque. Bente Hansen, an expert on tooth brushing, says that it is a good idea to hold the toothbrush the way you hold a pen. "Start in one corner and brush your way along the whole row," she says. "Don't forget your tongue either! It can actually contain loads of bacteria that may cause bad breath."

What is this article about?
A. The best way to brush your teeth.
B. The best kind of toothbrush to use.
C. The importance of good teeth.
D. The way different people brush their teeth.
Correct answer: A. The best way to brush your teeth.

Sources: OECD 2010, 2013a.

TABLE 1.2: Share of students scoring at the top and bottom on PISA mathematics, 2012

	Level 6	Level 5	Level 2	Level 1 and below
Shanghai (China)	30.8	24.6	7.5	3.8
Korea, Rep.	12.1	18.8	14.7	9.1
Finland	3.5	11.7	20.5	12.3
Chile	0.1	1.5	25.3	51.5
Uruguay	0.1	1.3	23.0	55.8
Brazil	0	0.7	20.4	67.1
Mexico	0	0.6	27.8	54.7
Costa Rica	0.1	0.5	26.8	59.9
Peru	0	0.5	16.1	74.6
Argentina	0	0.3	22.2	66.5
Colombia	0	0.3	17.8	73.8

Source: OECD 2013b.
Note: PISA = Program for International Student Assessment.

in reading, and 72 points in science—the last gap representing almost two years of science education. Considering that the eight LAC countries willing to benchmark themselves against the OECD in an international test are the region's strongest performers, a far greater gap in average learning levels across the region as a whole may be assumed.

Recent work by Hanushek and Woessmann (2012) has confirmed this. By integrating data from two Latin American regional assessments of student learning into their global database of international test results, a much larger number of LAC countries can be benchmarked against OECD learning levels. Almost all countries in the region participated in one or both of the UNESCO regional tests, which covered third- and fourth-grade math and reading performance in 1997 (Latin American Laboratory for Assessment of the Quality of Education [LLECE]) and third- and sixth-grade math and reading in the 2006 Second Regional Comparative and Explanatory Study (SERCE). As seen in figure 1.7, the average learning performance in LAC countries that have not participated in PISA is substantially lower than in those that have. Except in Costa Rica, the average student in Latin America learns much less during each year of schooling than the average student in the rest of the world. Uruguay is the only other country close to the regression line for the international sample. Countries such as Honduras, República Bolivariana de Venezuela, and Bolivia are very far off track in terms of the amount of globally relevant learning a year of schooling produces.

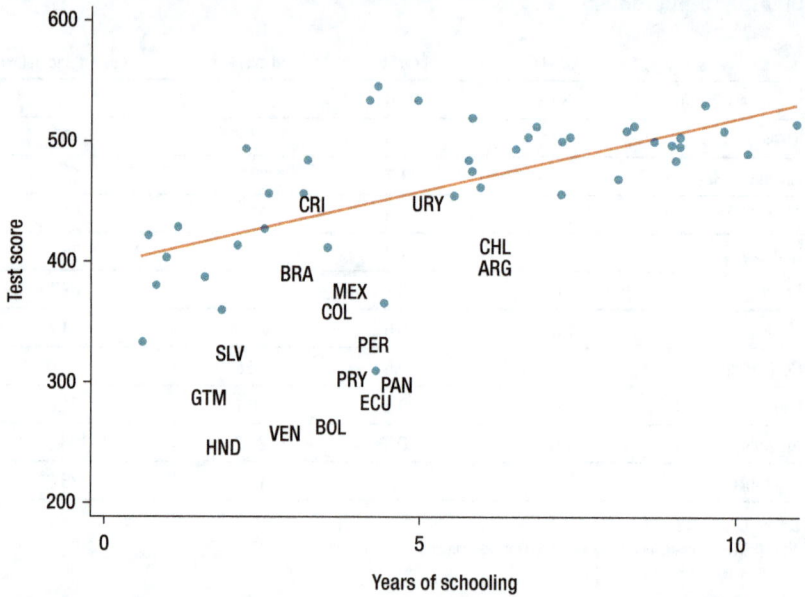

FIGURE 1.7: Comparative learning achievement in Latin America

Source: Hanushek and Woessmann 2012, 502.
Note: Years of schooling and educational achievement in Latin America and the world. Scatter plot of average years of schooling in 1960 against average scores on international student achievement tests (extended with regional test measures). Latin American countries are labeled by acronyms (ISO 3166 standard), and non-Latin American countries by dots. Regression line relates to non-Latin American countries only.

Third, despite LAC's overall poor performance, some countries are making sustained progress. Three LAC countries that have participated in PISA since 2000—Chile, Brazil, and Peru—are closing the gap with the OECD. Between 2000 and 2012, Chile raised its math, reading, and science scores by 39, 31, and 30 points, respectively, a gain of about one year of academic mastery in all areas. Brazil's 57-point increase in math was one of the largest in the entire PISA sample, and the country also raised its reading and science scores by 14 and 30 points, respectively. Despite ranking last in the 2012 sample, Peru registered huge improvement from its 2000 performance, with a 76-point increase in math, 57-point increase in reading, and 40-point increase in science. When trend rates of progress are analyzed, the annual gains in math and reading performance by the top three LAC "improvers"—Chile, Brazil, and Peru—from 2000–12 are well above annual rates of improvement in the United States, Korea, and most other OECD countries (Hanushek, Peterson, and Woessmann 2012).

Other LAC countries, however, show that PISA gains are by no means assured. After earlier progress, Mexico and Colombia saw math scores decline in 2012, as did

Costa Rica. Most striking is the continuous decline or stagnation in PISA results for Uruguay and Argentina. Two countries that were the highest performers in the region in 2000 have now been overtaken by Chile and Mexico, and in Argentina's case, also by Brazil.

In sum, all LAC countries still trail the OECD, East Asia, and many other upper middle-income countries on PISA by substantial margins, and the deficit of students performing at the highest levels is a grave concern. But the progress registered by Chile, Brazil, and Peru suggests relevant lessons from within the region on how to raise education quality and learning results.

Finally, it is clear that no country in the region has room for complacency. As figure 1.8 shows, LAC's top improvers as well as the other countries in the region made far less improvement on the 2012 round of PISA than in prior rounds. This suggests that while other countries in the region may have something to learn from the policies adopted in Chile, Brazil, and Peru over the past decade, those countries also need to do more. Close analysis of PISA data shows that a significant part of the progress seen in Brazil and Peru has come from a higher share of 15 year olds reaching ninth grade on time (rather than repeating grades) and not because ninth graders are learning more. There is a natural limit to PISA gains from reductions

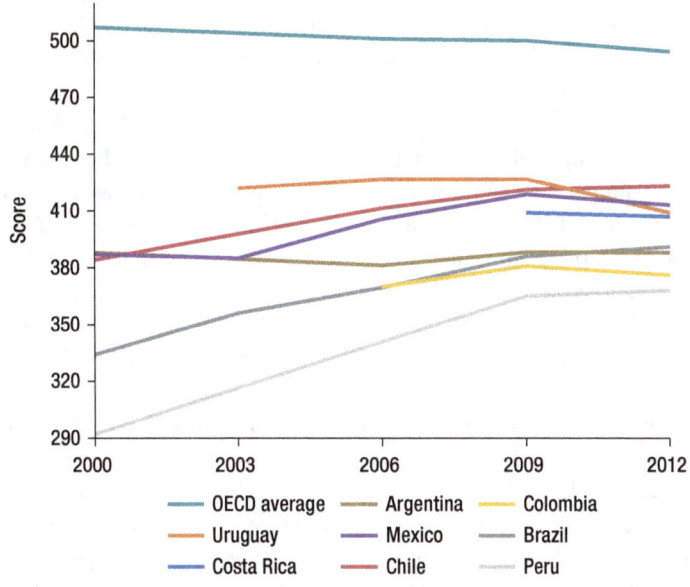

FIGURE 1.8: Comparative PISA math improvement, 2000–12

Source: OECD 2013b.
Note: OECD = Organisation for Economic Co-operation and Development; PISA = Program for International Student Assessment.

in age-grade distortion, and these countries may be reaping the last of this "low-hanging fruit." Given Brazil's history of the highest repetition rates in the region, it is undeniable progress that more students are progressing on schedule through the school system. But for all three countries, the PISA 2012 results suggest that staying the course on the current set of policies may not be enough to raise student learning at the same pace in the future. They, as well as other countries, need to look for new strategies.

What drives student learning?

If the economic benefits from education investments hinge on their effectiveness in producing student learning, the critical question becomes, what drives learning? Research continues to confirm that students' family background (parent education, socioeconomic status, and conditions at home such as access to books) is an important predictor of learning achievement in school. Indeed, neuroscience research on the plasticity (or malleability) of the brain during infancy and early childhood is drawing increasing attention to the earliest phases of family life, as well as to prenatal care. There is broad global evidence that large developmental deficits can arise if children do not have adequate access to nutrition, health care, cognitive stimulation, and socio-emotional support during their earliest years or if maternal health and nutrition are jeopardized during pregnancy (Engle et al. 2011). By tracing the development of cognitive skills (word recognition and vocabulary) among children in Ecuador, Peru, Chile, Colombia, and Nicaragua, Schady et al. (2014) show that large gaps develop before age five between children from the richest and poorest families.

Longitudinal studies also show the importance of childhood nutrition for educational attainment, employment, and incomes. Hoddinott et al. (2013) and Maluccio et al. (2009) find that the nutritional status of Guatemalan children age two to three is significantly correlated with their employment and incomes as adults. Data from Peru show that malnutrition during the first two years of life and during later childhood has significant impacts on cognitive skill development (Crookston et al. 2013; Crookston et al. 2011; Crookston et al. 2010). It is clear that the challenges school systems face in ensuring "learning for all" can be significantly aggravated by deficits in children's development during their earliest years.

Research is also producing a more nuanced understanding of the interaction between student learning outcomes and a set of "character skills" (sometimes called "noncognitive skills" or "socioemotional competencies") that are also essential for success in life (Heckman and Kautz 2013). Even relatively broad tests of thinking and reasoning such as PISA capture only a subset of the cognitive, social, and emotional competencies that individuals need for productive engagement in the workplace, their families, and communities. There is growing understanding that character skills such as conscientiousness, perseverance, sociability, emotional stability, and curiosity are important drivers of both educational success and other life outcomes (employment, family formation, healthy behaviors, avoidance of criminality, etc.).

Heckman and Kautz (2013) review currently available academic literature and program experience and conclude that character skills can be measured and, while stable at any particular age, are malleable across an individual's life. There is an important genetic influence, but schools, families, communities, and specific remedial programs can all impart or enhance character skills. Given the important interaction between students' character skills—especially conscientiousness—and their cognitive development, current evidence suggests that high-quality early child development programs that build a base of character skills in early childhood may be highly cost-effective strategies for promoting success in school and in later life.

Taken together, these bodies of evidence suggest that productive strategies for raising student learning in LAC—as in other countries—will have to include cost-effective investments in early child development programs, especially for the most vulnerable children. Expanding the coverage of such programs is a major challenge for all countries in the region. In 2012, no country in the region except Cuba had more than 30 percent of all children enrolled in crèche care (services for children age six months to four years old). Home visit and parent education programs are also relatively limited, despite evidence that these can be a cost-effective alternative strategy to center-based care. At the preschool level, no country except Cuba has universalized preschool coverage for four and five year olds, although several countries in the region have achieved universal enrollment of five and six year olds in half-day preschool.

Notwithstanding the crucial importance of protecting early child development and the strong public pressure in most LAC countries for expanded services, it is beyond the scope of this book to focus on this segment. Early child development services in most LAC countries include, and will likely continue to include, a wide variety of providers, service standards, and delivery models. In this environment, establishing the appropriate standards, support, and supervision for caregivers differs considerably from the challenges of raising teacher quality and learning results in formal, basic education systems.

This book focuses on the latter challenges. It also concentrates on publicly financed education. Although in every LAC country there exists a basic education market that includes private schools, many teachers work in both public and private schools, and private schooling provision is growing significantly in some urban areas, over 85 percent of basic education enrollments in Latin America and the Caribbean in 2013 were in public schools. The primary audience for this study is government policy makers across the region seeking to raise the quality of the systems they manage.

What does research tell us about the role of teachers in raising school quality? The short answer: in just the past decade, a tremendous amount. As student test score data at the classroom level have become more abundant, researchers for the first time have been able to measure directly the "value added" of individual teachers over the course of a school year. This work has documented eye-opening evidence of widely varying teacher effectiveness, even within the same school and same grade. While students with a weak teacher may master 50 percent or less of the curriculum for that grade; students with a good teacher get an average gain of one year; and students with great teachers advance 1.5 grade levels or more (Hanushek and Rivkin 2010; Rockoff 2004). A series of great or bad teachers over several years compounds these effects and can lead to unbridgeable gaps in student learning levels. *No other attribute of schools comes close to having this much impact on student achievement.*

A growing number of studies in the United States document powerful "teacher effects" that explain variations in student performance—especially in math. Looking across these studies suggests that a 1-standard deviation improvement in teacher quality implies a 0.13 standard deviation (SD) improvement in student reading and a 0.17 SD improvement in student math performance (table 1.3).[4] In other words, if your teacher is at the 84th percentile of the teacher performance distribution rather than the 50th percentile, your class will enjoy average learning gains approximately 0.15 standard deviations higher each year, which is a significant impact. It would require a hugely expensive 10-student reduction in average class size—from 25 to 15—to achieve the same improvement. (Hanushek and Rivkin 2010)

Within the LAC region, data from the 2006 SERCE regional learning assessment show similarly large variations in student learning results across third-grade classrooms within the same school (table 1.4). The average difference across classrooms ranges from 0.25 standard deviations in Costa Rica to 0.41 in Nicaragua and 0.43 in Cuba. These are not value-added measures and to some extent undoubtedly reflect

TABLE 1.3: Impact of teachers' relative effectiveness on student test scores

Study	Location	Reading (SD)	Math (SD)
Rockoff 2004	New Jersey	0.10	0.11
Nye, Konstantopoulos, and Hedges 2004	Tennessee	0.26	0.36
Rivkin, Hanushek, and Kain 2005	Texas	0.10	0.11
Aaronson, Barrow, and Sander 2007	Chicago	N.A.	0.13
Kane, Rockoff, and Staiger 2008	New York City	0.08	0.11
Jacob and Lefgren 2008	Undisclosed	0.12	0.26
Kane and Staiger 2008	Los Angeles	0.18	0.22
Koedel and Betts 2009	San Diego	N.A.	0.23
Rothstein 2010	North Carolina	0.11	0.15
Hanushek and Rivkin 2010	Undisclosed	N.A.	0.11
Average		0.13	0.17

Source: Hanushek and Rivkin 2010.
Note: N.A. = not applicable.

TABLE 1.4: Average difference in third-grade math scores across different classrooms in the same school

Country	Mean	Country	Mean
Argentina	0.29	Guatemala	0.30
Brazil	0.30	Mexico	0.36
Colombia	0.29	Nicaragua	0.41
Costa Rica	0.25	Panama	0.33
Cuba	0.43	Paraguay	0.34
Chile	0.33	Peru	0.32
Ecuador	0.35	Dominican Republic	0.33
El Salvador	0.32	Uruguay	0.28

Source: World Bank calculations from UNESCO 2006 (SERCE) test data for schools with two or more classrooms in the tested grade.

school system policies of streaming children by ability into different classrooms. But average learning gaps this large underscore how profoundly which teacher you are assigned to shapes your educational experience, even within the same school.

New research from the United States provides evidence that individual teachers critically impact not only children's immediate learning progress but also their longer-term development and life choices. In massive "big data" studies tracing the teacher and class assignments and annual test scores for 2.5 million primary school children in U.S. school districts from 1989 through 2009, Chetty, Friedman, and Rockoff (2014a) find clear differences between "high value-added" teachers (whose classrooms consistently registered above-average learning gains) and "low value-added" teachers. They also find no evidence that teachers' differential performance is because of student sorting (e.g., better students assigned to the better teachers). By studying thousands of classrooms where teachers are replaced from one year to the next, the researchers generate dramatic evidence of how quickly average student learning declines when a class loses a top teacher (from the top 5 percent of the distribution) and, conversely, how much learning can rise when a poor quality teacher (bottom 5 percent) is replaced by a good one (figure 1.9).

Another powerful contribution of this research is evidence that highly effective teachers affect students' entire life trajectories. By following students for 20 years—through completion of their education and entry into the labor market—Chetty et al. (2011) and Chetty, Friedman, and Rockoff (2014b) document that children exposed to even a single highly effective teacher during primary school are significantly more likely to go to college, attend better colleges, earn higher incomes, have higher savings rates, live in higher income neighborhoods, and (among females) are less likely to become teenage mothers. Consistent with other research (Rothstein 2010; Carrell and

FIGURE 1.9: Impact on student test scores of a change of teacher

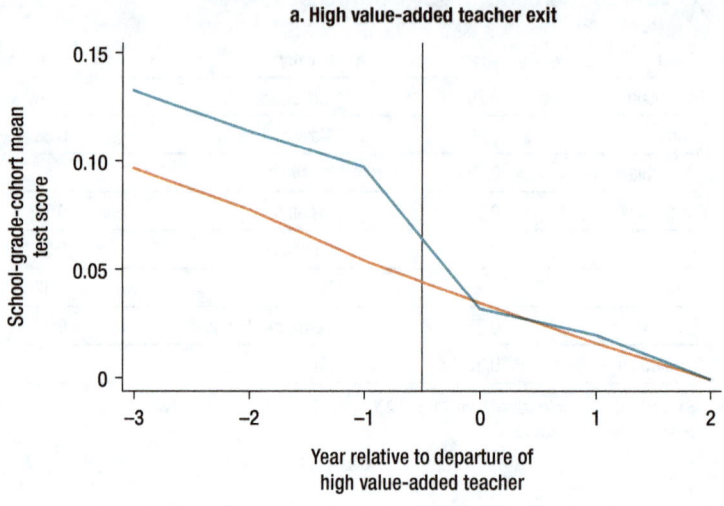

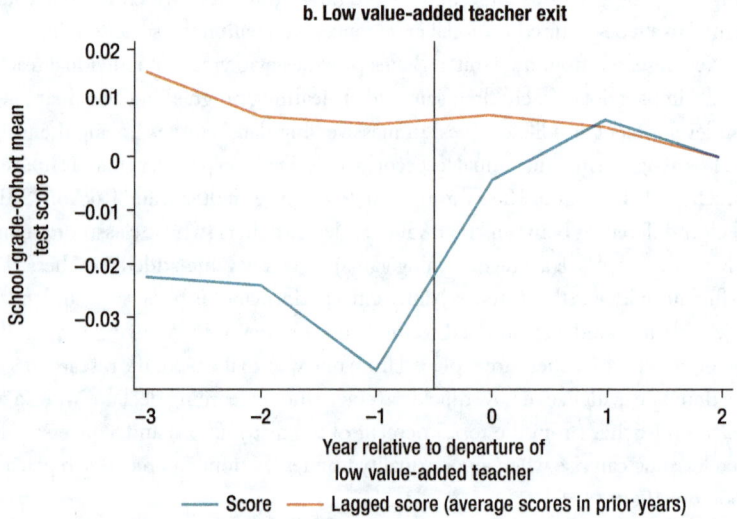

Source: Chetty, Friedman, and Rockoff 2014a (page 59, annex figure 3).

West 2010; Jacob, Lefgren, and Sims 2010), the impacts of highly effective teachers on students' learning can appear to fade out in subsequent years of schooling, but positive differentials persist in students' later lives (Chetty et al. 2011; Chetty Friedman, and Rockoff 2014b). The current evidence suggests that great teachers not only raise student learning in areas captured on standardized tests but also develop students' human capital in broader and deeper dimensions that have a lifelong payoff. Exposure to even a single highly effective teacher (value-added impact on student learning 1 SD above the mean) in a child's primary school career is correlated with $350 per year higher earnings at age 28, or 1.65 percent higher than the sample average (figure 1.10) (Chetty, Friedman, and Rockoff 2014b). This differential may not seem huge, but a result this clear and persistent from exposure to a single highly effective teacher at least 15 years earlier is striking. Exposure to multiple teachers in the top of the distribution (something their data set could not analyze) might significantly compound these positive impacts. This research presents the most compelling evidence to date on two profound findings. First, effective teachers appear to develop students' human capabilities in dimensions that have important long-term economic and social benefits. Second, even though these impacts appear to extend beyond the dimensions of learning that are captured on standardized tests, value-added test scores are a valid way of identifying effective teachers.

Pathbreaking research currently in progress in Ecuador paints a very similar picture. Araujo et al. (forthcoming) worked with the Ministry of Education to study 204 preschools in which 15,000 children in 2012 were randomly assigned to 451 different teachers. The research goes beyond prior studies in two important dimensions. First, children were tested at the beginning and end of the school year on a broad range of cognitive and socioemotional competencies, including language and early literacy skills, math, and executive function (impulse control, attention, cognitive flexibility, and working memory). Second, in an effort to understand exactly how highly effective

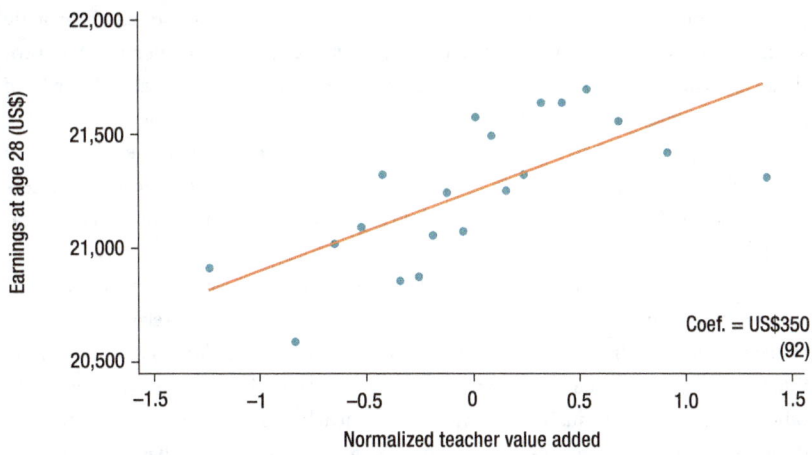

FIGURE 1.10: Long-term economic benefits of exposure to an effective teacher

Source: Chetty, Friedman, and Rockoff 2014b (page 73, annex figure 2).

teachers produce superior outcomes, all teachers were videotaped and their practice analyzed using a standardized instrument called CLASS (Classroom Assessment Scoring System).

The researchers found substantial teacher effects: a 1 SD increase in teacher quality resulted in 0.13, 0.11, and 0.06 SD higher test scores in language, math, and executive functioning, respectively. They also found clear evidence that teacher behaviors explained the better outcomes. Approximately one-third of the differences in student outcomes within a given school can be linked to differences in teachers' practice on the three dimensions that CLASS measures (emotional support, classroom organization, and instructional support). Echoing the Chetty et al. (2011) results, results in Ecuador also indicate that better teachers are better for students in *all* dimensions measured— the same teachers produce higher math, language, and executive function scores. Children from across the socioeconomic distribution responded to better teachers. While better teachers did not have an appreciable impact on absences from school, they clearly produced more learning per days of school attended. Finally, surveys showed that parents recognized better teachers, even though they did not change their behaviors—for example, by trying to move their children into different classrooms or schools. (Araujo et al. forthcoming.)

What makes teachers effective?

The evidence that teachers vary widely in their ability to produce student learning gains has intensified the focus of both policy makers and researchers on how to identify effective teachers. As the most recent research indicates, outstanding teachers influence their students' development more broadly and deeply than can be captured by academic test score gains. However, no evidence to date indicates any tradeoff between teachers' ability to promote student learning and other positive impacts. In fact, research strongly supports the notion that an individual teacher's quality, measured by her ability to produce superior average improvements in student learning, is a sine qua non for both students and nations to reap economic and social benefits from education.

Subsequent chapters will examine in more depth the latest evidence and experience—particularly from Latin America—with policies aimed at making teachers more effective. We summarize here three important findings from global research that create a context for these policies.

First, teachers' observable characteristics (age, level of formal education, certification status, and years of experience teaching) *are not* well correlated with their effectiveness (Goldhaber 2002; Kane, Rockoff, and Staiger 2008; Hanushek et al. 2005). Numerous studies have now confirmed the lack of consistent association. In other words, there is much wider variation in teacher performance *within* each of these categories (i.e., teachers with advanced degrees, teachers who have received formal certification) than *across* teachers with and without these characteristics. This is significant because in Latin America, as elsewhere in the world, these are still the main criteria applied in teacher hiring and promotion decisions. An exception, to some extent, is years of experience: numerous studies have documented that virtually all teachers increase their effectiveness during their first years on the job. However, the improvement tends to plateau off after four to five years. Moreover, for many teachers these "experience gains" are not very large. Indeed, they are typically smaller than the variation in performance that can be seen across a cohort of entering teachers even from day one.

Second, teachers' knowledge *is* correlated with effectiveness. It is intuitively plausible that teachers who "know their stuff" may be able to teach it more effectively. While relatively few studies have been able to examine the academic ability of teachers in service by testing them directly, the studies that have done so find positive correlations between teachers' test scores and those of their students (Marshall and Sorto 2012; Hanushek and Rivkin 2006; Hill, Rowan, and Ball 2005; Eide, Goldhaber, and Brewer 2004).

The importance of teacher knowledge appears to be even stronger in developing countries. A 2011 review of the developing country evidence on how different educational inputs affect educational outcomes finds that teachers' knowledge of the subjects they teach is one of the few variables consistently correlated with student learning. Across 20 different studies of the impact of teachers' knowledge (as measured by test scores) on their students' learning performance, all found a positive correlation and 13 were significantly positive. The researchers concluded that of all the education inputs that have been evaluated—including school infrastructure, learning materials, teacher and principal characteristics, and school organization—only three are consistently and significantly correlated with learning outcomes: teacher knowledge, teacher absence rates, and the availability of desks. (Glewwe et al. 2011)

The size of the effects documented to date is not always large. In rural Guatemala, Marshal and Sorto (2012) find that a 1 SD higher performance by mathematics teachers on a fourth-grade math test—a large differential—is correlated with 0.05 SD to 0.08 SD higher performance by their students in math, which is a relatively small increase. In Peru, Metzler and Woessmann (2012) find that 1 SD higher performance by teachers on a sixth-grade math test correlates with 0.09 SD higher math scores for their students, while effects in reading were not significant. In Mexico, a 1 SD higher test performance by teachers on the Carrera Magisterial competency test is associated with 0.08 SD higher learning outcomes for students in the case of primary teachers and 0.25 SD higher learning in the case of secondary school teachers (Santibanez 2006). In São Paulo, Brazil, a 1 SD higher test performance by teachers on the Prova de Promoção competency exam is associated with 0.045 SD higher student test scores (Fernandes and Ferraz 2014). While these differential learning gains are relatively small, they are typically calculated for a single cohort of students; teachers with superior content mastery will produce above-average learning results for many cohorts of students over their careers.

A more compelling picture emerges from studies that look across countries. Researchers who have focused on analyzing international test data have consistently correlated the superior performance of countries such as Finland, the Netherlands, Singapore, Japan, Korea, and China (Shanghai) with the relatively high academic performance of teacher candidates in these countries. Teacher candidates in these countries score in the top one-third of university students and face tight competition for entry into the profession. These patterns have led numerous policy analysts (Barber and Mourshed 2009; Clotfelter, Ladd, and Vigdor 2007; OECD 2005) to conclude that teachers' academic quality is a major factor in teacher effectiveness, even if there is relatively little direct correlation evidence.

Third, teachers' interpersonal qualities *may be* correlated with effectiveness, but the evidence is limited. Some research has focused on teachers' interpersonal qualities, beliefs, and attitudes, such as perseverance and "grit" (OECD 2009). These studies are limited in number but generally conclude that highly effective teachers tend to have positive attitudes toward themselves and their students and exhibit above-average levels of perseverance and resilience (Rockoff et al. 2011; Wayne and Youngs 2003; Stipek et al. 2001). A study of Teach For All (TFA) teachers assigned to high-poverty schools in Chile, for example, found that 43 percent of the TFA teachers were "confident that their students with behavioral problems will learn" while only 30 percent of traditionally recruited teachers believed this (Alfonso, Santiago, and Bassi 2010).

Who are LAC's teachers?

What do we know about the performance and characteristics of teachers in Latin America? First and foremost, while standardized measurement of student learning outcomes has increased greatly over the past 20 years, most countries do not have the quantity of classroom-level data necessary to research the "value added" of individual teachers, as has been possible in the United States. In subsequent chapters, we discuss in detail the evidence about teacher effectiveness in Latin America that is emerging from direct observations at the level of the classroom and from the experience of Chile, which has implemented the region's most advanced system of teacher performance evaluation.

This section provides a context for that discussion by examining what we know about the individuals who become teachers in LAC, and how their academic preparation, working conditions, and compensation compare, both across different countries in the region, and with other regions.

Teachers' characteristics

Academic preparation

Average education levels for teachers have continued to rise across the LAC region, with particularly sharp increases in Brazil and Costa Rica. Costa Rica, Panama, and

Peru today have the highest levels, with teachers averaging more than 16 years of education. Despite Brazil's progress, the formal educational level of its teachers remains on par with Nicaragua and Honduras, at 13 years. In all 10 of the countries for which comparable household survey data are available, the formal educational level of teachers is higher than for all other professional and technical workers, and it is considerably higher than the average schooling of office workers as a whole.

The evidence that teachers have become more highly educated, however, is undercut by evidence that the pool of individuals that enters teaching in Latin America is academically weaker than the overall pool of students in higher education. Figure 1.11 shows that 15-year-old students who identify themselves as interested in a teaching career score below the national mean on PISA in every country except Uruguay and well below the average score for students who are prospective engineers in all countries. The 120-point difference between prospective teachers and prospective engineers in Argentina is equivalent to the gap in average PISA performance between Peru and the United States and three years of math education. Potential teachers in Brazil also score well below potential engineers. Only in Uruguay, traditionally one of the highest education performers in LAC, are the math skills of prospective teachers above the national average and relatively close to those of prospective engineers.

Data on higher education students in Chile, Colombia, and Brazil paint a similar picture. The average score on the Chilean university entrance exam (Prueba de Selección Universitaria) for education students is 505 (500 for those preparing to teach at the preschool level), while the average for law is 660; engineering, 700; and

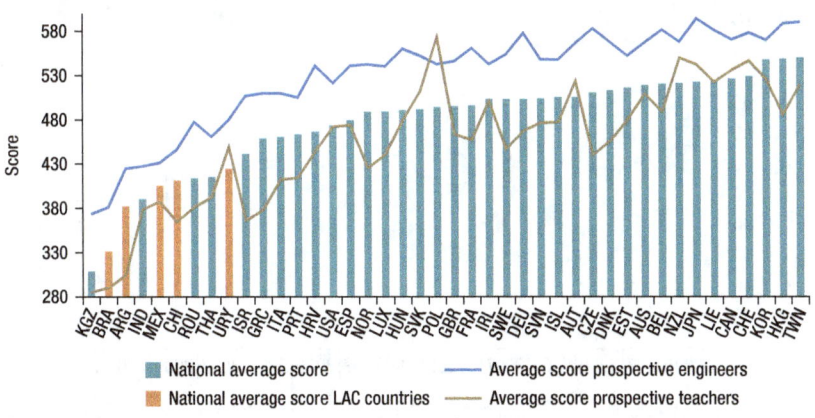

FIGURE 1.11: Comparative PISA math performance of prospective teachers and engineers

Source: OECD, PISA (2000–06). Data are from PISA 2006, except for Brazil (from PISA 2000).
Note: LAC = Latin America and the Caribbean; PISA = Program for International Student Assessment. Country acronyms are ISO 3166 standard.

medicine, 745. In Colombia, Barón et al. (2014) find average university entrance exam scores for teachers are 14.5 percent below those of students in other disciplines, with an even larger gap for female teachers.

At Brazil's prestigious University of São Paulo (USP), where students in all disciplines represent the country's academic cream, entering scores of students pursuing education degrees fall significantly below those of other disciplines. No program besides education admits students scoring below 50 percent, let alone 40; the very highest-scoring teacher education candidates perform below the lowest entering medical school students (figure 1.12). More sobering still is the fact that 90 percent of Brazil's teachers would not qualify for acceptance to a program such as USP's and instead receive their teaching degrees from institutions of lower academic quality.

Gender and family background

About 75 percent of Latin America's teachers are female, but this ranges from a low in Mexico (62 percent female) to 82 percent female in Uruguay, Brazil, and Chile. In a significant number of countries, the teaching profession is becoming increasingly "feminine," with teachers under 30 years old more likely to be female than their older cohorts (age 50 and older). The shift has been particularly sharp in Mexico, where 49 percent of older teachers are male but only 25 percent of new ones are. Similar patterns are playing out in El Salvador, Peru, Panama, Costa Rica, and Chile. The one exception in the region is Nicaragua, where the female share of the teaching force is dropping.

Teachers are also poorer than the overall pool of university students. In Costa Rica, the average household income of university students in teacher education programs is lower than in any other discipline. In Peru's San Marcos University, students

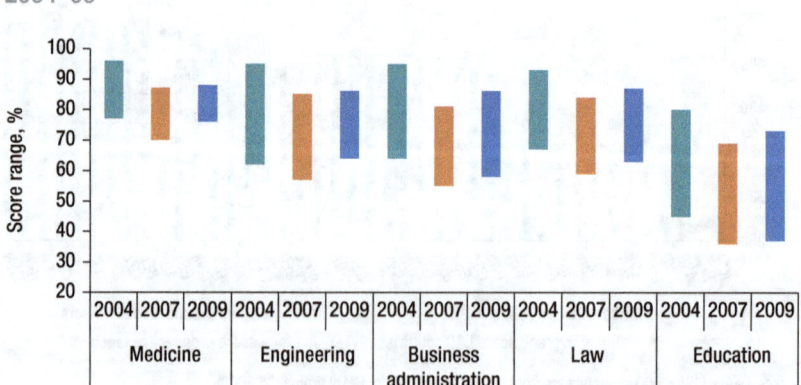

FIGURE 1.12: University of São Paulo entrance exam scores, by field of study, 2004–09

Source: World Bank analysis of data from the University of São Paulo EXAME Fuvest: Fundacao Universitaria para o Vestibular.

majoring in education have lower household income and less-educated parents than students in any other field (figure 1.13). While over 60 percent of entering medical students have parents who completed tertiary education, the vast majority of teacher candidates are first generation college goers.

Finally, the teaching force in most of Latin America is aging. In Peru, Panama, and Uruguay, by the late 2000s, the average teacher was more than 40 years old. The "youngest" teaching corps in the region, in Honduras and Nicaragua, averaged 35 years old. Only one country in the region, Chile, saw a decline in the average age of the teaching force between 2000 and 2010: from 41 to 39 years.

Content knowledge

There are relatively few direct studies of the content mastery of Latin America's teachers, but those available paint a dismal picture. The analysis of Metzler and Woessmann (2012), which found the math performance of Peruvian sixth graders to be significantly correlated with their teachers' performance on the same sixth-grade test, also served to expose the weak overall performance of Peruvian teachers (figure 1.14). Fully 84 percent of teachers scored below level 2 in math, and 48 percent did so in language. Performance below level 2 is defined by the Ministry of Education as "unable to make basic inferences from a text" and "unable to establish mathematical relationships and adapt routine and simple mathematical procedures and strategies" (Peru, Ministry of Education 2007). On a more comprehensive test of teachers' content mastery and understanding of pedagogical practice in Peru, only 8,744 of 183,100 teachers achieved the Ministry of Education's threshold passing score.

FIGURE 1.13: Socioeconomic background of university students in Peru, by discipline, 2000

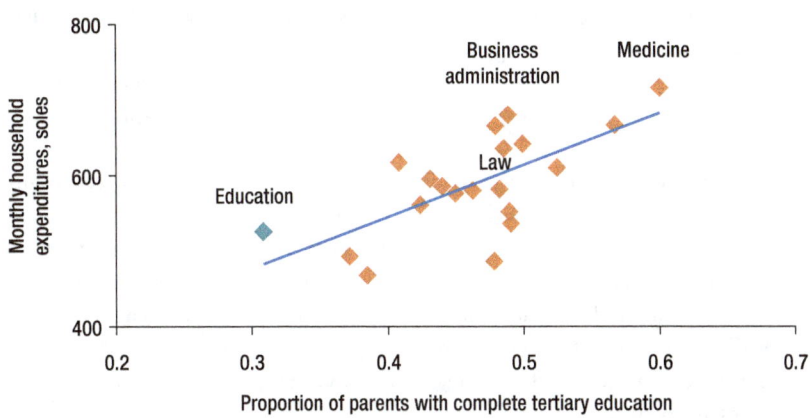

Source: World Bank analysis of data from the Universidad Mayor San Marcos, Peru.

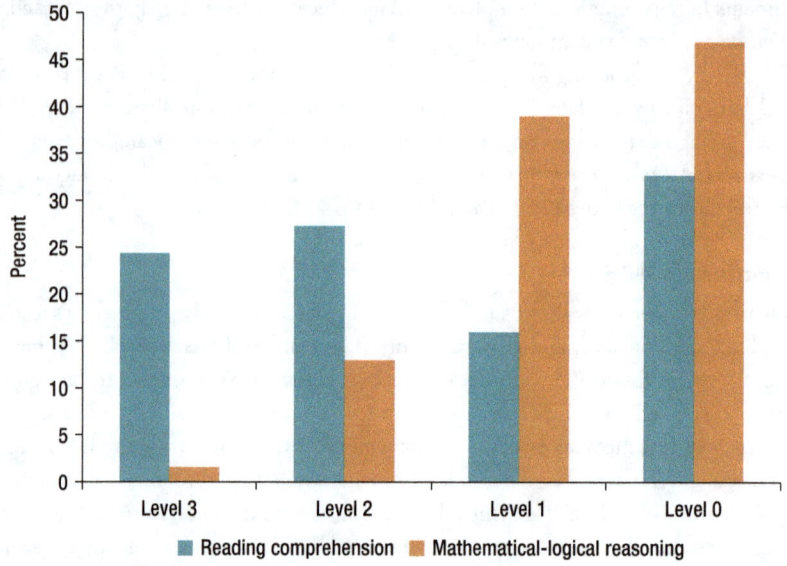

FIGURE 1.14: Teacher performance on sixth-grade reading and math in Peru

Source: Peru, Ministry of Education.

The clearest data on how the content mastery of Latin American teachers compares with teachers in other countries comes from a multicountry research program on the quality of mathematics teaching, known as TEDS-Math (Teacher Education and Development Study in Mathematics). Chile was the only country in the region to participate in the program, which applied content tests and interviews to representative samples of prospective math teachers in each country. As can be seen from figures 1.15–1.18, Chile's future secondary school teachers performed the lowest in the group on tests of math content mastery as well as math pedagogy (effective strategies for secondary level math instruction). Future Chilean primary school teachers were the second worst performers in both areas, ahead of only Georgia.

The countries participating in TEDS-Math are admittedly a select group, including several of the world's highest performers on PISA, Trends in International Mathematics and Science Study (TIMMS), and other international tests. But there is a truly sobering gap between the measured competency of future teachers in Singapore or Taiwan, China, and those in Chile, especially in mathematics content knowledge. Given that Chile is the LAC region's highest performing country on international tests, these data leave little doubt that the region as a whole faces deep issues in raising the quality of its teachers.

majoring in education have lower household income and less-educated parents than students in any other field (figure 1.13). While over 60 percent of entering medical students have parents who completed tertiary education, the vast majority of teacher candidates are first generation college goers.

Finally, the teaching force in most of Latin America is aging. In Peru, Panama, and Uruguay, by the late 2000s, the average teacher was more than 40 years old. The "youngest" teaching corps in the region, in Honduras and Nicaragua, averaged 35 years old. Only one country in the region, Chile, saw a decline in the average age of the teaching force between 2000 and 2010: from 41 to 39 years.

Content knowledge

There are relatively few direct studies of the content mastery of Latin America's teachers, but those available paint a dismal picture. The analysis of Metzler and Woessmann (2012), which found the math performance of Peruvian sixth graders to be significantly correlated with their teachers' performance on the same sixth-grade test, also served to expose the weak overall performance of Peruvian teachers (figure 1.14). Fully 84 percent of teachers scored below level 2 in math, and 48 percent did so in language. Performance below level 2 is defined by the Ministry of Education as "unable to make basic inferences from a text" and "unable to establish mathematical relationships and adapt routine and simple mathematical procedures and strategies" (Peru, Ministry of Education 2007). On a more comprehensive test of teachers' content mastery and understanding of pedagogical practice in Peru, only 8,744 of 183,100 teachers achieved the Ministry of Education's threshold passing score.

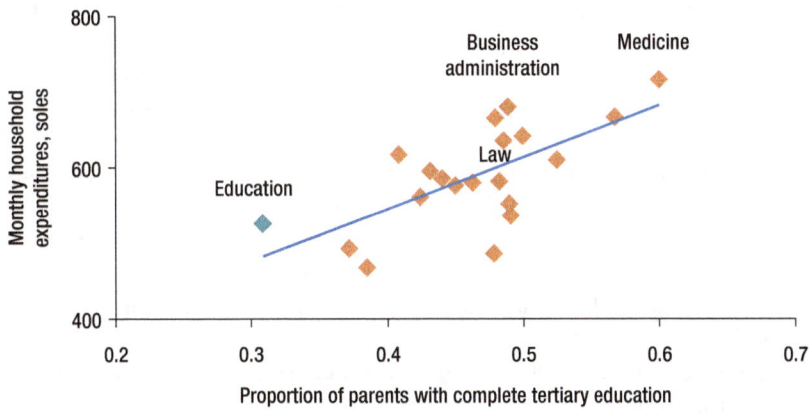

FIGURE 1.13: Socioeconomic background of university students in Peru, by discipline, 2000

Source: World Bank analysis of data from the Universidad Mayor San Marcos, Peru.

FIGURE 1.14:  Teacher performance on sixth-grade reading and math in Peru

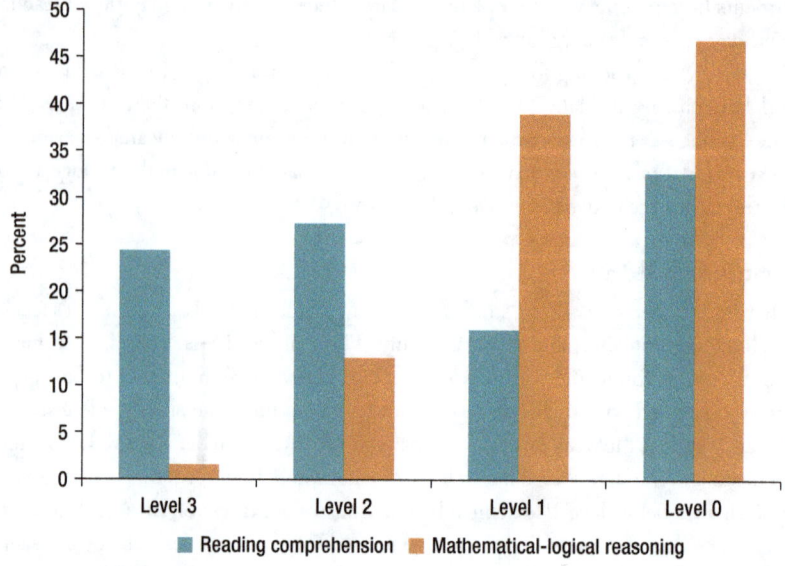

Source: Peru, Ministry of Education.

The clearest data on how the content mastery of Latin American teachers compares with teachers in other countries comes from a multicountry research program on the quality of mathematics teaching, known as TEDS-Math (Teacher Education and Development Study in Mathematics). Chile was the only country in the region to participate in the program, which applied content tests and interviews to representative samples of prospective math teachers in each country. As can be seen from figures 1.15–1.18, Chile's future secondary school teachers performed the lowest in the group on tests of math content mastery as well as math pedagogy (effective strategies for secondary level math instruction). Future Chilean primary school teachers were the second worst performers in both areas, ahead of only Georgia.

The countries participating in TEDS-Math are admittedly a select group, including several of the world's highest performers on PISA, Trends in International Mathematics and Science Study (TIMMS), and other international tests. But there is a truly sobering gap between the measured competency of future teachers in Singapore or Taiwan, China, and those in Chile, especially in mathematics content knowledge. Given that Chile is the LAC region's highest performing country on international tests, these data leave little doubt that the region as a whole faces deep issues in raising the quality of its teachers.

FIGURE 1.15: Math content knowledge of future secondary school teachers, 2008

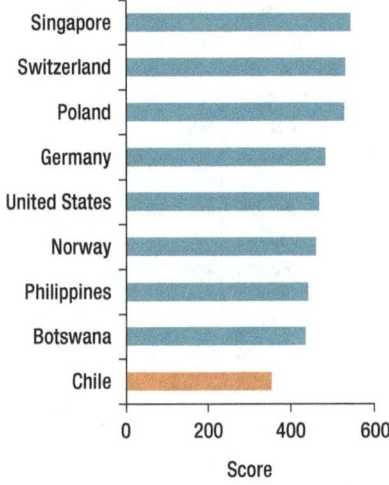

Source: TEDS-M 2008 (test scores).

FIGURE 1.16: Math pedagogy knowledge of future secondary school teachers, 2008

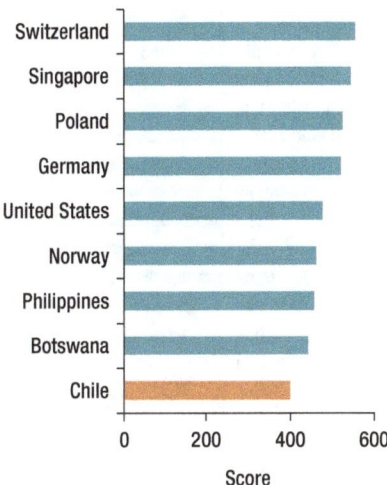

Source: TEDS-M 2008 (test scores).

Teacher compensation

Teacher compensation is a core policy issue in education. Given the size of the teaching force—20 percent of all professional and technical workers—and the predominance of public provision, teacher salaries account for roughly 3 to 4 percent of GDP and 15 percent of total public spending across Latin America. Teacher salary adjustments and pension policies have non negligible fiscal implications. Given the strength of teachers' unions in Latin America, teacher compensation is also often a politically charged and visible issue.

In light of evidence that the quality of Latin America's teachers is low, it is logical to explore whether salary levels are the binding constraint on teacher quality. There is continuing controversy over this, despite a large number of studies, because researchers use different comparison occupations and adjust or fail to adjust for teachers' work hours. We attempt a comprehensive treatment. First, we look at teacher salary trends in long-term perspective. Second, we compare teachers' wages to a variety of different occupational and professional alternatives, both on a monthly and hourly adjusted basis. Finally, we examine the issue of salary differentiation within the profession.

FIGURE 1.17: Math content knowledge of future primary school teachers, 2008

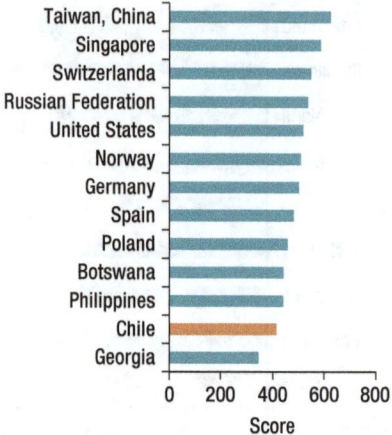

Source: TEDS-M 2008 (test scores).
a. Switzerland: Cantons where teachers are prepared for grades 1–6.

FIGURE 1.18: Math pedagogy knowledge of future primary school teachers, 2008

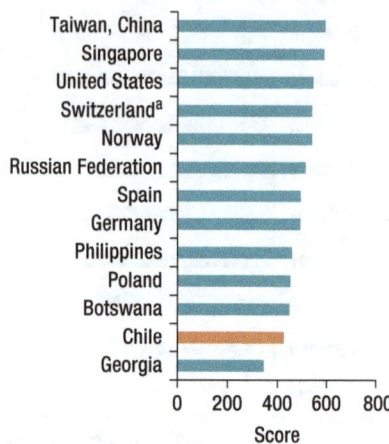

Source: TEDS-M 2008 (test scores).
a. Switzerland: Cantons where teachers are prepared for grades 1–6.

Long-term trends

There are relatively limited long-term data on teacher salary trends in Latin America, but what exist appear consistent with long-term studies of the market for teachers in OECD countries. Several influential studies in the United States have depicted two striking trends: a sharp decline in the returns to teacher education over the past 60 years relative to other professions and the development of an extremely compressed teacher-wage distribution (Corcoran, Evans, and Schwab 2004; Eide, Goldhaber, and Brewer 2004; Hoxby and Leigh 2004). An interesting recent study of Swedish education demonstrates that these long-term trends are not unique to the United States (Fredriksson and Ockert 2007). Since many elements of the Swedish case appear consistent with long-term trends in Latin American countries and the researchers have documented these with exceptional thoroughness, we highlight their findings in some detail here.

First, as seen in figure 1.19, the economic returns to teacher education in Sweden were on par with other professions in the late 1960s, but by 2002 were dramatically lower. Second, as figure 1.20 shows, by 2004 the teacher-wage distribution diverged substantially from that of individuals with the same educational background who engaged in other occupations. In contrast with other sectors, teachers' average salaries are highly concentrated in the middle of the wage distribution, showing almost no

FIGURE 1.19: Long-term decline in returns to university-level teacher education in Sweden, 1968–2003

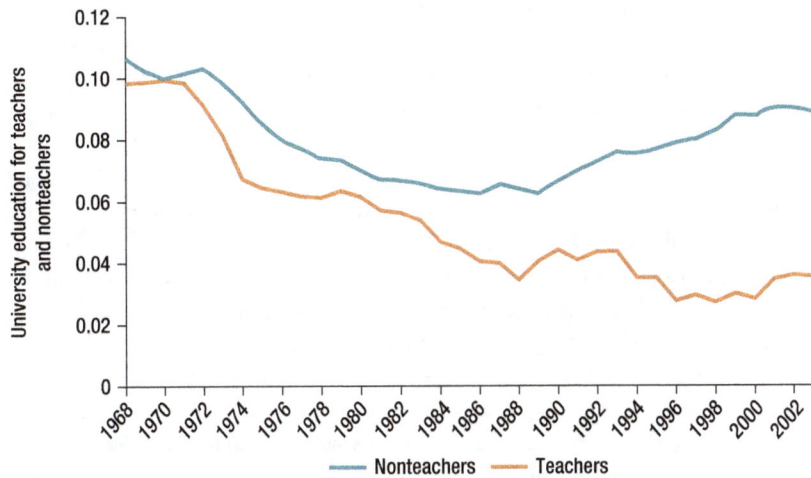

Source: LINDA (Longitudinal INdividual DAta for Sweden) database, quoted in Fredriksson and Ockert 2007.
Note: The regressions include controls for gender, potential experience, immigrant status, and years since immigration. Estimates for 1968–91 are imputed using the relative changes in the return to schooling estimated from earnings regressions.

FIGURE 1.20: Teacher-wage distribution in Sweden compared with nonteachers, 2004

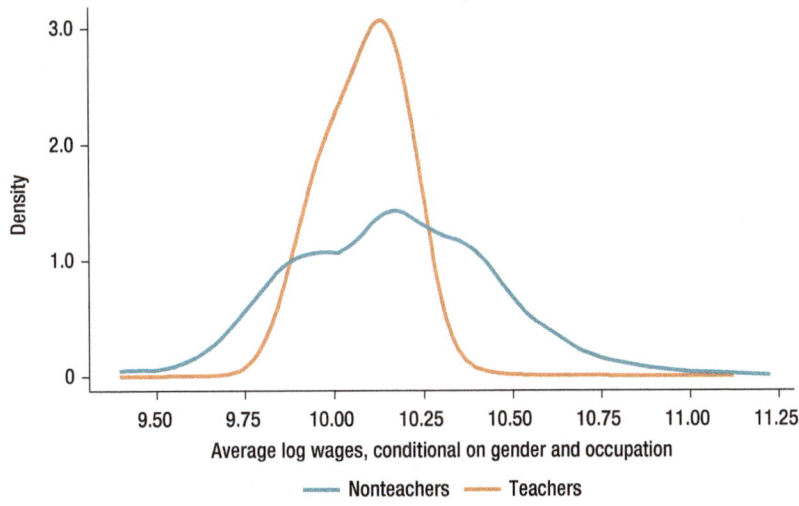

Source: Fredriksson and Ockert 2007.
Note: The figure shows Kernel density estimates.

differentiation in line with differential skills or effort. Third, teachers face a "flat" salary trajectory over the course of a career, while salaries for other professionals rise significantly as they accumulate experience (figure 1.21).

Exploiting a unique data set that collected cognitive test score data from successive cohorts of 13 year olds and followed these children through their subsequent educations and careers, Fredriksson and Ockert were able to measure the impact of the teaching profession's deteriorating incentives on not only the *quantity* of teacher supply but also its *quality*. First, they document a substantial decline in the number of university students applying for teacher education programs over the 40-year period of declining relative wages. Second, they document a steady drop in the fraction of new teachers from the highest ability group. Third, they find evidence that the "deskilling" of teachers happens through two separate routes: the average cognitive ability of university students getting a teaching degree declines *and* higher-ability individuals already in teaching leave the profession at a higher rate.

Although no database permits a similarly detailed analysis for Latin America, a number of the long-term trends experienced in Sweden have parallels in the region. Figure 1.22 shows the deep decline in teacher salaries in real terms in Peru from the 1960s to early 2000s, except for a short, highly inflationary period of rapid public sector wage increases in the late 1980s.

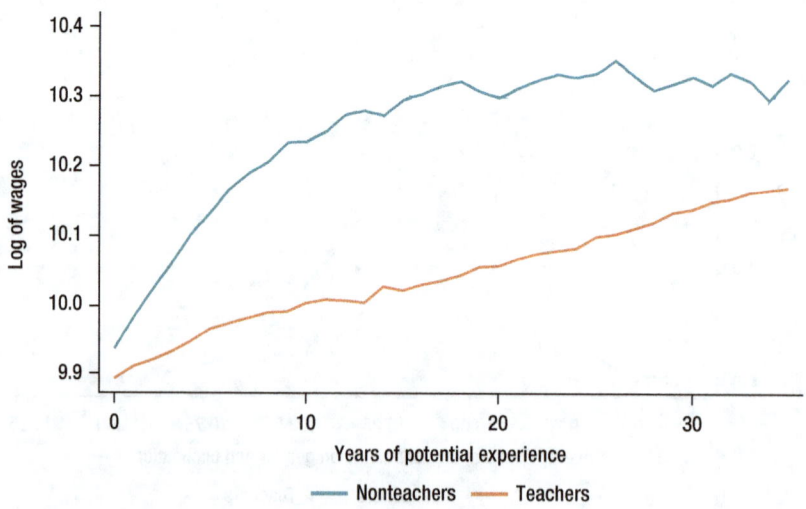

FIGURE 1.21: Career salary trajectories for teaching and alternative professions in Sweden, 2004

Source: Fredriksson and Ockert 2007.
Note: Average log wages conditional on gender and occupation.

FIGURE 1.22: Evolution of teacher salaries in Peru, 1960–2010

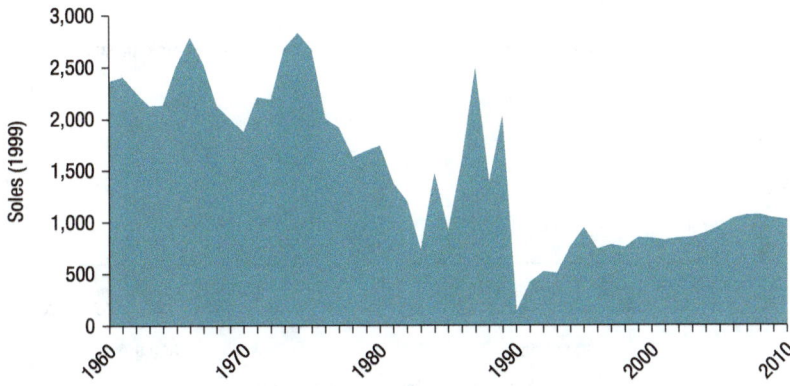

Source: Data on teachers salaries for the 1960–99 period are from Saavedra Chanduvi (2004). Data salaries for 2000–10 are from Encuesta Nacional de Hogares (ENAHO [Peru Household Survey]). Price deflators for all periods are from GRADE (Grupo de Análisis para el Desarrollo), Peru.

In Peru and elsewhere in the region, the "massification" of basic education coverage over the past 50 years put pressure on public budgets, creating downward pressures on salaries, and eventually forced education systems to hire less-educated teachers. The teaching profession gradually lost status in most of Latin America. While there are no data to permit a direct comparison of the cognitive ability of today's teachers with those of 50 years ago, a common observation is that the teaching profession was traditionally the highest prestige profession accessible to educated women (and a large number of men) and attracted individuals of high intellectual caliber.

What we *do* know is that today the teaching profession in most of Latin America does not attract high-caliber students. A clear challenge is to reverse a decades-long erosion of incentives to enter teaching that has produced a low-quality teacher stock.

Job stability

As we discuss in detail in chapter 5, extensive research indicates that individuals are motivated to become teachers by powerful nonsalary, or "intrinsic," incentives: the mission of helping children, the satisfaction of professional mastery, collegial interaction, and other factors. Employment in teaching also has some distinctive characteristics: it is known for long vacations and a "family-friendly" short official working day. Perhaps most important, since most teaching positions are in the public sector and have civil service status, the profession enjoys a high degree of job security and relatively generous health and pension benefits. Thus, the analysis of teachers' salaries relative to other professions must be nested in broader analysis.

Household survey data from 10 LAC countries confirm that teaching offers a higher degree of job stability than other sectors, especially for women

FIGURE 1.23: Chance of being employed, by age, for teacher graduates compared with other graduates in LAC

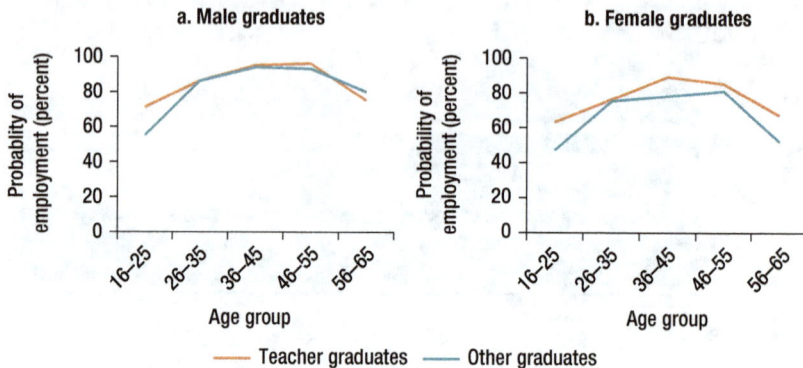

Source: World Bank analysis of household survey and labor market data for 10 LAC countries, circa 2010.
Note: LAC = Latin America and the Caribbean.

(figure 1.23). Both male and female teacher graduates have better prospects of immediate employment upon completing their studies than other graduates. For males graduating from teacher preparation, the subsequent employment trajectory is similar to other sectors. But women who graduate from teacher education are significantly more likely to be become employed and stay employed than women with other degrees.

However, the probability of employment by age 25 is still only about 75 percent for female teacher graduates and 85 percent for males across the 10 countries in our sample, and there is substantial underlying heterogeneity. In Uruguay and Costa Rica, unemployment among teacher graduates (age 25 to 35) is under 5 percent, well below the 11 to 12 percent unemployment rate for graduates in other fields. In Peru, by contrast, unemployment among teacher graduates (8 percent) is as high as for other graduates, and in El Salvador and Panama it is only slightly lower for teachers than for other graduates (7 percent and 10 percent, respectively).

A second core attraction of teaching is shorter working hours. Teachers' reported hours of work per week vary from a high of 40 in Chile and 38 in Costa Rica and Panama to 30 or less in Brazil, Peru, Mexico, and Uruguay. Other occupational groups—whether professional and technical or office workers—all report considerably higher hours. Males in other professions report 50 hours per week of work across most of their careers, while women report 40. In teaching, hours worked are similar for men and women. All three of these factors—high job stability, higher initial employability, and shorter working hours—are incentives for teaching that powerfully complement salary incentives, particularly for risk-averse individuals.

Relative salaries

Average salaries for teachers in Latin America, as in other regions, tend to decline in relation to per capita GDP as country income increases. When salaries across the region are compared with predicted values from a fitted regression, it appears that annualized teachers' pay in Nicaragua, Honduras, Costa Rica, Uruguay, and Chile is slightly higher that would be predicted, and salaries in El Salvador, Brazil, Mexico, and especially Peru are relatively low (figure 1.24). For global comparison, teacher salaries in the United States and Finland in 2010 were about 1 time GDP per capita; in the United Kingdom and Japan, about 1.4 times GDP per capita; and in Korea, 1.6 times GDP per capita. However, as shown by the case of Norway, where teacher salaries are only 0.7 times GDP per capita, for countries with a high share of GDP generated in extractive industries—which would apply to Chile, Peru, and Mexico in our sample—this measure can be misleading.

The most robust measure of the attractiveness of teacher compensation is in comparison with salaries for other professional occupations. We updated the analysis of Mizala and Ñopo (2011), which analyzes household survey data for nine LAC countries through 2009, to analyze survey data through 2010 for ten LAC countries. Following their methodology, we analyze teachers' wages in comparison with

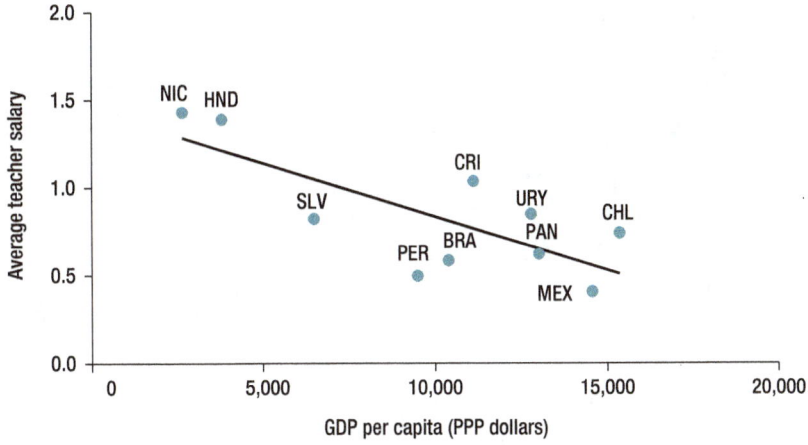

FIGURE 1.24: LAC teacher salaries in relation to GDP per capita, circa 2010

Source: Teacher salary data compiled from household survey data. Country GDP in PPP terms from World Bank Atlas of Global Development (database).
Note: GDP = gross domestic product; LAC = Latin America and the Caribbean; PPP = purchasing power parity. The regression line indicates the projected average teacher salary for each country; circles indicate the actual average salary circa 2010. Annual salary estimated as 12 times monthly salary reported on household income surveys.

matched sets of other workers, controlling for all observable characteristics reported in household survey data, such as formal educational level, age, gender, and years of experience.

Similar to Mizala and Ñopo and previous studies (Hernani-Limarino 2005; Saavedra Chanduvi 2004; Mizala and Romaguera 2005; Maul Rivas and Lavarreda 2008; Lopez-Acevedo 2004; Piras and Savedoff 1998) results are heterogeneous across countries and across urban and rural regions within countries, depending upon the comparison groups used. Figure 1.25 presents wage data for teachers and other matched professionals, adjusted for hours worked, in the 10 LAC countries for which comparable household surveys are available. It shows that teachers in 2010 were paid, on average, 18 to 30 percent more than other professional workers with equivalent education in Mexico, Honduras, and El Salvador. Teachers' earnings were on par with other professions in Costa Rica, Uruguay, and Chile, and were 10 to 25 percent lower than for matched workers in other professional occupations in Peru, Panama, Brazil, and Nicaragua.

Figure 1.25 also shows the movement in relative salaries over the 2000s. In most countries, the relationship in 2010 is not too different from that of the beginning of the decade, although there could have been variations in-between. Teachers' relative salaries improved in El Salvador, Uruguay, and Nicaragua. In Panama, and especially Peru, however, teachers clearly lost ground.

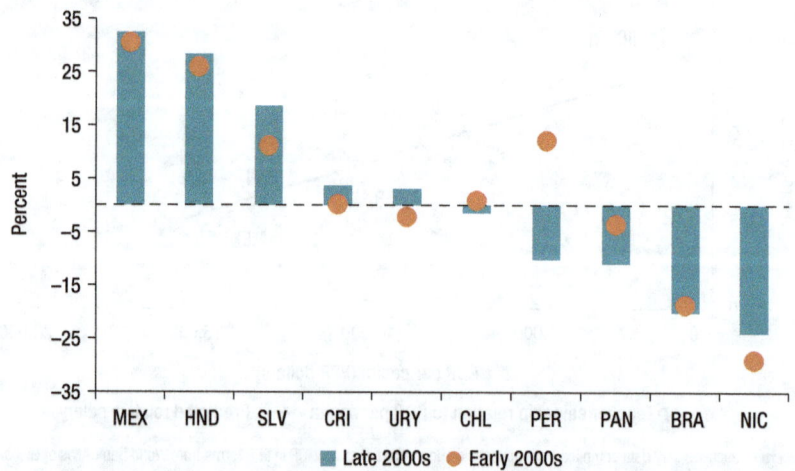

FIGURE 1.25: Average salary for teachers relative to other professional workers, adjusted for hours worked, circa 2000 and 2010

Source: World Bank analysis of household survey and labor market data for 10 Latin America and Caribbean countries.
Note: Comparisons are for matched sets of workers, controlling for all observable characteristics reported in household survey data, such as formal educational level, age, gender, and years of experience.

If salaries are compared on a monthly basis, without adjustment for hours worked, the relative position of teachers looks much worse. While in all countries except Peru and Panama, teachers' relative compensation improved over the decade, in 2010 it still fell between 5 and 55 percent below monthly salaries for other professionals. Although teachers themselves report fewer working hours, the tendency of teachers to think of—and compare—salaries in terms of the monthly amount received is in many ways understandable. As figure 1.26 shows, no country in the region pays teachers monthly salaries that are competitive with salaries in other professions. Political negotiations with teachers' unions typically focus on this parameter, and the nonpecuniary advantages of a teaching career fall out of the calculus. Surveys consistently show that teachers in the region are dissatisfied with their salaries.

There is some question, though, about the most appropriate counterfactual for teacher employment. From the standpoint of formal education, the closest labor market comparator is "other professional and technical occupations" as the average educational attainment of these workers approaches—but is still not as high as—teachers. Mizala and Ñopo (2011) observe that teachers are more educated than other professionals and technicians, but their years of education are not rewarded in the labor market. In fact, they find that, given the wage compression that characterizes the profession, the very highest-educated teachers (with postgraduate degrees) are penalized in the top percentiles of the earnings distribution. But our analysis suggests that teachers' years of formal education is a poor proxy for their actual level of human capital. The average salary for other professional and technical occupations

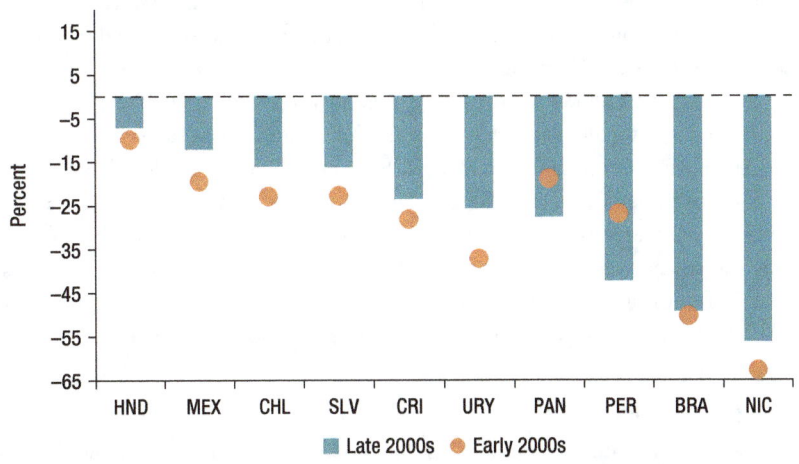

FIGURE 1.26: Average monthly salary for teachers relative to other professional workers, 2000 and 2010

Source: World Bank analysis of household survey and labor market data for 10 Latin America and Caribbean countries.

includes engineering, medicine, and law, and university entrance data suggest that all of these professions demand higher cognitive abilities than Latin America's current teachers can claim.

There are indications that the region continues to produce an excess number of teacher graduates, despite the perception of relatively low compensation. The most recent data for Uruguay suggest that only 61 percent of graduates from teacher training schools are actually working as teachers, only 59 percent in Panama, 55 percent in Costa Rica, and 51 percent in Peru. There are several alternative explanations for this phenomenon. First, students may retain interest in the teaching profession despite lower relative salaries because of the nonpecuniary advantages of teaching jobs that Mizala and Ñopo (2011) point out, including a higher degree of job stability, shorter working hours, and longer vacation periods. A second possibility is that enrollment in teacher education reflects a lack of academic alternatives more than a positive interest in teaching. The low average university entrance scores of prospective teachers make these candidates uncompetitive for many other programs. Third, the evidence that students entering teacher education programs are of lower average socioeconomic status and more likely to be first-generation university students than entrants in other fields suggests a pool of students whose lives have may afforded them limited experience with other professions and, consequently, more limited academic aspirations. Teaching is the one profession that everyone has some direct knowledge of, which can make it a more tangible goal. The most troubling aspect of these data, however, is the suggestion that as much as half of the investment individuals—and the public sector—are making in teacher education in countries such as Peru, Costa Rica, and Panama may be wasted.

Salary differentiation

From an incentives standpoint, the lifetime earnings profile and differentiation of salaries may be even more important than the average level. We look at two dimensions: career trajectories and wage compression.

As figure 1.27 shows, similar to Sweden, the career trajectory of teachers' earnings in Peru is lower and flatter than in other professions. This is largely driven by the differential experienced by male teachers. Salaries for women employed as teachers are equal to those of women in other sectors—and distinctly lower than salaries for their male counterparts—until about age 55, when earnings begin to decline sharply for female teachers while continuing to rise for women in other professions. For males, teaching represents significantly lower earnings across the career, although the gap begins to diminish when earnings for both groups begin to decline after about age 50.

Wage compression

Teacher wages in Latin America also exhibit the compression observed in Sweden. As figure 1.28 shows, landing a teaching position in Panama guarantees a salary within a

FIGURE 1.27: Wage-experience profiles for teachers and other professional workers in Peru, 2010

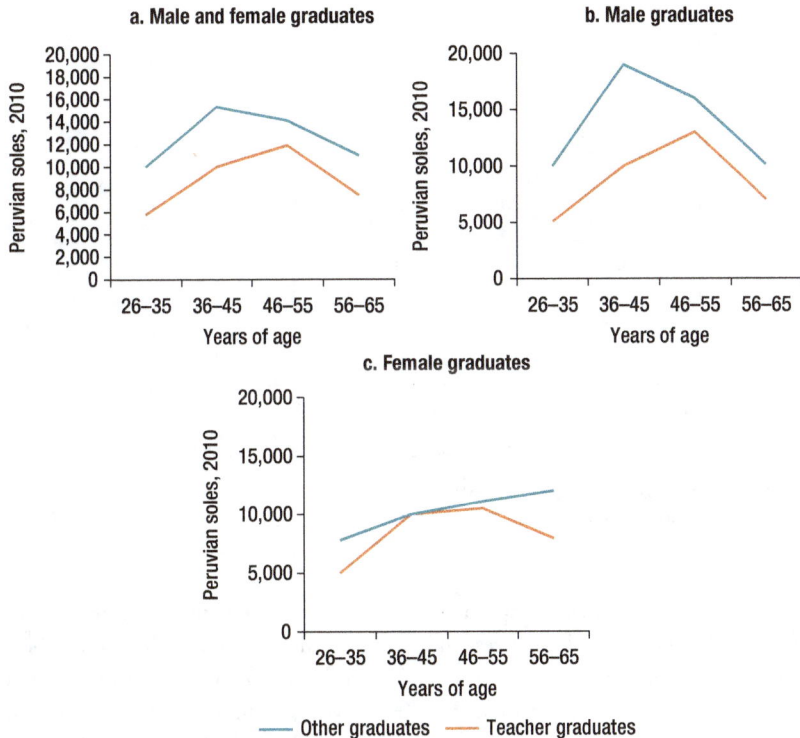

Source: World Bank analysis of 2010 household survey data for Peru.

fairly narrow band, with little risk of a very low wage and little chance of a high one. Research by Hernani-Limarino (2005) predicted the compensation that individuals in Latin America and the Caribbean can command in and outside the teaching profession, using a statistical methodology designed to account not only for observable individual factors such as labor market experience and education levels that can be expected to affect pay levels directly but also for unobserved factors that can influence individuals' compensation through their relative productivity. The analysis suggests that in most countries in the region individuals who tend to be less productive will earn relatively more as teachers and those with attributes that make them highly productive will tend to earn relatively less. This finding echoes U.S. research by Hoxby and Leigh (2004), which finds that the major factor driving talented women out of teaching is the "push" of a highly compressed wage scale, which is unattractive to more ambitious and talented individuals.

FIGURE 1.28: Wage distribution for teachers compared with other professional occupations in Panama, 2009

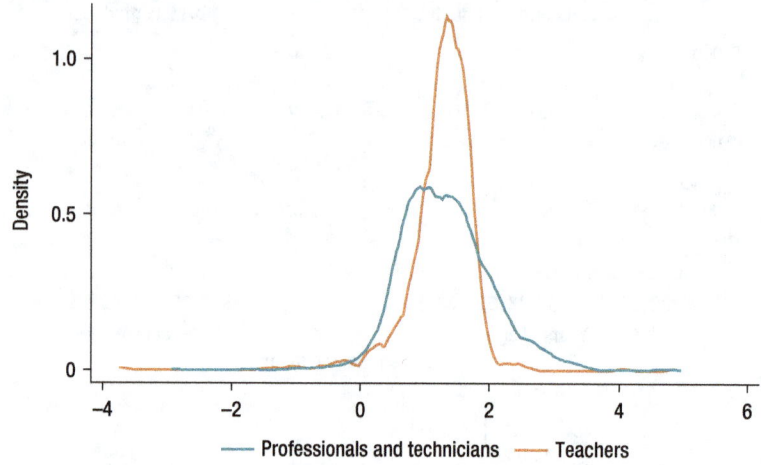

Source: World Bank analysis of household survey and labor market data.
Note: Log hourly wage unconditional distribution by occupational group.

Interestingly, however, it appears that in some countries in the region teacher wages are beginning to "decompress" into a broader distribution. In the case of Chile, the shift between 2000 and 2009 is marked, approaching a bimodal distribution (figure 1.29). This shift is consistent with the analysis of Behrman et al. (2013), which found a widening gap in wages between teachers employed in the private-subsidized (voucher) and fully private schools—which have the flexibility to differentiate teacher salaries in line with their productivity—and wages in municipal schools, which follow a seniority-based, single-salary schedule with little differentiation. The voucher school segment grew from 45 to almost 60 percent of total enrollments over the 2000s, and now employs 48 percent of all Chilean teachers. This can explain the perceptible shift in the overall teacher-wage distribution seen in figure 1.29.

Behrman et al. (2013) show that salaries in the voucher and fully private schools, particularly for men, are significantly higher than municipal teacher salaries, attract better-prepared candidates, and rise more quickly with each year of teaching. In modeling different policy responses, they find that raising municipal teachers' wages by 20 percent would not increase average teacher quality because it would simply draw more low-productivity teachers into the municipal sector—unless the salary rise were accompanied by an increase in standards. While the analysis confirms that municipal schools face a challenge in attracting talented teachers, the authors conclude that eliminating the voucher sector would adversely impact education quality, because the private voucher sector improves the overall pool of individuals entering the profession.

FIGURE 1.29: Wage distribution for teachers compared with other professions in Chile, 2000 and 2009

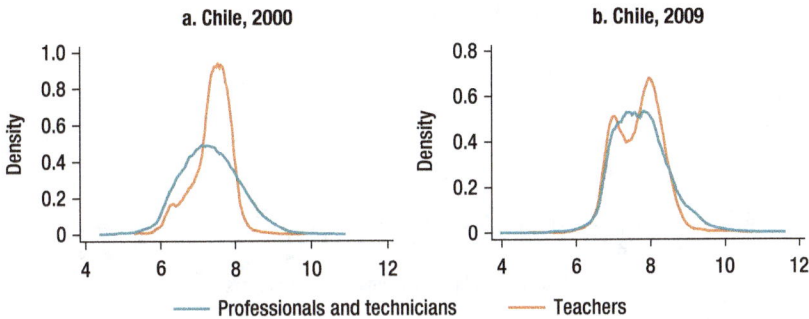

Source: World Bank analysis of household survey and labor market data.
Note: Log hourly wage unconditional distribution by occupational group.

In Costa Rica, the teacher-wage distribution also widened considerably between 2001 and 2009, along with a perceptible improvement in average salaries (figure 1.30). Irrespective of the average salary, increasing salary differentiation typically creates stronger incentives for the most talented and ambitious workers. Unfortunately, there is no research at present on the impact of these trends in Costa Rica, which would be valuable to explore.

Conclusions

Available evidence suggests that Latin America is not attracting the high-caliber individuals it needs to build world-class education systems. Virtually all countries in the region appear trapped in a low-level equilibrium of low standards for entry into teacher education programs, low quality candidates, low and undifferentiated salaries, low professionalism in the classroom, and poor education results. Moving to a new equilibrium will be difficult. No Latin American school system today is very close to high standards, high academic talent, high or at least adequate compensation, and high professional autonomy that characterizes the world's most effective education systems—in Singapore; Shanghai, China; Korea; the Netherlands; Finland; Ontario, Canada; and Germany.

Raising the stakes further are the sweeping transformations occurring in global education. The traditional goals of national education systems and the traditional paradigm of teacher-student interaction placed teachers at the center of the transmission of a discrete body of knowledge to students in classrooms and schools. The emerging paradigm is that teachers are not the only or even the major source of information and knowledge available to students. A core role of teachers today is to equip students to

FIGURE 1.30: Wage distribution for teachers compared with other professions in Costa Rica, 2001 and 2009

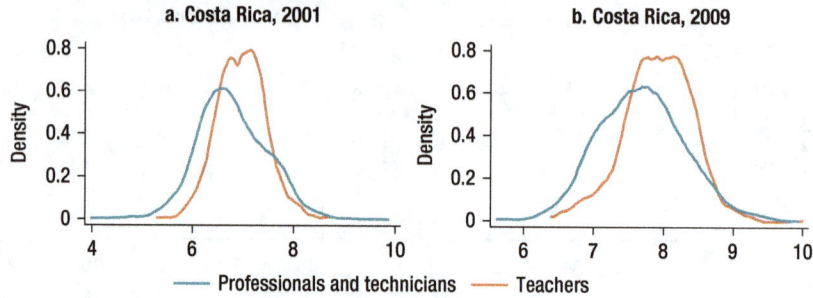

Source: World Bank analysis of household survey and labor market data.
Note: Log hourly wage unconditional distribution by occupational group.

seek, analyze, and effectively use vast amounts of information that are readily available online. Teachers must also develop students' competencies in the broad range of areas valued in an integrated global economy: critical thinking; problem-solving; working collaboratively in diverse environments; adapting to change; and the capacity to master new knowledge, skills, and changing employment demands across their lifetimes. These functions demand that teachers trained today have much more sophisticated information and communications technology skills than those trained even five years ago, plus the intellectual confidence to demonstrate critical and analytical thinking to their students and the interpersonal skills to work collaboratively with colleagues on continuous refinement of an evolving curriculum. No teacher preparation programs in LAC—or even in most OECD countries—are fully prepared to produce this profile of teacher today, let alone a profile for the next decade. But virtually all OECD countries are responding to this complex challenge by raising their expectations, and standards, for teachers.

Countries across Latin America and the Caribbean are also responding. Virtually all aspects of teacher policy are under review and reform in different LAC countries, and in some areas the region is in the vanguard of global policy experience. By drawing together in one volume the key teacher policy reforms being undertaken in the region today and the best available evidence on their impact, this book hopes to stimulate and support the faster progress that is needed.

Notes

[1] Chapter Annexes to the book may be found at http://www.worldbank.org/lac/teachers.

[2] Participation by South Asian countries in international tests over the period was too limited to include that region in the database.

[3] The OECD PISA secretariat estimates that one academic year of content (in OECD countries) equals approximately 38 points on the PISA test scale.

[4] These studies typically regress student achievement on past student achievement, school and peer factors, family and neighborhood inputs, and a teacher fixed effect (Hanushek and Rivkin 2010). Rothstein (2010) demonstrates that sorting of students may lead to upward bias on some of these, but studies that guard against sorting such as Rothstein (2010) and Rivkin, Hanushek, and Kain (2005) also show significant impacts.

References

Aaronson, D., L. Barrow, and W. Sander. 2007. "Teachers and Student Achievement in the Chicago Public High Schools." *Journal of Labor Economics* 25 (1): 95–135.

Alfonso, M., A. Santiago, and M. Bassi. 2010. *Estimating the Impact of Placing Top University Graduates in Vulnerable Schools in Chile.* Washington, DC: Inter-American Development Bank.

Araujo, M. C., P. Carneiro, Y. Cruz-Aguayo, and N. Schady. Forthcoming. "A Helping Hand? Teacher Quality and Learning Outcomes in Kindergarten." Inter-American Development Bank, Washington, DC.

Atlas of Global Development (database). World Bank, Washington, DC. http://data.worldbank.org/atlas-global.

Barber, M., and M. Mourshed. 2009. "Shaping the Future: How Good Education Systems Can Become Great in the Decade Ahead." Report on the International Education Roundtable, Singapore Ministry of Education and McKinsey, July 7.

Barón, J., L. Bonilla, L. Cardona, and M. Ospina. 2014. *Quienes Eligen la Disciplina de la Educación en Colombia? Caracterización desde el Desempeño en las Pruebas SABER 11.* Bogotá: Lecturas de Economía.

Barro, R. J., and J. W. Lee. 2012. "A New Data Set of Educational Attainment in the World, 1950–2010." *Journal of Development Economics* 104 (2013): 184–98.

Behrman, J. R., M. Tincani, P. E. Todd, and K. I. Wolpin. 2013. "The Impact of School Voucher Systems on Teacher Quality in Public and Private Schools: The Case of Chile." Unpublished manuscript. http://www.homepages.ucl.ac.uk/~uctpmt1/Behrman_Tincani_Todd_Wolpin_revised_2014.pdf.

Carrell, Scott E., and James E. West. 2010. "Does Professor Quality Matter? Evidence from Random Assignment of Students to Professors." *Journal of Political Economy* 118 (3): 409–32.

Chetty, R., J. N. Friedman, N. Hilger, E. Saez, D. W. Schanzenbach, and D. Yagan. 2011. "How Does Your Kindergarten Classroom Affect Your Earnings? Evidence from Project STAR." *Quarterly Journal of Economics* 126 (4): 1593–660.

Chetty, R., J. N. Friedman, and J. E. Rockoff. 2014a. "Measuring the Impacts of Teachers I: Evaluating Bias in Teacher Value-Added Estimates." Forthcoming. *American Economic Review.*

———. 2014b. "Measuring the Impacts of Teachers II: Teacher Value-Added and Student Outcomes in Adulthood." Forthcoming. *American Economic Review.*

Clotfelter, C., H. Ladd, and A. J. Vigdor. 2007. "How and Why Do Teacher Credentials Matter for Student Learning?" Working Paper 12828, National Bureau of Economic Research, Cambridge, MA.

Corcoran, S. P., W. N. Evans, and R. M. Schwab. 2004. "Women, the Labor Market, and the Declining Relative Quality of Teachers." *Journal of Policy Analysis and Management* 23 (3): 449–70.

Crookston, B. T., K. A. Dearden, S. C. Alder, C. A. Porucznik, J. B. Stanford, R. M. Merrill, T. T. Dickerson, and M. E. Penny. 2011. "Impact of Early and Concurrent Stunting on Cognition." *Maternal & Child Nutrition* 7 (4): 397–409.

Crookston, B. T., M. E. Penny, S. C. Alder, T. T. Dickerson, R. M. Merrill, J. B. Stanford, C. A. Porucznik, and K. A. Dearden. 2010. "Children Who Recover from Early Stunting and Children Who Are Not Stunted Demonstrate Similar Levels of Cognition." *Journal of Nutrition* 140 (11): 1996–2001.

Crookston, B. T., W. Schott, S. Cueto, K. A. Dearden, A. Georgiadis, E. A. Lundeen, M. E. Penny, A. D. Stein, and J. R. Behrman. 2013. "Post-Infancy Growth and Cognitive Achievement and Schooling at Age 8 Years: Observational Cohort Study for Ethiopia, India, Peru and Vietnam." *American Journal of Clinical Nutrition* 98 (6): 1555–63.

Eide, E. G., D. Goldhaber, and D. Brewer. 2004. "The Teacher Labour Market and Teacher Quality." *Oxford Review of Economic Policy* 20 (2): 230–44.

ENAHO (Encuesta Nacional de Hogares [Peru Household Survey]). Instituto Nacional de Estadísticas e Informática, Lima, Peru.

Engle, P. L., L. C. H. Fernald, H. Alderman, J. Behrman, C. O'Gara, A. Yousafzai, M. Cabral de Mello, M. Hidrobo, N. Ulkuer, I. Ertem, and S. Iltus. 2011. "Strategies for Reducing Inequalities and Improving Developmental Outcomes for Young Children in Low-income and Middle-income Countries." *The Lancet* 378 (9799): 1339–53.

Fernandes, M., and C. Ferraz. 2014. "Conhecimento ou Práticas Pedagógicas? Medindo os Efeitos da Qualidade dos Professores no Desempenho dos Alunos." Manuscript. PUC-Rio, Rio de Janeiro. http://www.econ.puc-rio.br/uploads/adm/trabalhos/files/td620.pdf.

Fredriksson, P., and B. Ockert. 2007. "The Supply of Skills to the Teacher Profession." Manuscript. Uppsala University, Uppsala, Sweden.

Glewwe, P., E. A. Hanushek, S. Humpage, and R. Ravina. 2011. "School Resources and Educational Outcomes in Developing Countries: A Review of the Literature from 1990 to 2010." Working Paper 17554, National Bureau of Economic Research, Cambridge, MA.

Goldhaber, D. 2002. "The Mystery of Good Teaching: Surveying the Evidence on Student Achievement and Teachers' Characteristics." *Education Next* 2 (1): 50–55.

Hanushek, E. O., J. F. Kain, D. M. O'Brien, and S. G. Rivkin, 2005. "The Market for Teacher Quality." Working Paper 11154, National Bureau of Economic Research, Cambridge, MA.

Hanushek, E., P. Peterson, and L. Woessmann. 2012. *Achievement Growth: International and U.S. State Trends in Student Performance*. PEPG Report 12-03, Program on Education Policy and Governance, Harvard University, Cambridge, MA.

Hanushek, E., and S. Rivkin. 2010. "Using Value-Added Measures of Teacher Quality." Policy Brief 9, National Center for Analysis of Longitudinal Data in Education Research, Washington, DC.

Hanushek, E. A., and S. G. Rivkin. 2006. "Teacher Quality." In vol. 2. of *Handbook of the Economics of Education*, edited by F. Welch, 1051–78. Amsterdam: North-Holland.

Hanushek, E. A., and L. Woessmann. 2007. "The Role of Education Quality for Economic Growth." Policy Research Working Paper 4122, World Bank, Washington, DC.

———. 2012. "Schooling, Educational Achievement, and the Latin American Growth Puzzle." *Journal of Development Economics* 99 (2): 497–512.

Heckman, J. J., and T. Kautz. 2013. "Fostering and Measuring Skills: Interventions that Improve Character and Cognition." Working Paper 19656, National Bureau of Economic Research, Cambridge, MA.

Hernani-Limarino, W. 2005. "Are Teachers Well Paid in Latin America and the Caribbean? Relative Wage and Structure of Returns of Teachers." In *Incentives to Improve Teaching: Lessons from Latin America*, edited by E. Vegas, 63–102. Washington, DC: World Bank.

Hill, H., B. Rowan, and A. D. Ball. 2005. "Effects of Teachers' Mathematical Knowledge for Teaching on Student Achievement." *American Educational Research Journal* 42 (2): 371–406.

Hoddinott, J., J. R. Behrman, J. A. Maluccio, P. Melgar, A. R. Quisumbing, M. Ramirez-Zea, A. D. Stein, K. M. Yount, and R. Martorell. 2013. "Adult Consequences of Growth Failure in Early Childhood." *American Journal of Clinical Nutrition* 98 (5): 1170–78.

Hoxby, C. M., and A. Leigh. 2004. "Pulled Away or Pushed Out? Explaining the Decline of Teacher Aptitude in the United States." *American Economic Review* 94 (2): 236–40.

Jacob, B. A., and L. Lefgren. 2008. "Can Principals Identify Effective Teachers? Evidence on Subjective Performance Evaluation in Education." *Journal of Labor Economics* 26 (1): 101–36.

Jacob, B. A., L. Lefgren, and D. P. Sims. 2010. "The Persistence of Teacher-Induced Learning." *Journal of Human Resources* 45 (4): 915–43.

Kane, T. J., J. E. Rockoff, and D. O. Staiger. 2008. "What Does Certification Tell Us about Teacher Effectiveness? Evidence from New York City." *Economics of Education Review* 27 (6): 615–31.

Kane, T. J., and D. O. Staiger. 2008. "Estimating Teacher Impacts on Student Achievement: An Experimental Evaluation." Working Paper 14607, National Bureau of Economic Research, Cambridge, MA.

Koedel, C., and J. R. Betts. 2009. "Does Student Sorting Invalidate Value-Added Models of Teacher Effectiveness? An Extended Analysis of the Rothstein Critique." Department of Economics Working Paper 0902, University of Missouri, Columbia, Missouri.

Lopez-Acevedo, G. 2004. "Teachers' Salaries and Professional Profile in Mexico." Policy Research Working Paper 3394, World Bank, Washington, DC.

Maluccio, J. A., J. Hoddinott, J. R. Behrman, R. Martorell, A. R. Quisumbing, and A. D. Stein. 2009. "The Impact of Improving Nutrition During Early Childhood on Education Among Guatemalan Adults." *Economic Journal* 119 (537): 734–63.

Marshall, J. S., and M. A. Sorto. 2012. "The Effects of Teacher Mathematics Knowledge and Pedagogy on Student Achievement in Rural Guatemala." *International Review of Education* 58 (2): 173–97.

Maul Rivas, H., and J. Lavarreda. 2008. *Análisis de las remuneraciones de los docentes del sector público en Guatemala*. Ciudad de Guatemala: Informe Final para el Ministerio de Educación de Guatemala.

Metzler, J., and L. Woessmann. 2012. "The Impact of Teacher Subject Knowledge on Student Achievement: Evidence from Within-Teacher Within-Student Variation. *Journal of Development Economics* 99 (2): 486–96.

Mizala, A., and H. Ñopo. 2011. "Teachers' Salaries in Latin America: How Much Are They (Under or Over) Paid?" IZA Discussion Paper 5947, Institute for the Study of Labor, Bonn.

Mizala, A., and P. Romaguera. 2005. "Teachers' Salary Structure and Incentives in Chile." In *Incentives to Improve Teaching: Lessons from Latin America*, edited by E. Vegas, 103–50. Washington, DC: World Bank.

Nye, B., S. Konstantopoulos, and L. V. Hedges. 2004. "How Large Are Teacher Effects?" *Educational Evaluation and Policy Analysis* 26 (3): 237–57.

OECD (Organisation for Economic Co-operation and Development). 2005. *Teachers Matter: Attracting, Developing and Retaining Effective Teachers*. Paris: OECD Publishing.

———. 2009. "Teaching Practices, Teachers' Beliefs and Attitudes." In *Creating Effective Teaching and Learning Environments: First Results from TALIS*, 88–120. Paris: OECD Publishing.

———. 2010. Vol. 1 of *PISA 2009 Results: What Students Know and Can Do—Student Performance in Reading, Mathematics and Science*. Paris: OECD Publishing.

———. 2013a. *Education at a Glance 2013: OECD Indicators*. Paris: OECD Publishing. http://dx.doi.org/10.1787/eag-2013-en.

———. 2013b. Vol. I of *PISA 2012 Results: What Students Know and Can Do—Student Performance in Mathematics, Reading and Science*. Paris: OECD Publishing. http://www.oecd-ilibrary.org/education/pisa-2012-results-what-students-know-and-can-do-volume-i-revised-edition-february-2014_9789264208780-en.

Piras, C., and B. Savedoff. 1998. "How Much Do Teachers Earn?" Working Paper 375, Inter-American Development Bank, Washington, DC.

Rivkin, S. G., E. A. Hanushek, and J. F. Kain. 2005. "Teachers, Schools, and Academic Achievement." *Econometrica* 73 (2): 417–58.

Rockoff, J. E. 2004. "The Impact of Individual Teachers on Student Achievement: Evidence from Panel Data." *American Economic Review* 94 (2): 247–52.

Rockoff, J. E., B. A. Jacob, T. J. Kane, and D. O. Staiger. 2011. "Can You Recognize an Effective Teacher When You Recruit One?" *Education Finance and Policy* 6 (1): 43–74.

Rothstein, J. 2010. "Teacher Quality in Educational Production: Tracking, Decay, and Student Achievement." *Quarterly Journal of Economics* 125 (1): 175–214.

Saavedra Chanduvi, J. 2004. "La situación laboral de los maestros respecto de otros profesionales. Implicancias para el diseño de políticas salariales y de incentivos." In *¿Es posible mejorar la educación peruana?: evidencias y posibilidades*, edited by P. Arregui, M. Benavides, S. Cueto, J. Saavedra, and B. Hunt, Lima: Grupo de Análisis para el Desarrollo (GRADE).

Santibañez, L. 2006. "Why We Should Care if Teachers Get A's: Teacher Test Scores and Student Achievement in Mexico." *Economics of Education Review* 25 (5), 510–20.

Schady, N., J. Behrman, M. C. Araujo, R. Azuero, R. Bernal, D. Bravo, F. Lopez-Boo, K. Macours, K. Marshall, C. Paxson, and R. Vakis. 2014. "Wealth Gradients in Early Childhood Cognitive Development in Five Latin American Countries." IDB Working Paper 482, Inter-American Development Bank, Washington, DC.

Stipek, D. J., K. B. Givvin, J. M. Salmon, and V. L. MacGyvers. 2001. "Teachers' Beliefs and Practices Related to Mathematics Instruction." *Teaching and Teacher Education* 17 (2): 213–26.

TEDS-M (Teacher Education and Development Study in Mathematics) 2008 (database). International Association for the Evaluation of Achievement. http://rms.iea-dpc.org/.

Wayne, A. J., and P. Youngs. 2003. "Teacher Characteristics and Student Achievement Gains: A Review." *Review of Educational Research* 73 (1): 89–122.

2
Inside the Classroom in Latin America and the Caribbean

The magic of education—the transformation of schooling inputs into learning outcomes—happens in the classroom. Every element of an education system's expenditure, from curriculum design through school construction, book procurement, and teacher salaries, comes together at the moment when a teacher interacts with students in the classroom. How efficiently this instructional time is used is a core determinant of the productivity of education spending.

A schematic description of the "results chain," or production function, for education outcomes is shown in figure 2.1. A substantial body of research confirms that each of the elements pictured contributes to student learning. The importance of student socioeconomic background, as discussed in chapter 1, is particularly well-established. No single school-level factor has as strong and consistent a correlation with learning outcomes and schooling attainment as students' family income and parental education. Recent research also points to the importance of student motivation, which is correlated with socioeconomic background, but also reflects character skills such as conscientiousness and perseverance. Cross-country research on the Program for International Student Assessment (PISA) outcomes has established that a common feature of high-performing countries is the existence of high-stakes examinations at the end of secondary school, which determine university prospects and create strong incentives for students to apply themselves to their studies (Woessmann 2004). Experimental evidence from contexts as different as the United States, Israel, Kenya, and Mexico also shows that cash incentives for students can stimulate more effort and in some cases substantially raise learning outcomes (Angrist and Lavy 2009; Kremer, Miguel, and Thornton 2009; Fryer 2011; Levitt, List, and Sadoff 2011; Behrman et al. forthcoming).

This chapter was coauthored with Soledad de Gregorio and Jessica Rodriguez.

FIGURE 2.1: Education results chain and reduced form education production function

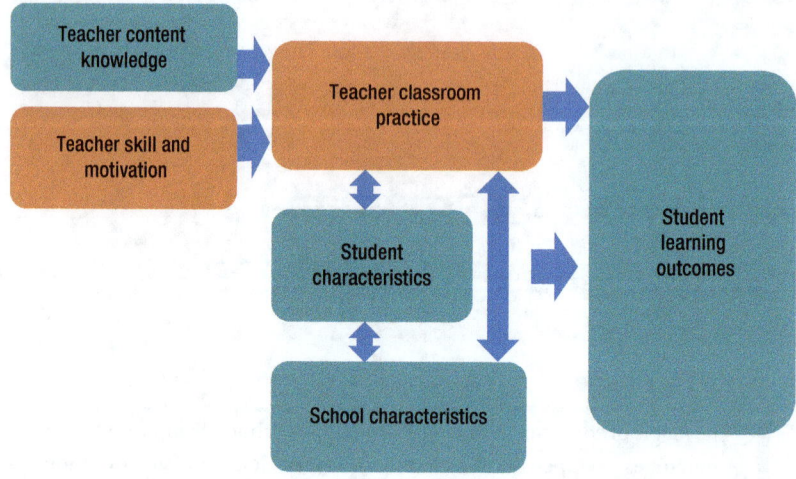

But unpacking the relative importance of "student" and "school quality" factors has been complicated by the near-complete lack of data for two key elements of the delivery chain: teacher skill and motivation and teacher classroom practice. These vectors are omitted from most reduced form analyses of the determinants of learning outcomes, which typically rely on the elements for which data—or reasonable proxy information—are available. Teachers' level of formal education, for example, is typically used as a proxy for their content knowledge, parents' education and student socioeconomic background as a proxy for the differential "readiness to learn" that students bring to the classroom, and school-level spending on inputs as a proxy for the quality of the service delivered by the school. However, focusing on these more easily measured elements pictured in turquoise in figure 2.1 typically leaves a large share of the variance in learning outcomes unexplained.

In the conceptual framework of figure 2.1, it is intuitively suggestive that a robust quantitative measure of teacher classroom practice—as the central "output" in the chain from education inputs to student learning outcomes—might have important explanatory power. And in fact, research interest in developing such a measure has grown enormously over the past few years. A number of instruments for capturing some measure of classroom dynamics exist, most of which were developed for purposes of teacher performance evaluation. Efforts by education economists to use these for large-scale research on what makes teachers effective are a quite recent phenomenon. The most notable example in the U.S. context to date is the Measures of Effective Teaching (MET) program, launched in 2011 to analyze teacher-student dynamics in 3,000 secondary school classrooms, funded by the Bill & Melinda Gates Foundation

(Kane et al. 2013). The emerging research on Ecuadorean preschools, discussed in chapter 1, is another pathbreaking effort (Araujo et al. forthcoming).

Early results from this shift in research attention are encouraging. The evidence is still quite limited and almost entirely from the U.S. context. But it does confirm that measures of teacher-student dynamics in the classroom can explain why some teachers are more effective than others in raising student learning outcomes. Broadbrush results are that students learn more when their teachers spend more class time on academic activities ("on-task") and when teachers are able to keep them engaged for longer periods of time (Lavy 2012; Vieluf et al. 2012; Kane et al. 2010; Stallings, Johnson, and Goodman 1985).

Latin America and the Caribbean classroom observation sample

For this study, the World Bank collaborated with seven Latin American and the Caribbean (LAC) countries between 2009 and 2013 on the largest-scale effort to date to build reliable, globally comparable data on teacher classroom practice. The research had three objectives. The first was to benchmark teacher practice in representative national and subnational samples of schools in Latin America against comparable data from each other and from school systems in the United States. The second was to contribute to the global evidence base on the links between classroom dynamics and student learning outcomes, drawing on the increasing amount of high-quality student assessment data available in these LAC countries. The third was to deepen ongoing impact evaluations of key teacher policy reforms by generating intermediate variables on how reforms affect teacher practice in the classroom, as a conduit to their ultimate impact on student learning. With the help of carefully trained national teams of observers, we amassed data on over 15,000 classrooms in 3,015 different schools across the region. Participating countries include Brazil, Colombia, Honduras, Jamaica, Mexico, and Peru and a pilot effort in the Dominican Republic (table 2.1).

In Colombia, Honduras, Jamaica, and Peru, school samples were representative at the national level. The samples in Brazil and Mexico were representative at the level of participating subnational governments: the states of Pernambuco and Minas Gerais and the municipality of Rio de Janeiro in Brazil; and the Federal District (Distrito Federal) in Mexico. (Details of the protocols for the stratified random selection of representative samples of schools and the random selection of classrooms within schools are included in Annex 2.3.)[1] Observations focused on tested grades and subjects to facilitate research on the correlations between classroom practices and student learning, but individual classrooms were randomly selected from within the targeted grades and subjects. Schools were not informed of their selection and not advised of visits in advance. Teachers received no advance notice that they would be observed, but just before the observation teachers were informed that the visit was for research purposes and they were guaranteed anonymity.

TABLE 2.1: LAC classroom observation sample

Country	Region	Year	Grades	Schools	Classrooms
Brazil	Minas Gerais	2011	8–9, 11–12	604	3,020
	Minas Gerais pilot	2009	5, 9, 12	75	150
	Pernambuco	2009	2–5, 8, 9	228	1,100
		2010	2–5, 8, 9	301	1,505
	Rio de Janeiro (Municipality)	2010	4–6, 8, 9	100	896
		2011	3–9	131	665
	Rio de Janeiro (state) pilot	2012	9, 10–12	60	281
Colombia	National	2011	5, 9, 11	200	1,091
	Antioquia	2011	5, 9, 11	84	995
Dominican Republic	Pilot	2012	1–8	10	51
Honduras	National	2011	3, 6, 9	153	758
Jamaica	National	2011	4, 5, 9, 10	200	1,000
Mexico	Distrito Federal	2011	1–9	201	2,335
Peru	National	2012	4	400	1,195
	Callao, pilot	2011	2	201	313
	San Martin, pilot		2	67	320
Total				3,015	15,675

Source: World Bank and government data.
Notes: LAC = Latin America and the Caribbean. Results presented throughout the chapter are for full samples only (i.e., not including pilot observations in Minas Gerais and Rio de Janiero State, Brazil; Callao and San Martin, Peru; or the Dominican Republic). Approximately half of the schools in the Peru sample were multigrade schools in which a single teacher was observed delivering several different classes, each of which is recorded as a "classroom" observed.

Observation method and instrument

The observations used a slightly adapted and internationally validated version of the Stallings Classroom Snapshot instrument, originally developed by Jane Stallings for research on the efficiency and quality of basic education teachers in the United States in the 1970s (Stallings 1977; Stallings and Mohlman 1988). The Stallings instrument generates robust quantitative data on the interaction of teachers and students in the classroom, with a high degree of inter-rater reliability (0.8 or higher) among observers with relatively limited training, which makes it suitable for large-scale samples in developing country settings (Abadzi 2007; DeStefano, Adelman, and Moore 2010; Schuh Moore, DeStefano, and Adelman 2010). In comparison with observation instruments such as the Classroom Assessment Scoring System (CLASS), which generates data on the quality of teachers' instructional interaction and emotional support for students as well as their classroom management, the Stallings instrument captures a much more limited range of teacher behaviors. But its simplicity allows for easier implementation, and the language- and curriculum-neutral instrument means that results are directly comparable across different types of schools and country contexts. Box 2.1 provides more detail on the Stallings instrument and observation protocol.

The Stallings instrument generates quantitative measures of four main variables:

- Teachers' use of instructional time
- Teachers' use of materials, including information and communication technology (ICT)
- Teachers' core pedagogical practices
- Teachers' ability to keep students engaged

BOX 2.1: *How the Stallings Classroom Snapshot works*

The Stallings method uses a standardized coding grid to register the activities and materials being used by a teacher and students over the course of a single class. Ten separate observations or "snapshots" are made at regular intervals over the course of each class period. If a class is 50 minutes long, observations are made every 5 minutes. Each observation takes 15 seconds.

During those 15 seconds, the observer scans the room in a 360-degree circle starting with the teacher and codes four key aspects of classroom dynamics in detail: (a) how the teacher is using the class time within three broad categories: instruction, classroom management, or other activities (considered "off-task"); (b) if the time is being used for instruction, which specific pedagogical practices are being used; (c) if time is being used for instruction, which specific learning materials are being used; and (d) how many students are visibly engaged in the activity being led by the teacher or are engaged in off-task behaviors (such as social interaction with other students or visibly "tuned out" of the activity at hand). Table B2.1.1 lists the specific teaching, classroom management, and off-task activities captured in a Stallings Classroom Snapshot.

The coding grid has a matrix format in which different activities are listed along the vertical axis and materials used along the horizontal axis. Within each activity, there are two lines: the top line captures whom in the classroom the teacher is engaging with—whether it is the entire class, a large group of students, a small group, or only one student (e.g., checking a student's work at his or her desk). The bottom line registers what different students are doing, in the event that the entire class is not engaged with the teacher.

(continued on next page)

BOX 2.1: *How the Stallings Classroom Snapshot works (continued)*

TABLE B2.1.1: Activities captured in Stallings Classroom Snapshot

Use of time	Specific practice
Academic activities	Reading aloud
	Exposition/demonstration
	Question and answer/discussion
	Practice and drill
	Seatwork
	Copying
Classroom management	Verbal instruction
	Discipline
	Classroom organization (alone)
	Classroom organization (with students)
Teacher off-task	Teacher absent from classroom
	Teacher in social interaction with students
	Teacher uninvolved or in social interaction with others

Options for the students include "social interaction" and "disengaged." We define a large group as six or more students.

The utility of the Stallings method is that it generates quantitative data from the observation of classroom dynamics. Although many school systems collect some form of classroom observation data from school supervisors, these observations are usually qualitative, subjective, and cannot be meaningfully aggregated. The collection of 10 15-second snapshots from each classroom with the Stallings coding grid creates standardized measures of key variables. All Stallings results, therefore, are expressed as a percentage of total class time. At the school system level, Stallings results represent a percentage of the nationally established total annual days of instruction.

Between observations, the observer also fills out a classroom demographic sheet reporting on other useful information, such the number of students and their gender, the state of classroom infrastructure, availability of books and materials, and the official start and end times of the class. (The full coding grid and demographic sheets used are presented in Annexes 2.1 and 2.2.) A final part of our protocol was a structured interview of the school director or substitute to gather additional information about the school, its student population, teachers, priorities, and the perspectives of school personnel on system policies and recent reforms.

(continued on next page)

BOX 2.1: *How the Stallings Classroom Snapshot works* (continued)

FIGURE B2.1.1: Excerpt from Stallings Classroom Snapshot coding grid: Time use, materials use, and level of student engagement

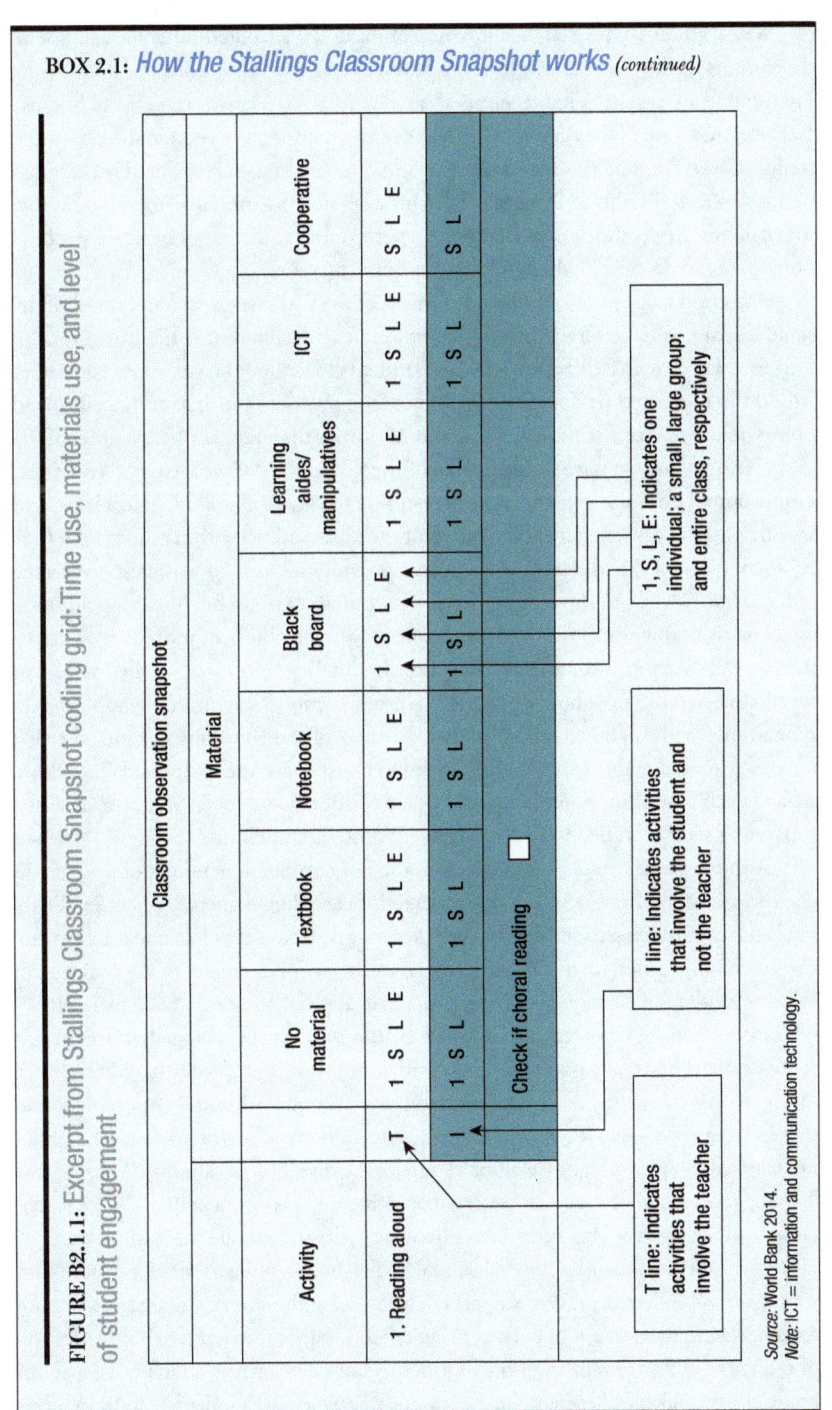

Source: World Bank 2014.
Note: ICT = information and communication technology.

Key features of the Stallings instrument make it well suited to large-scale use in developing country contexts. However, several factors need to borne in mind when interpreting its results. First, there is clear potential for Hawthorne effects because teachers are aware of the observer (and sometimes pair of observers) in the classroom (unlike observation methods that place a video camera in the classroom for extended periods so as to minimize these effects). One operating assumption, therefore, is that the Stallings observations capture teachers performing at their very best—or production possibility frontier—which is in fact useful to measure.

A second issue is the potential noisiness of the variables being measured; if the same teacher were observed on different days or with different student sections on the same day or with a different cohort of students the following year, how consistent would the measured performance be? Since the protocol for this study prioritized observing large cross-sections of classrooms, rather than repeat observations of the same classrooms, we have no estimates of the scope for "within-teacher" variance. Our protocol does not generate robust results at the level of individual teachers, and we do not share the teacher-level data. Multiple observations within each school (our protocol calls for five different classrooms) provides a basis for estimating variance at the school level, but repeat visits at different times of the school year would obviously be desirable for more robust estimates of the noisiness of individual schools' data as well. At the system level, however, the Stallings protocol applied to a representative sample of schools generates a cross-sectional picture of school-system functioning with high statistical validity. For two of the Brazilian systems, we also have two annual rounds of data for the same classrooms and schools. While these data in each case show some statistically significant changes over time, our basis for separating secular trends from measurement noise is still limited.

A third, and more important, issue is the nonrandom assignment of teachers to classes in most of the school systems observed. Even when students are not explicitly tracked by ability, classroom assignment rules may de facto result in some teachers facing much more gifted or docile students than others. For example, in many Brazilian systems, students are assigned to classrooms by age, which means that older students—who have typically repeated one or more grades—are clustered together. In Brazil's school system, like many others, teachers with more seniority typically have first choice of which class to teach. This results in nonrandom "sorting" of students and teachers at the classroom level. As a result, when we evaluate the correlations between teacher practices and student learning, we cannot be sure of the direction of causality. Are students learning more because their teachers are managing the classroom better? Or are teachers able to manage the classroom better because their students are more motivated?

Last, and most important, what makes the Stallings instrument versatile and robust across different grades, subjects, languages, and countries is that it does not try to measure the content of what is being taught—either the depth or sophistication of the curriculum content itself or the teacher's mastery of that content. Two sixth-grade classrooms in different countries in our sample could appear identical in terms of the classroom dynamics measured by the Stallings instrument, even though one is teaching a much higher level of science content than the other. Similarly, a teacher's practice may look highly interactive while he or she is making factual errors. In fact, observer teams regularly reported distressing examples of weak content mastery by teachers, such as a fourth-grade math teacher instructing a class that "2.17" is greater than "2.2," "because 17 is greater than 2."

Referring to figure 2.1, it is clear that the dimensions of "classroom practice" captured by the Stallings instrument are not a complete measure of the quality of teacher-student interaction and cannot be expected to explain all of the variance in teacher effectiveness (whether measured as value-added learning gains or average student learning performance) across different classrooms. The research conducted for this report is in fact the largest scale and most comprehensive global effort to date to explore just how much of measured differences in teacher effectiveness can be correlated with the dimensions of teacher classroom practice captured by Stallings method observations.

What are we learning from classroom observations in LAC?

Application of the Stallings instrument in U.S. school districts over several decades led Stallings and Knight (2003) to observe that high-performing schools achieve an average of 85 percent of class time spent on instruction. They set this as a "benchmark" for good classroom practice. Their research also led them to conclude that the most effective teachers used "active" instructional methods, directly engaging with students through lecture and explanation and question and answer interaction. They accordingly recommend that teachers use the bulk of their instructional time (50 percent of total class time) on "active" instruction. Correspondingly, not more than 35 percent of total class time should be spent on "passive" instruction, such as students doing assignments at their seats with the teacher circulating the classroom and monitoring progress. Up to 15 percent of class time is necessarily absorbed by classroom management activities: passing out papers, taking attendance, explaining the schedule for the week, etc. But an effective teacher would keep this time to a minimum and would never be observed "off-task"—engaged in neither teaching nor classroom management activities. Stallings and Knight observe that highly effective teachers do a good job of keeping students engaged in learning throughout the class, but acknowledge that a realistic benchmark for a school is to keep the share of time students are off-task below 6 percent (table 2.2).

The "good practice" benchmarks proposed by Stallings and Knight are grounded in several decades of practical experience observing classroom dynamics in the U.S. context. However, their research did not have access to the classroom-level student learning data (which was much less abundant at that time) that could validate the correlation between "best practice" classroom dynamics and student learning outcomes. Some influential recent studies have been able to do this (Kane et al. 2013),

TABLE 2.2: Stallings good practice benchmarks for instructional time use

			Stallings benchmarks for effective time use (U.S. research)
	Instruction		85%
Teachers	Active instruction		50% or more
		Reading aloud	
		Demonstration/lecture	
		Discussion/question and answer	
		Practice and drill	
		Cooperative projects	
	Passive instruction		35% or less
		Monitoring copying	
		Monitoring seatwork	
	Classroom management		15% or less
		Verbal instruction (e.g., giving assignments)	
		Managing with students (e.g., passing out papers)	
		Disciplining students	
		Managing alone (e.g., grading homework)	
	Off-task		0%
		Absent from the room	
		Socializing with students	
		Socializing with others	
Students	Off-task		6% or less
		Socializing	
		Uninvolved	
		Acting out	

Source: Stallings and Knight 2003.

but these studies have used different observation instruments, all of which are more sophisticated and require significantly longer training for observers. We found these less practical for large-scale, cross-country research in developing country settings.

Therefore, we use the Stallings and Knight proposed benchmarks as an interesting point of reference for our observation results in LAC countries, but rely on evidence generated by our own study to document their importance for student learning.

What have we learned from more than 150,000 different "snapshots" of classrooms in over 3,000 schools in seven different countries over the past three years? The evidence supports five important conclusions.

Low time on instruction

The first and overwhelming finding is that none of the countries studied comes close to the Stallings benchmark of 85 percent of total class time used for instruction. As figure 2.2 shows, the highest averages recorded—65 percent for the

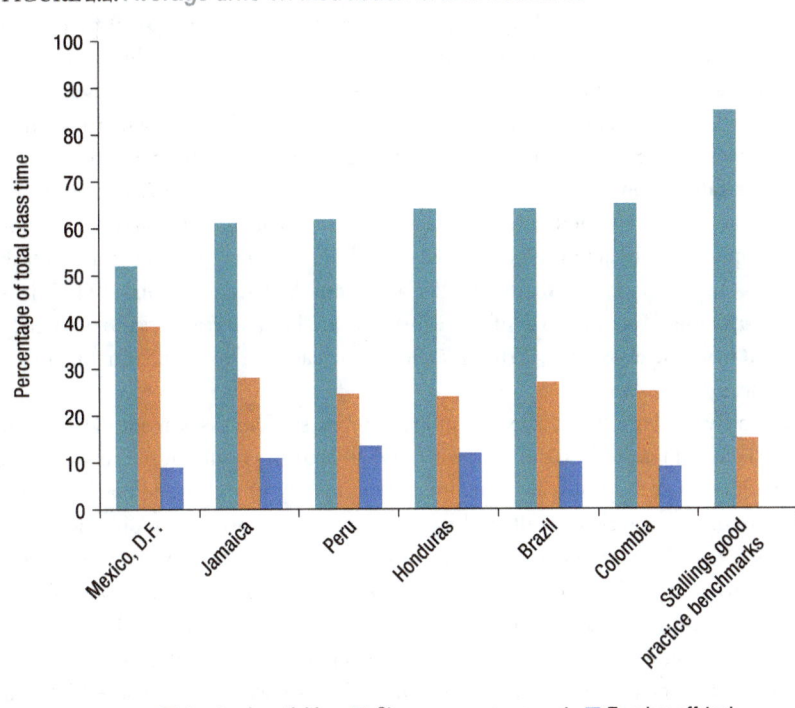

FIGURE 2.2: Average time on instruction in LAC countries

Source: World Bank classroom observation database.
Note: Values for Brazil in this and subsequent figures are pooled data from Pernambuco, Minas Gerais, and the municipality of Rio de Janeiro. Results for the Dominican Republic and Rio de Janeiro state are not included because the samples were pilots. D.F. = Distrito Federal; LAC = Latin America and the Caribbean.

national sample in Colombia and 64 percent each for Brazil and Honduras—are a full 20 percentage points below the Stallings benchmark. Since Stallings measures are statistically representative of the functioning of the school system as a whole, this implies that 20 percent of potential instructional time is being lost across Latin America compared with the good practice goal. *This is the equivalent of one less school day per week.*

Most of the time being lost to instruction is used on classroom management activities—which absorb between 24 percent and 39 percent of total time—well above the 15 percent Stallings benchmark. Mexico's Distrito Federal (D.F.) marks the extreme of the spectrum, with a striking amount of potential class time tied up in activities such as taking attendance, passing out materials, or collecting homework. It is interesting to observe the emphasis that the international nongovernmental organization Teach For All places on training its Latin American teachers to manage classroom transitions and administrative processes as efficiently as possible, with the mantra that "instructional time is a school's most expensive resource." Most classroom teachers in Latin America appear to operate with little of this pressure.

The Stallings benchmarks assume that there is no time teachers are completely off-task, but every LAC country in the sample loses at least 9 percent of total instructional time because teachers are engaged in neither teaching nor classroom management. The highest shares are 14 percent in Peru and 12 percent in Honduras. Figure 2.3 presents data on what teachers are doing when recorded as off-task. In some countries, as much as 6 to 11 percent of the time the teacher is physically absent from the classroom. In other countries, over 7 percent of the time teachers are engaged in social interaction with someone at the classroom door or simply not interacting with the class at all. The average teacher time off-task across the sample means that in a 200-day school year, students miss 20 full days of instruction. More than half of those lost days are because teachers are physically absent from the classroom, arriving late to class, leaving early, or conducting other business during class time.

In Brazil, Honduras, Mexico, and Colombia, student assessment data permit correlation of teachers' use of time with student learning results at the school level. Since the research protocol maintains the anonymity of individual teachers, it is not possible to correlate results at the classroom level. In most cases, one classroom of each tested grade and subject was randomly selected for observation. Thus, the analysis typically correlates average student test scores for all classes of that grade and subject in a school with the dynamics of one randomly selected classroom teaching that grade and subject at that school. The high degree of variance across classrooms within a school on the Stallings measures—discussed later in this chapter—is one factor that weakens the correlations. In the case of Mexico, however, richer administrative data available at the classroom level permit the correlation of classroom-level learning outcomes with Stallings observations for the same classroom (box 2.2).

FIGURE 2.3: Breakdown of teacher time off-task, by country

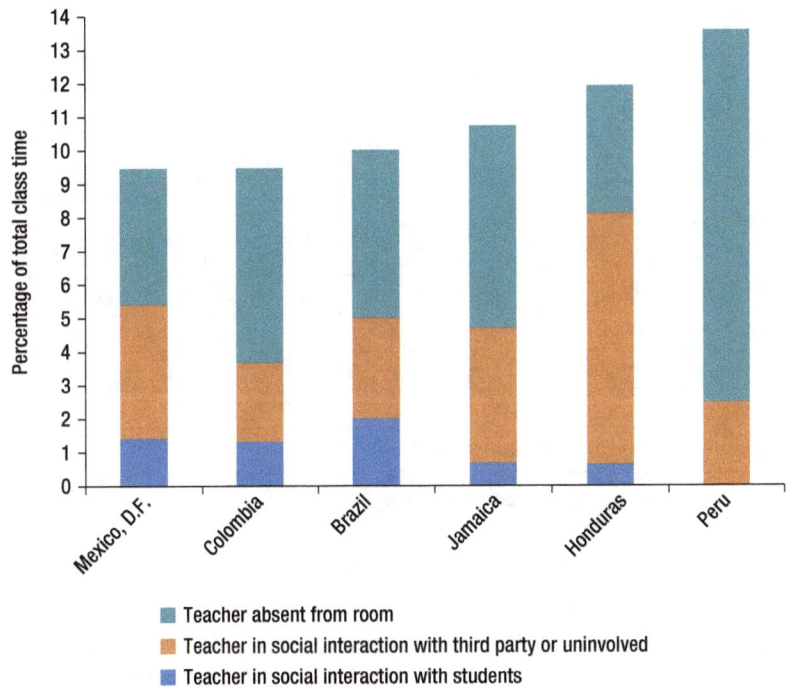

Source: World Bank classroom observation database.
Note: D.F. = Distrito Federal, or Federal District.

BOX 2.2: *Explaining learning improvements in Mexico, D.F.*

Classroom observations employing the Stallings instrument generate robust data on teachers' practice in the classroom. But these dynamics are also influenced by student and school characteristics, such as the type of school, the role of the school principal, teachers' characteristics, and students' socioeconomic background and prior learning.

For the Mexico Federal District, detailed administrative data and annual student test score data with unique student identifiers allow us to add extra controls to the analysis (table B2.2.1) and assess how much of student learning performance is explained by classroom dynamics, compared to other factors. For each classroom observed, we control for the prior–year test results for all of the students in that class as well as students' gender. We also control for teachers' educational level and age, and school level characteristics (afternoon/night school, class size, and school effects). Afternoon and evening shifts in Mexico City schools tend to serve students of lower socioeconomic background.

(continued on next page)

BOX 2.2: *Explaining learning improvements in Mexico, D.F.* (continued)

TABLE B2.2.1: Classroom dynamics and student learning outcomes at the classroom level, Mexico, D.F., 2011

	Math		Spanish	
Data at the student level	1	2	1	2
Teacher practice				
Time on instruction with most or all students engaged	0.162**	0.131**	0.157**	0.142**
	(0.075)	(0.063)	(0.077)	(0.064)
School-level effects	No	Yes	No	Yes
Number of observations	19232	19232	19232	19232
R2	0	0.11	0	0.1

Source: World Bank classroom observation database.
Note: Robust standard errors in parenthesis clustered at the school level: *** significance <1%, ** significance<5%, * significance<10%. Regression also includes grade effects.

In table B2.2.1, we analyze student learning results only for the classrooms that were observed. The correlations are statistically significant at the 5 percent level and are robust even controlling for school effects, as presented in the second column, for both math and Spanish.

Next we introduce controls for students' gender and previous achievement on standardized tests; teachers' gender, age, and educational background; and class size. These characteristics could also be related to teacher practice. For example, teachers with a higher level of training (university degree) may have better classroom practice, or it may be easier for teachers with small classes to keep students engaged. Or "good students"—those with have higher learning outcomes in previous years—may also be easier to teach. But table B2.2.2 shows that the correlation between classroom practice and student results holds, even after controlling for all of these other factors, although statistical significance is reduced.

While students' prior-year test scores are the single strongest predictor of their test performance, teachers' performance—in terms of their ability to engage students in learning—is also among the strongest factors. The relationship between student results and classroom practice is positive and statistically significant for both math and Spanish in the specification without school effects and remains statistically significant for Spanish even with controls for school characteristics. These results can be interpreted as confirming that there are important differences in teachers' ability to manage classrooms effectively,

(continued on next page)

BOX 2.2: *Explaining learning improvements in Mexico, D.F.* (continued)

TABLE B2.2.2: Classroom dynamics and other factors that explain student learning outcomes, Mexico, D.F., 2011

Data at the student level	Math		Spanish	
	1	2	1	2
Student characteristics				
Student gender (male)	0.010	0.015	−0.087***	−0.085***
	(0.010)	(0.009)	(0.009)	(0.010)
Previous test scores (t−1)	0.657***	0.654***	0.649***	0.643***
	(0.012)	(0.011)	(0.011)	(0.010)
Teacher characteristics				
University degree	0.006	−0.011	0.049	0.038
	(0.041)	(0.046)	(0.043)	(0.046)
Teacher gender (male)	0.020	0.032	0.067	0.054
	(0.047)	(0.043)	(0.042)	(0.042)
Age	0.019	0.010	0.005	−0.000
	(0.015)	(0.015)	(0.014)	(0.012)
Age 2	−0.000	−0.000	−0.000	0.000
	(0.000)	(0.000)	(0.000)	(0.000)
Teacher practice				
Time on instruction with most or all students engaged	0.127*	0.081	0.138*	0.114*
	(0.075)	(0.070)	(0.075)	(0.073)
School level				
Class size	−0.004	−0.003	−0.006*	−0.004
	(0.003)	(0.006)	(0.003)	(0.006)
School fixed effects	No	Yes	No	Yes
Number of observations	19232	19232	19232	19232
R2	0.43	0.49	0.44	0.43

Source: World Bank data.
Note: Robust standard errors in parenthesis clustered at school level: *** significance <1%, ** significance<5%, * significance<10%. Regression also included grade effects.

irrespective of their students' ability level and socioeconomic status. The analysis provides reassurance of the utility of the simple but powerful indicators of teacher performance generated by the Stallings method.

Source: Luque and Hernandez forthcoming.

TABLE 2.3: Instructional time use in Rio de Janeiro schools, fifth grade, 2010

	Use of class time			
	Time on instruction (percent)	Classroom organization (percent)	Teacher off-task (percent)	Teacher out of the classroom (percent)
Total: Rio municipality	58	37	6	1
Top 10 percent of schools on IDEB	70	27	3	0
Bottom 10 percent of schools on IDEB	54	39	7	3
Difference	0.16	−0.13	−0.03	−0.03
	[0,09]*	[0,09]*	[0,02]	[0,01]**

Source: World Bank classroom observation database.
Note: Robust standard errors in brackets. * refers to statistically significant at 10%, ** refers to statistically significant at 5%. IDEB = Index of Basic Education Development, Brazil's national measure of school quality based on student test scores and student flows.

Table 2.3 shows a characteristic result. The pattern of time use in the highest-performing 10 percent of schools in Rio de Janeiro is distinctly different from schools in the bottom 10 percent of the distribution on the national education quality index of test scores and pass/graduation rates. Top schools average 70 percent of class time on instruction and 27 percent of time on classroom management. Teachers are off task only 3 percent of the time and are never absent from the classroom. In the lowest-performing schools, only 54 percent of time is spent on instruction, with 39 percent of teachers' time absorbed in classroom management. Teachers are off-task 7 percent and physically absent from the classroom 3 percent of the time. These data mean that students in high-performing schools receive an average of 32 more days of instruction over the 200-day school year than their counterparts in low-performing schools. As noted earlier, we cannot establish the direction of causality, but it is obvious that differences in opportunities to learn of this magnitude could contribute to the gap in school results.

Comparison of schools at the top and bottom ends of the performance distribution in almost all of the countries showed statistically significant differences in instructional time. In Honduras, schools in the top 10 percent of the learning distribution on the national assessment averaged 68 percent of time on instruction, while the bottom 10 percent of schools averaged 46 percent (see Annex 2.4). In Mexico, D.F., the 10 percent of schools with the highest student assessment scores averaged 62 percent of time on instruction compared with 51 percent in the lowest performing schools.

Scatter plots of student test results and time spent on instruction across the full distribution of schools show results that are less sharp, but consistently correlated: students perform better on standardized tests in schools where teachers devote more time to academic activities (figure 2.4). A positive correlation holds in all four countries, across all tested grades and subjects, with very few exceptions. This may

FIGURE 2.4: Instructional time and student learning across LAC countries

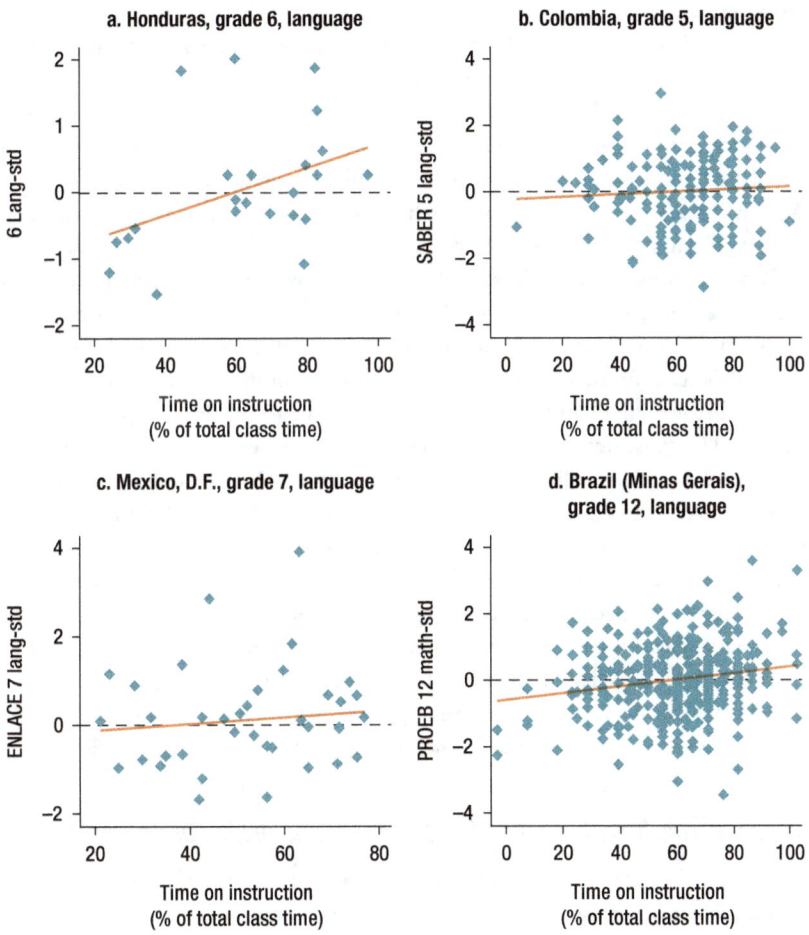

Source: World Bank classroom observation database.
Note: LAC = Latin America and the Caribbean; SABER = standardized test, Colombia; ENLACE = National Assessment of Academic Achievement in Schools, Mexico; PROEB = Assessment Program for Public Basic Education, Minas Gerais, Brazil; assessment for Honduras administered by the Ministry of Education.

seem intuitively obvious: if a teacher is dedicating more time to instruction, students have more opportunities for learning. But this is the first robust evidence we know that supports the intuition across a diverse set of countries. (The full set of results, by country, grade and subject is included in Annex 2.5.)

In some cases where the positive correlation between teacher's time on-task and student learning is not strong, it becomes stronger if learning results are correlated with the share of time the teacher is successfully engaging a large group of students or the entire class in learning activities. Teachers who successfully involve the majority of the class in the task at hand have better control of the class, fewer problems with discipline, more time to impact student learning, and afford a larger share students the opportunity to learn (see Nystrand and Gamoran 1991 for findings with respect to student discipline). Figure 2.5 shows the tighter correlation for some countries between learning outcomes and the Stallings variable "teacher time on task with all students engaged."

Across the region, however, the share of time spent on interactive instructional methods is well short of the Stallings/Knight recommendation of 50 percent. As can be seen from figure 2.6, teachers use "exposition/demonstration" and "debate/discussion" only about 30 percent of total class time, and in countries such as Peru and Mexico, much less. Two of the most widely used teaching activities are still having students copy from the blackboard and do individual work at their seats. Students in Peru and Honduras spend over 10 percent of total class time (and 20 percent of the total time spent on instruction in Peru) copying. In every country in the sample, students spend even more time—from 20 to 30 percent of the time used for "instruction"—doing individual work at their seats. The scarce hours of a school day are typically most productive if children have completed homework assignments prior to class and the teacher uses class time to check for understanding, address questions, and reinforce what has been practiced and learned. In every country, many enumerators report the impression that teachers give students seatwork assignments because they are not prepared to use class time otherwise.

The single most consistent finding across the whole sample is the negative correlation between time off-task and student achievement. As discussed earlier, approximately 10 percent of the time teachers are not engaged in either teaching or classroom management. Figure 2.7 suggests that this has negative consequences for LAC's students.

Teachers rely heavily on the blackboard and make little use of technology

A second finding of the research is that many learning materials available in LAC classrooms are not being used intensively by teachers. Descriptive data collected by the observers shows that schools in these countries offer students a relatively enriched learning environment. Students are almost universally equipped with workbooks and writing materials; textbooks are generally available; schools have libraries; some classrooms have book corners; and a fast-growing share of schools have visible information and communication technology (ICT) in the classroom—ranging from televisions to liquid-crystal display (LCD) projectors and screens to individual laptops. It appears from this research that the LAC region has made very substantial progress over the past decade in supplying its schools with books and materials. In Mexico D.F., textbooks and other learning materials appear to be relatively well-integrated into teachers' practice (figure 2.8). But in most of the countries, teachers continue to rely heavily on a single, very traditional, learning aid: the blackboard. For about one-third of all time spent on teaching activities, teachers use the blackboard and nothing else.

FIGURE 2.5: Instructional time with high student engagement and student learning outcomes in LAC

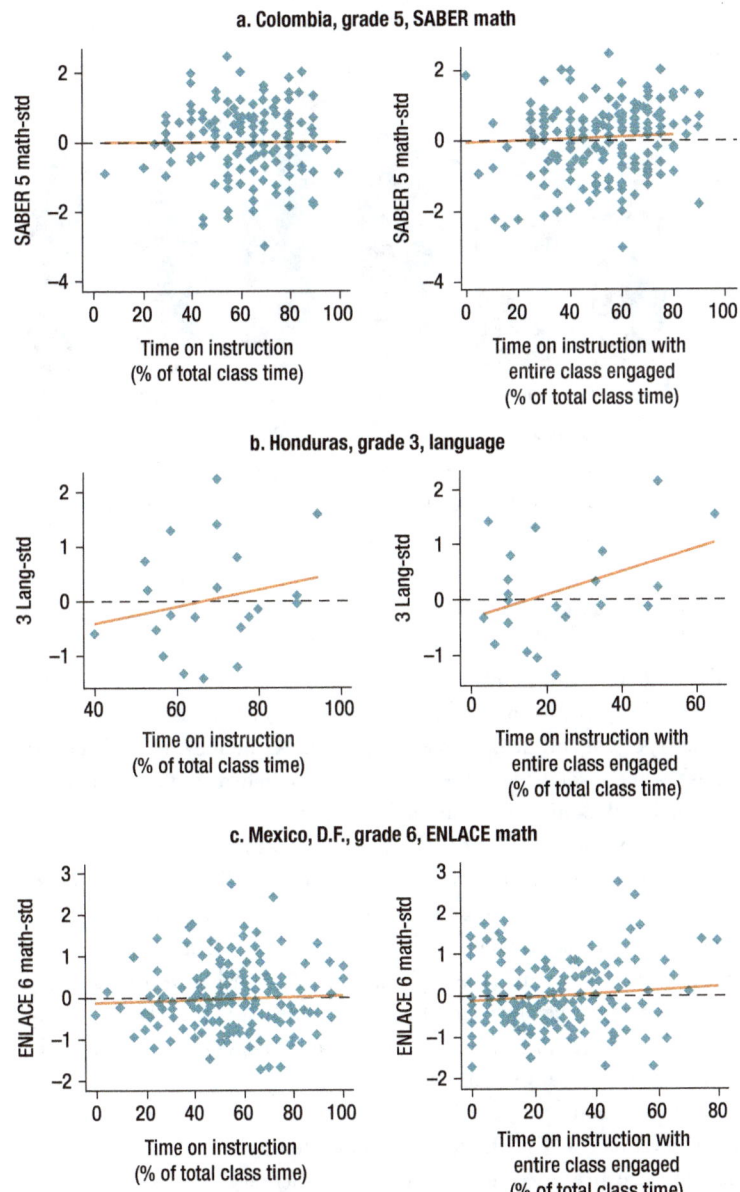

Source: World Bank classroom observation database.
Note: LAC = Latin America and the Caribbean; SABER = standardized test, Colombia; ENLACE = National Assessment of Academic Achievement in Schools, Mexico.

FIGURE 2.6: Core pedagogical practices across LAC countries

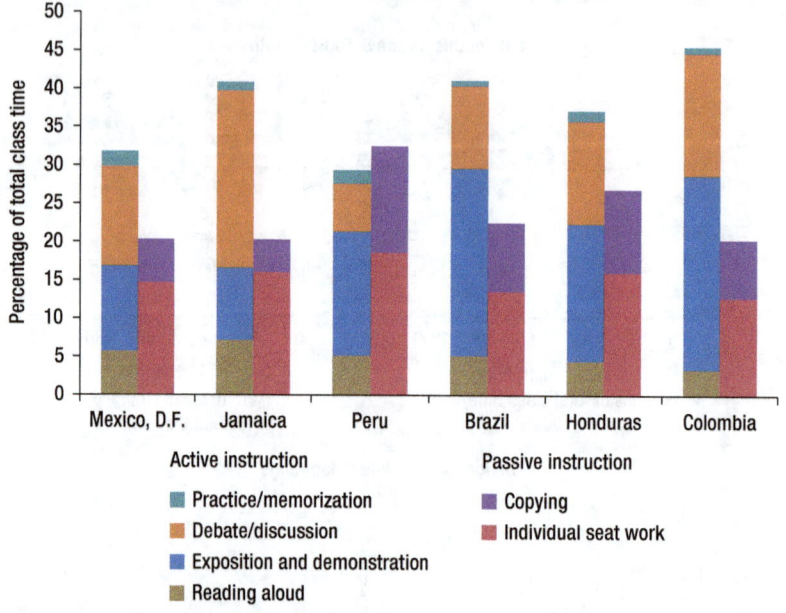

Source: World Bank classroom observation database.
Note: LAC = Latin America and the Caribbean.

Also striking is the significant share of time that teachers lecture their classes without the aid of *any* learning materials. In lower grades, it is difficult to maintain student engagement and demonstrate new concepts—be they the alphabet or math problems—without some type of learning materials. In higher grades, where curriculum content becomes more sophisticated, it is difficult to deliver well-organized, substantive lectures without reference materials (such as textbooks, workbooks, handouts, maps, or diagrams) or a written outline of the content being covered, whether on a blackboard or whiteboard. In the absence of such supports, the teacher is simply chatting with the class. In fact, a common piece of qualitative feedback from observer teams is that the great majority of classes appear to lack a clear lesson plan and structure. Observers (who are generally education system supervisors or pedagogical coordinators) report being struck by the limited amount of content delivered and the disorganized presentation in many classrooms.

While education systems in these countries are beginning to invest heavily in classroom-level use of ICT, the research shows that this use has not yet impacted teachers' practice. In every country in our sample, there are programs in place to equip classrooms with audiovisual equipment and computers. The most common equipment is LCD projectors and screens and whiteboards. Peru and Honduras have introduced one laptop per child. The other countries typically have a single computer in

FIGURE 2.7: Teacher time off-task and student learning in LAC countries

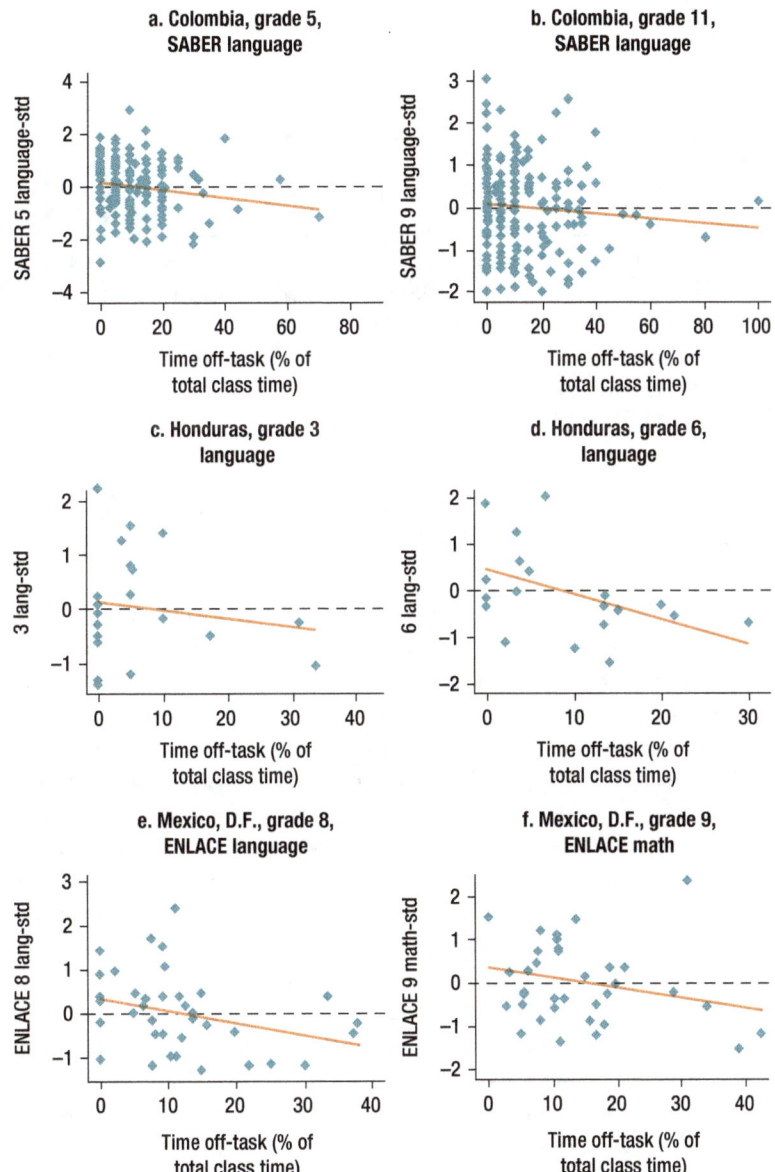

Source: World Bank classroom observation database.
Note: LAC = Latin America and the Caribbean; SABER = standardized test, Colombia; ENLACE = National Assessment of Academic Achievement in Schools, Mexico.

FIGURE 2.8: Teachers' use of learning materials

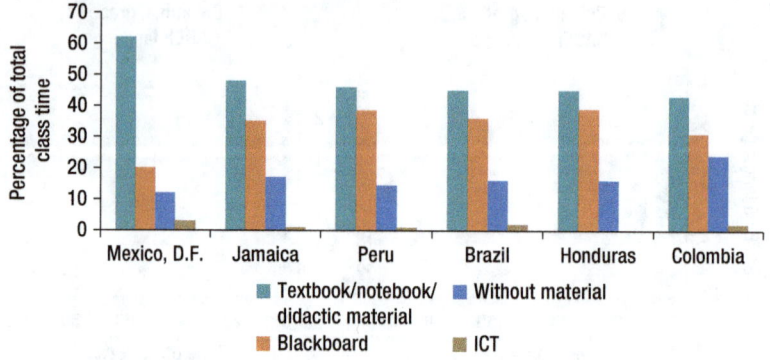

Source: World Bank classroom observation database.
Note: ICT = information and communication technology.

the classroom for the teachers' use and dedicated computer labs that students rotate through during the day.

On average, across the entire sample, teachers use available classroom-level ICT only 2 percent of the time. In Honduras and Peru—the countries with the largest investments in one-to-one computing in this sample—the share of total class time spent using these materials is in fact the lowest in the sample, 1 percent in Peru and less than 1 percent in Honduras.

In contrast, the two rounds of observations carried out in Pernambuco state and Rio de Janeiro municipal schools in Brazil give a more encouraging sense that with adequate support for teachers, new technologies can penetrate the classroom. Figure 2.9 shows teachers' use of ICT in Pernambuco and Rio de Janeiro municipality.

In the case of Pernambuco's Escolas de Referência, the introduction of LCD projectors, microscopes linked to projectors for science classes, and computer labs in schools is part of a comprehensive strategy to equip these schools as demonstration schools for the entire system. The Escolas de Referência program also includes important corresponding reforms such as full-day schooling, full-time contracts for teachers (so that they teach in only one school), and explicit time built into teachers' contracts for collaborative work with other teachers on curriculum and lesson planning. The 2010 observations in Pernambuco clearly showed more intensive use of ICT in the Escolas de Referência than in the rest of the state system.

In the case of Rio, a program called Educopédia has equipped schools with LCD projectors that teachers use to display engaging multimedia presentations of curriculum modules designed by teams of teachers. The modules generally blend videos and interactive exercises for students, with a clear structure and repeated reinforcement questions. Our 2010 round of observations showed very limited uptake

FIGURE 2.9: Teachers' use of ICT in Pernambuco and Rio de Janeiro, 2010–11

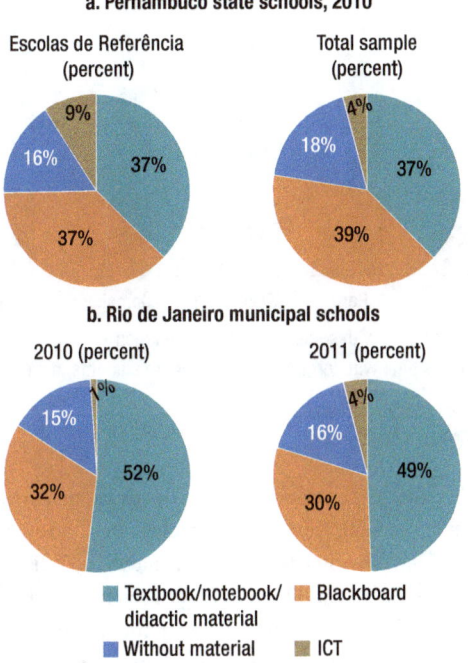

Source: World Bank classroom observation database.
Note: ICT = information and communication technology.

of the new resources by Rio municipality teachers—using ICT only 1 percent of the time. The Secretariat responded with a targeted effort to provide teachers with individualized support through roving resource teachers. One year later, utilization had quadrupled.

Students are unengaged

The third key finding is that across all countries in our sample, during more than half of all class time at least some students are not engaged (figure 2.10). Between one-fifth and one-quarter of total class time, a large group of students (six or more) is visibly not involved in the activity the teacher is leading. With an average class size of 25 across these countries, six students represent a significant part of the class. Sometimes students off-task are quiet—looking out the window, doodling, or sleeping. Sometimes they are chatting, passing notes, and disrupting the work of other students. Sometimes the degree of disruption leads to a total breakdown of learning activity. Observers in every country have sat in classrooms that are badly out of control, even with the teacher present.

INSIDE THE CLASSROOM IN LATIN AMERICA AND THE CARIBBEAN   119

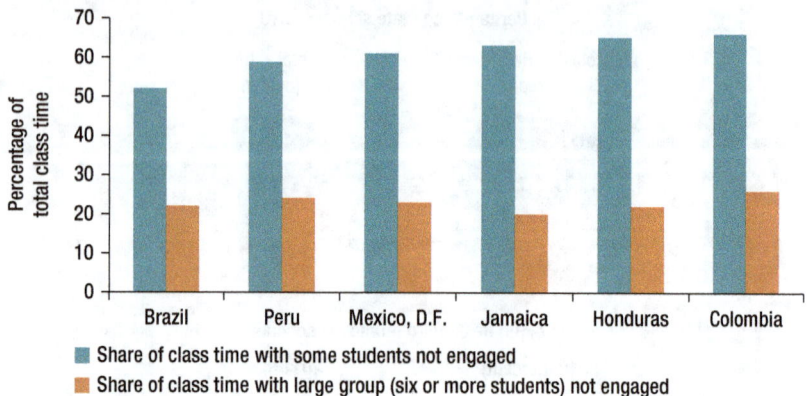

FIGURE 2.10: Share of total class time with students not engaged

■ Share of class time with some students not engaged
■ Share of class time with large group (six or more students) not engaged

Source: World Bank classroom observation database.
Note: D.F. = Distrito Federal.

As noted earlier, the single strongest and most consistent correlation in our data is the negative impact on learning results when teachers (and students) are off-task. This may appear so intuitively obvious as to not bear mention. What does bear mention, and policy focus, is the degree of difficulty LAC's teachers currently have in keeping their classes engaged in learning. In no country in the sample do teachers on average keep the entire class engaged in learning more than 25 percent of class time (Peru), and in Colombia and Honduras teachers achieve this less than 20 percent of time (figure 2.11). This could reflect the conscious choice of teaching strategies that divide the class into groups working on parallel activities. But this strategy is reported rarely by observer teams. More consistent with the classrooms observed in this study is that teachers arrive at school without the detailed class preparation that would be required to manage multiple activities simultaneously. More commonly, it appears that a single teacher-led activity "pitched to the middle" of the learning distribution leaves some students bored and others falling behind. Both sets typically react by disengaging.

The observation evidence suggests that working with teachers on this issue should be a top priority for LAC school systems. Given high repetition rates in a number of countries, LAC's teachers face special challenges in dealing with heterogeneous classes that span different ages and learning levels. Well-trained teachers, however, do learn to handle such classes and with well-designed lesson plans teachers can be expected to do much better than the 20 percent rate of student engagement observed currently. One of the clearest findings of this research is that poor student learning results can be directly and strongly linked to the failure of teachers to keep students engaged.

A study in Colombia provides some data on how little LAC's teachers focus on engaging their students in learning. A questionnaire applied to a sample of students across both high-performing and low-performing schools detected differences in how

FIGURE 2.11: Teacher time on instruction with the entire class engaged

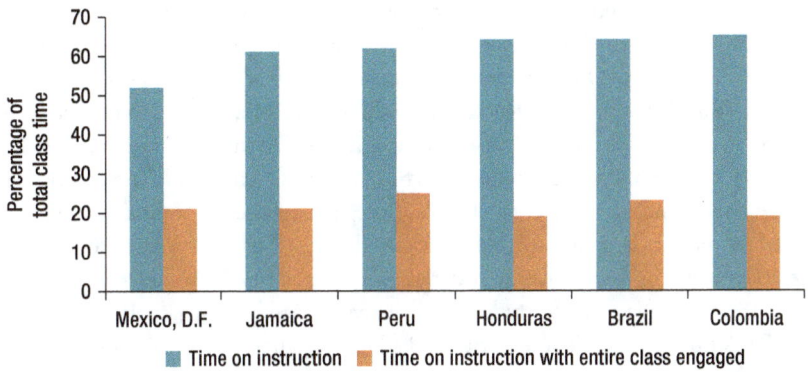

Source: World Bank classroom observation database.
Note: D.F. = Distrito Federal.

much students like their teachers, how fair or caring they are perceived to be, and whether or not they grade homework: 94 percent of students in high-performing schools, for example, said they "got along" with their teachers, while only 82 percent of students in low-performing schools agreed with this. But on many important dimensions of pedagogical practice, students' perceptions were remarkably consistent: in both high- and low-performing schools, less than 50 percent of students reported that teachers regularly "ask questions about the texts they are reading," "connect material to students' own life experiences," "link new materials to what they already know," "explain what they expect of students," or "give timely feedback." Only slightly more than half of students in both groups say teachers regularly "discuss students' work" or "ask questions that challenge them to learn" (Garcia et al. 2014).

Research in São Paulo, Brazil, has also focused on student feedback about teachers' instructional practices. Drawing on the state's high-quality administrative data, Fernandes and Ferraz (2014) have been able to analyze student test score gains at the classroom level and identify highly effective teachers (in terms of their ability to produce value-added learning gains)—one of the first analyses of this kind in LAC. As discussed in chapter 1, they find that teacher content mastery, as measured on the São Paulo teacher promotion exam (Prova de Promoção), explains part of the difference in individual teachers' effectiveness. But they find a much larger effect derives from teacher practices, independent of teachers' content mastery. Student learning gains in math were between 0.13 and 0.22 standard deviation (SD) higher (a very strong effect) for teachers who (a) regularly assign homework, (b) correct homework, (c) explain material until all students understand it, (d) give a variety of examples to solve, and (e) relate math content to everyday situations. Student learning gains in Portuguese were between 0.09 and 0.13 SD higher for teachers who (a) regularly assign homework, (b) correct homework, (c) explain material until all students understand it, and (d) suggest books for outside reading. Part of the impact of these practices may relate to their rarity. Only 14 percent of students reported that their math teachers "always or almost always" assign homework, and only 5 percent reported that language teachers did so. Only one-third of students reported that teachers who assigned homework actually returned it with corrections. Only 6 percent of students said their math teachers "always or almost always" relate math content to real-world situations and only 4 percent said their language teachers recommend outside reading books. It is unfortunate that classroom observation data has not been collected in São Paulo state schools, to examine whether these teacher practices reflecting effort and preparation outside of the classroom are mirrored in the classroom dynamics measured by the Stallings instrument, such as teachers' use of instructional time, materials, and the ability to keep students engaged.

But the pattern of low student engagement evident in our sample, the limited feedback from their students reported by Colombian students, and the São Paulo evidence that a core set of teacher practices can powerfully affect student learning point to important challenges for both pre-service and in-service teacher training programs in LAC. A first challenge is to ensure that teachers recognize the importance of drawing all students into the learning process; a second is to equip teachers with a wide range of strategies to achieve this.

Average classroom practice varies tremendously across schools

A fourth important finding is the huge range in average classroom practice across schools. In every system studied, there are some schools whose teachers' average use of instructional time exceeds the Stallings 85 percent benchmark and others where instructional time is disastrously low—below 20 percent of total class time. Imagine attending a school where four days per week there is no instruction. Figure 2.12 gives a sense of the variation. Mexico, D.F. stands out as having the narrowest distribution, which is good news on the low end but raises questions about why almost no schools manage to devote more than 80 percent of class time to instruction. In cases such as this, structural features of the way the school day is organized may create barriers to the more efficient time use. For example, if students in the primary grades change classrooms between subjects—rather than the more typical pattern of remaining in the same room with a single teacher all day—it not only builds "transit time" into the school day but it obliges teachers to spend more time "settling" students at the beginning of each class and perhaps take attendance multiple times per day. These issues may seem trivial, but compounded over a school year can substantially impact instructional time.

It is evident from these results that school systems are not focused on the issue of instructional time. Within a given national or subnational education system, all schools operate in the same institutional and policy environment—with the same policies for the selection of school directors, and the same curriculum, teacher standards and preparation, and student assignment rules—yet this research shows that these policies are playing out at the school level in widely different ways. And these

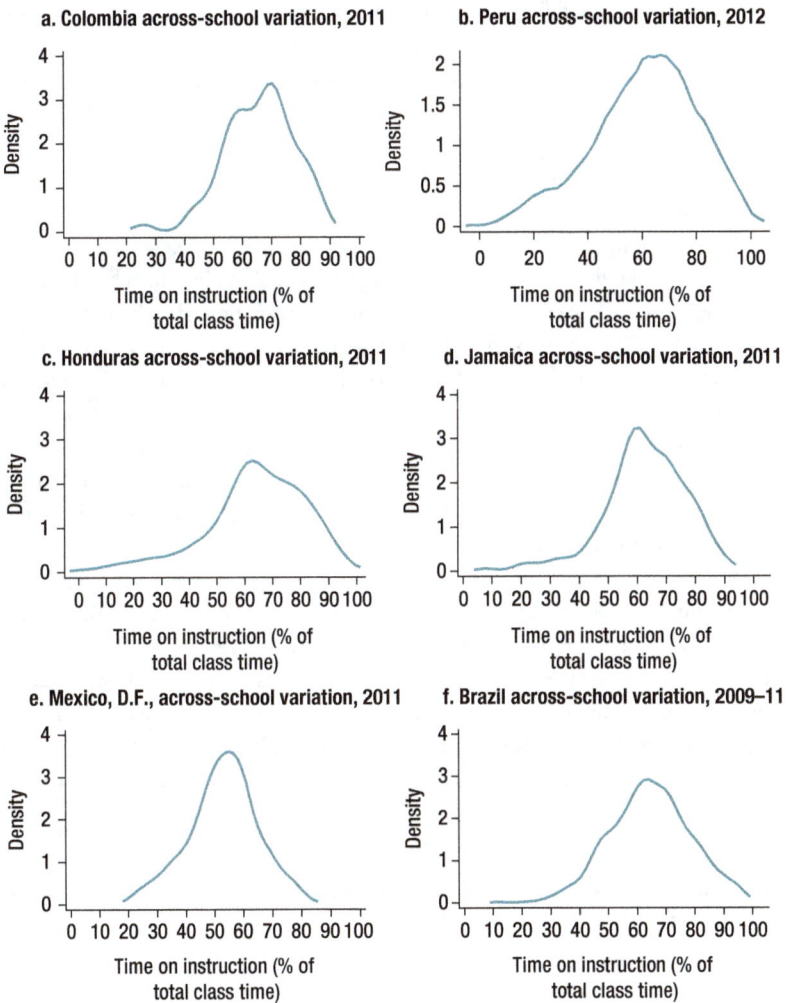

FIGURE 2.12: Distribution of schools by average time spent on instruction

Source: World Bank classroom observation database.

differences can have important consequences for students. In Honduran schools, 64 percent of time is spent on instruction, on average, across the system. But schools in the top quintile of the distribution (of instructional time use) average 85 percent, the Stallings benchmark. Schools in the bottom quintile average 37 percent. This 48-percentage point difference means that students in top quintile schools receive an average of 96 more days of instruction than students in the bottom quintile of schools in every 200-day school year. The consequences for a student spending several years in a school that consistently delivers much less instruction will be cumulative and highly unfair.

What drives these differences in schools' average use of time? In some countries, schools in different districts or regions show distinctly different performance. In Honduras, for example, there are extreme differences between the province with the best average performance, Copán (83 percent), and the worst, Colón (33 percent) (figure 2.13).

Some of the differences across Honduran provinces and in rural Peru appear linked to the special challenges faced by small rural schools, in which a single teacher must handle multiple grades. Managing time efficiently in such a setting is difficult, and disaggregating the Stallings results by type of school in Honduras bears this out. While regular schools average 69 percent of time on instruction, Honduran multigrade schools average 58 percent. But it is interesting to contrast these results with the opposite pattern observed in Colombia. Colombia has a 40-year tradition of providing special training, curriculum materials, and support to multigrade teachers in rural areas in a schooling model especially designed for these settings, called the Escuela Nueva (discussed further in chapter 4). In Colombia, the average time spent on instruction in multigrade schools (71 percent) is actually higher than in regular schools (65 percent), although the multigrade sample is small.[2]

Other patterns appear linked to the differential school-level impacts of government policies. Peru's 2007 reform of the teacher career path (Carrera Pública Magisterial [CPM]) introduced a more stringent review process, including competency tests, for new teachers. The objective was to raise the bar for teacher quality by combining higher standards at entry with higher incentives. In the 2011 pilot sample in Peru, the government team collected teacher background information that permitted a disaggregated analysis, and it showed that these teachers

FIGURE 2.13: Average instructional time in different provinces of Honduras, 2011

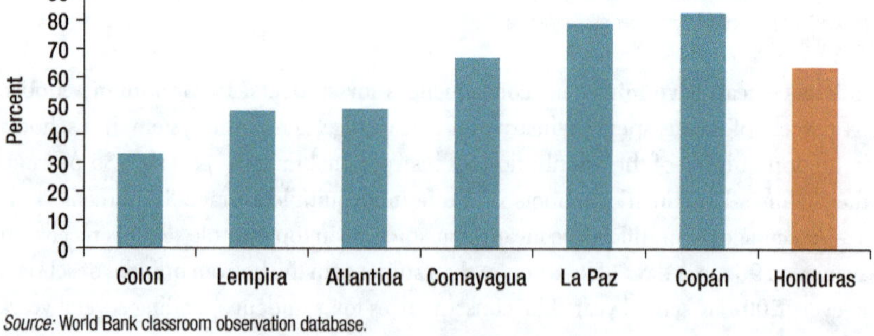

Source: World Bank classroom observation database.

performed differently. CPM teachers used 66 percent of time for instruction, compared with 55 percent for regular teachers, and spent 7 percent of time off-task, compared to 13 percent for regular teachers.

Finally, two rounds of observations were conducted in a panel of 228 schools in Pernambuco to deepen ongoing research on how the introduction of bonus pay linked to school performance affects teacher practice in the classroom. The first finding is that schools observed in late 2009 that went on to achieve their performance targets for that year and earn the bonus (based on improved test scores and graduation rates) demonstrated better classroom dynamics than schools that failed to gain the bonus (figure 2.14). In the successful schools, 63 percent of time was used for instruction, compared with 54 percent in schools that failed to achieve the bonus. In the unsuccessful schools, teachers were off-task 16 percent of the time; in the bonus schools, 11 percent.

Interestingly, in observations exactly one year later, classroom dynamics across the entire sample improved. The gap in instructional time use between schools that earned

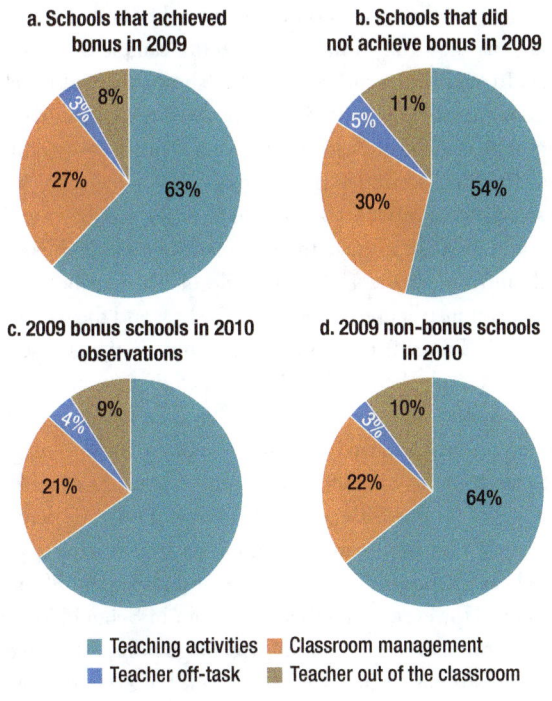

FIGURE 2.14: Classroom dynamics with the introduction of bonus pay in Pernambuco, Brazil (distribution of total class time, in percent)

Source: World Bank classroom observation database.

INSIDE THE CLASSROOM IN LATIN AMERICA AND THE CARIBBEAN   125 the bonus in 2009 and schools that did not virtually disappeared. With only two rounds of observations, we cannot read too much into these changes. However, the pattern is consistent with a hypothesis that incentive pay stimulates greater effort by *all* teachers, reflected in better preparation for classes and more effective use of available time for learning. Less consistent is the fact that time off-task and teacher absence from the classroom did not decline in either group, as one of the most straightforward ways to exert more work effort is to arrive on time. One hypothesis is that, given the high share of Brazilian teachers who hold positions in two different schools, competing schedules may genuinely constrain their ability to respond to performance pay incentives along this margin. It is interesting to note that a rigorously evaluated teacher bonus program in India that produced strong effects on student learning also showed no impacts on teacher absence rates (Muralidharan and Sundararaman 2011). The researchers found that although absence rates remained high, teachers used school time more intensively on the days they were present and conducted reinforcement classes after school.

Average classroom practice varies tremendously within schools

Perhaps the most surprising finding of the research is the degree of variation found in teacher practice across different classrooms *inside* a single school. In every school system studied, the difference between the performance of the best teacher in a school (in terms of instructional time use) and the worst teacher in that same school is over four-fifths as large as the variation across the entire sample of classrooms—a truly staggering range. In statistical terms, as table 2.4 shows, the within-school standard deviation (last column) ranges from 0.19 to 0.23 across these countries, while the distributions of the entire sample of classrooms in each country have standard deviations ranging from 0.21 to 0.26 (second to last column).

To give a sense of this variation, we ranked all of the schools in each national (or subnational) sample by their average time on instruction and chose two schools— one at the 25th and one at the 75th percentile of the distribution—in each. We compared the time on instruction achieved by the best and the worst teacher inside each of these schools. Figure 2.15 presents the results. In the 201-school sample in Mexico's D.F., for example, School No. 49 averaged 60 percent of time on instruction, but the best teacher spent 80 percent of time on learning activities and the lowest-performing teacher achieved only 30 percent—a 50 percentage point difference from one classroom to another in the same school. Even more surprisingly, while School No. 147, at the 75th percentile averaged only 46 percent of time on instruction across all classrooms in the school, its best teacher equaled the performance of the best teacher in School No. 49, and also spent 80 percent of class time on instruction. However, in another classroom in School No. 147, observers recorded zero time on instruction—an 80 percentage point difference in the use of time across two classrooms in the same school on the same day. We observe the identical phenomenon in Jamaica. In both School No. 50 and School No. 150, the

TABLE 2.4: Within-school and across-school variation in average teacher time on instruction (full samples only)

Country	Region	Number of schools observed	Number of classrooms observed	Minimum and maximum values observed (entire sample)	Minimum and maximum values observed (school average)	School-level average	Standard deviation of school values	Standard deviation of classroom values	Average within-school standard deviation
Brazil	Various states	1,439	7,336	0–100	5–97	64	0.18	0.21	0.19
Colombia	National	200	1,091	0–100	25–88	66	0.12	0.22	0.19
Honduras	National	153	758	0–100	3–96	64	0.18	0.25	0.19
Jamaica	National	200	1,000	0–100	0–90	61	0.17	0.25	0.19
Mexico	Distrito Federal	201	2,335	0–100	22–80	52	0.11	0.25	0.23
Peru	National	400	1,195	0–100	0–100	61	0.19	0.26	0.19
Total observations		2,593	13,715						

Source: World Bank classroom observation database.
Note: In Brazil, observations were drawn from representative samples in Minas Gerais, Pernambuco, and Rio de Janeiro municipality.
In Peru, approximately half of all "classrooms" observed were in multigrade schools and represent a single teacher observed during two or three different class hours.

FIGURE 2.15: Range in teacher time on instruction within schools (comparison of schools at the 25th and 75th percentile of the distribution in terms of school-average time on instruction)

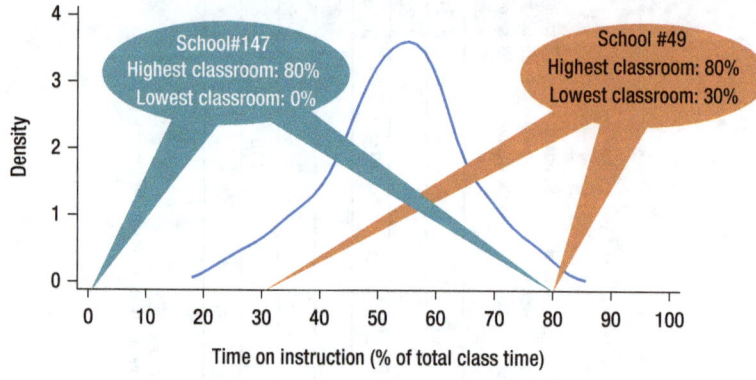

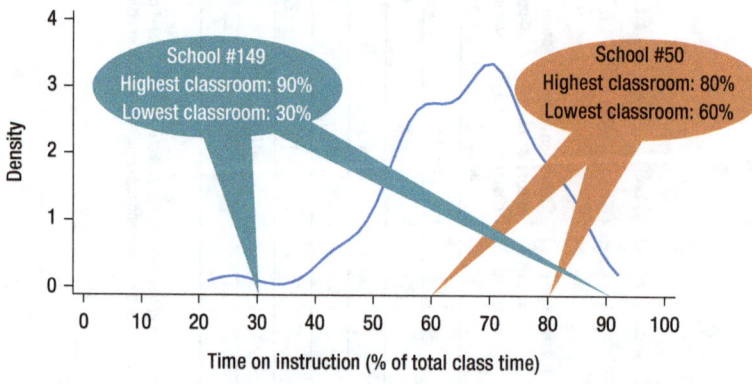

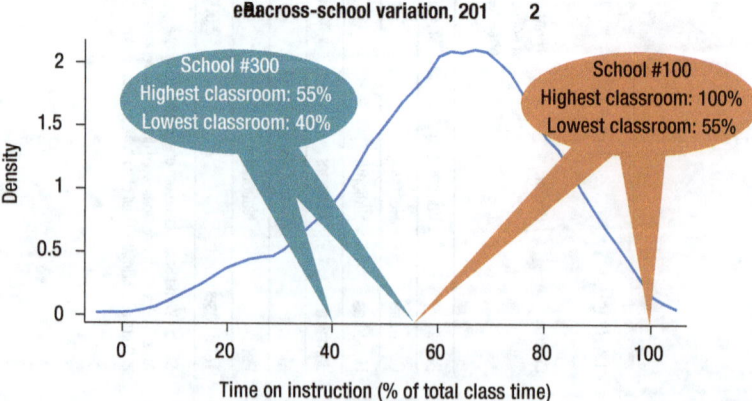

(continued on next page)

FIGURE 2.15: Range in teacher time on instruction within schools (comparison of schools at the 25th and 75th percentile of the distribution in terms of school-average time on instruction) *(continued)*

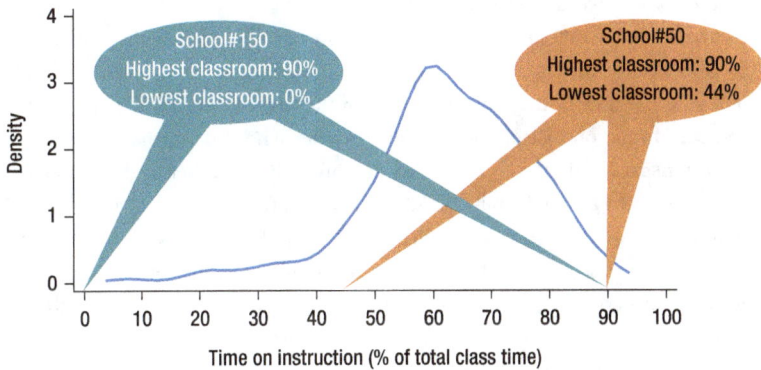

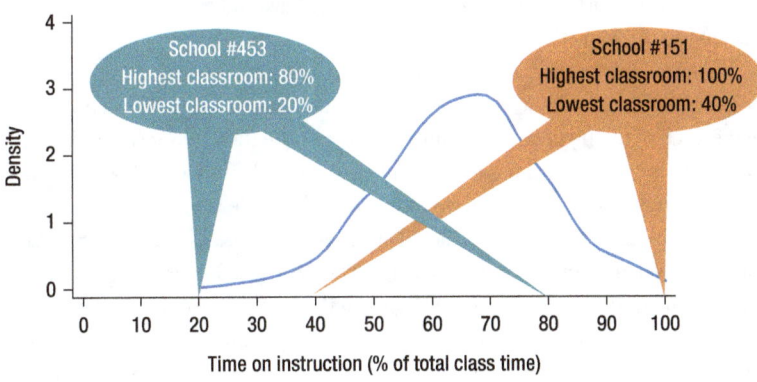

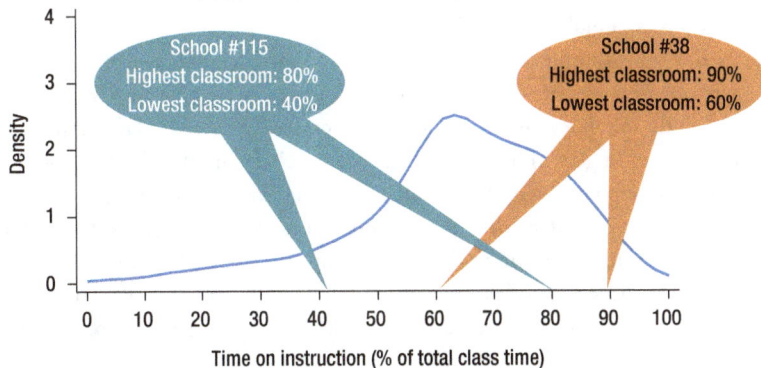

Source: World Bank classroom observation database.

best-performing classrooms achieved 90 percent of time on instruction—higher than the Stallings benchmark. However, while in School No 50, the lowest-performing classroom used 44 percent of time (a 56 percentage point differential), in School No. 150, observers saw a class with zero time on task. A difference of 90 percentage points in the use of class time between two teachers in the same school is truly striking and in some sense unfathomable.

Virtually every country shows evidence of extreme and inexplicable variations in teachers' use of instructional across different classrooms in the same school. In Colombia, the school at the 75th percentile of the distribution, which averaged only 58 percent of time on instruction, had one teacher whose performance (90 percent of time on instruction) actually exceeded that of the best teacher in the school at the 25th percentile. In Minas Gerais, Brazil, inside both the better-performing school at the 25th percentile and the school at the 75th percentile of the distribution there was a gap of 60 percentage points between the best- and worst-performing teachers. In Honduras and Peru, the gaps observed were smaller, which likely reflects the small size of many of the schools in those samples, a significant share of which were actually multigrade (one or two teacher) schools.

Looking across these data as a whole, the most powerful conclusion is that even schools with extremely low average time on task have individual teachers doing an excellent job of using class time for instruction.

Figure 2.16 (a. and b.) analyzes these patterns further. For each quintile of schools in the overall distribution, we compare the school-average time on instruction with the average of all of the highest-performing teachers inside these schools and the average of all of the lowest-performing teachers in these schools. In Colombia, for example, the average time on instruction across the national sample is 65 percent, but schools in the top quintile of the performance distribution (of time use) average 82 percent, while schools in the bottom quintile average 49 percent—a 33 percentage point differential. But an even greater range exists between the best- and worst-performing teachers *inside* these schools. For schools in the lowest quintile, the best teacher in each school uses 78 percent of time for instruction—not far from the Stallings benchmark—while the worst teachers average 18 percent. This 60 percentage point difference in time on-task across different classrooms within these schools dwarfs the difference observed across quintiles of schools.

In the top quintile of schools, the gap in time use between the best- and worst-performing teachers is much smaller, 34 percentage points. While the top teachers in these schools are teaching an impressive 97 percent of time, their performance is not hugely different from the top teachers in schools in the bottommost quintile, who average 78 percent. What truly distinguishes schools in the top of the distribution from those in the bottom is consistency: good schools have less variation from classroom to classroom in one very basic parameter of teacher performance—the share of class time used for education. Whether the country has relatively high across-school variation (such as Honduras, Jamaica, or Brazil) or

FIGURE 2.16: Variance in instructional time within schools in Colombia and Honduras, 2011

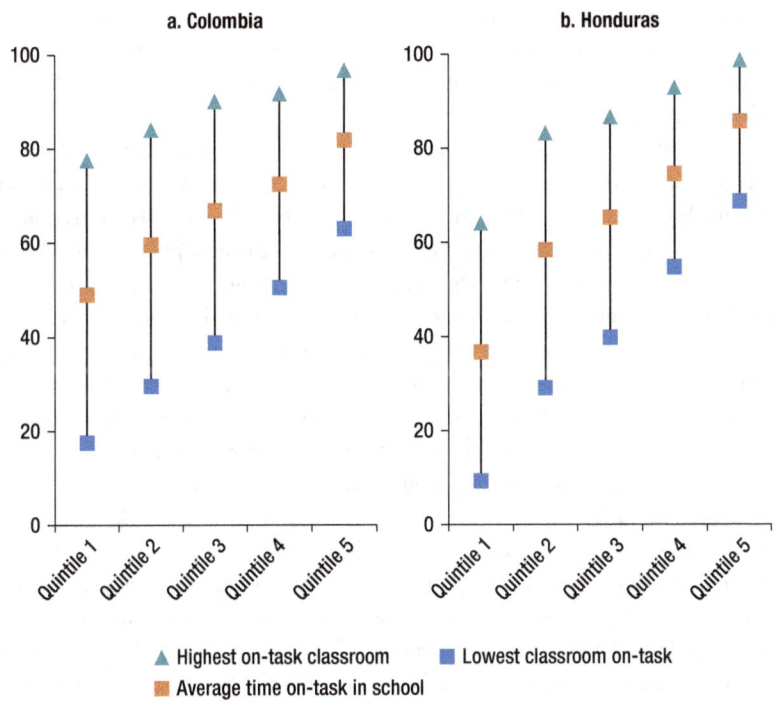

Source: World Bank classroom observation database.

low (Mexico, D.F., and Colombia), the top quintile of the distribution is characterized by more consistent teacher performance.

The implications of these data are profound. As noted earlier, the substantial variation in time use across schools clearly indicates that school systems are not focused on the issue of instructional time. In some sense, this is understandable. No school systems today collect standardized data on classroom dynamics, and no individual supervisor in a large school system can be expected to have first-hand experience with a systemwide sample of schools. Indeed, the universal reaction of ministers and education secretaries to this research has been surprise at the magnitude of the variations across schools. While disparities in school quality and learning results are known to exist, this is the first concrete evidence that average teacher practice in different schools is so different.

But variations in classroom practice at the school level are another matter. Direct observation of all of the classrooms within a single school is not only technically feasible but is also an implicit responsibility of school directors. A 45-percentage point difference between classroom A and classroom B in the time spent on instruction in a school system whose official calendar is 200 days per year implies 90 fewer days of instruction per year for the unfortunate students in classroom B. A standardized observation instrument is not, in fact, necessary to detect differences this large in how teachers within a single school are managing class time, using materials, and keeping students engaged.

The findings raise questions about the accountability and capacity of school directors in these countries. One possibility is that directors do not believe they are accountable for raising the quality of instruction in their schools. Directors' responses on questionnaires administered as part of this research provide support for this. Across these countries, school directors report that the majority of their time is absorbed by administrative duties. In Peru, for example, 87 percent of directors state that they spend more time on administrative tasks than anything else. In Minas Gerais, Brazil, which has a long tradition of substantial school-level autonomy and where directors are directly elected by the community, the sample of 604 school directors ranks "observing classrooms" last on a list of eight priority activities and reports that it absorbs only 2.5 percent of their time (Instituto Hartmann Regueira 2011, 56).

A second possibility is that school directors feel accountable for the quality of instruction but do not have the capacity either to identify or promote it. In most countries, school directors are promoted from within the ranks of teachers, but they are not necessarily promoted for exceptional teaching skill—or the ability to cultivate it in others. Even directors who do spend time in the classrooms of their own school may have little perspective on what truly great teaching looks like or how their school compares with the average across the system.

Most likely, both factors contribute to the observed school-level results in these countries. School systems in East Asia are well-known for focusing attention on classroom practice, whether through the Japanese "lesson study" method discussed in chapter 4 or Shanghai's requirement that for teachers, teacher mentors, or school directors to be promoted, they must demonstrate their capacity to raise instructional quality by "turning around" a low-performing classroom or school. As discussed in detail in the next chapter, pre-service teacher education programs in Latin America and the Caribbean include little to no training in classroom observation or the effective use of instructional time. Few in-service training programs focus on these issues either.

Conclusions

The research conducted for this study provides evidence that differences in teacher effectiveness at the classroom level in LAC are large, visible, and can have important consequences for student learning. Several partner countries have embraced this result and are taking actions to address it.

First, some countries have decided to mainstream periodic classroom observations using the Stallings instrument into their regular school supervision processes. Jamaica has trained its entire corps of supervisors in the method. After a pilot program in two provinces, Peru also trained a core team in the Stallings method and carried out its own observations in 2012 in a national sample of schools. The Peruvian ministry is also proposing direct classroom observation as part of its new teacher evaluation system. As described in detail in chapter 4 (box 4.1), Rio de Janeiro municipality was inspired to reform its teacher hiring process after seeing the Stallings evidence of weak instructional practice. It now requires new teacher candidates to teach a sample class, observed by a bank of evaluators who rate candidates' effectiveness in managing instructional time and classroom dynamics. Mexico's D.F. has developed a computerized version of the Stallings instrument, which has the advantage of generating real-time data on the individual classroom being observed as well as a range of useful comparative metrics, including on that classroom's prior performance, other classrooms in the same school, and other schools across the district. In addition to the speed with which results and feedback are generated in the field at the point of observation, the D.F.'s innovation eliminates the costs of recovering and scanning paper coding sheets and improves quality because of inbuilt consistency checks that eliminate the need for subsequent data cleaning. Management of the all-electronic database is very efficient (see box 2.3).

Second, the Stallings observation results are leading school systems to revisit in-service teacher development programs. Several are returning to classrooms with the highest performance on the Stallings variables to videotape these teachers. Letting teachers "see" what good practice looks like is one of the most powerful ways to stimulate and model improvement. Equally powerful is letting less-prepared

---

BOX 2.3: *Innovations in system monitoring: Digitized Stallings observations*

In 2011, education managers in Mexico's Distrito Federal (D.F.) developed a computerized version of the Stallings instrument to facilitate its systemwide application on a regular basis. All of the D.F.'s school supervisors were trained in the Stallings method and the use of the electronic coding sheet. Through 2012, as part of the D.F.'s revamped strategy for school supervision, supervisors visit schools monthly and register the 10 "snapshots" per class hour on electronic coding sheets on their laptops (see figure B2.3.1). The program instantly generates data on how effectively a given teacher is using time and materials and keeping students engaged. These data are compared with other teachers in the same school, previous observations of the same teachers, average patterns for that school and neighboring schools, and average patterns for the district as a whole.

(continued on next page)

BOX 2.3: *Innovations in system monitoring: Digitized Stallings observations (continued)*

FIGURE B2.3.1: Snapshot of instant results

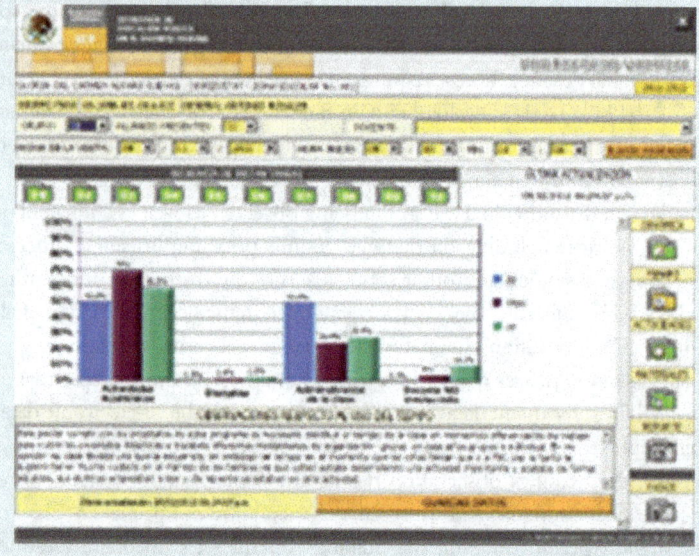

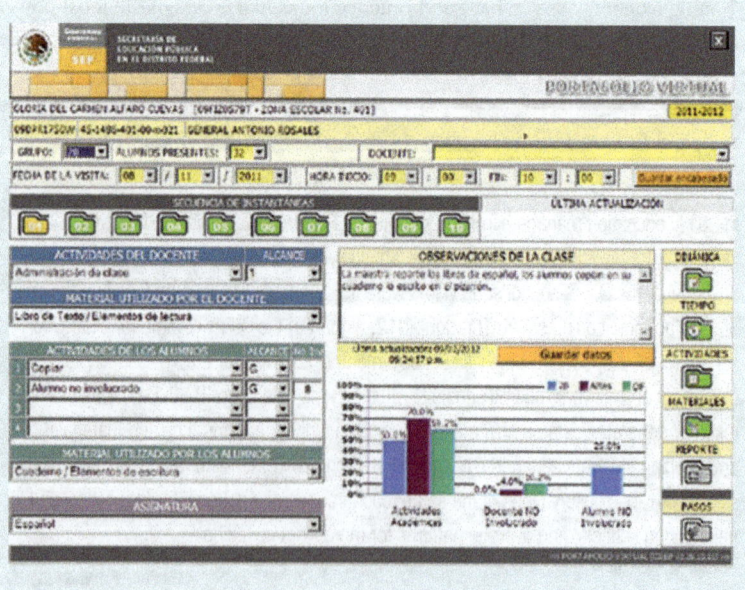

teachers view and analyze their own performance. Systematic classroom observation data gives school systems an objective way to identify where—and how—their most effective teachers are working. It provides a barometer that most systems have lacked. Combined with student test scores and other school results, classroom observation data can pinpoint where schools with the most efficient instructional practice are located, which teachers within schools are doing the best job of keeping their students engaged, and exactly *how* they do it.

In a particularly innovative application of the Stallings method, the Brazilian state of Ceará is launching a randomized evaluation of a school-level training program designed to promote collaboration among teachers in sharing and improving instructional practice. Schools will be provided with feedback on their Stallings observation results as well as a "tool kit" of good practice techniques and videos and log books for teachers to use in observing and evaluating each others' practice. The goal is to see whether explicit feedback and supports can help schools build a professional learning community among teachers in which good practices are quickly shared and the performance of weaker teachers is raised. Results are expected in 2016.

The seven-country research program conducted for this study has established that instructional time and teachers' practice in the classroom are important elements of the quality of education being delivered to LAC's children. It has established that there is wide variation in teacher effectiveness from one classroom to another, and that a significant part of what makes some teachers better than others can be detected simply by taking the time to observe them at work in the classroom.

The degree of variation in teacher practice observed across different classrooms within the same school suggests that there is substantial scope for directors to promote more exchange of practice within their schools. The costs of identifying the best teacher practice within a single school and ensuring that other teachers can observe and learn from these examples are much lower than the in-service development that most school systems invest in, as they avoid the logistical costs of bringing teachers off site and hiring trainers. This form of teacher development is integral to most East Asian school systems, but is only beginning to take hold in LAC, as in Ceará's new program and Rio municipality's Ginásios Experimentais Cariocas discussed in chapter 4. Our research results suggest that wider experimentation with this approach—and careful studies to evaluate its impact such as Ceará's—would be valuable.

Raising the average and reducing the variance in teacher practice observed across different schools are the responsibilities of school system managers. Many different policy approaches can be imagined, from providing comparative classroom observation data back to schools as an input to their development planning, to new forms of teacher training, to incentives for teachers directly linked to their classroom practice as observed on video or by trained observers. Most policy makers involved in this program have taken the results as a stimulus to action along several of these lines. This research has created a baseline picture of what LAC's students encounter inside the classroom of their schools today. It also gives us a unique basis for deeper analysis of how ongoing and new reforms in these countries succeed in reshaping that reality.

Notes

[1] Chapter Annexes to the book may be found at http://www.worldbank.org/lac/teachers.

[2] Despite efforts to ensure a nationally representative sample of schools, multigrade schools were undersampled in Colombia, due to logistical constraints.

References

Abadzi, H. 2007. "Absenteeism and Beyond: Instructional Time Loss and Consequences." Policy Research Working Paper 4376, World Bank, Washington, DC.

Angrist, J., and V. Lavy. 2009. "The Effects of High Stakes High School Achievement Awards: Evidence from a Randomized Trial." *The American Economic Review* 99 (4): 1384–414.

Araujo, M. C., P. Carneiro, Y. Cruz-Aguayo, and N. Schady. Forthcoming. "A Helping Hand? Teacher Quality and Learning Outcomes in Kindergarten." Inter-American Development Bank, Washington, DC.

Behrman, J., S. Parker, P. Todd, and K. Wolpin. Forthcoming. "Aligning Learning Incentives of Students and Teachers: Results from a Social Experiment in Mexican High Schools." *Journal of Political Economy*.

DeStefano, J., E. Adelman, and A.-M. Schuh Moore. 2010. *Using Opportunity to Learn and Early Grade Reading Fluency to Measure School Effectiveness in Nepal*. Washington, DC: EQUIP2, AED, and USAID.

Fernandes, M. and C. Ferraz. 2014. "Conhecimento ou Práticas Pedagógicas? Medindo os Efeitos da Qualidade dos Professores no Desempenho dos Alunos." Manuscript, PUC-Rio, Rio de Janeiro, Brazil. http://www.econ.puc-rio.br/uploads/adm/trabalhos/files/td620.pdf.

Fryer, R. G. 2011. "Financial Incentives and Student Achievement: Evidence from Randomized Trials." *Quarterly Journal of Economics* 126 (4): 1755–98.

Garcia, S., D. Maldonado, G. Perry, C. Rodriguez, and J. Saavedra. 2014. *Tras la Excelencia Docente: Cómo Mejorar la calidad de la educación para todos los colombianos*. Bogota: Fundacion Compartir.

Instituto Hartmann Regueira. 2011. *Pesquisa sobre a qualidade do ensino nas escolas do Estado de Minas Gerais*. Belo Horizonte, Brazil: IHR.

Kane, T., D. McCaffrey, T. Miller, and D. Staiger. 2013. "Have We Identified Effective Teachers? Validating Measures of Effective Teaching Using Random Assignment." Measures of Effective Teaching (MET), Bill & Melinda Gates Foundation, Seattle, WA.

Kane, T., E. Taylor, E. Tyler, and A. Wooten. 2010. "Identifying Effective Classroom Practices Using Student Achievement Data." NBER Working Paper 15803, National Bureau of Economic Research, Cambridge, MA.

Kremer, M., E. Miguel, and R. Thornton. 2009. "Incentives to Learn." *Review of Economics and Statistics* 91 (3): 437–56.

Lavy, V. 2012. "Expanding School Resources and Increasing Time on Task: Effects of a Policy Experiment in Israel on Student Academic Achievement and Behavior." NBER Working Paper 18369, National Bureau of Economic Research, Cambridge, MA.

Levitt, S., J. List, and S. Sadoff. 2011. "The Effect of Performance-Based Incentives on Educational Achievement: Evidence from a Randomized Experiment." Unpublished manuscript, University of Chicago, Chicago.

Luque, J., and M. Hernandez. Forthcoming. "Analysis of Classroom Dynamics in Mexico's Distrito Federal." Manuscript, World Bank, Washington, DC.

Muralidharan, K., and V. Sundararaman. 2011. "Teacher Performance Pay: Experimental Evidence from India." *Journal of Political Economy* 199 (1): 39–77.

Nystrand, M., and A. Gamoran. 1991. "Instructional Discourse and Student Engagement." *Research in the Teaching of English* 25 (3): 261–90.

Schuh Moore, A.-M., J. DeStefano, and E. Adelman. 2010. *Using Opportunity to Learn and Early Grade Reading Fluency to Measure School Effectiveness in Ethiopia, Guatemala, Honduras, and Nepal*. Washington, DC: EQUIP2, AED, and USAID.

Stallings, J. 1977. *Learning to Look: A Handbook on Classroom Observation and Teaching Models*. Belmont, CA: Wadsworth Publishing.

Stallings, J., R. Johnson, and J. Goodman. 1985. "Engaged Rates: Does Grade Level Make a Difference?" Paper presented at the Annual Meeting of the American Educational Research Association, Chicago, IL.

Stallings, J., and S. Knight. 2003. "Using the Stallings Observation System to Investigate: Time on Task in Four Countries." Unpublished paper for the International Time on Task Project, World Bank, Washington, DC.

Stallings, J., and G. Molhlman. 1988. "Classroom Observation Techniques." In *Educational Research, Methodology, and Measurement: An International Handbook*, edited by J. Keeves, 469–74. Oxford: Pergamon.

Vieluf, S., D. Kaplan, E. Klieme, and S. Bayer. 2012. *Teaching Practices and Pedagogical Innovation: Evidence from TALIS*. Paris: OECD Publishing. http://dx.doi.org/10.1787/9789264123540-en.

Woessmann, L. 2004. "The Effect Heterogeneity of Central Exams: Evidence from TIMSS, TIMSS-Repeat and PISA." CESifo Working Paper 1330, Center for Economic Studies of the Institute for the Promotion of Economic Research, Munich.

World Bank. 2014. *Conducting Classroom Observations Using the Stallings Classroom Snapshot Method: Manual and User Guide*. Washington, DC: World Bank.

3
Recruiting Better Teachers

There are three core challenges in raising teacher quality: recruiting, grooming, and motivating better teachers. Of these, recruiting—raising the caliber of teachers at the point of recruitment—is likely to be the most complicated challenge for Latin America and the Caribbean (LAC) countries, because it depends on raising the prestige and selectivity of the profession, which requires the alignment of a complex set of factors that are difficult and slow to change.

Global research on high-performing education systems consistently points to the ability to attract top talent into teaching as a critical underlying factor that takes education systems from "good to great" (Barber and Mourshed 2007). But attracting high-talent individuals into teaching requires aligning salaries and the salary structure, the social prestige of the profession, the selectivity of entry into teacher education, and the quality of that education. If underlying fundamentals such as salaries and prestige are not adequate to attract a pool of talented candidates, it is impossible to be selective at entry into teacher education. If teacher standards at the point of recruitment are not selective, investments in higher salaries are wasted and prestige will not rise. If the academic quality of teacher training is not high, it is impossible to sustain selectivity over time; graduates will not be successful in their work as teachers or in demand from school systems; and good students with alternative career options will look elsewhere.

Figure 3.1, adapted from Barber and Mourshed, shows three key stages in teacher recruitment. Two involve screening: at entry to teacher education programs and, upon exit from those programs, at the point of hiring. The third, intervening, stage is the process of teacher education: preparing talented students for careers as effective teachers through high-quality pre-service training.

In countries with high-performing education systems, such as Finland, Japan, the Republic of Korea, the Netherlands, and Singapore, there is a high degree of

---

This chapter was coauthored with Guillermo Toral, David Evans, and Soledad de Gregorio.

FIGURE 3.1: Key steps in the recruitment of high-quality teachers

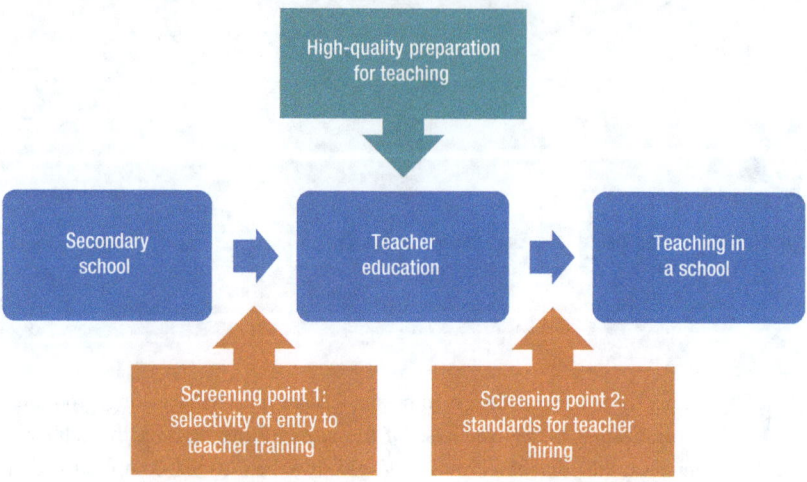

Source: Adapted from Barber and Mourshed 2007.

selectivity at the first screening point—entry into teacher education. These countries all have significant control over which graduates from secondary education have access to teacher training institutions. The number of accredited institutions is limited, and the fundamentals of the career (salary and nonsalary rewards and high employment prospects) combine with selectivity at this point of entry to attract high-caliber candidates.

In Finland, public opinion polls consistently rate teaching as the most admired of professions. Teacher training schools accept only one of every ten applicants for primary-level teachers, and one in four at the secondary level—all of whom are drawn from the top of the academic distribution (Sahlberg 2011). In Singapore, only 20 percent of secondary school students who apply to teacher education programs are accepted, and all come from the top third of secondary students (figure 3.2). High selectivity at entry to teacher education makes the remaining phases much more efficient. Motivated students are less likely to drop out, and the number of trainees can be calibrated to the number of new teachers needed, guaranteeing that all new graduates find jobs.

Latin American and Caribbean countries are characterized by a lack of selectivity at the first screening point. Rather than large numbers of students wanting to become teachers but not being able to, just the opposite is true. Data from the Young Lives Longitudinal Survey in Peru compare what students intended to study in tertiary education with what they actually studied. Far more students end up in teacher training programs than initially desired them: education ranks tenth as an intended course of study, but fourth as an actual (Annex 3.5[1]). Rather than exclude interested but

FIGURE 3.2: Teacher recruitment in Singapore

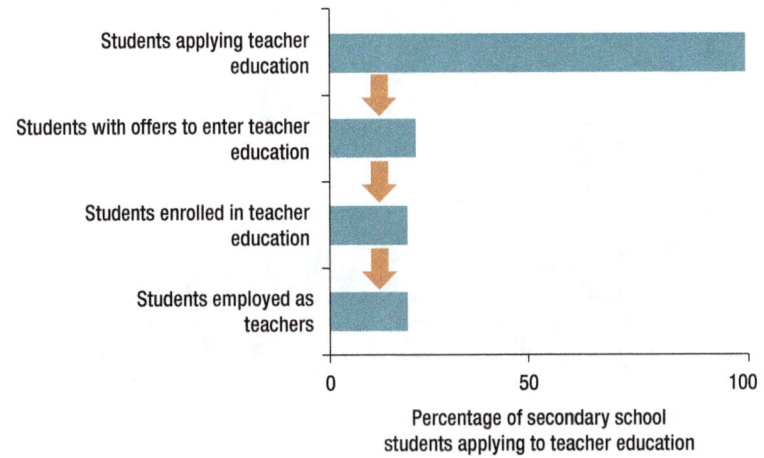

Source: National Institute of Education, Singapore.

unqualified candidates, education schools today absorb students who cannot qualify for other courses of study.

Our analysis of comparative teacher salaries in chapter 1 suggests that salary increases may be necessary in some countries to make teachers' average salaries—and the structure of teacher salary incentives—competitive with salaries in other professional and technical fields. But salary increases will raise quality only if they are accompanied by policies to raise the selectivity of teacher education programs. This is a crucial issue in the LAC region that gets far too little attention. Indonesia in 2008 introduced a teacher certification program that doubled teacher salaries but did not substantively change teacher standards. A rigorous impact evaluation of the reform in 2014 found that although the higher salaries had a large fiscal impact, they produced no improvement in student learning outcomes (Dee Ree et al., forthcoming). Closer to home, improved incentives led to a doubling of enrollments in teacher preparation programs in Chile over the 2000s, but most of the enrollment expansion was in institutions with low academic standards, and the country saw no improvement in the average quality of graduates. The share of tertiary education students in Latin America enrolled in teacher training is much higher than observed in East Asia or Europe, because there is almost no winnowing of teacher candidates at the point of entry into teacher training (figure 3.3).

A lack of selectivity in teacher education leads to an enormous reserve of teachers (i.e., people trained as teachers who are working in other fields) and comes with major costs. In Peru, only 50 percent of teacher graduates are employed as classroom teachers, and in Costa Rica, only 55 percent (figure 3.4). Surveys conducted by Chile's Ministry of Education in 2013 found that half of all students graduated from teacher

FIGURE 3.3: Percentage of tertiary graduates who studied education

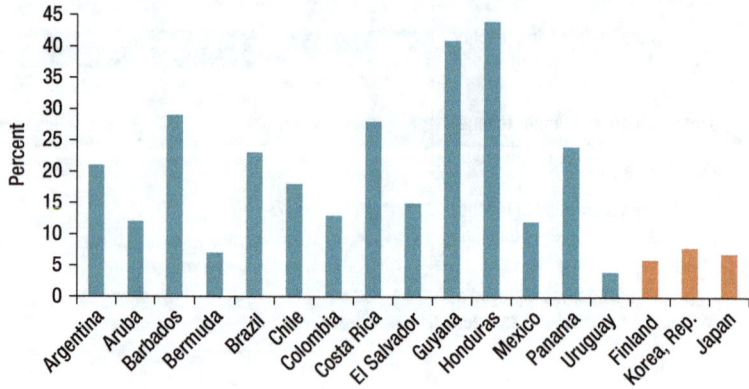

Source: UNESCO 2012.
Note: Data are most recent available year between 2009 and 2012.

FIGURE 3.4: Share of recent teacher graduates employed in teaching

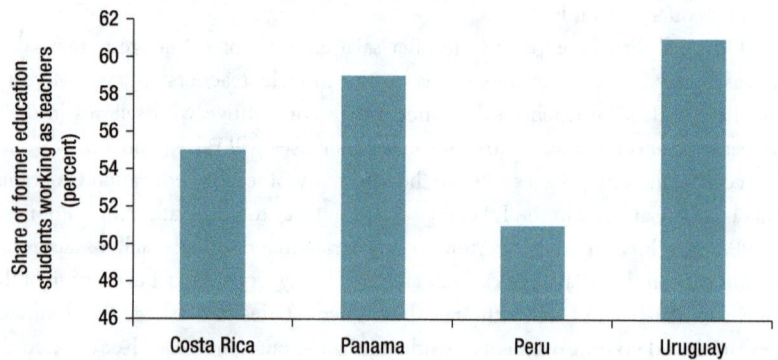

Source: World Bank construction using household survey data for 2009–12.

education institutions since 2008 were currently employed in retail. As teacher education is often subsidized by the public sector, producing an excess of teachers diverts resources from other, more productive investments in student learning. In countries such as Chile, where many students finance teacher education with loans, the overproduction of graduates from a five-year program of study that does not lead to relevant employment is even more problematic. In countries with inefficient or nontransparent recruiting processes, an excess pool of teacher graduates may even reduce the chances for the most talented teachers to find a post. Most fundamentally, a lack of selectivity undermines the prestige of the profession and makes teacher education less attractive for top students.

It is important to realize that the selectivity and status of the teaching profession are not immutable qualities of an education system. Finland made raising teacher selectivity a cornerstone of its education reform strategy in the 1970s. Within 20 years, it successfully transformed its labor market for teachers from one in which a large number of teacher training institutions of low or variable quality produced an excessive number of teachers to one with a much smaller number of high-quality institutions producing just enough high-talent teachers (box 3.1).

BOX 3.1: *How top education systems attract talented teachers*

Finland. Finland's high performance on international learning assessments has attracted substantial attention, and there is a tendency to think that this performance is somehow culturally ingrained. But a generation ago the Finnish education system looked and performed very differently. What changed was a conscious national strategy to raise the quality of basic education through a focus on attracting and training better teachers. Two main reforms drove the change: actions to raise the quality of pre-service education and a redefinition of the teaching profession to grant teachers increased autonomy and accountability. Pre-service education was made more selective by raising degree requirements to the master's level and raising accreditation standards sharply, which resulted in the closure of all teacher training programs outside of top research universities. This was politically difficult and controversial at the time, but it has had huge payoffs.

Teacher education programs became more intellectually challenging but also strongly focused on teacher practice in the classroom. Students now spend substantial time working in primary and secondary schools affiliated with their university programs. Independent research on how children learn and the effectiveness of alternative teaching methods is part of the degree requirements for all future teachers. To attract top students into these challenging programs, students' tuition expenses and living costs are fully funded by the government. Given the quality of the training institutions and the limits on teacher quantity, graduates are certain of employment as teachers. These changes reinforced each other and created a virtuous circle in which the challenge and prestige of Finland's teacher education programs began to attract high-caliber students, and demanding admissions standards further ensured institutions' quality. Applicants undergo written tests of content mastery, aptitude tests, and interviews. In some universities, the admissions process also includes evaluations of individuals' personality in group dynamics and an optional teaching demonstration.

Singapore. Singapore is known for its strategic approach to identifying and nurturing teaching talent. It has developed a comprehensive system for selecting, training, compensating, and developing both teachers and principals, thereby creating tremendous

(continued on next page)

> **BOX 3.1:** *How top education systems attract talented teachers (continued)*
>
> capacity at the point of education delivery. Singapore has a single national teacher training university, the National Institute of Education, which produces all of the country's teachers. Prospective teachers are carefully selected from the top one-third of the secondary school graduating class by panels that include current school principals. Strong academic ability is essential, but students are also assessed on their commitment to the profession and to serving diverse types of students. Prospective teachers receive a monthly stipend throughout their education that is competitive with the monthly salary for fresh graduates in other fields. They must commit to teaching for at least three years. Interest in teaching is seeded early through teaching internships for high school students; there is also a system for midcareer entry into teaching, which is a way of bringing real-world experience to students.
>
> *Sources:* OECD 2011, 2012b; Eurydice 2011; Sahlberg 2011.

Raising the selectivity of teacher education

If Latin American countries wish to transform the education profession, raising the selectivity of teacher education will be key. Tighter control of the content, quality, and selectivity of teacher education programs will save resources, increase prestige, and allow reallocation of resources currently spent on low-quality preparation for a large number of candidates to high-quality preparation for a more elite group of candidates.

A major constraint to this transformation is the principle of university autonomy that prevails in Latin America, which legally prevents most ministries of education from unifying or standardizing admissions into pre-service training. The most prestigious universities in the region do screen teacher education applicants and use a combination of tests and interviews effectively to select the best possible students (e.g., the University of Costa Rica, Catholic University of Peru, Mexico's National Pedagogical University). But the majority of LAC's teachers are not produced by these institutions. In Colombia, only 18 percent of university programs producing teachers are accredited. Most graduates come from nonaccredited programs, and only 31 percent of these students achieve the threshold score on the national SABER Pro examination (Compartir 2013). Across the region, the dominant landscape is huge heterogeneity in the quality and admissions standards of different institutions—particularly among low-cost private providers and nonuniversity teacher training institutes—and very weak government quality assurance.

There are four main strategies open to ministries of education in this area:

- Close low-quality schools under direct control of the ministry (typically nonuniversity teacher education institutions).

- Establish a national teacher university directly controlled by the ministry of education (similar to Singapore's National Institute of Education).
- Create special financial incentives to attract top students into the best existing programs.
- Raise accreditation standards for university-based programs, forcing closure or adaptation.

Close low-quality nonuniversity programs

Peru. During the 1990s, Peru experienced a proliferation of pre-service teacher training institutions dependent on the Ministry of Education, called Institutos Superiores Pedagógicos (ISPs). Within one decade, 235 of these institutions were created, and by 2003 they represented 75 percent of all teacher education enrollments (Piscoya 2004). By the mid-2000s, serious concerns had arisen about the quality of these institutions and the large number of graduates they produced. A 2004 assessment by the Ministry of Education concluded that less than 22 percent of these institutions exhibited an "optimum" level of quality (Sánchez and National Directorate of Teacher Training 2006, 29). A further study estimated that "every year about 30,000 teachers graduate from pre-service training institutions, whereas only about 3,100 are needed per year to serve new enrollments and 3,700 to cover for those who retire" (Peru, Consejo Nacional de Educación 2006, 83).

In response, the ministry in 2007 established a unified national standard for admission into ISPs. The admissions process had two stages: a first "national phase" where candidates' general knowledge, capacity for logical thinking, math, and communication skills were tested through multiple-choice tests and a second "regional phase," implemented by provincial education authorities, where candidates' vocation, personality, and specialized knowledge were evaluated through written tests and an interview. The national phase was given a weight of 70 percent, and the regional phase 30 percent. To pass the admissions process, candidates had to obtain a score of at least 14 (out of 20) in each stage.

Setting a national bar for admissions had a dramatic effect on ISP enrollments. While total higher education enrollments in Peru remained at roughly 1 million, enrollments in both university and nonuniversity teacher education programs between 2006 and 2008 dropped from 38,000 to about 12,000, with the sharpest decline by far in the ISPs (figure 3.5).

However, the admission process faced opposition; many ISPs in rural zones that could not fill their programs with qualified candidates faced closure, and indigenous groups challenged the tighter standards as insensitive to Peru's cultural and educational diversity. The ministry was forced to reverse elements of the reform in 2010 and give institutions increased flexibility over their entry standards. In 2012, candidate selection was fully decentralized back to the institutions, which are now responsible for the design and implementation of admission tests covering general knowledge, aptitude for the profession, personality, and mastery of specialty subjects. To compensate somewhat for the lowering of standards, the reform also established a compulsory remediation program of two months for all students admitted. The result is a compromise between a national admissions policy and a decentralized process: institutions control admissions processes but these must be consistent with national guidelines and are subject to a cap on enrollment set by the ministry every year. The impact of this compromise is visible in the enrollment figures for ISPs, which saw their sharp downward trend begin to be reversed in 2012 (figure 3.6).

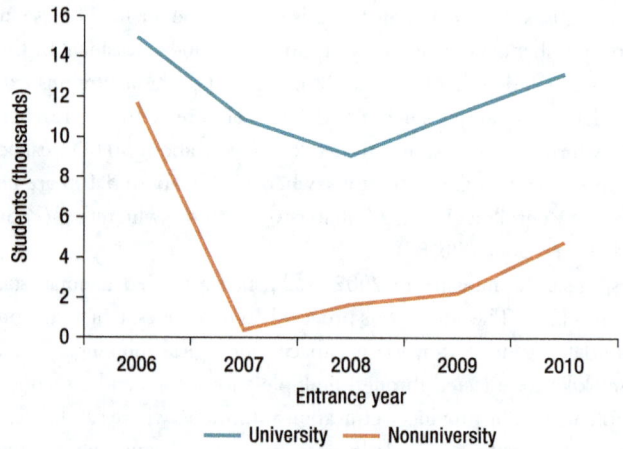

FIGURE 3.5: Students admitted into teacher education programs in Peru, 2006–10

Source: World Bank construction using data from Peru's national household survey (ENAHO).

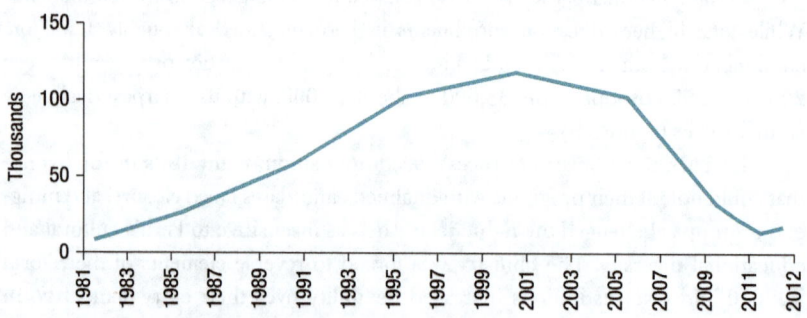

FIGURE 3.6: Students enrolled in ISPs in Peru, 1981–2012

Source: World Bank construction using data from Peru's Ministry of Education.
Note: ISP = Institutos Superiores Pedagógicos.

Establish a national teacher education university

Ecuador. Ecuador is the first country in the region to try to raise teacher quality by creating a new national university dedicated to teacher education. As part of a broader effort to raise tertiary education quality, the Ministry of Education in 2012 closed 14 universities after an 18-month quality assessment. It then created a new high-level pedagogic university, the Universidad Nacional de Educación (UNAE), expected to open in 2015. With an initial investment of US$440 million, this public university's mission is to train high-quality teachers, public education managers, and academic researchers in education who will work in a newly created education policy research center. The institution, which is currently being built, will work on the basis of frameworks and curricula designed through national and international consultations with stakeholders and experts. A central idea is that UNAE will become the link between national policy makers and the country's existing teacher training institutions, by producing highly qualified individuals who can move into leading faculty positions in other institutions over time (Ecuador, Ministerio de Educación 2011).

Create special incentives for top students

Strategies to raise teacher quality by forcing the closure of low-quality institutions or establishing a new institution model are necessarily relatively long term. A strategy that offers shorter term impacts is the use of targeted incentives to attract top secondary school graduates into the best available teacher training schools. In Finland; Hong Kong SAR, China; Singapore; and Sweden, teacher training is open only to select candidates, but these students receive free tuition plus a salary or stipend while they are in training (Garland 2008). In Scotland, teachers who complete their coursework successfully receive a year-long paid internship with school-based mentoring and peer-teacher support (OECD 2007). In the United Kingdom, a program of scholarships to highly prestigious institutions to lure top science students into teaching led to an increase of over 10 percentage points between 2010 and 2012 in the share of teacher education entrants with honors degrees (United Kingdom, Department for Education 2012a).

Chile's Beca Vocación de Profesor. The most interesting program of this type in LAC to date is the 2010 scholarship program introduced in Chile (Beca Vocación de Profesor [BVP], or Scholarship for the Teaching Profession). The program has been carefully followed by Chilean researchers, so there is some initial evidence on its effectiveness.

The BVP is offered in two forms. The first is aimed at students enrolling for the first time in eligible teaching programs. The second targets students finishing a bachelor's degree in other disciplines but who are open to becoming teachers. The vast majority of BVP recipients to date (94 percent in 2011) fall in the first category. For this group, the program offers scholarships covering full tuition and registration fees for students scoring 600 points or more on the university entrance examination, the Prueba de Selección Universitaria (PSU).[2] Given the high costs of tertiary education in Chile, full tuition is a significant incentive: the average yearly tuition for a general pedagogy program at university in 2012 was Ch$1.8 million (approximately US$3,800). Students who score above 700 receive an additional stipend for living expenses of Ch$80,000 (about US$160) per month. Students with scores of 720 or above may also receive financing for one semester of study abroad (Chile, Ministerio de Educación 2012a) To ensure quality, the scholarship can be used only for degree programs in institutions that have been accredited for longer than two years and accept no students scoring below 500.

Students applying for the BVP agree to work full time in a public or subsidized school for at least three years after obtaining their degree. They must complete this service within 12 years and sign a promissory note for the total amount of the scholarship as a guarantee of this commitment. In 2011, 28,179 students applied for the BVP, of which 3,385 (12 percent) were awarded the scholarship and 3,252 (96 percent of awarded students) accepted.

A study analyzing the results of the BVP's first year found that the program was successful in attracting students with higher academic performance than the average for teacher training candidates. The proportion of students enrolled in education programs from the top 30 percent of the PSU distribution increased from 10.7 percent (on average, from 2007–10) to 18.1 percent in 2011. The probability that a student with a PSU score of 600 points or more entered teaching has risen between 30 and 40 percent and by 100 percent for students over 700 points, although this latter impact is over a very small base. The positive impact of the program on the average PSU score of entrants into teacher training is larger for students coming from public high schools (Alvarado, Duarte, and Neilson 2011). The BVP has clearly succeeded in its first stage goal of attracting more academically qualified students into teacher education programs. A second impact ministry officials report is feedback from top universities that the introduction of the "BVP cohort" of students into their programs has raised the quality of academic interaction and stimulated higher performance from all students.

The next step is to see if BVP students perform systematically better on Chile's teacher exit exam, and ultimately, whether they are more effective on average than other teachers in helping students learn. Research on the first question will be possible when the first cohort of BVP beneficiaries graduates from teacher education in 2015 and takes the Inicia exam. Building evidence on the second question will take longer, but that is the ultimate test of this promising reform.

Colombia's loan-scholarships for high performing students who choose teaching. Colombia recently established a similar program to attract talent into teacher education. In 2012, the government allocated over US$70 million to award 6,000 loan-scholarships to three cohorts of students scoring in the top quintile of the university admission test (SABER 11) who chose to study in one of the 56 education degree programs in Colombia accredited as "high quality." The scholarships cover tuition fees for the total duration of the degree in the form of a loan through Colombia's student loan entity, (Instituto Colombiano de Crédito Educativo y Estudios Técnicos en el Exterior, or ICETEX).[3] The loan is forgiven in its entirety for students who complete the degree. Beneficiaries who are eligible for support on socioeconomic grounds or who must move to a different city to study also receive a nonreimbursable monthly grant equivalent to between one and five minimum salaries. The initial result of Colombia's effort is similar success as Chile's in attracting academically stronger candidates into teacher education, but the longer term impacts on these teachers' quality is also yet to be evaluated.

Raise accreditation standards

Low infrastructure costs and demand from the rapidly growing pool of secondary graduates in most LAC countries has made the teacher education sector attractive to for-profit private providers. As seen in figure 3.3, in a number of LAC countries over 20 percent of all higher education students are enrolled in teacher education programs. Uncontrolled growth of these programs is producing a glut of graduates in many countries that school systems cannot absorb.

Governments' main instrument for controlling the quality and size of legally autonomous universities and other tertiary-level institutions is a national quality assurance system, designed to certify, monitor, and improve tertiary education quality and ensure institutions' consistency with public policy goals.

Quality assurance systems are usually based on a process of institutional self-evaluation, external evaluation by a group of experts, and accreditation decisions by a public oversight authority, based on quality criteria established by the authority. The specific quality criteria and standards defined, together with the consequences of accreditation decisions, are among the most important pieces in the design of an adequate quality assurance system. The cases of Chile and Peru illustrate the importance of establishing strong overall quality assurance systems for tertiary education and the importance of ensuring that these pay sufficient attention to teacher education programs.

Chile. Chile has had a mandatory accreditation system in place since 2006 for teaching programs. Accredited status is important in Chile because it allows students to obtain government loan or grant support for their studies. Institutions and programs can be accredited for up to seven years according to the degree to which they meet the evaluation criteria. External reviewers have criticized this feature of Chile's current accreditation system (e.g., OECD 2013) because it fails to impose a minimum quality threshold. As shown in figure 3.7, about 5 percent of Chile's teacher education programs in 2013 were nonaccredited, and almost 12 percent had only two years of accreditation. Less than 10 percent of programs attained the highest standard of

FIGURE 3.7: Number of teacher training programs by accreditation status in Chile, 2013

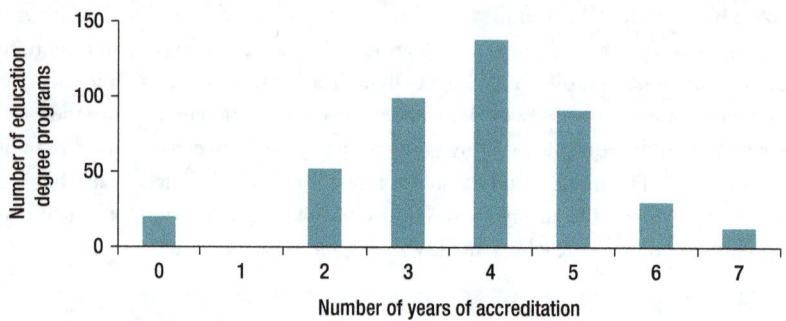

Source: Chilean National Accreditation Commission.
Note: Includes all degree programs in education (in universities and professional institutes) as of May 1, 2013, except for those in their first accreditation process.

quality (six or seven years of accreditation). However troubling, this represents progress from 18 months earlier, when more than 30 percent of all teacher education programs were not accredited and only 2 percent reached the highest quality standard (Chile, Consejo Nacional de Educación 2011).

Chile's experience shows how significantly accreditation standards and the market signals they create affect student enrollment decisions (figure 3.8). In just three years after 2006, the market shifted massively from 77 percent of enrollments in nonaccredited programs to 66 percent of enrollments in accredited programs (as of 2010). However, there is a surprisingly persistent market for low-quality providers, with almost 34 percent of all teacher training candidates in 2010 remaining in programs that did not receive accreditation in the first round of reviews. These students are not eligible for public financing (either grants or loans) and hence finance their studies by other means, usually family income and private loans without a government guarantee.

Peru. Peru is also pursuing a policy of higher accreditation standards for teacher education programs, but its experience is a reminder that this route can be a long-term process, especially in countries where comprehensive tertiary education accreditation systems are being developed for the first time.

A 2006 law in Peru established the National System for the Evaluation, Accreditation, and Certification of Education Quality (Sistema Nacional de Evaluación, Acreditación y Certificación de la Calidad Educativa [SINEACE]), and a 2007 bylaw established compulsory evaluation and accreditation for programs in education and medicine. The implementing entities—Consejo de Evaluación, Acreditación y Certificación de la Calidad de la Educación Superior No Universitaria (CONEACES), for nonuniversity programs, and

FIGURE 3.8: Enrollment in teacher education programs by accreditation status in Chile, 2007–10

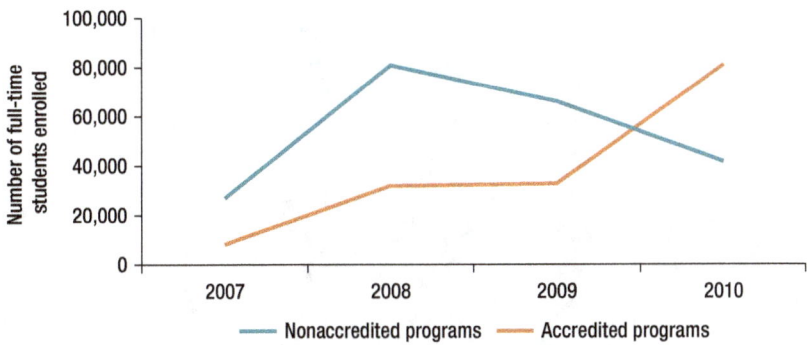

Source: World Bank construction using Chile's Ministry of Education enrollment data.

Consejo de Evaluación, Acreditación y Certificación de la Calidad de la Educación Superior Universitaria (CONEAU), for university programs—began intensive work to define quality standards and the processes for institutional self- and external evaluation. In 2011, the first external evaluations of education degree programs began. But SINEACE's current projection is that by 2016—10 years after the legislation passed—still only about one-fourth of university education programs and one-fifth of Institutos Superiores Pedagógicos will have received an accreditation decision on the basis of the new standards.

Raising the quality of teacher education

Latin America has seen a significant "upskilling" of teachers' formal qualifications over the past few decades, as seen in Brazil (figure 3.9). Thirty years ago, teachers in most LAC countries were trained at the secondary level, in *escuelas normales*. Today, only a few countries in the region (Guatemala, Haiti, Honduras, Nicaragua, and Suriname) still provide teacher training at the secondary level, and these countries are also experiencing a push toward tertiary-level preparation (UNESCO 2012).[4] Table 3.1 summarizes the level and length of pre-service training in a selection of countries in the region.

However, the accumulated evidence from various tests of teacher content mastery is that more years of formal education have not necessarily translated into higher capacity teachers. The Dominican Republic, for example, in 1997 raised the bar for teacher preparation to three years of tertiary education, which raised the costs of educating new teachers as well as their salaries at entry. Eighty-five percent of all teachers have now acquired this standard. But Dominican students still scored the lowest in

FIGURE 3.9: Rise in formal education of primary school teachers in Brazil, 1995–2010

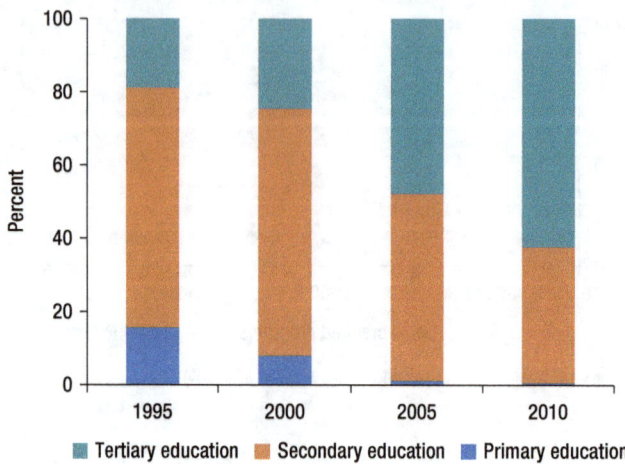

Source: World Bank construction from Brazil's Ministry of Education (INEP) data.

the region on the Second Regional Comparative and Explanatory Study (SERCE) reading and math assessment. The study of math and reading skills among Peruvian sixth-grade teachers, discussed in chapter 1, demonstrates deplorably weak mastery of basic content among teachers who almost universally have tertiary-level preparation (Metzler and Woessmann 2012).

There is little available research on the quality of teacher pre-service education in LAC, and almost no data that can meaningfully be compared across countries. Qualitative accounts of pre-service training in Latin America consistently describe it as failing to provide sufficient content mastery and student-centered pedagogy; being isolated from the school system and education policy making; and including actual classroom experiences only toward the end of the degree, if at all (UNESCO 2012, 44–5).

Building teacher practice into pre-service education

A key issue in LAC countries is the relevance of pre-service training. Ministries of education staff and many teacher graduates characterize university programs as ideological and theoretical, with little emphasis on the skills and techniques that teachers need to be effective in the classroom. Related to this is the candidates' limited exposure to schools and classrooms during their academic training. A study of the links between teacher preparation and student achievement using data from New York City schools finds that pre-service training programs that focus on the work teachers will

TABLE 3.1: Level and length of pre-service training in Latin America and the Caribbean countries

Country	Minimum required years of pre-service training	
	Nonuniversity tertiary	University
Argentina	4	5
Brazil	4	4
Chile	4	5
Colombia	2.5	5
Costa Rica	N.A.	4
Cuba	5	N.A.
Dominican Republic	3	3.5
Guatemala	N.A.	3
Honduras	3	4
Jamaica	3	N.A.
Mexico	4	4
Peru	5	5
Paraguay	3–4	4
St. Vincent and the Grenadines	2	N.A.
St. Kitts and Nevis	2	N.A.
Uruguay	4	4–5

Source: Franco 2012.
Note: N.A. = not applicable.

actually face in classrooms (for instance, by providing students with field experience in schools and extensive feedback from teacher mentors or by requiring students to present a capstone project stemming from their practice) lead to more effective first-year teachers (Boyd et al. 2009).

Most Latin American and Caribbean countries lack a national minimum threshold of practice teaching for future teachers and leave it to institutions to define. While a few universities in the region have ambitious practicum programs for their teacher trainees, many others provide future teachers with minimal or no real contact with schools. For those countries that do set national thresholds, the minimum length established varies a lot (figure 3.10). The Cuban system stands in distinct contrast to the rest of the region, with its very heavy emphasis on teaching practice. Teacher candidates spend 72 percent of their time over a five-year program doing practice teaching in schools. The next highest country in the region, Mexico, requires 25 percent of time spent on pre-service practice teaching, while countries such as Brazil and Peru have formal requirements that demand very little.

FIGURE 3.10: Compulsory pre-service teaching practice, in a selection of Latin America and the Caribbean countries

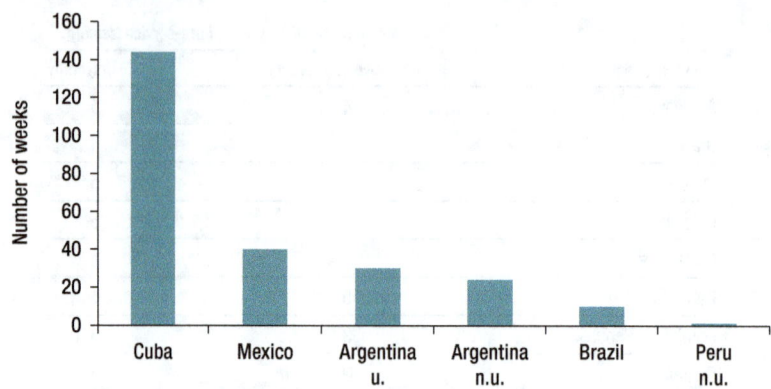

Source: Franco 2012.
Note: u. = university level; n.u. = nonuniversity level. Figures assume 40 program hours per week and 40 weeks per year.

Similar patterns in the United States provoked a national blue ribbon panel in 2010 to call for a redesign of teacher education "from beginning to end" to "place practice at the center of teacher preparation." The panel argued that teaching, like medicine, is a "practice," and that teacher education must follow the structure of medical education and create "abundant opportunities for candidates to develop their own practice and observe that of mentors while working in schools and classrooms under the tutelage of expert clinical educators." (NCATE 2010)

Quality of practice is as important as quantity. It is rare in LAC countries to see teacher trainees given a chance to teach and be videotaped, observed, and critiqued by expert teachers. Unless teachers have the opportunity to develop and deliver lessons themselves and receive feedback that promotes their reflection, the practicum may have limited impact on the quality of their teaching. Moreover, practice is often isolated from the other components of pre-service training. Clinical experiences usually take place at the end of the degree, which precludes further work to analyze situations encountered and develop new alternatives. Here the Cuban model proves exemplary. Cuba's future teachers are assigned to a school from their second year of studies and complement their theoretical studies with daily practice in a diversity of settings, supported by experienced mentors who provide them with systematic feedback (García Ramis 2004).

While university autonomy can make it difficult to introduce formal minima for practice within teacher education programs, innovative solutions can help bridge the gap. In Brazil, the federal government's Institutional Program of Grants for Induction into Teaching (Programa Institucional de Bolsa de Iniciação à Docência [PIBID]) offers grants for teacher education students to get experience in public schools and connect their understanding of theory with practice. The program provides funding not only to the student teachers but also to the classroom teachers who supervise them and the university professors who coordinate the subprojects, which is essential for compensating these partners for their time and effort. Although there is no evidence yet on the impact of the program on new teachers' skills, it has been popular with tertiary education institutions: 104 of them had projects approved by PIBID in 2010 (Gatti, Barretto, and André 2011, 129–30).

Competitive funds for innovation in teacher education

A promising instrument for stimulating improvements in teacher education is competitive funding. LAC countries have used this successfully to promote policy goals in higher education, such as expanded research collaboration in science. Chile is making active use of this approach in teacher education.

Chile. Chile's Program for Strengthening Pre-Service Teacher Training (Programa de Fortalecimiento de la Formación Inicial Docente) was implemented between 1997 and 2002 with the participation of 17 traditional and prestigious Chilean universities (all members of Consejo de Rectores de las Universidades de Chile) and supported investments totaling US$25 million. The winning projects included curriculum reforms that increased students' teaching practice in schools and improved the linkages between theory and practice (Avalos 2000). While the impact of the program on teacher effectiveness has never been systematically researched, Avalos concludes that the program did motivate leading universities to review the quality of their teacher preparation programs and adopt changes.

In 2012, the ministry announced a new line of competitive funding for improvements in teacher training as part of the Improvement of Quality and Equity in Higher Education program (Mejoramiento de la Calidad y la Equidad en la Educación Superior). This time the fund has specific objectives and selection criteria: reforming teacher education by incorporating lessons from research; strengthening remediation programs for teacher trainees; improving the quality of teaching in math, language, and science; and enhancing managerial and analytic capacity among the relevant university authorities. Ministry officials state they hope to stimulate a radical rethinking of teacher education with the new program, including, for example, proposals to cut the current five-year teacher education curriculum to a shorter cycle, with less emphasis on theory and more emphasis on classroom practice. Between 2012 and 2016, the government will invest US$45 million on the most innovative proposals. All accredited institutions can submit proposals, which are assessed and ranked by a panel of experts. Those selected then go through a negotiation phase with the ministry to establish explicit performance agreements, with specific targets that the president of the institution must take responsibility for achieving.

Peru. Peru is also establishing a competitive fund for tertiary education institutions, with a specific line of support for teacher training institutions. A unique feature of the Peruvian fund for quality enhancement (Fondo de Estímulo de la Calidad), which will invest US$39 million from 2013 to 2018, is that it will have separate competitions for low-quality and high-quality institutions. The objective is to raise the minimum bar among low-quality institutions while promoting excellence and international benchmarking among high-quality universities.

Raising hiring standards

The low overall quality of many teacher education programs in LAC makes it all the more important that countries screen effectively at the second stage: selecting the best available candidates for teaching positions. There are three main policy instruments to ensure this selection: (a) teacher standards to guide hiring decisions, (b) tests of teachers' skills and competencies, and (c) alternative certification.

Teacher standards

Articulation of clear standards for "what makes a good teacher"—such as the definition of what a "teacher should know and be able to do"—is an important step in developing a more professional teaching corps. Clear standards can make teacher hiring transparent and meritocratic. They can also, over time, influence how education schools prepare new teachers. Over the past 20 years, most Organisation for Economic Co-operation and Development (OECD) countries have put serious effort into developing standards for teachers. (Annex 3.3 includes leading examples from across the world.) Although they cover many common areas, such as expectations for teacher content mastery, understanding of students' needs, responsibilities to the school, and personal integrity, a review of different economies' standards (e.g., from Finland; Japan; Korea; Shanghai, China; and Singapore) shows variety in priorities and tone, reflecting national education goals and culture.

Chile's 2002 Marco para la Buena Enseñanza (MBE) is considered one of the best examples of national teacher standards in the LAC region. The MBE was developed through a three-year process of consultation between a national commission and the teachers' union. Chile's framework divides teaching into four domains: preparation or "readiness to teach," creating a favorable learning environment in the classroom, tailoring instruction to the needs of all students, and professional responsibilities beyond the classroom (Flotts and Abarzúa 2011). Each component is divided into subdomains—for example, content mastery in the subjects taught is a subdomain of preparation for teaching—and for each subdomain, the framework provides a rubric classifying teacher practice in that area. Figure 3.11 shows the domains and subdomains in Chile's framework.

Tests of teachers' skills and competencies

Countries in Latin American and the Caribbean have traditionally not had the kind of compulsory national certification process for the teaching profession that is common

FIGURE 3.11: Chile's framework for good teaching

Preparation
- Knowledge of the content and curriculum
- Knows the students
- Dominates the didactics
- Organizes objectives and contents coherently
- Coherent evaluation strategies

Learning environment
- Creates an environment of acceptance, equity, confidence, and respect
- Manifests high expectations about all students' learning and development possibilities
- Classroom norms
- Organized work environment and physical setting

Professional responsibilities
- Reflects systematically on teaching
- Professional and team relationships with colleagues
- Takes on responsibility in orienting students
- Favors collaboration with parents and guardians
- Knows updated information about the profession, the education system, and current policies

Instruction for all students
- Communicates learning objectives
- Uses challenging, coherent, and significant teaching strategies
- Content of class is treated with conceptual thoroughness and is comprehensible for all students
- Optimizes use of time
- Promotes thinking
- Evaluates and monitors student learning

Source: Chile, Ministerio de Educación 2008.

in medicine or law—that is, a test that prohibits those who do not meet its standards from being hired into the profession. The proposal to establish a Jamaica Teaching Council would, however, give this body the authority to establish a mandatory test for those who want to register as teachers (table 3.2).

More common in the region is the use of tests by individual hiring authorities (*concursos*) to rank or otherwise assess applicants' relative quality. While these two models are not incompatible, the cleavage between them reflects a tension between teaching as a civil service position and teaching as a profession. A salient difference is that tests used by hiring agencies are rarely standardized and therefore cannot serve as a barometer of changes in the quality of teachers over time.

But an increasing number of LAC countries are moving in the direction of national teacher competency tests, either as exit exams upon completion of teacher training or as screening exams prior to hiring. Either can be useful in permitting governments to monitor the quality of pre-service training. The cases of Mexico, which introduced mandatory national hiring exams for civil service teachers; El Salvador and Colombia, which have introduced mandatory national university exit exams; and Chile and Brazil, which have voluntary national teacher certification exams, are reviewed below.

Mexico's teacher hiring based on competency tests. Recent research from Mexico provides the strongest evidence to date on the importance of clear competency

TABLE 3.2: **Post-training tests for teachers (in primary education)**

Country	Tests as part of a competitive hiring evaluation	Mandatory national exit exam (from teacher education)	Voluntary national certification test	Mandatory national certification test
Argentina	No			
Brazil	Yes, at subnational level		Proposed	
Chile	Yes		Yes	Proposed
Colombia	Yes	Yes		
Costa Rica	Yes			
Cuba	No			
Dominican Republic	Yes			
El Salvador	Yes	Yes		
Honduras	Yes			
Jamaica	No			Proposed
Mexico	Yes		Yes	
Paraguay	Yes			
Peru	Yes			Proposed
Uruguay	Yes			

Source: Franco 2012.

standards for teachers (Estrada 2013). In 2008, the Calderón government mandated that all new civil service teachers be hired by states on the basis of performance on nationally designed tests of competency, which cover content mastery and pedagogical knowledge relevant to the level of education and discipline they will teach. This marked a sharp change from the prevailing system of teacher hiring through nontransparent processes controlled by state-level committees in which the teachers' union has a dominant voice. Several states desisted from the new hiring process, and others implemented it only gradually.

Researcher Ricardo Estrada was able to exploit this variation and carefully construct a six-year database of 1,148 small, rural junior secondary schools in 13 states that received no new teachers in 2008 or 2009 but in 2010 received either one new test-hired teacher or one new traditionally hired teacher. He focused on small rural schools (called Telesecundaria schools because they implement a TV-based distance learning curriculum), reasoning that the marginal impact of a single new teacher will be stronger in such schools. Annual National Assessment of Academic Achievement in Schools (ENLACE) student test data for the period 2005–10, which established parallel trends in his sample prior to 2010, permitted a robust difference-in-differences analysis that isolates the effects of merit-based teacher hiring. Administrative data also allowed Estrada to control for class size, school size, the share of indigenous students in the school, the principal's level of education, and state-specific time trends.

The results are striking. First, schools with test-hired teachers were 50 percent less likely to be flagged for suspected cheating on the end-of-year ENLACE exam. (The Federal Ministry of Education measures exam cheating using a detection algorithm designed to identify suspect strings of correct and incorrect answers within classrooms.) Second, in schools where no exam cheating was suspected and thus measured learning outcomes were more reliable, the introduction of a test-hired teacher was associated with an increase of .66 standard deviation (SD) in math scores and .78 SD increase in Spanish; these are huge effects. Estrada concludes that the federal policy of transparent, merit-based teacher hiring indeed produces better teachers, and that even in a relatively short (one-year) period, introducing a better-qualified teacher into a small school can have a dramatic effect on student learning.

El Salvador's Assessment of Academic and Pedagogic Competencies. In 2000, El Salvador established a mandatory exam for teachers exiting teacher training programs, called the Evaluación de las Competencias Académicas y Pedagógicas (ECAP). No teacher may be hired in any public or private school without passing this examination. Although only 39 percent of students passed the test at its first application in 2001, that share has risen over time (figure 3.12).

The upward trend is encouraging, but there is regrettably no evaluation evidence as yet on whether higher scoring teacher candidates perform more effectively as teachers. The country has not seen improvement in overall student learning outcomes over this period, but on the other hand, the teachers who have passed through the ECAP still constitute only a part of the overall stock of teachers. Given the database that ECAP has established, it would be possible to use tracer studies to research these questions, which could be of benefit to El Salvador as well as other countries considering this type of teacher exit exam. For both legitimacy and efficiency reasons, it is important to research whether the exam tests areas of teacher knowledge and skills that are meaningful predictors of their future performance on the job.

Colombia's SABER Pro for teacher education. In Colombia, all tertiary education graduates must take an exit exam of skills and competencies. SABER Pro is organized by the Colombian Institute for Educational Evaluation (Instituto Colombiano para la Evaluación de la Educación [ICFES]) and gives every student a score based on competency across five key areas (writing, quantitative reasoning, critical reading, citizen skills, and English). Since 2009, it is a legal prerequisite for all tertiary education students to take the SABER Pro examination to obtain their degree.

Colombia has been one of the most active countries in the region in testing tertiary education graduates, and ICFES is advancing toward the ability to measure the value added of different tertiary education institutions, since students' scores on the SABER Pro test may be compared with their scores on the SABER

FIGURE 3.12: Pass rate of teacher college exit exam in El Salvador, 2001–12

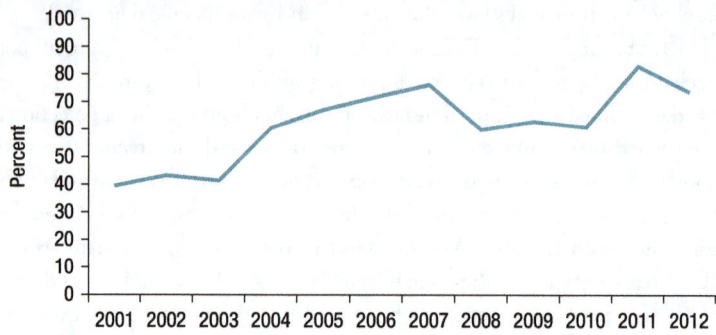

Source: Picardo 2012.

11 tests taken at the end of secondary school. Since 2011, the SABER Pro test has also included discipline-specific modules, including three modules (on teaching, educating, and assessing) that evaluate teachers' mastery of the content of teacher education programs. The results of 2009 SABER Pro test of reading, which is taken by graduates in all disciplines, demonstrate that Colombia's teachers—like those in other countries—have weaker average content mastery than graduates in other disciplines. In 2009, graduates from nonuniversity teacher training programs and from university programs preparing preschool teachers ranked at the bottom of all test takers in reading. Across 21 different tertiary programs, the graduates from nonuniversity teacher training programs ranked lowest, and graduates from university education programs ranked third-lowest (Barrera-Osorio, Maldonado, and Rodríguez 2012).

Chile's Prueba Inicia. In 2008, Chile introduced an exit exam for students graduating from teacher education programs, called the Prueba Inicia. The content of the test was developed by the Ministry of Education on the basis of Chile's teacher standards (MBE) and consultations with leading universities on appropriate expectations for teachers completing their preparation. The first test, in 2008, focused on primary school teachers, but subsequent applications have included tests for preschool teachers and high school teachers in different disciplinary areas. The test focuses on content mastery and pedagogy for the respective level of education (disaggregated by discipline in the case of secondary education) and on writing skills. Between 2009 and 2011, Inicia also covered information and communication technology (ICT) skills. Scores are divided in three ranges: outstanding, acceptable, and insufficient. A score of "acceptable" signals that a candidate is fully prepared to meet Chile's national teaching standards.

Given that the exam is voluntary and only about 40 percent of graduating teachers opt to take it, the results are discouraging (figure 3.13). In 2011, 42 percent of test takers from basic education teaching programs scored insufficient on the test of pedagogic knowledge, and 69 percent were insufficient on the test of content mastery. The ministry's policy since 2011 of publicizing the results also provides a window into the relative quality of different institutions. Among institutions with more than 20 graduates taking the basic education exam in 2011, some schools report 100 percent of their students score in the "acceptable" or "outstanding" range while other schools have less than 25 percent reach this threshold. On the tests of content mastery, the share of test takers scoring in the "insufficient" range is 12 percent for the best institution and 94 percent for the weakest.

The low share of teachers who opt to take the Inicia exam, coupled with the poor performance of those who do, has raised serious concern in the Ministry of Education and inspired a proposal in 2012 to make the exam mandatory (still pending in the legislature as of 2014).

Brazil's national test for entry into teaching. In 2014, Brazil will launch a Prova Nacional de Concurso para o Ingresso na Carreira Docente (National Test for Entry into the Teaching Profession) as a voluntary certification test for graduates of pre-service teacher training. The exam, to be administered yearly by the National Institute of Educational Studies and Research (Instituto Nacional de Estudos e Pesquisas Educacionais [INEP]), is based on a set of nationally relevant teacher standards (called the National Reference Matrix) elaborated in consultation with local and state governments, teacher unions, university faculties of education, and educational researchers. The test covers content mastery in (a) math, Portuguese, history, geography, science,

FIGURE 3.13: Teacher graduates' performance on Prueba Inicia exit exam in Chile, 2011

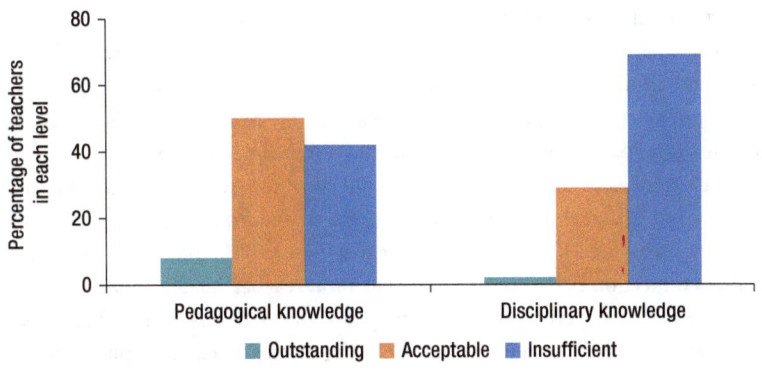

Source: Chile, Ministerio de Educacion 2012b.
Note: Results are for basic education teachers.

art, and physical education and (b) classroom management, education policy, child development, and the psychology of learning. It was designed principally as a support to smaller states and municipalities, which manage school systems but do not have the technical or financial capacity to implement the same kind of competitive teacher hiring examinations (*concursos*) as are conducted in larger states and municipalities. For teacher candidates, a nationally valid test increases the opportunities for mobility across the country. Last but not least, the test is designed to facilitate research and policy making regarding the quality of pre-service training.

Global evidence. The experience of New York City provides some encouraging evidence that raising teacher standards with a mandatory certification exam at entry can positively affect the quality of new teachers in a relatively short time. It also shows that students in the most disadvantaged schools may benefit most from actions to raise teacher quality. In 1998, the New York State Assembly mandated that by 2003 all newly hired teachers must pass a Liberal Arts and Sciences Teacher (LAST) certification exam. A study by Boyd et al. (2008) finds that immediately after the certification test was established, a high share of new teachers could not pass it. As a temporary measure, school districts were allowed to hire uncertified teachers (temporary license). Prior to 2003, New York City hired about 5,000 temporary license teachers per year, and these teachers were concentrated in the highest poverty schools (measured by student eligibility for free lunches and the minority share of students); temporary license teachers accounted for 63 percent of new hires in the poorest quartile of schools. After 2003, however, the city was able virtually to eliminate such hiring, and uncertified teachers fell to less than 1 percent of new hires in the poorest quartile of schools (figure 3.14).

A similarly rapid transition occurred with teacher performance on the LAST certification exam. When the test was first introduced, over 30 percent of teachers hired into high poverty schools failed it on their first attempt, compared with a failure rate of 15 percent for teachers hired into the richest quartile of schools. But by 2003, the performance of new teachers on the certification exam was about the same across all categories of schools (figure 3.15).

Boyd et al. (2008) show that as the gap in teacher qualifications narrowed, the gap in student performance across high and low poverty schools also fell. In 2000, 74 percent of students in the highest poverty schools failed to reach state reading proficiency standards (compared with 30 percent of students in the lowest poverty schools). By 2005, failure rates declined for all schools but the improvement was greatest in high poverty schools, and the gap in performance narrowed from 44 percentage points to 32 percentage points. The researchers note that these correlation data cannot establish a causal connection between the improvement in teacher qualifications and student outcomes in high poverty schools. But they do observe that New York City was able to make striking progress in narrowing the gap in average teacher qualifications in less than five years as the result of three policy changes: (a) the state policy abolishing temporary licenses for teachers who could not pass the certification exam, (b) the state

FIGURE 3.14: Elimination of temporary license teachers in New York City, 2000–05

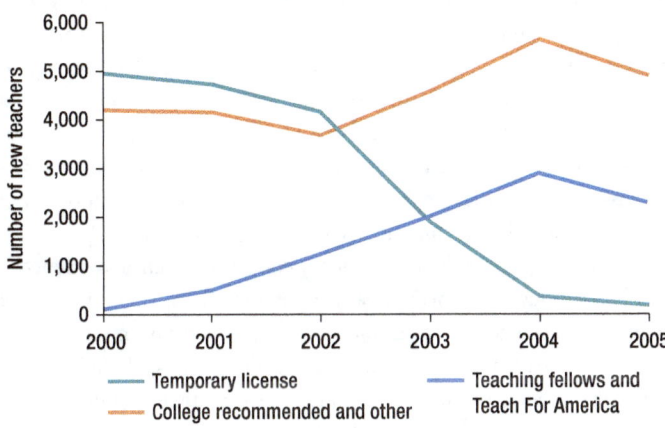

Source: Boyd et al. 2008.

FIGURE 3.15: Failure rate on LAST certification exam for new teachers in New York City, by poverty quartile of school's students, 2000–05

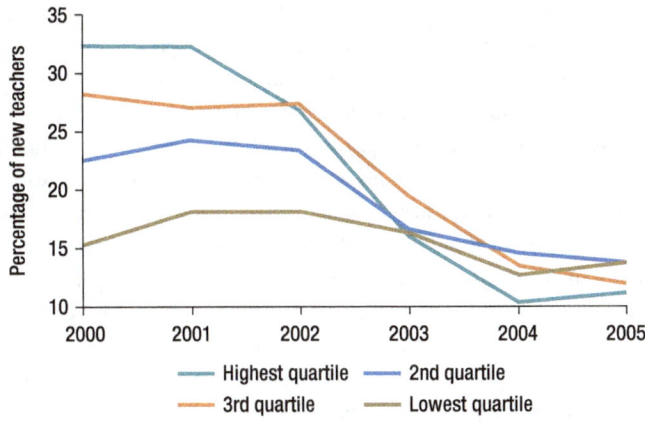

Source: Boyd et al. 2008.

policy allowing school districts such as New York City to offer "alternative certification" to teachers who *could* pass the teacher certification exam whether or not they had completed teacher training programs, and (c) New York City's proactive effort to recruit teachers from high-caliber alternative certification programs such as Teach For America and the New York Teaching Fellows Program (Boyd et al. 2008).

Alternative certification

As the experience of New York City demonstrates, a final strategy for raising the quality of new teachers is to bypass low-quality education schools entirely and recruit teachers prepared in other disciplines, a practice known as alternative certification. A number of education systems around the world have opened their recruitment processes to individuals not formally trained as teachers. In some countries, this policy has grown out of concerns over the low academic quality of teacher education programs and a belief that individuals with higher education degrees in specific content areas may have stronger expertise than graduates from teacher education programs. A second motivation is difficulty finding enough conventionally trained teachers to meet specific skills needs, particularly for secondary education, math, and sciences. A third motivation is a shortage of conventionally trained teachers willing to teach in challenging environments, such as disadvantaged urban schools or in remote rural areas. In all of these instances, school systems in the United States, United Kingdom, and many other OECD countries have opened teacher recruitment to professionals with alternative certification. Such programs have been lauded for bringing smart, experienced professionals into the classroom and for ensuring that high-needs schools are adequately served. They have been criticized by teachers' unions for circumventing the standard certifications in place to ensure quality.

To date, alternative certification has not been widely used in LAC, and there is limited evaluation evidence on its impact. One exception is Honduras's Tutor-Learning schools (Sistema de Aprendizaje Tutorial [SAT]), managed by a leading nongovernmental organization (NGO), the Asociación Bayan. To expand middle school coverage (grades 7–9) in rural areas, the government allows SAT schools to recruit teachers from the community who do not have university education or conventional teaching credentials. While the government approves the SAT schools' curriculum and pays teacher salaries, the NGO hires, trains, and supervises the alternative teachers. The SAT school model combines many elements that distinguish it from conventional middle schools in rural Honduras, including improved instructional materials, an emphasis on close teacher-student interaction, six weeks of annual in-service training for the locally recruited teachers, and flexible contracts, which make it easier to dismiss teachers who do not perform well. Thus, it is difficult to unpack how much each element contributes to the program's results. But a careful recent evaluation finds that test scores of children in villages served by SAT schools are significantly (0.2 SD) higher than in villages with traditional public middle schools, and that per-student costs of SAT schools were 18 percent lower (McEwan et al. forthcoming). In this case, at least, the evidence indicates that neither the lower formal qualifications nor the lower salaries of the alternative teachers jeopardize their effectiveness.

The most widespread experiment with alternative certification in the region to date is the launch of national branches of Teach For All (TFA) in six LAC countries since 2007. TFA is modeled on Teach For America, one of the best-known programs of alternative certification in the United States. In Argentina, Brazil, Chile, Colombia, Mexico, and Peru, TFA programs have recruited outstanding university graduates—across a range of disciplines—who are willing to commit to two years of teaching in highly disadvantaged schools. In every country to date, the program has proved to be attractive to high-talent university students: each branch receives hundreds of applicants for every opening.

The programs operate on similar lines: (a) publicizing the program in top universities and through social media; (b) screening and selecting top candidates from these universities; (c) assigning candidates to vulnerable schools that have requested participation in the program; (d) preparing the candidates through a one-month, practice-focused, intensive training program; (e) providing weekly mentoring of teachers once they start in their schools; and (f) ensuring ongoing monitoring of student progress in TFA classrooms. The training is a four-week program based in an actual school, where trainees work daily preparing and delivering lessons that are videotaped and then analyzed in detail under the tutelage of expert teachers. The program also uses data intensively—tracking attendance and student learning progress each day and providing visible comparative feedback on teacher performance (openly posted on walls) each week on how each new teacher's students are doing.

In its focus on the "mechanics" of teaching—lesson planning, techniques for keeping students engaged, efficient management of class time and transitions, constant assessment of students' learning progress, videotaped classes to dissect in detail—TFA's training looks very different from formal teacher education in most LAC countries, but similar in some ways to the Honduras SAT program. TFA's approach to teacher induction, which is relatively expensive as it involves weekly observation and mentoring of each teacher by a master teacher, is also an interesting example. The TFA model is based on over 20 years of program experience in the United States and, in essence, implies that for academically talented individuals with undergraduate specialization in subjects other than teacher education, several years of formal teacher education may be efficiently substituted by a much shorter period of intensive, school-based, practice-oriented training and a high-quality program to mentor new teachers.

The most rigorous evaluation of a TFA program in LAC is underway in Chile—measuring the impact that Enseña Chile (ECh) teachers have on student learning, student self-esteem, motivation, and school directors' and parents' satisfaction in a subset of schools randomly chosen from all of the schools that applied for the program in 2013. Results are expected in 2016. A 2010 evaluation by Alfonso, Santiago, and Bassi documents that the TFA programs in LAC have generally succeeded in attracting high-talent university graduates. In Enseña Perú, students in the top third of their university class are more likely to be selected into the program (Alfonso and Santiago 2010). The researchers also studied a closely matched set of teachers from ECh and comparable traditional teachers and have found higher student test scores in language and math, both for novice (first-year) and more experienced (second-year)

ECh teachers. Students of ECh teachers also have better socio-emotional results, including higher self-esteem and self-efficacy. Surveys of teachers reveal that the ECh teachers have more positive attitudes about their students' ability to learn and higher expectations for them (Alfonso, Santiago, and Bassi 2010).

The evidence base on the Teach For America model is more established in the United States. The most rigorous study, in which Teach For America and traditionally recruited teachers were randomly assigned to primary school classrooms, finds significantly higher mathematics achievement for students of Teach For America teachers than for other teachers, although reading results were not different across the two groups (Decker, Mayer, and Glazerman 2004). A more recent study focused on the performance of Teach For America teachers at the secondary school level. The study could not use random assignment, but drew on extensive value-added test score data at the classroom level. It finds that even though Teach For America teachers are much more likely to be assigned to classrooms of minority students with lower starting academic performance, their students register larger gains in learning than students of traditionally recruited teachers, particularly in math and science classes (Xu, Hannaway, and Taylor 2011).

A number of other U.S.-based studies have found that teachers hired through alternative pathways are basically equivalent to traditionally certified teachers (Sass 2011; Goldhaber and Brewer 2000), or that alternatively certified teachers are better in some subjects or worse in others (Darling-Hammond et al. 2005; Boyd et al. 2006; Xu, Hannaway, and Taylor 2011). A study in New York City, the largest school district in the United States, finds that students of alternatively certified teachers did slightly worse than students of traditionally certified teachers during teachers' first few years of teaching. An exception, however, were Teach for America teachers, whose students performed slightly better (Kane, Rockoff, and Staiger 2008). This finding points to the obvious fact that where many different models of alternative certification exist, their impact will stem from specific program design elements that affect the talent they attract and the efficiency with which they prepare teachers for the classroom.

As a whole, the current global evidence on alternative certification suggests that allowing teachers to enter the profession through an alternative route can be a tool for addressing teacher shortages in underserved areas or specialty subjects without raising costs or jeopardizing quality, if the alternative preparation programs are well designed and managed. The evidence clearly shows that student learning can benefit from bringing teacher candidates with high cognitive abilities and strong subject-area knowledge into the classroom, regardless of the particular path they follow. But rigorous evidence from the ECh program will likely be more convincing to LAC policy makers than evidence from the U.S. setting. The Teach For All experience appears particularly relevant for LAC because its core strategy for raising teacher quality directly addresses two of the clearest points of weakness in most LAC education systems: teachers' poor mastery of academic content and the limited emphasis that traditional teacher education programs place on preparing teachers for effective practice in the classroom.

Recruiting better teachers over the next decade

Demographic change will play a more important role in Latin American and Caribbean education systems over the next decade than many policy makers have realized. In contrast to the past three decades, when all countries in the region struggled to expand education coverage for a rapidly growing student population, many will face shrinking cohorts of school-age children over the next 15 years. Several countries, particularly in the southern cone, are already experiencing this. Projections of the demand for teachers in LAC countries by 2025 that reflect these demographic trends are presented in figure 3.16. They indicate that—if nothing else changes—the region will need 8 percent fewer preschool, primary, and secondary teachers in 2025 than were employed in 2010. However, the projected demand for teachers also depends upon two additional factors—education coverage and the ratio of pupils to teachers. Table 3.3 reveals the substantial heterogeneity across the region in these key underlying factors in 2010.[5]

Coverage. A more realistic assumption, however, is that all countries in the region will continue to make progress toward the goals of universal coverage at the preschool, primary, and secondary levels. At the primary level, as table 3.3 indicates, virtually all countries in the LAC region have achieved universal coverage; gross enrollment ratios exceed 100 percent for all of the countries in the United Nations Educational, Scientific, and Cultural Organization (UNESCO) dataset. Their main challenge now is to increase system efficiency—reducing repetition and dropout rates so that gross enrollment ratios converge downward to 100 percent and net enrollment ratios and primary school completion rates rise to 100 percent.

At the preschool level, there is huge heterogeneity across the region. Countries such as Paraguay, the Dominican Republic, Honduras, and Colombia report 50 percent or less of all children age four to six enrolled in preschool, while a few countries exceed 100 percent.[6] At the secondary level, no country has achieved 100 percent coverage. In addition, since enrollments at this level are also swollen with a large number of over-age students who have repeated grades, enrollments on a net basis (only students of official secondary school age divided by the total number of children in the population of that age) are considerably lower, so both coverage and efficiency must improve.

For the purposes of estimating what the maximum demand for teachers over the period to 2025 might be, we prepared a set of projections based on ambitious assumptions of country progress toward the goals of universal education coverage. For all countries, no matter how far they currently are from these goals, we assume the following:

- *Universal primary education completion, Millennium Development Goal 2, is achieved by 2025 in all countries.* For the countries analyzed here, this implies steady improvements in system efficiency to eliminate repetition and dropout and the expansion of access to all pockets of children not currently enrolled so as to achieve a 100 percent gross enrollment ratio, 100 percent net enrollment ratio, and 100 percent primary completion by 2025.

FIGURE 3.16: Projected change in the stock of teachers needed in LAC, 2010–25

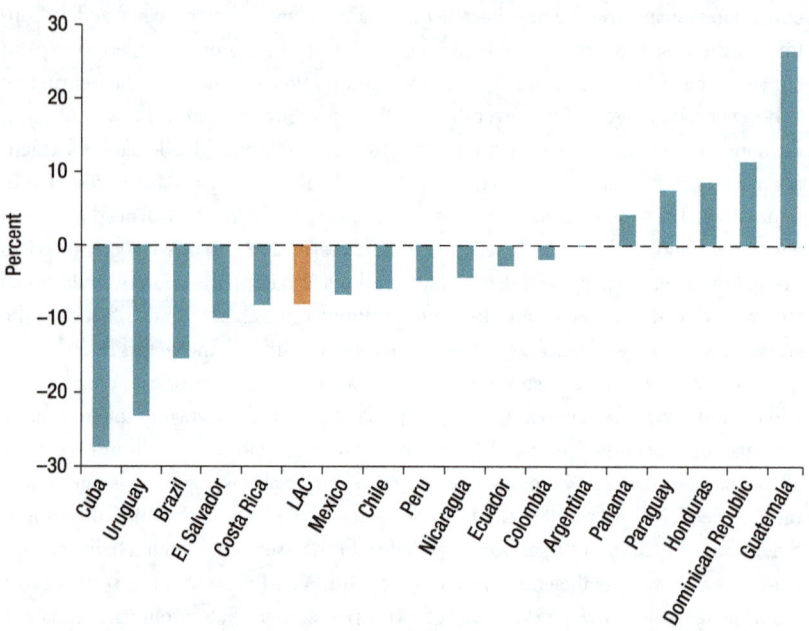

Source: World Bank elaboration with data from UIS.Stat (UNESCO Institute for Statistics database) and UNESCO 2009.
Note: LAC = Latin America and the Caribbean. Assumes no change in enrollment ratios at preschool, primary, and secondary levels and constant pupil-teacher ratios.

- *Rapid expansion of secondary education coverage.* We project a 90 percent gross enrollment ratio or higher in secondary education for all countries by 2025. This is much faster than past trends for most countries in the region, but is arguably an imperative for the economic competitiveness of middle-income countries.
- *Rapid expansion of preschool coverage.* We project a 90 percent gross enrollment ratio for the 4-to-6 age group by 2025. This is also much faster than past trends in most countries but is a justified target given the payoffs to early childhood development.

Even with these highly ambitious targets for overall schooling expansion, the region would need about 735,000 fewer teachers in 2025 than in 2010 (Annex 3.2, tables 3.9–3.11). Because of the declining size of the school-age population in the largest countries in the region, the total number of students enrolled at all three levels would still decline from 143 million in 2010 to 132 million in 2025.

TABLE 3.3: Projected change in the stock of teachers needed from 2010 to 2025, because of demographic trends, assuming constant enrollment ratios and pupil-teacher ratios

Country	Projected change in the student population aged 4–18, 2010–2025 (percent)	Projected change in number of teachers needed, 2010–2025 (percent)	Preschool education coverage 2010	Preschool education PTR circa 2010	Primary education coverage 2010	Primary education PTR circa 2010	Secondary education coverage 2010	Secondary education PTR circa 2010
Argentina	0.1	−0.1	74	19	118	16	88	12
Brazil	−15.8	−15.4	67	18	131	21	92	15
Chile	−5.5	−5.9	91	12	105	24	91	23
Colombia	−1.9	−1.9	50	27	116	28	94	26
Costa Rica	−8.7	−8.1	72	14	110	18	95	15
Cuba	−27.2	−27.4	102	14	102	9	89	9
Dominican Republic	9.1	11.4	38	24	109	25	80	28
Ecuador	−3.1	−2.8	145	12	118	18	88	11
El Salvador	−6.3	−9.9	62	23	114	30	65	24
Guatemala	25.7	26.4	66	23	116	28	58	15
Honduras	8.1	8.6	43	28	102	32	72	11
Mexico	−7.3	−6.7	103	25	114	28	89	18
Nicaragua	−4.0	−4.4	56	21	118	30	69	31
Panama	2.9	4.2	66	18	108	23	74	15
Paraguay	7.5	7.5	36	26	100	28	67	12
Peru	−5.0	−4.8	78	19	107	20	91	18
Uruguay	−21.3	−23.2	88	25	113	14	83	13
Regional average	−7.9[a]	−8.0[a]	72.8	20.5	111.8	23.1	81.5	17.4

Sources: UNESCO Institute for Statistics 2010, World Bank population data, and World Bank projections.

Notes: PTR = pupil-teacher ratio. Preschool coverage is the gross enrollment ratio (GER) for children age four to six in all countries; basic education coverage is the GER for primary education (includes lower secondary in some countries) relative to the official age for this segment in each country; secondary education coverage is the GER relative to the official age for that segment in each country.

[a] Regional average for percentage change in number of teachers needed is population weighted. All other columns are unweighted averages.

Under these assumptions, the total stock of teachers (in all three levels of education) would also fall—from 7.35 million in 2010 to 6.61 million in 2025. This presents an opportunity for the region to pay higher average salaries to a smaller stock of teachers, which could help raise the attractiveness of the profession. The size of the salary increment would be relatively small, however, given the number of additional teachers who would need to be hired in the countries that currently have low enrollments to achieve the ambitious expansion of coverage we project.

Pupil-teacher ratios. The potential "fiscal space" for raising average salaries depends heavily on an assumption that pupil-teacher ratios (PTRs) do not decline in countries where they are already relatively low. It is important to note that the inertial tendency in most school systems experiencing a declining student population is to allow the PTR to fall. It requires active management to trim the size of the teaching force pari passu with demographic decline—thus maintaining a stable PTR—and both teachers unions (who fight to protect job stability) and parents (who believe that smaller class size is better for their children) resist this (box 3.2).

Exactly this transition has occurred in the United States over the past four decades: while the student population has declined, the number of teachers has actually increased and the PTR has declined by 31 percent between 1970 and 2011. This managerial inertia has had high costs. Increased spending on education over this period in real terms has been entirely absorbed by higher teacher numbers rather than higher teacher salaries, which in fact have declined in real terms. As researchers have documented, despite higher spending, a falling pupil-teacher ratio, and shrinking average class size, the United States has seen no improvement in student learning outcomes. In other words, school systems in the United States have locked in an unproductive pattern of education spending (Hanushek 2002).

The contrast with East Asian countries is sharp. Countries such as Singapore, Korea, China, and Japan have consciously prioritized higher teacher salaries, a longer school day, and cost-effective nonsalary investments over smaller class size. Teacher salaries in Korea average 1.6 times per capita gross domestic product (GDP), in contrast to less than 1 times per capita GDP in LAC. Although Korea could clearly afford to hire more teachers, it has focused instead on maintaining a pupil-teacher ratio of 21 and an average class size of 27. Education spending in these Asian countries has not only prioritized higher average teacher salaries, but also salaries differentiated by competency and performance, which attracts more talented individuals.

To explore the implications of this trade-off in LAC, we prepared a set of projections assuming the same ambitious growth in enrollments as above, but also assuming that LAC countries adopt policies to manage the PTR similar to those employed by high-performing East Asian countries. For these projections, we assume target PTRs of 18 to 1 for preschool education, 20 to 1 for primary education, and 20 to 1 for secondary education. For all countries, we assume gradual progress toward these target levels in a linear path from their current PTRs such that countries reach

> **BOX 3.2:** *Pupil-teacher ratio and average class size*
>
> The *average class size* for a school system is estimated by dividing the number of students enrolled by the number of classes, whereas the *pupil-teacher ratio (PTR)* is calculated by dividing the number of students enrolled by the total number of teachers employed (both in full-time equivalent units). The two measurements are related but conceptually and statistically different. Average class size is typically higher than the PTR, because the PTR counts teachers who are not assigned to classrooms, such as special subject teachers (art, music, literacy specialists, etc.). Differences in the way countries organize their schools cause average class size and the PTR to diverge more in some countries than others. For example, Japan and the Republic of Korea both currently have an average class size of 27 in primary education (public schools), but Japan's PTR for primary education is 18 to 1 and Korea's is 21 to 1. On a conceptual level, the PTR is more relevant for teacher demand projections because it captures the total number of full-time equivalent teachers a school system will require and thus is directly linked to the fiscal consequences of how the teaching force is managed.
>
> While many parents believe that smaller classes and a lower PTR lead to better teaching and hence improved learning outcomes, the mixed empirical evidence on this has fed continuing academic controversy. Results depend on the range being considered: there is fairly consistent evidence that average class size above 40 impedes average student learning, while the incremental learning gains from reductions in the range from 30 to 20 may not be significant. Average class size below 20 is a luxury that even most Organisation for Economic Co-operation and Development (OECD) countries cannot afford: the OECD average for primary education is 21 (OECD 2012b). While the estimated learning benefits from smaller classes have varied in different studies, a consistent finding is that the costs of lowering class size are high compared to alternative investments in education quality. A good overview of the research evidence is presented by Hanushek (2002).

the target PTRs only in 2025. For countries in the region currently below those targets, the projections chart a gradual move upward. For countries currently above those levels, the projections chart a move downward that implies the need to hire more teachers.

As figure 3.17 shows, 8 of the 17 countries analyzed would be able to achieve our ambitious coverage targets as well as relatively low PTRs by 2025 with no increase in teacher numbers—and in fact with very large reductions in Costa Rica, Brazil, Argentina, Uruguay, Ecuador, and Cuba. Other countries, however, would need to hire substantially more teachers to meet the projected goals of close to universal coverage and lower pupil-teacher ratios than they currently enjoy. Driven by the reductions in larger countries, the overall size of the teaching force in LAC would still decline by 11 percent.

The declining teacher numbers that would result from policies to manage the pupil-teacher ratio combined with demographic trends would permit significant increases in teacher salaries. In Brazil, for example, this scenario would result in a 27 percent decline in the number of teachers—from 2.9 million in 2010 to 2.1 million in 2025—and would allow for a 37 percent average increase in teachers' salaries in real terms (table 3.4). This would move teachers' relative salaries from the 76th percentile of the wage distribution in 2010 to the 85th percentile in 2025, compared to the 90th percentile for other professional workers—a very significant improvement (Annex 3.6). In Uruguay, it would permit an even larger 65 percent real increase in teachers' salaries, bringing them 12 percentage points higher in the salary distribution. For countries such as Chile and Mexico, demographic trends will also produce a decline in teacher numbers that could be used to finance higher salaries if these countries maintain their current PTRs, which are higher than our target values. But as a comparison of the middle and last columns of table 3.4 shows, under the more generous PTRs we assume, their fiscal space for salary increases would be lower.

For countries still far from universal preschool, primary, and secondary coverage and with relatively high PTRs currently—Guatemala, the Dominican Republic, Nicaragua, Colombia, Honduras, Paraguay, and El Salvador—these projections imply a massive need for new teachers that is frankly unlikely to be met. In table 3.4, which estimates the change in average salaries from the 2010 level that would be

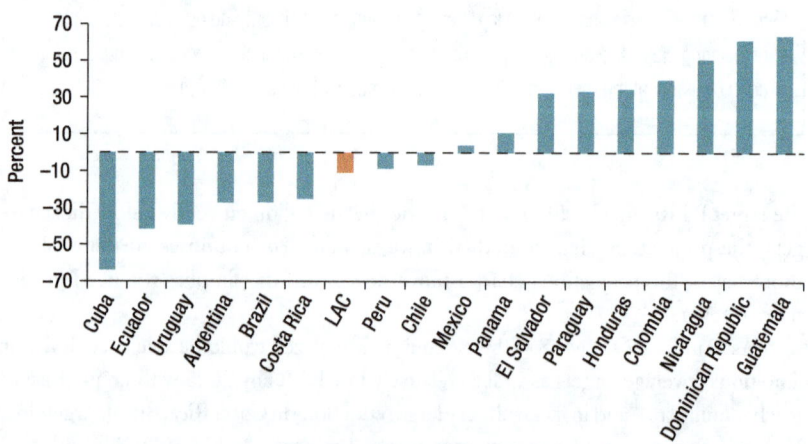

FIGURE 3.17: Change in stock of teachers needed, assuming expanded coverage and efficient pupil-teacher ratios, 2010–25

Sources: World Bank projections with data from UNESCO 2009, UIS.Stat, and World Bank population data.
Notes: LAC = Latin America and the Caribbean. Projections assume that all countries reach target gross enrollment ratios of 100 percent for primary and 90 percent for preschool and secondary education by 2025, and pupil-teacher ratios of 18 to 1 for preschool education and 20 to 1 for primary and secondary education by 2025.

required to finance the much higher teacher numbers needed in these countries in 2025 under an assumption of constant real spending on education, the large real decreases in salaries that result are implausible. More realistic assumptions are that these countries will make slower progress in expanding education coverage—particularly at the preschool and secondary levels—than our scenario projects. They would also likely prioritize expansion of coverage and not try to reduce their pupil-teacher ratios at the same time, which would make the demand for new teachers more manageable. And they may respond to demand pressure with increases in overall education spending.

In sum, these estimates show the potential benefits of a conscious strategy to raise teacher quality by capitalizing on the declining size of the school-age population over the next decade. With careful management of teacher recruitment and the pupil-teacher ratio—even with significantly higher schooling coverage—the total number of teachers in Latin America and the Caribbean could fall by 11 percent,

TABLE 3.4: Potential changes in teacher salaries possible with efficient pupil-teacher ratios, 2025

Country	Average salaries circa 2010 (percentile of the national salary distribution)		Average teacher salaries in 2025, with constant PTR and adjusted GER		Average teacher salaries in 2025, with adjusted PTR and adjusted GER	
	Teachers	Other professionals	Real change compared with 2010 (percent)	Teachers percentile ranking (in overall wage distribution)	Real change compared with 2010 (percent)	Teachers percentile ranking (in overall wage distribution)
Brazil	76	90	32	82	37	85
Chile	78	90	8	79	7	79
Costa Rica	83	87	8	83	34	87
Honduras	88	88	−25	78	−26	78
Mexico	85	88	9	88	−4	85
Nicaragua	71	91	−7	68	−34	37
Panama	81	90	−17	70	−10	76
Peru	70	90	4	72	9	73
El Salvador	86	90	5	89	−25	77
Uruguay	69	92	29	76	65	81

Source: World Bank calculations from UNESCO enrollment data, World Bank population data, and compiled household survey data.
Note: GER = Gross enrollment ratio; PTR = pupil-teacher ratio. Assumes constant real spending on education and constant spending on teacher salaries as a share of education spending. Salaries are expressed as the percentile in the national salary distribution in the country. Starting (2010) PTRs for each country are detailed in table 3.3; adjusted PTRs are 18 to 1 for preschool, and 20 to 1 each for primary and secondary education; adjusted GERs are 90 percent or higher for preschool, 100 percent for primary education, and 90 percent or higher for secondary education.

from 7.35 million in 2010 to 6.55 million in 2025. Several countries have a major opportunity to raise teacher quality though higher salaries, stronger incentives, and higher nonsalary spending at constant spending per student, if they manage teacher numbers in favor of higher quality. As our assumptions are based on constant spending on teacher salaries in real terms, countries that increase spending on education as a share of GDP would have even more resources per teacher to finance the move to higher quality.

But heterogeneity in countries' current education coverage and pupil-teacher ratios combined with demographic trends will create very different teacher policy challenges in different parts of the region. Some countries will struggle to recruit and train large numbers of new teachers. Others will not need a net increase, but will have to replace a large number of retiring teachers, given the age structure of their current force. Others will have to manage a shrinking overall teaching force, with an especially large reduction in primary education teachers. In the latter countries, some primary teachers can probably be retrained as preschool teachers; it is less clear that these would be able to transition into positions teaching at the secondary level.

Conclusions

Education systems in Latin America and the Caribbean today are caught in a vicious circle in which academically talented students do not apply for teacher education programs and teacher education programs have increased in level, cost, and length, but do not efficiently prepare students to become effective teachers. Changing this reality is not an easy task; it involves complex and sensitive reforms in a range of arenas. However, a number of countries in the region are moving in these directions, and there is much that others can learn from these experiences.

First, despite an excess of teacher education graduates in much of the region, in most countries there is a shortfall of talented candidates for teaching. Efforts to attract more talented teachers must be multidimensional: as discussed in subsequent chapters, financial rewards are not the only incentives that motivate potential teachers—social perceptions of the prestige of the profession are also important, and these are deeply connected to its academic selectivity, which is currently low.

Raising the selectivity of entry into teacher training in LAC is one of the biggest challenges the region faces. There has been a massive growth of enrollments in low-cost, low-quality teacher training institutions in many LAC countries, and reversing this is a political and institutional challenge. Governments have direct control over nonuniversity teacher training institutions, but face political pressures in closing these. Reforming university-level teacher education is complicated by the legal autonomy these institutions enjoy, a valuable tradition that nonetheless can hinder legitimate government efforts to raise academic standards. Higher accreditation standards and tighter enforcement of standards are needed in both subsectors—nonuniversity and university teacher preparation programs. An alternative, interesting model to watch is

Ecuador's new National Teacher University, an effort by the Ministry of Education to take direct responsibility for production of the high-caliber teachers it seeks. Finally, as a shorter-term strategy, targeted scholarship programs to attract high-talent candidates into the best existing teacher education programs can work: Chile's Beca Vocation Professor has succeeded in drawing academically stronger students into teacher education, and university faculties report positive spillover effects on their programs. It is interesting to note that a recent survey in Chile showed a significant percentage increase between 2010 and 2012 in the share of parents who think that teachers are valued by society (Salazar 2013).

Second, the quality of teacher education must be upgraded. Despite widespread progress in raising the formal level and length of pre-service training, quality has lagged behind. Teacher education systems in the region generally fail in providing future teachers with a 21st-century knowledge base and ICT skills, plus the practical skills in preparing engaging lessons, assessing student progress, and using classroom time and resources effectively that teachers need from day one. The evidence from classroom observations presented in chapter 2 is that teachers fail in simple dimensions. Teacher education programs in Latin America and the Caribbean, except for Cuba, give little emphasis to practice-based training, and future teachers spend little time working and doing research in schools under the guidance of master educators. A promising strategy for promoting innovation and a bottom-up transformation of teacher education is to use competitive funding programs, such as in Chile and Peru.

Third, more stringent standards for teacher hiring will have ripple effects on teacher education programs and the caliber of students attracted to the profession. Standards for teaching—a clear articulation of what a high-quality teacher must know and be able to do—are the backbone that can pull teacher education into alignment with other teacher policies, since they are at the base of the selection, training, certification, and career-long evaluation and promotion of teachers. The absence of clear standards can negatively affect the quality of teacher training.

The challenges laid out in this chapter—raising the selectivity of teacher education, raising the quality of teacher education programs, and developing effective systems for screening teacher applicants to recruit the best—exist in all LAC countries. But they will play out against a very different demographic backdrop. Projected declines in the student population in more than half of the region—including all of its largest countries—will make it easier for these to finance higher teacher quality, but will pose the political challenge of pruning low performers out of the force to make room for new talent. In the context of a potential decline in some cases of more than 15 percent in the size of the teaching force by 2025, managing both teacher exits and recruitment with a strategic focus on quality is critical. In countries where increased need for teachers is projected over the next decade, the major challenge is the financial burden of raising education spending to support the recruitment of new teachers at higher standards. For these countries, an efficient ratio of pupils to teachers is a critical policy choice.

Notes

[1] Chapter Annexes to the book may be found at http://www.worldbank.org/lac/teachers.

[2] The Chilean university entrance examination, PSU, has scores standardized to a mean of 500 points and a standard deviation of 110. In 2012, given the existence of some bias in the PSU (Pearson 2013), students with a score of at least 580 points and in the top decile of their high school grade point average distribution were also eligible for the BVP.

[3] Tuition fees are considerable in most tertiary education institutions in Colombia. The average yearly fees in 2010 were US$617 in public universities and US$3,297 in private universities (OECD 2012a).

[4] For instance, in Guatemala, three years of university-level preparation will be required for new teachers after 2013, and in Honduras the new Education Act establishes that from 2018 all teachers must have tertiary education degrees.

[5] Annex 3.2 presents the basis for these projections in detail, disaggregating the teacher needs stemming from retirements as well as net changes in the stock of teachers from 2010 to 2025.

[6] In some cases, such as Mexico, this is because preschool is offered to children age three to six, so UNESCO's enrollment estimates (designed to be internationally comparable) compare the total number of children enrolled (including many three year olds) to the total number of children age four to six in the population.

References

Alfonso, M., and A. Santiago. 2010. "Selection into Teaching: Evidence from Enseña Perú." Technical Note IDB-TN-193. Inter-American Development Bank, Washington, DC.

Alfonso, M., A. Santiago, and M. Bassi. 2010. "Estimating the Impact of Placing Top University Graduates in Vulnerable Schools in Chile." Technical Note IDB-TN-230. Inter-American Development Bank, Washington, DC.

Alvarado, M., F. Duarte, and C. Neilson. 2011. "Efectos de la Beca Vocación de Profesor." Working Paper 1603490, Ministerio de Educación, Gobierno de Chile, Santiago.

Avalos, B. 2000. "Policies for Teacher Education in Developing Countries." *International Journal of Educational Research* 33 (5): 475–74.

Barber, M., and M. Mourshed. 2007. *How the World's Best-Performing School Systems Come Out on Top.* London: McKinsey. http://mckinseyonsociety.com/downloads/reports/Education/Worlds_School_Systems_Final.pdf.

Barrera-Osorio, F., D. Maldonado, and C. Rodríguez. 2012. *Calidad de la Educación Básica y Media en Colombia: Diagnóstico y Propuestas.* Bogota: Universidad de los Andes.

Boyd, D., P. Grossman, S. Lankford, S. Loeb, and J. Wyckoff. 2006. "How Changes in Entry Requirements Alter the Teacher Workforce and Affect Student Achievement." *Education Finance and Policy* 1 (2): 176–216.

———. 2009. "Teacher Preparation and Student Achievement." *Educational Evaluation and Policy Analysis* 31 (4): 416–40.

Boyd, D., H. Lankford, S. Loeb, J. Rockoff, and J. Wyckoff. 2008. "The Narrowing Gap in New York City Teacher Qualifications and Its Implications for Student Achievement in High-Poverty Schools." *Journal of Policy Analysis and Management* 27 (4): 793–818.

Chile, Consejo Nacional de Educación. 2011. "Estadísticas 2011: Acreditación Carreras." Ministerio de Educación, Santiago. http://www.cned.cl/public/Secciones/SeccionIndicesEstadisticas/doc/Estadisticas2011/023_AcreditacionCarreras.pdf.

Chile, Ministerio de Educación. 2008. "Marco para la Buena Enseñanza." Ministerio de Educación, Santiago (accessed July 24, 2012). http://www.docentemas.cl/docs/MBE2008.pdf.

———. 2012a. "Beca Vocación de Profesor," website. Ministerio de Educación, Santiago (accessed September 13, 2012). http://www.becavocaciondeprofesor.cl.
———. 2012b. *Evaluación Inicia: Presentación de Resultados 2011*. Santiago: Ministerio de Educación.
Compartir. 2013. *Tras la Exelencia docente: Como Mejorar la calidad de la educación para todos los colombianos?* Bogota: Compartir.
Darling-Hammond, L., D. J. Holtzman, S. J. Gatlin, and J. V. Heilig. 2005. "Does Teacher Preparation Matter? Evidence about Teacher Certification, Teach for America, and Teacher Effectiveness." *Education Policy Analysis Archives* 13: 42.
De Ree, J., K. Muralidharan, M. Pradhan, and H. Rogers. Forthcoming. "Double for Nothing? The Impact of Unconditional Teacher Salary Increases on Performance." World Bank, Washington, DC.
Decker, P. T., D. P. Mayer, and S. Glazerman. 2004. *The Effects of Teach For America on Students: Findings from a National Evaluation*. Princeton, NJ: Mathematica Policy Research Institute.
Ecuador, Ministerio de Educación. 2011. "Estrategia UNAE." Ministerio de Educación, Quito (accessed March 9, 2013), http://www.educacion.gob.ec/formacion-inicial-e-induccion/unae-siprofe/estrategia-p.html.
Estrada, Ricardo. 2013. "Rules Rather than Discretion: Teacher Hiring and Rent Extraction." Manuscript, Paris School of Economics.
Eurydice. 2011. *National System Overview on Education Systems in Europe: Finland*. Brussels: European Commission.
Flotts, M. P., and A. Abarzúa 2011. "El modelo de evaluación y los instrumentos." In *La Evaluación Docente en Chile*, edited by J. Manzi, R. González, and Y. Sun, 33–61. Santiago, Chile: MIDE UC, Centro de Medición.
Franco, M. 2012. "Pre-Service Training in Latin America and the Caribbean: A Background Study for the World Bank LAC Study on Teachers." Manuscript, World Bank, Washington, DC.
García Ramis, L. J. 2004. *Situación de la Formación Docente Inicial y en Servicio en la República de Cuba*. Paris: UNESCO (accessed March 9, 2013).
Garland, S. 2008. "Reform School." *Daily Beast*, December 17. http://www.thedailybeast.com/newsweek/2008/12/17/reform-school.html.
Gatti, B. A., E. S. S. Barretto, and M. E. D. A. André. 2011. *Políticas Docentes no Brasil: Um estado da arte*. São Paulo: UNESCO.
Goldhaber, D. D., and D. J. Brewer. 2000. "Does Teacher Certification Matter? High School Teacher Certification Status and Student Achievement." *Educational Evaluation and Policy Analysis* 22 (2): 129–45.
Hanushek, E. 2002. "Evidence, Politics, and the Class Size Debate." In *The Class Size Debate*, edited by L. Mishel and R. Rothstein, 37–65. Washington, DC: Economic Policy Institute.
Kane, T. J., J. E. Rockoff, and D. O. Staiger. 2008. "What Does Certification Tell Us about Teacher Effectiveness? Evidence from New York City." *Economics of Education Review* 27 (6): 615–31.
McEwan, P. J., E. Murphy-Graham, D. Torres Irribarra, C. Aguilar, and R. Rápalo. Forthcoming. "Improving Middle School Quality in Poor Countries: Evidence from the Honduran Sistema de Aprendizaje Tutorial." *Educational Evaluation and Policy Analysis*.
Metzler, J., and L. Woessmann. 2012. "The Impact of Teacher Subject Knowledge on Student Achievement: Evidence from Within-Teacher Within-Student Variation. *Journal of Development Economics* 99 (2): 486–96.
NCATE (National Council for Accreditation of Teacher Education). 2010. *Teacher Education Through Clinical Practice: A National Strategy to Prepare Effective Teachers*. Report of the Blue Ribbon Panel on Clinical Preparation and Partnerships for Improved Student Learning, Washington, DC. http://www.ncate.org/LinkClick.aspx?fileticket=zzeiB1OoqPk%3D&tabid=715.

OECD (Organisation for Economic Co-operation and Development). 2007. *Reviews of National Policies for Education: Quality and Equity of Schooling in Scotland*. Paris: OECD.
———. 2011. "Building a High-Quality Teaching Profession: Lessons from Around the World." Background report for the International Summit on the Teaching Profession, OECD, Paris.
———. 2012a. *Tertiary Education in Colombia*. Paris: OECD.
———. 2012b. *Education at a Glance 2012: OECD Indicators*. Paris: OECD.
———. 2013. *Quality Assurance in Higher Education in Chile*. Paris: OECD.
Pearson. 2013. *Final Report: Evaluation of the Chile PSU*. New York (accessed November 12, 2013). http://www.mineduc.cl/usuarios/mineduc/doc/201301311057540.Chile_PSU-Finalreport.pdf.
Peru, Consejo Nacional de Educación. 2006. *Proyecto Educativo Nacional al 2021: La educación que queremos para el Perú*. Lima: Consejo Nacional de Educación. http://www.cne.gob.pe/docs/cne-pen/PEN-Oficial.pdf.
———. 2009. *Proyecto Educativo Nacional en el 2009: Balance y recomendaciones*. Lima: Consejo Nacional de Educación. http://www.cne.gob.pe/images/stories/consejo%201-42baja.pdf.
Picardo J. O. 2012. "La formación de docentes en América Latina y El Caribe: caso El Salvador." Manuscript, San Salvador.
Piscoya, L. A. 2004. "La formación docente en Perú." Manuscript, IESALC-UNESCO, Lima.
Sahlberg, P. 2011. "Lessons from Finland." *American Educator* 35 (2): 34–38.
Salazar, P. 2013. "Encuesta revela una mejora en la valoración de los docentes." *La Tercera*, April 7 (accessed May 29, 2013). http://www.latercera.com/noticia/educacion/2013/04/657-517591-9-encuesta-revela-una-mejora-en-la-valoracion-de-los-docentes.shtml.
Sánchez Moreno Izaguirrue, G., and National Directorate of Teacher Training. 2006. *Construyendo una Política de Formación Magisterial*. Lima: Peru, Ministerio de Educación.
Sass, T. 2011. "Certification Requirements and Teacher Quality: A Comparison of Alternative Routes to Teaching." Manuscript, Georgia State University Department of Economics, Athens.
UNESCO (United Nations Educational, Scientific, and Cultural Organization). 2009. *Projecting the Global Demand for Teachers: Meeting the Goal of Universal Primary Education by 2015*. Montreal: UNESCO Institute for Statistics.
———. 2012. *Antecedentes y Criterios para la Elaboración de Políticas Docentes en América Latina y el Caribe*. Santiago: UNESCO.
UIS.Stat (UNESCO Institute for Statistics database). Montreal, Canada. http://data.uis.unesco.org/.
United Kingdom, Department for Education. 2012a. "Highest Quality of Graduates Going into Teacher Training." Press release, London. http://www.education.gov.uk/inthenews/inthenews/a00217134/teaching-agency-census-.
———. 2012b. *Teachers' Standards*. London (accessed July 19, 2012), https://www.education.gov.uk/publications/eOrderingDownload/teachers%20standards.pdf.
Xu, Z., J. Hannaway, and C. Taylor. 2011. "Making a Difference? The Effects of Teach For America in High School." *Journal of Policy Analysis and Management* 30 (3): 447–69.

4
Grooming Great Teachers

Once teachers are hired, it is the task of a school system to make them as effective as possible. This involves both supporting individual teachers' development of their craft and building a professional community of teachers within schools and across the school system. Critical tasks in this process include the following:

- *Induction*: support for teachers' development during the critical first five years of teaching
- *Evaluation*: robust systems for periodic assessment of individual teachers' strengths and weaknesses
- *Professional development*: effective training to remedy teachers' identified weaknesses and leverage the skills of top performers
- *Management*: matching teacher assignments to schools' and students' needs, and building effective schools through shared practice and professional interaction

Teacher induction and probationary periods

One of the most consistent findings of education research is that new teachers face a steep learning curve in their first three to five years on the job (Boyd et al. 2006; Chingos and Peterson 2010; Hanushek and Rivkin 2010). No matter what teachers' starting level of effectiveness, in most cases it improves during the first few years of teaching and then typically reaches a plateau. In cases where this early improvement does not occur, it is a signal that the teacher is likely to unlikely ever to reach high effectiveness. During this window, school systems have a critical opportunity to support and maximize the development of new teachers and to identify those who should

---

This chapter was coauthored with David Evans, Guillermo Toral, Noah Yarrow, and Soledad de Gregorio.

be counseled out of the profession. As teachers are typically hired into civil service positions that make dismissal on performance grounds difficult, there is a high payoff to avoiding mistakes in recruitment. Both of these goals are served by a well-organized induction program and the use of probationary periods.

Despite this, formal induction programs are not widespread even among Organisation for Economic Co-operation and Development (OECD) countries. A recent review by the European Commission has found that only 11 of 27 European Union member states have formal induction programs. While most of the other countries have some guidelines or recommendations for the support of entry-level teachers, their implementation is uneven (European Commission 2010; European Commission/EACEA/Eurydice 2013). In the United States, a few programs that assigned mentors or coaches to new teachers have been rigorously evaluated, and the evidence suggests that such interventions can improve the learning outcomes of students assigned to new teachers, but that the quality and intensity of the mentoring is important (Rockoff 2004; Glazerman et al. 2010a).

Few countries in Latin America have formal induction programs for entry-level teachers. The English-speaking Caribbean countries are an exception. Most countries of the Organization of Eastern Caribbean States (OECS) have adopted formal induction programs, but these are strikingly short compared to the multiyear induction periods found in OECD countries that use them. Except for Belize, the OECS induction programs range from ten days to four months (table 4.1).

TABLE 4.1: Induction programs for new OECS teachers

Country	Are all teachers inducted?	What is the duration of induction?	What are the key aspects?
Anguilla	Yes	4 months	Lesson planning, classroom management, assessment, teaching of reading, literacy, and numeracy strategies
Antigua and Barbuda	Yes	1 week, sometimes shorter	Orientation to the world of teaching: classroom management, lesson plans, knowledge of civil service regulations
Belize	Yes	1 year	Mentoring, professional development activities, performance assessment
Grenada	No	10 days (about 40 hours	Modes of instruction, lesson planning, classroom management, assessment, teacher professionalism
St. Kitts and Nevis	Yes	2 weeks	Classroom management, teacher professionalism, work preparation
St. Vincent and the Grenadines	Yes		Short induction period before the opening of each academic year

Source: World Bank 2012.
Note: OECS = Organization of Eastern Caribbean States.

Belize's teacher induction program is one year long and includes tutoring (observation of classroom practice and feedback) and mentoring (support from a senior colleague), professional development activities (including development of a portfolio as well as the design and implementation of an action-research project), and assessments. The program is "designed to provide [incoming teachers] with sufficient support and structure to enable them to apply what was learnt during their college based study and to refine it in the specific context of the new teacher's school and classroom" (Belize, Ministry of Education 2009). Belize's program appears well designed and consistent with global best practice, but there is unfortunately no research evidence on its implementation or impact.

A key ingredient of effective induction is expert appraisal of new teachers' performance in the classroom and detailed formative feedback. Unfortunately this is rarely embedded in induction programs in a systematic manner. Of the new teachers surveyed under the OECD's Teaching and Learning International Survey (TALIS) 2008, about 75 percent have worked in schools that have formal mentoring or induction programs. However, these teachers report no more frequent assessment and feedback than do teachers without formal induction or mentoring programs (OECD 2013). In fact, TALIS shows wide variation in the amount of mentoring different countries provide to new teachers.

One of the best-regarded programs is Scotland's Teacher Induction Scheme, established in 2002. The program is compulsory for new teachers and lasts one year. During this period, every incoming teacher dedicates at least 30 percent of his or her time to professional development activities outside of class, including whole school initiatives; each teacher also receives 3.5 hours a week of individual mentoring support from an expert teacher. Another feature of the best induction and mentoring programs is strong links to pre-service teacher education. In Scotland, Norway, and the Netherlands, for example, teacher education faculties are partners in the induction and mentoring of new teachers, which generates valuable feedback for the schools on the strengths and weaknesses of their programs in producing qualified new teachers (European Commission 2010).

Effective induction programs go hand in hand with consequential probationary periods. Many more school systems recognize the importance of the latter tool: 80 percent of OECD countries reviewed in 2005 use probationary periods for incoming teachers (OECD 2005). In most of these countries, such as the United Kingdom and New Zealand, probationary periods last for one to two years. In the United States the length of the probationary period varies by state but is about three years on average, with some school systems having recently raised it (for instance, in Chicago it is now four years, and in Michigan, five years). The rationale is to allow more time for assessing new teachers' performance and growth potential and to avoid mistakes in hiring that are difficult to undo. Investing in a well-designed induction program to support new teachers during a multiyear probationary period can help school systems make their new teachers maximally effective as well as spot performance problems early enough to deal with them (OECD 2013).

In Latin America and the Caribbean (LAC), formal probationary periods are rare. Out of seven countries reviewed in a regional study of teacher policies, only two (Colombia and the Dominican Republic) have consequential probationary periods that include a comprehensive assessment of new teachers (Vaillant and Rossel 2006).[1] Many states in Brazil have a formal probationary period before new teachers acquire full civil service status (for instance, two years in Rio Grande do Sul and three in Paraná), but cases of teachers being evaluated and dismissed during these years are exceedingly rare. However, the city of Rio de Janeiro in 2012 launched an innovative and rigorous approach to new teacher induction (box 4.1).

Teacher evaluation

At the heart of most top schools and high-performing education systems is effective evaluation of teachers' performance on a regular basis. At the school level, teacher evaluation plays a critical role in supporting and improving the quality of teachers and in holding them accountable. It plays formative and accountability roles at the system level as well: teacher evaluation identifies overall weaknesses in an education system; it can be used for school and system accreditation; it is an essential platform for rewarding high performers; and it is especially valuable in targeting in-service training to the areas—and the teachers—needing the most help (table 4.2).

For these reasons, many top education systems invest heavily in teacher evaluation. Japan; Republic of Korea; Shanghai, China; and Singapore all have strong systems for comprehensive evaluations of individual teachers' performance at least every few years. As SABER benchmarking data (compiled in Annex 4.1[2]) demonstrates, the experience in Latin America to date is much more limited. Mexico was the first country in the region to introduce a national teacher evaluation and promotion program, the Carrera Magisterial, but the government is currently reshaping its design. Ecuador began implementing teacher performance evaluations in 2007, and Peru is currently designing a comprehensive system. Elsewhere in the region, countries have some elements in place, but they are less comprehensive and systematic. Chile stands out for having put in place in 2003 a comprehensive system of teacher performance evaluation that remains the region's best practice example.

Because teacher evaluation systems are often implemented with other reforms, identifying the impact of an evaluation program on teacher performance is a challenge. However, research on an evaluation system quite similar to Chile's that was adopted in Cincinnati's school district found that the introduction of comprehensive teacher evaluation resulted in higher math scores for students of those teachers randomly selected for performance evaluation in the year of evaluation (0.07 standard deviation

> **BOX 4.1:** *Raising teacher quality through rigorous induction in Rio de Janeiro*
>
> The Rio de Janeiro municipal school system in 2012 introduced a rigorous induction process into the hiring of new teachers. Under the new approach, the traditional process of teacher selection based on formal qualifications and tests of content mastery (*concurso*) has been supplemented with a second stage selection process that focuses on teachers' ability to master new professional development content and the quality of their classroom teaching practice.
>
> The first phase of the selection process requires that candidates obtain a score of at least 60 percent on tests of content mastery and pedagogical theory, with minimum thresholds in each section. Those who pass the first phase take an 80-hour training course on effective classroom management, child development, class preparation, and other hands-on topics. The course content was developed by the city's new Teacher Training Institute (Escola de Formação do Professor Carioca Paulo Freire) and was inspired by the deficiencies in teacher practice identified through classroom observations conducted with the World Bank and good practice techniques presented in books such as *Aula Nota 10* (the Portuguese adaptation of U.S. educator Douglas Lemov's [2010] book *Teach Like a Champion*). The two-week course covers child development and learning styles, classroom management, and teaching practices that keep students engaged. Candidates must score above 60 points on a final exam covering this phase as well.
>
> The final phase is to prepare and teach a sample class to a panel of expert teachers. By integrating a hands-on demonstration of teaching practice into the induction program, the new process seeks to ensure that all new recruits are fully prepared to be effective in the classroom.
>
> The program is too new for data on how the more rigorous induction and two-stage selection process affects teachers' transition to work in schools. But the Rio de Janeiro municipal secretariat reports a significant number of cases where candidates who scored highly on the theory and multiple-choice tests that used to constitute the entire selection process have been eliminated after poor performance on the classroom management and demonstration class segments. This suggests that building these elements into the hiring process allows for a more comprehensive evaluation that may better identify high-potential teachers.

[SD]) and that these impacts increased in subsequent years (0.11 SD, on average). This is important direct evidence that investing in well-designed systems to evaluate teachers at regular intervals and give them feedback on their performance contributes directly to their effectiveness with positive benefits for their students (Taylor and Tyler 2012).

TABLE 4.2: Roles of teacher evaluation

Level ↓	Purpose →	
	Improvement/formative	Accountability/summative
Teacher	Individual staff development	Individual personnel decisions (e.g., promotion)
School	School improvement strategies	School status decisions (e.g., accreditation)
System	Training priorities and targeting	Policy making and resource allocation

Source: World Bank, building on Wise et al. 1985.

Further and more powerful evidence on how well-designed evaluation systems can raise teacher quality comes from a rigorous study of the first three years of experience in Washington, DC, with a teacher evaluation system that is widely considered a best-practice example in the United States. We discuss this later in this chapter (box 4.4).

Key steps in the design of a teacher evaluation system include the following:

- Defining good teaching (creation of national or subnational teaching standards)
- Identifying how good teaching can be measured (developing instruments and processes that can produce valid estimates of different teachers' effectiveness)
- Defining different levels of teacher quality on each dimension of performance
- Linking evaluation results to career development

Defining good teaching

As discussed in chapter 3, the first step in developing a teacher evaluation system is to establish national teaching standards that clearly articulate the competencies and behaviors that good teachers are expected to have and demonstrate. Formally adopted teacher standards are the natural starting point not only for the design of a teacher evaluation system but also for hiring standards, promotion criteria, accreditation standards for pre-service training institutions, and many other core functions. The majority of OECD countries have adopted national teacher standards (European Commission/EACEA/Eurydice 2013).

Most LAC countries do not have teacher standards in place today. It is possible to evaluate some aspects of teacher performance in the absence of explicit standards. The competency tests given to teachers in Ecuador in 2007 as a first effort to benchmark their quality is a good example of a pragmatic approach. However, it is difficult to design a comprehensive teacher evaluation system without a full articulation of what a good teacher must know and be able to do, and the research evidence thus far suggests that teacher evaluation systems based on comprehensive measures of performance have higher validity than evaluations based on a single dimension (such as tests of content mastery) alone. The starting point for countries seeking to raise teacher quality is the definition of teacher standards.

Developing instruments for measuring teacher quality

Once the profile of "what makes a good teacher" has been defined, the second step is to develop valid instruments for measuring key dimensions of this profile. The spectrum includes measures of inputs (teacher content knowledge and teacher preparation) to outputs (teacher practice in the classroom, peer feedback on a teacher's contribution to school processes) to outcomes (student test scores and student or parent feedback). There is growing evidence that combined measures predict teacher quality more accurately than any single measure, and that direct observation of teacher practice in the classroom is a particularly important dimension for robust evaluation (Kane and Staiger 2012). Box 4.2 summarizes recent research on alternative classroom observation instruments for use in teacher evaluation.

BOX 4.2: *Measuring teacher quality with classroom observation instruments*

A three-year research program on how to assess teacher performance (called the Measures of Effective Teaching Project, or MET), funded by the Bill & Melinda Gates Foundation, has studied the use of five different teacher observation tools in almost 3,000 classrooms. This is the second-largest observational study of classroom practice in the world, after the study in Latin American classrooms conducted for this report. An interesting dimension of the MET study is explicit analysis of alternative classroom observation instruments on two criteria: (a) reliability, or the portion of the variance due to differences in teacher practice, rather than variability from the observer, students, or other factors; and (b) correlations between teachers' classroom practice and student outcomes, including test scores, student effort, and students' enjoyment of learning activities led by the teacher.

The classroom observation methodologies studied include (a) the Danielson Framework for Teaching, (b) the Classroom Assessment Scoring System (CLASS), (c) the Protocol for Language Arts Teaching Observations, (d) the Mathematical Quality of Instruction, and (e) the UTeach Teacher Observation Protocol. As each method requires a relatively high degree of training to ensure an adequate degree of inter-rater reliability among observers, the study used videotapes of teachers, which could then be scored multiple times using different instruments. In total, 1,333 teachers were videotaped 7,491 times, with each video scored by at least three different reviewers. Observation results

(continued on next page)

> **BOX 4.2:** *Measuring teacher quality with classroom observation instruments (continued)*
>
> were then correlated with student achievement gains in math and language. Here are the key findings:
>
> - Consistency across the different classroom observation instruments is high: from 85 to 88 percent concordance, suggesting that any of them can be a useful tool for assessing teacher practice.
> - Reliably characterizing an individual teacher's quality requires averaging scores over multiple observations of that teacher's classroom practice.
> - Combining classroom observation scores with students' feedback about their teachers improves the predictive power and reliability of correlations with learning outcomes.
> - Combined measures (e.g., classroom observations plus student feedback) are a more robust predictor of teachers' relative effectiveness than any of the underlying measures alone and are much more robust than formal qualifications, such as years of teaching experience or level of education (graduate degrees).
>
> While the consistency across the different classroom observation instruments is encouraging, the study finds that teacher evaluation is still an imperfect science. Only 7 to 37 percent of the variance in teacher ratings across the observation tools are attributable to persistent differences among teachers. The authors conclude that while classroom observation is a key dimension for a robust system of teacher evaluation, other measures, such as feedback from teachers' peers and students, are important complements that can boost assessments' overall reliability.
>
> *Source:* Kane and Staiger 2012.

Chile now has a decade of experience with its national teacher evaluation program, the Sistema de Evaluación del Desempeño Profesional Docente (Teacher Professional Performance Assessment System), also called Docentemas. The evaluation is mandatory for municipal school teachers, which comprised 44 percent of all basic education teachers in 2012 (Centro de Estudios MINEDUC 2012a). Teachers are evaluated using four instruments, all constructed with Chile's teacher standards (Marco de la Buena Enseñanza [MBE]) as their foundation.

These are the four instruments and their relative weights in the overall assessment score:

- *Self-assessment*: structured questionnaire to prompt teachers to reflect on their teaching performance (10 percent)

- *Portfolio*: teachers submit a written lesson plan and a professionally made videotape of one of their classes (60 percent)
- *Peer interview*: structured questionnaire to examine how the teacher being evaluated would handle different pedagogical challenges, applied by a similar teacher trained to conduct these interviews following a set protocol (20 percent)
- *Third-party reports*: structured questionnaire completed by the school director and a district pedagogical supervisor (10 percent)

The unit cost of each teacher evaluation is approximately US$400; the major cost driver is the labor involved in scoring the portfolios, which requires specially trained teachers, careful review of videotaped lessons, and ongoing supervision from a high-caliber research team that develops and oversees the evaluation exercise (Taut and Sun, forthcoming). Twenty percent of portfolios are double-rated to check consistency, and substantial attention is paid to secure processes for storing and accessing evaluation data.

The evaluation cycle is one school year, from drawing up the list of the approximately 15,000 teachers to be evaluated each year, through communication of final results back to individual teachers. Teachers are given about three months to complete their portfolios, and researchers estimate that the average teacher spends 40 hours on this part of the exercise. More than 70 percent of teachers cite lack of time as their principal difficulty in preparing the portfolio, but teachers also consistently report this as a useful and relevant professional development activity that causes them to interact in meaningful ways with their peers (Taut and Sun, forthcoming). Some of the costs of the evaluation process also have professional development benefits for the participants. For example, approximately 1,300 teachers each year are trained to carry out the peer interviews.

An effective teacher evaluation system meets certain tests. First, it must have technical validity—in that it is able to distinguish between high-, average-, and low-performing teachers in a robust and consistent manner across different evaluators and over time. Second, its results should have consequences for teachers—positively influencing teachers' professional growth and contributing to improved practice, and triggering actions for poor performers. Finally, the results should inform system-wide policy, especially in identifying priority areas for in-service teacher training and targeting specific types of training to the teachers who need them most.

The value of a set of teacher assessment instruments stems from its reliability and validity. That is to say, the instruments must permit consistent measurements regardless of who makes the scoring (reliability) and should measure precisely what it claims to be measuring (validity). Moreover, the instruments should capture elements of teachers' skills and practice that are meaningfully linked to teachers' ability to help students learn and other important system goals. While systematic efforts to validate teacher evaluation systems are rare, they are particularly important with high-stakes evaluations.

In Chile, the university research team contracted to implement Docentemas has made significant efforts to assess the technical validity of its measurements. The researchers have found good alignment between the teacher assessment instruments and the standards for good teaching on which it is based (the MBE), but the domain of content mastery is captured least well. One concern the researchers have raised is that despite the use of a high-caliber academic team with extensive training to evaluate the quality of teachers' portfolio (the sample lesson plan and videotaped lesson), the inter-rater reliability for this component remains below the generally accepted value of 0.8. For this reason, researchers have recommended that teachers' portfolios all be scored by more than one rater, instead of the current protocol of only 20 percent of cases randomly selected to be reviewed twice. The recommendation has significant cost implications, however, which are currently under consideration by the ministry (Taut et al. 2011).

Defining different levels of teacher quality

The third step is to define benchmarks for quality in each performance area. In Chile's teacher evaluation system, scores are calculated for each domain of the MBE framework according to four defined levels of performance: unsatisfactory, basic, competent, and outstanding. Teachers receive scores for each instrument, each domain, and an overall rating (Flotts and Abarzúa 2011) (figure 4.1).

FIGURE 4.1: Performance levels in Chile's teacher evaluation system

Outstanding
Professional performance that clearly and consistently stands out with respect to what is expected in the evaluated indicator. Usually it is characterized by a wide repertoire of behaviors or by pedagogical richness.

Competent
Adequate professional performance. Fulfills what is required to teach professionally. Even though it is not exceptional, it is good performance.
[MINIMUM EXPECTED PERFORMANCE]

Basic
Professional performance that fulfills what is expected but irregularly or occasionally.

Unsatisfactory
Performance that presents clear weaknesses in the evaluated indicator, and these weaknesses affect the teaching significantly.

Source: MINEDUC 2012a.

Underlying each dimension measured by each instrument are specific rubrics and examples, which guide evaluators in differentiating teacher performance levels. Careful definition of the performance domains, rubrics, and examples is essential to increase the reliability of ratings and orient teachers about performance expectations. These definitions are also a tool for training and supervision since they give qualitative information and distinctions that allow for professional discussion and suggested areas of growth.

Figure 4.2 illustrates how each indicator is operationalized, through a detailed rubric that guides evaluators in scoring the portfolio instrument.

Since Docentemas began, more than 70,000 teachers have been evaluated and 14,000 have been evaluated twice (MINEDUC 2012a). In 2012, the most recent round, about 10 percent of teachers were rated outstanding and 67 percent competent, as compared with 6.6 percent and 52.7 percent, respectively, in 2005. It is encouraging that these shares have shown an upward (although not monotonic) trend since the program was introduced. Similarly, the share of unsatisfactory teachers has decreased from 3.5 percent in 2005 to 0.9 percent in 2012 (figure 4.3). It may be premature to conclude that these trends are irreversible, but the ministry believes it reflects progress in consolidating a culture of teacher evaluation and the impact of policies adopted in 2011 (discussed in the next section) to strengthen performance incentives associated with evaluation results.

FIGURE 4.2: Sample performance benchmarks in Chile's teacher evaluation system

Dimension F: classroom learning environment	Indicator: "promoting students' participation in the lesson"
Outstanding	Competent elements PLUS: The teacher encourages student participation in the lesson and explicitly recognizes the value of different opinions and answers as a source of enrichment for the learning process. OR If some students do not spontaneously participate in classroom activities, the teacher uses strategies or actions to promote student involvement.
Competent	The teacher offers opportunities for participation by all students, not just a few. AND **All** opportunities offered by the teacher for student participation are related to the learning objectives and/or content of the lesson.
Basic	The teacher offers opportunities for participation by all students, not just a few. AND **Most** of the opportunities offered by the teacher for student participation are related to the learning objectives and/or content of the lesson.
Unsatisfactory	Does not accomplish some of the Basic elements. OR Most of the time, the teacher does not answer students' questions during the lesson.

Source: Taut and Sun forthcoming.
Note: Actual portfolio scoring rubrics used in the Chilean evaluation system are confidential. This example shows a preliminary version of a rubric used in the past.

FIGURE 4.3: Change in teacher evaluation ratings in Chile,

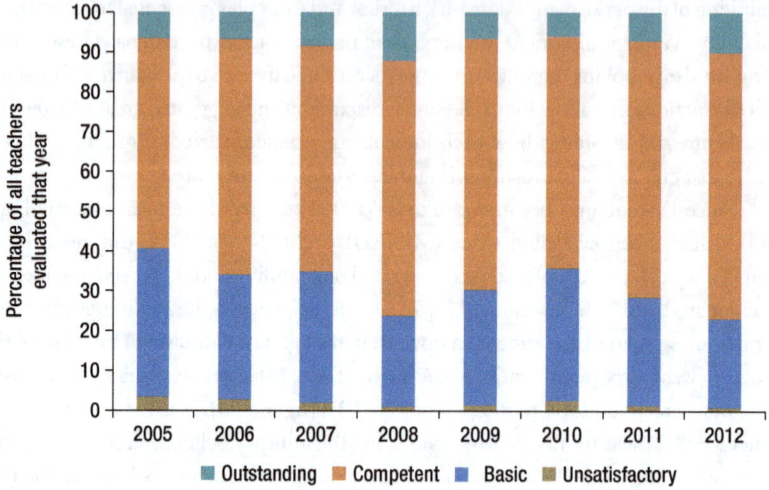

■ Outstanding ■ Competent ■ Basic ■ Unsatisfactory

Source: World Bank, using data from Chile, Ministerio de Educación.

Linking teacher evaluation to career development

The fourth step in establishing a teacher evaluation system is to define its links with teachers' career progression. Investing in a comprehensive system of teacher evaluation is expensive, but it can make other important education system functions more efficient. First, the evaluation process helps teachers improve their performance, by making them more aware of what is expected, and encouraging them to reflect on their classroom practice, pedagogic knowledge, and content mastery. It provides direct, individualized feedback to teachers in contrast to feedback that may not be as forthcoming or insightful from their direct supervisors and peers.

Second, it can make investments in teacher training more efficient and even reduce overall training costs. Teacher evaluation results allow school systems to identify the specific areas where teachers most need training and to develop courses, materials, and methods tailored to these issues. Korea's Teacher Appraisal for Professional Development program requires all teachers to prepare a professional development plan on the basis of their evaluation results and submit it to their school's appraisal management committee. Proposals are consolidated at the level of the local authority and guide the design of professional development programs for the coming year (OECD 2013). In addition to getting overall priorities aligned with system needs, evaluation results allow school systems to target specific types of training to the teachers who need them most.

Third, teacher evaluation systems are an essential platform for performance incentives, as discussed further in chapter 5. When it builds the capacity for systematic evaluation of teacher performance, a school system also gains the power to identify and reward top performers. Chile, Singapore, Finland, Japan, United Kingdom, and different school systems in Germany and the United States all offer financial rewards to teachers evaluated as outstanding. But rewards can also be nonfinancial. In Korea, highly rated teachers are rewarded with a one-year sabbatical to conduct research, which further deepens the system's professional capacity. In addition to supporting positive performance incentives, teacher evaluation systems can strengthen accountability systems. They allow school system managers to identify teachers in need of improvement and create strong incentives for these teachers to pursue the training offered and apply it to their work. Teacher evaluation also gives school systems the data it needs to deal with consistent poor performers forthrightly and transparently. If the general results of schools' teacher evaluations are shared with parents and students, as in Korea (something relatively few systems do), it additionally strengthens school-level accountability.

Finally, evaluation systems provide the soundest basis for long-term grooming of individual teachers' potential and the fairest basis for promotions. Rather than promoting teachers on the basis of seniority alone—as most systems currently do—teachers can be promoted on the basis of recognized competence. A salary structure aligned with evaluated performance creates the right incentives for current teachers and makes the profession more attractive to talented candidates in the future.

Singapore provides an excellent example of a teacher evaluation system fulfilling all of these functions (box 4.3).

In Chile, as in most LAC countries, alternative career streams within education are not as clearly defined as in Singapore. But Chile's teacher evaluations have both positive and negative consequences for teachers (figure 4.4). Teachers rated as outstanding or competent are not evaluated again for four years and are eligible to apply for an individual performance bonus, Asignacion Variable por Desempeño Individual (AVDI), by taking a test of content mastery.

Teachers rated basic must take part in Professional improvement plans (Planes de Superación Profesional [PSPs]), which are delivered by their municipal education system, and be evaluated again in two years (MINEDUC 2012a). Teachers rated unsatisfactory must participate in a PSP and be reevaluated the following year. If on the second evaluation their rating remains unsatisfactory, teachers are dismissed from the public teaching force, receiving a payout proportional to their current salary. If on three consecutive evaluations teachers receive basic ratings, or alternate between basic and unsatisfactory, they are also dismissed (MINEDUC 2012b). In 2012, 42 teachers had to leave the system: 36 as a result of 2 consecutive unsatisfactory ratings, and 6 as a result of 3 consecutive basic ratings. Even though these numbers are low, researchers report evidence that the evaluation's signaling effect leads significantly more low-performing teachers to leave the municipal school system of their own volition, after

BOX 4.3: *Teacher evaluation in Singapore*

Singapore constitutes global best practice in linking teacher evaluation to other aspects of teacher development. Its Enhanced Performance Management System (EPMS), established in 2005, is used as the basis for awarding both short-term monetary rewards (one-year bonuses for outstanding performance) and long-term career planning and promotions. The EPMS evaluates teachers and school directors against the essential competencies (knowledge and skills) required for each of the three professional tracks in Singapore's teaching career: (a) the teaching track, which allows teachers to advance toward the level of "master teacher"; (b) the leadership track, which allows teachers to take on management roles in schools or in the ministry; and (c) the senior specialist track, which allows teachers to support other teachers as pedagogical specialists (see figure B4.3.1). All three tracks provide substantial room for professional growth and financial compensation. The focus of EPMS is the development of teachers and future leaders and involves a cycle of yearly performance planning, coaching and support, evaluation, and promotion decisions.

FIGURE B4.3.1: Singapore's three professional tracks in education

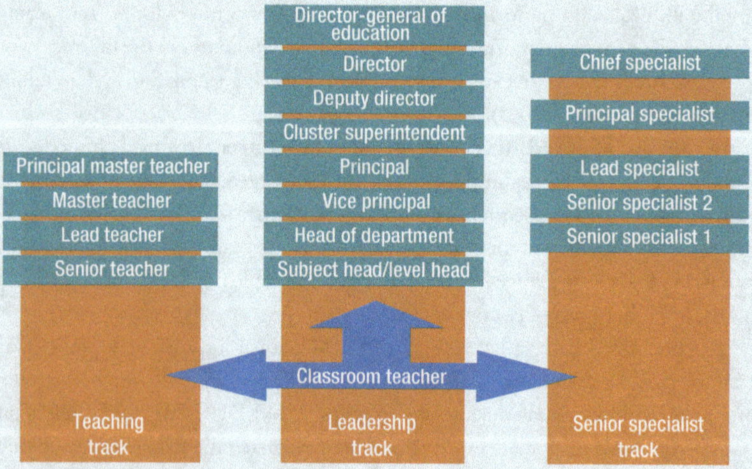

Teaching track	Leadership track	Senior specialist track
Principal master teacher	Director-general of education	Chief specialist
Master teacher	Director	Principal specialist
Lead teacher	Deputy director	Lead specialist
Senior teacher	Cluster superintendent	Senior specialist 2
	Principal	Senior specialist 1
	Vice principal	
	Head of department	
	Subject head/level head	

Classroom teacher

Sources: OECD 2013; Singapore, Ministry of Education.

FIGURE 4.4: Consequences of teacher evaluations in Chile

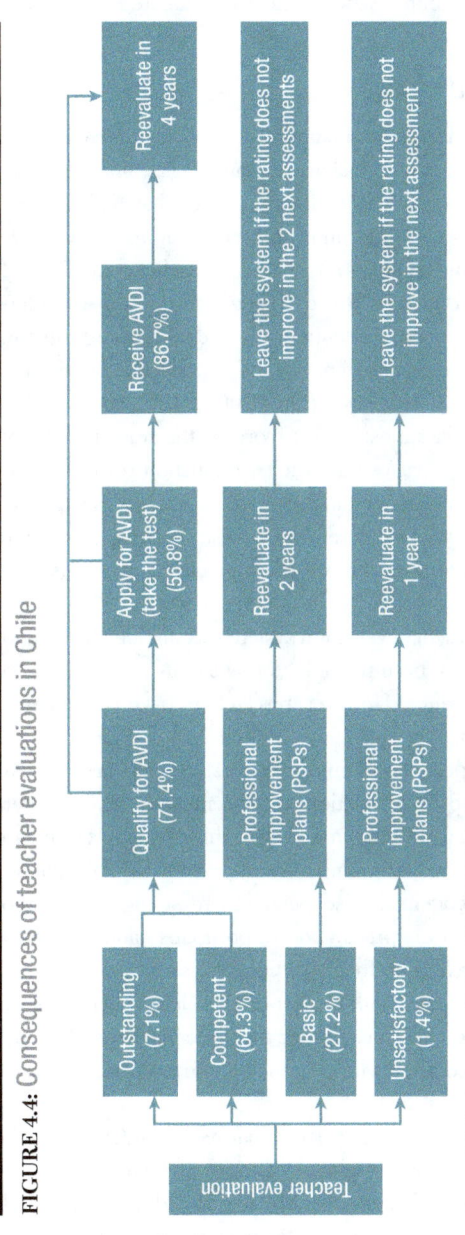

Source: World Bank, based on data from Chile, Ministerio de Educación.
Note: AVDI = Asignación Variable por Desempeño Individual; PSP = Planes de Superación Profesional. Teachers rated outstanding or competent may apply for the AVDI performance bonus at any point in the next three years. Hence, the number of AVDI applicants in a given year may be higher than the number of teachers rated outstanding or competent in that year. When teachers from previous cohorts are included, the share of eligible applicants who take the AVDI test is 36 percent.

one unsatisfactory rating or two consecutive basic ratings. Data from 2007–09 show that teachers who have received at least one unsatisfactory rating have a 32 percent probability of leaving the public school system, as compared to 11 percent among those who never received such a rating.

Implementation and impact

Given their high stakes, teacher evaluation systems—like student assessment systems—pose important implementation challenges. Protecting the integrity of system processes and system data is fundamental. Colombia's 2002 Estatuto de Profesionalización Docente (EPD), discussed further in chapter 5, introduced new systems for teacher certification, training, and compensation based on teacher evaluations performed at the school level by school directors. However, in the decade since its adoption, the EPD has not shown evidence of positive impacts on student learning outcomes; researchers point to a lack of rigor and consistency in the implementation of teacher evaluations by school directors as a likely reason (Ome 2009; Galvis and Bonilla 2011). Almost all public teachers receive almost perfect scores in the evaluation. It appears from the experience in Colombia that vesting teacher evaluation responsibility exclusively in school directors poses reliability and incentive issues. It is difficult to ensure consistency in the standards used by different directors and, perhaps more important, school directors face mixed incentives if they believe positive evaluations may help motivate their team and negative ones may create conflict.

Because Chile's teacher evaluation system was implemented nationally (with no control group), it has not been possible to evaluate its causal impact on teacher and school system performance. However, researchers have studied several important aspects of the program. First, qualitative studies show that initial teacher resistance to the program has disappeared over time; a recent study of 30 schools across 10 municipalities reveals overall positive reactions to Docentemas. School leaders report using the results to give special recognition to their highly evaluated teachers and to develop remedial actions for lower performing teachers, even beyond the nationally mandated consequences. The program is also perceived to strengthen collaboration among teachers—particularly in the preparation of portfolios—and to improve teaching by requiring teachers to reflect on their practice. In most schools, school leaders report that this reflection takes place both at the individual level and in a coordinated fashion at the school level. In teachers' perception, the principal downside to the system is the increased workload associated with carrying out the evaluations, especially in preparing the portfolio (Taut et al. 2011).

The studies available to date suggest that results of Chile's teacher evaluations are a reasonably robust predictor of student achievement on the national standardized student test Sistema de Medición de la Calidad de la Educación (SIMCE). Regression analysis shows statistically significant differences between the scores of students who had teachers rated insufficient and students of teachers rated competent (3.8 points or 0.08 SD higher for the latter) or outstanding (9.3 points or 0.19 SD higher).[3]

Correlations with learning outcomes are highest for teachers' scores on the portfolio, where 1 extra point in a teacher's score is associated with 8 extra points in math and 6 in reading for the teacher's students. For the supervisor assessment, 1 extra point in the teacher's score is associated with 4.2 extra points in math and 2.2 in reading, and for the peer interview, 1 extra point in the teacher's score is correlated with 2.6 extra points in math and 1 in reading. Teachers' self-evaluation results show no association with student learning (Centro de Estudios MINEDUC 2012b). A study using hierarchical models to analyze panel data with SIMCE scores between 2004–06 finds that teachers' value-added learning results in math and (to a lesser extent) in reading had a significant correlation with their evaluation results, again particularly with those of the portfolio (Taut et al. 2011).

A study looking at the cumulative effects of students' exposure to highly rated teachers also finds positive correlations at all levels of socioeconomic status (figure 4.5). On average, grade 4 students exposed to three or four competent or outstanding teachers during their first four years of schooling have test scores about 0.24 SD higher than those with no such exposure to high-quality teachers. At the secondary level, the cumulative effects are even higher: students with two competent or outstanding teachers over their schooling career have average scores 15 points (about 0.3 SD) higher than those without such exposure, which is a large effect. The size of these effects is also relatively larger and shows more robust levels of statistical significance for students from lower socioeconomic backgrounds (MINEDUC 2009).

Core strengths of Docentemas are that it is grounded in clear standards and rubrics, includes objective performance evidence such as the teacher portfolio, and uses external observers who are extensively trained to improve reliability.[4] However, Chile's system also faces implementation issues. Researchers note that there exists a black market for portfolios (sample lesson plans and videotaped classes); there is no law against the sale of these materials; and if a teacher is found to have submitted false instruments, his or her evaluation for that year is nullified, but there are no other consequences (Taut and Sun, forthcoming). There are also concerns that the rubric used in peer evaluations may be leaked to some teachers, which aids them in preparing for the interview.

Perhaps most important, the stakes around Chile's evaluations—both positive and negative—have to date been relatively low. Teacher promotions continue to be determined by seniority, with no link to performance evaluations. Positive evaluations allow teachers to pursue the AVDI performance bonus. But despite an increase in 2011, the bonus size is relatively small, and the test of content mastery required to access it is perceived as challenging. A significant share of eligible teachers decided it was not worth the effort. For teachers receiving poor evaluations (basic or unsatisfactory), oversight of follow-up actions is often weak. While these teachers are required to participate in remedial training programs, the PSPs, a study found that in 2009 only half of them actually did so, and there is no sanction for noncompliance (Cortés and Lagos 2011).

FIGURE 4.5: Test scores for students exposed to outstanding or competent teachers in Chile, by socioeconomic level of students)

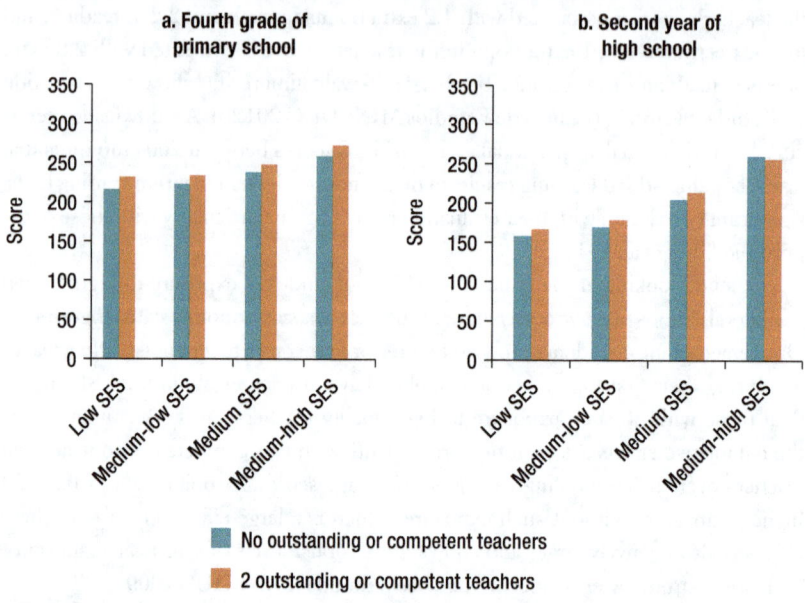

Source: MINEDUC 2009.
Note: All differences are statistically significant except for students in the top quintile in the second year of high school. SES = socioeconomic status.

Delivering on the goals of a well-conceived teacher evaluation system clearly depends not only on getting the design right but also on developing robust processes and ensuring that they are implemented with integrity. These tasks are capacity intensive and costly. However, the experience to date with Washington, DC's teacher evaluation system suggests that the payoffs to getting it right can be even larger (box 4.4).

In-service training

In every education system in Latin America, in-service teacher training is a major element of nonsalary spending. Although consolidated data are rarely reported, when the cost of staff time is added, total investments in training are very large. In Brazil and Mexico, secondary education teachers participate in 21 and 35 days of in-service professional development, respectively, representing more than one month of teacher time annually (OECD 2009).

Despite the resources invested in teacher training, rigorous evaluations of its effectiveness are rare across the OECD and almost nonexistent in LAC countries.

BOX 4.4: *Raising quality through teacher evaluation in Washington, DC*

The best-practice model of teacher evaluation in the United States is widely considered to be Washington, DC's system, called IMPACT. Although the teachers' union bitterly fought its initial adoption in 2009, IMPACT survived politically and is now in its fifth year of implementation. After the Obama Administration's US$5 billion Race to the Top grant competition made reform of teacher performance evaluation an explicit criterion, at least 20 states, including New York, and hundreds of U.S. school districts have begun to adopt systems similar to IMPACT.

IMPACT has three core elements: (a) establishment of clear teaching standards (called the "9 Commandments of Good Teaching"); (b) a comprehensive annual process for review of teachers' performance; and (c) high-powered performance incentives, with large financial rewards for effective teachers and strong negative consequences (outright dismissal) for ineffective ones. Prior to IMPACT, the DC chancellor observed, "Only 8 percent of DC's eighth graders were on grade level in math and only 12 percent in reading, yet the vast majority of teachers were 'exceeding expectations' on their annual performance reviews; the teacher evaluation system was broken" (Turque 2010).

Elements of the IMPACT design that have attracted praise include the use of multiple measures of teacher performance, with a strong emphasis on classroom practice; the use of highly experienced "master educators" for external assessment of teacher performance; provision of substantial, detailed feedback to teachers; one-on-one coaching available on demand to help teachers improve; and high-powered incentives and accountability for evaluation results. (Examples of IMPACT feedback to a teacher and a typical teacher evaluation report used in other urban school districts may be compared in Annex 4.3.)

Teachers are rated as highly effective, effective, minimally effective, and ineffective. Ratings are heavily based on direct observation of every teacher in the classroom on five different occasions each year, two by master educators and three by school administrators (75 percent of the evaluation). Other elements are (a) commitment to school community (assessed by principals, 10 percent); (b) core professionalism (assessed by principals, 10 percent); and (c) the school's value-added learning gains for the year (5 percent). For the 20 percent of teachers who teach math and language in grades that are tested every year, the classroom observation weight is reduced and complemented with the value-added learning gains for a teacher's students.

Much of the initial controversy around IMPACT stemmed from the strength of its performance incentives. Teachers deemed ineffective are fired immediately, and about 4 percent of the teaching force has been dismissed outright each year. Highly effective teachers receive very large one-time bonuses (up to US$25,000), and those rated highly

(continued on next page)

BOX 4.4: *Raising quality through teacher evaluation in Washington, DC*
(continued)

effective in two successive years receive permanent pay increases (up to US$27,000 per year). These are large financial rewards in relation to the US$50,000 average starting salary and have built political support for the system among teachers. Some elements of the IMPACT design—such as annual reviews of all teachers, multiple classroom observations by highly trained external experts, and high financial rewards—may not be easily transferable to larger school systems, however. Washington, DC, has only 120 schools and 2,600 teachers and has benefitted from an unusual degree of private sector support. After national attention was focused on the city's disastrous prior performance, with the lowest student test scores of any urban district, the Bill & Melinda Gates Foundation provided initial funding for IMPACT's substantial startup costs and outsized teacher bonuses.

In this context, the first rigorous academic study of the IMPACT program has attracted substantial attention. Using a regression discontinuity method to analyze the behavior of teachers just above and below the evaluation system's different performance thresholds, researchers Dee and Wyckoff (2013) documented a substantial, 10 point (.2 SD) improvement in overall teacher ratings over the first three years of the program. In other words, as shown in figure B4.4.1, the entire DC teaching force has shifted significantly in the direction of higher quality in this relatively short period.

Dee and Wyckoff (2013) conclude the improvement in teacher quality is a direct result of the evaluation system. They document the change in the teaching force that occurred through four main mechanisms: (a) voluntary attrition of teachers with low performance ratings (increased by over 50 percent compared with previous years); (b) low-rated teachers who decided to stay in the system achieved big improvements in performance (0.27 SD, on average); (c) a higher share of top teachers stayed in system than in previous years; and (d) teachers at the threshold for bonuses also made big improvements (0.24 SD, on average).

These different responses by teachers to their evaluation feedback are consistent with broader research evidence on the design of effective performance incentives, which suggests that it is critically important that individuals see the system as "effort responsive"—in this case, that teachers have the knowledge and support to believe that their efforts can result in desired improvements. Consistent with this, expectations for teacher performance are clearly communicated, and support to meet those expectations (instructional coaches) is available. Dee and Wyckoff (2013) also present early evidence that IMPACT is affecting longer term dynamics of teacher supply by attracting higher caliber

(continued on next page)

BOX 4.4: *Raising quality through teacher evaluation in Washington, DC*
(continued)

FIGURE B4.4.1: Change in Washington, DC's teacher quality since introduction of teacher evaluation

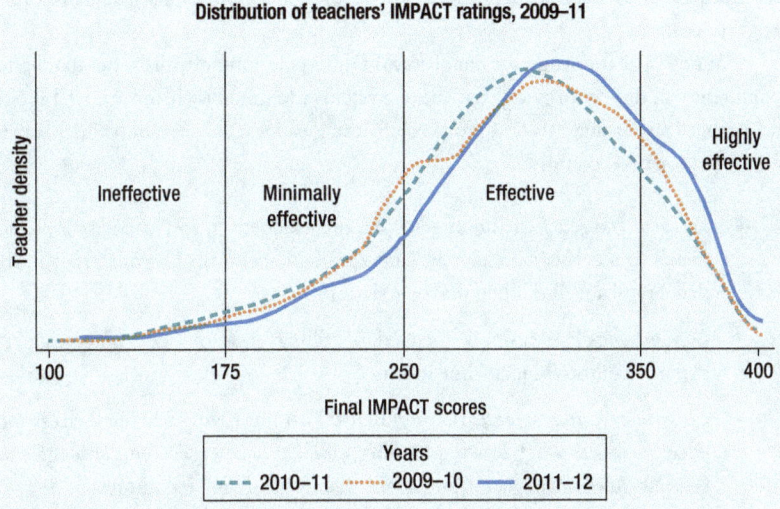

Source: Dee and Wyckoff 2013.

individuals into the system: teachers who left the DC public schools at the end of 2010–11 had average evaluation scores of 255 out of 400 in their last year, while newly hired teachers in 2011–12 averaged 281 out of 400 in their first year—a difference of 0.5 SD.

The researchers cannot disentangle the impact of teacher evaluation feedback alone from the strong incentives embodied in the DC program. But they conclude that Washington, DC's experience shows that high-powered incentives linked to a well-designed teacher evaluation system can substantially improve teacher quality in a relatively short period. Not only teacher quality has improved; since IMPACT was introduced, student learning gains in the Washington, DC, school system have been the largest of any urban district in the United States.

The evidence on the relatively small share of programs that have been evaluated rigorously is not encouraging (Glewwe et al. 2013). A few studies show student learning gains as a result of in-service teacher training programs (Cohen and Hill 2001). However, two meta-analyses actually find negative impacts for some programs (Kennedy 1998; Yoon et al. 2007). (The studies reviewed by Yoon et al. are summarized in Annex 4.4.)

Given huge heterogeneity in teachers' training needs, country contexts, program design, content, delivery mechanisms, and training intensity, it is perhaps not surprising that the evidence on impact is mixed. The most common conclusion of studies in this area is that the relevance of program content, the intensity and duration of the training, and the quality of the delivery are key for impact. However, these observations are unsatisfying as a guide to policy in this area because they abstract from the central question of how to design relevant program content.

Our review of the academic literature and different training approaches that figure prominently in the "improving" education systems identified by Mourshed, Chijioke, and Barber (2011) suggests that four broad strategies for teacher training are likely to be relevant for LAC countries:

- *Scripted approaches*: training to prepare teachers in low-capacity environments to use specific teaching strategies and accompanying materials in the delivery of a well-defined daily curriculum

- *Content mastery*: training focused on filling gaps or deepening teachers' expertise in the subjects they teach

- *Classroom management*: training focused on improving teachers' classroom effectiveness through lesson planning, efficient use of class time, strategies for keeping students engaged, and more effective teaching techniques

- *Peer collaboration*: school-based or cross-school structured opportunities for small groups of teachers to observe and learn from each other's practice and collaborate on curriculum development, student assessment strategies, research, and other activities that contribute to system quality as well as teachers' professional development

A fifth strategy, which is common in LAC, is to finance or otherwise incentivize teachers' pursuit of additional formal education, notably master's or even doctoral degrees. We do not include this in the discussion, because school systems do not have direct responsibility for designing and delivering these courses. But we know of no evaluations in this area that suggest this approach is cost-effective. Indeed, the current global evidence, presented in chapter 1, is that differences in teachers' individual effectiveness (i.e., ability to produce value-added learning gains) show little correlation with their formal level of education.

Table 4.3 highlights the small body of rigorous evaluation evidence (published academic studies) relating to the four categories above that is most relevant for Latin America's schools. Several of the evaluated programs overlap across categories. The Liberia program evaluated by Piper and Korda (2010) is probably the closest in design to programs currently being used in Haiti and to improve early grade literacy teaching in Brazil.

TABLE 4.3: Rigorous evaluation evidence on the impact of teacher training

Country and authors	Impact of teacher training on … (SD)			Type of training and evaluation design
	Teacher knowledge	Teacher practice	Student learning; subject area	
Scripted training				
Honduras (McEwan et al. forthcoming)	NM	NM	0.25 increase in math and 0.17 increase in language scores compared with students in nonprogram villages	2-week training course before each trimester for alternatively certified "tutors" in use of specially designed Sistema de Aprendizaje Tutorial (SAT) textbooks and workbooks (matching)
Liberia (Piper and Korda 2010)	NM	NM	0.79 improvement in reading skills (~3 years of schooling)	Week-long training in prepared daily reading lesson plans (random assignment)
Brazil (Ceará state) (Costa and Carnoy, 2014)	NM	NM	0.10 increase in language and 0.17 increase in math scores on national test	Monthly training for teachers in use of new early grade reading materials; financial rewards for municipalities with largest 3rd grade literacy gains (difference-in-differences)
Latin America[a] (Chesterfield and Abreu-Combs 2011)	Inconsistent	Positive significant effects	Positive significant effects	Continuous teacher training during school year in pedagogical materials, techniques, and diagnostic skills (staggered time series)
Content mastery				
United States (McCutchen et al. 2002)	7.5 percentage point increase	0.72 and 0.82 for a subset of activities	50 percent increase (one measure), 0 (another measure) in reading	2-week training in content mastery in literacy (random assignment)
United States (McCutchen et al. 2009)	0.50	0.64	0.44 to 0.49 improvement in reading	2-week training in content knowledge and content-specific pedagogy in literacy (random assignment)
United States (Garet et al. 2008)	0.37 (training) 0.38 (training, coaching)	0.33 (training) 0.53 (training, coaching)	Zero impact on reading	48 hours of training in content knowledge and subject-specific pedagogy in literacy; (for another group) 60 hours of coaching (random assignment)

(continued on next page)

TABLE 4.3: Rigorous evaluation evidence on the impact of teacher training *(continued)*

Country and authors	Impact of teacher training on ... (SD)			Type of training and evaluation design
	Teacher knowledge	Teacher practice	Student learning; subject area	
United States (Webster-Stratton et al. 2008)	NM	Significant improvement on measures of teaching style	Significant improvements in school readiness (discipline)	28 hours of training in classroom management focused on promoting positive behavior (random assignment)
United States (Raver et al. 2008)	NM	Significant improvement in positive climate	Significant improvement in behavior management	30 hours of training in classroom management focused on promoting positive student behavior (random assignment)
Professional interaction				
United States (Perry and Lewis 2009)	No change	NM	No change	Teachers academic content collaboratively (random assignment)

Notes: NM = not measured; SD = standard deviation. All impact estimates are in SD, except where noted.
a. The study included Bolivia, the Dominican Republic, Ecuador, El Salvador, Guatemala, Honduras, Jamaica, Nicaragua, and Peru.

Among the approaches considered global good practice in peer collaboration, teachers work jointly on strategies for math instruction in Japan (Lesson Study), or whole school teams work with external coaches to improve their instruction, as in Ontario, Canada. One application of the Japanese Lesson Study model in the United States (Perry and Lewis 2009) has not been effective, which suggests that this model may not be easy to transplant. But another form of peer collaboration, coaching, has been shown to be effective in Kenya (Hardman et al. 2009) and in the United States (Garet et al. 2008).

It is important to note that most of the carefully evaluated programs are small in scale, with training delivered directly to teachers by experts in the methodologies taught. It cannot be assumed that programs delivered in the "cascade" format that is much more common in developing countries—in which the experts who designed the program train a network of other "trainers" who deliver it to teachers—would have impacts as large as those in, say, the Liberia program. A study in Kenya provides qualitative evidence that teachers find this kind of cascade training—in which teachers are trained and then it is hoped that they will train other teachers in their school—completely ineffective (Hardman et al. 2009).

Scripted training

Many scripted training programs focus on early grade reading, which is both of central importance to learning and a domain where global evidence on effective approaches can guide teacher training design. A well-designed program in Liberia has had very large impacts on student learning across all measurements used: letter naming (0.52 SD), phonemic awareness (0.55 SD), oral reading fluency (0.80 SD), and reading comprehension (0.82 SD). The training program is intensive—involving multiple week-long workshops, monthly coaching sessions, scripted lesson plans for teachers, and corresponding student reading materials. The program also involves teacher outreach to parents to inform them of students' reading progress and strengthening of parent-teacher associations (Piper and Korda 2010). This broad and unified spectrum of intervention is not common in professional development and likely contributes to the large effect size observed.

Another study, this one from Latin America, shows strong positive results from a broad training program that provides detailed materials for teachers to incorporate in their teaching: the Centers of Excellence for Teacher Training program, an initiative supported by the U.S. Agency for International Development and implemented between 2002 and 2009 with the objective of improving early grade literacy levels in LAC through improved reading instruction skills of teachers in marginalized areas. The program uses a combination of training components that includes scripted training and materials, classroom management techniques, research-based reading methodologies, and diagnostic tools. Using data from 255 teachers, the study shows improvements in teaching practices (as measured through standardized classroom observations), teachers' knowledge of how to teach reading (as measured with teacher surveys), and student learning achievement (as measured with standardized tests) (Chesterfield and Abreu-Combs 2011).

A program developed in the Brazilian state of Ceará to promote early grade reading skills, Programa de Alfabetização na Idade Certa (PAIC), uses a well-designed set of workbooks and reading books, just-in-time monthly training sessions for teachers in how to deliver each chunk of the curriculum, and regular monitoring of student progress to ensure that all children acquire basic literacy by age eight. Costa and Carnoy (2014) used a careful difference-in-differences analysis to compare municipalities within the state of Ceará, which received the program, with similar municipalities in bordering states, which did not. They find that PAIC has had significant positive impacts on students' literacy and math skills. Since the Ceará state program combines technical support for scripted teacher training and literacy materials with financial incentives for those municipalities whose eight-year-old students register the largest literacy gains, the evaluation cannot disentangle the relative importance of these two components in the causal impacts. But it is a promising example of a well-designed, scripted literacy training program initially developed in a single Ceará municipality (Sobral) being successfully scaled up to hundreds of municipalities at the state-level. The Brazilian state of Minas Gerais has implemented a similar program over the past six years and has also seen significant improvements in early grade reading scores, although that program has not been rigorously evaluated (Bruns, Evans, and Luque 2012; Mourshed, Chijioke, and Barber 2011). In 2013, the Brazilian federal ministry launched an effort to scale up the PAIC approach nationally.

The Honduras program (Sistema de Aprendizaje Tutorial [SAT]) uses a scripted method to prepare tutors recruited from the community (with less formal training than traditional teachers) to deliver the middle school curriculum. The program is anchored by a well-designed set of workbooks and textbooks, and students work through them under the guidance of the tutors. Tutors receive two weeks of in-service training just prior to each trimester to prepare them to teach the next set of materials. A rigorous evaluation of student performance in communities served by the SAT compared to a control set of communities with traditional middle schools finds that SAT's model of well-designed learning materials combined with scripted training for relatively unskilled teachers produces higher learning results at lower per-student costs than in traditional middle schools.

Most of the evidence on other scripted learning programs is not rigorous, and many results are ambiguous (Glazerman et al. 2010b). While well-designed programs of scripted teacher in-service training can have positive impacts, not all programs do so. The most recent evidence from Liberia and Honduras is encouraging, however, as it suggests that providing teachers with well-designed modular learning materials and "real-time" training offering detailed guidance on what to teach each day can significantly improve student learning in contexts where few other approaches have worked.

Well-designed scripted training programs are a relevant and promising approach in many LAC countries, perhaps especially for early grade literacy instruction and math skills. Scripted training is part of the current strategy in Haiti, where many teachers lack in-depth subject and pedagogic knowledge. They can benefit from detailed guidance on the content that should be covered in each day's lesson, how topics should be presented, how classroom books and other learning materials can be used, and how students' progress can be assessed (World Bank 2011).

A particularly powerful example of a scripted training approach is Colombia's Escuela Nueva program. Developed in the 1970s to improve the quality of multigrade schools in Colombia's sparsely populated, mountainous rural areas, Escuela Nueva represents a deep transformation of the curriculum, materials, classroom organization, and functioning of multigrade schools, and spurred massive a effort to retrain Colombia's 30,000 rural teachers, as described in box 4.5.

Scripted training approaches are useful wherever teacher capacity is low, because they allow a well-designed curriculum and supporting materials such as teachers' guides and student workbooks to provide a "scaffolding" that compensates for weaknesses in teachers' content mastery and teaching skills—for example, in the preparation of effective lesson plans, homework assignments, and quizzes to assess students' progress. Even in high-income countries such as the United States, some well-known scripted methods (e.g., Success For All) are used at the primary and secondary level in many schools, particularly in large urban, low-achievement districts (Kirschner, Sweller, and Clark 2006; Gove and Wetterberg 2011).

Scripted training programs can also prepare teachers to use information and communication technology (ICT) in the classroom. The Roberto Marinho Foundation in Brazil over the past 10 years has trained thousands of teachers in almost every Brazilian state in the use of high-quality video-based instructional programs designed to help overage students get back on grade level by following an "accelerated" curriculum. These programs deliver a well-designed compressed curriculum through videos. Teachers are trained to support the program by facilitating group discussions of the content presented (using teacher guides) and administering and grading regular quizzes and other assessments to ensure that students keep pace. These programs appear to be especially valuable in compensating for weaknesses in teachers' content mastery at the secondary education level and in math and sciences. There have been no rigorous evaluations of the cost-effectiveness of these programs (and the video content and teacher support is fairly expensive), but their popularity with students and apparent effectiveness has led to widespread adoption across Brazil.

Content mastery

The second core strategy is training to deepen teachers' mastery of specific academic content. Several evaluated programs have focused on strengthening teachers' knowledge in the topic of instruction. All three reviewed here focus on content knowledge surrounding literacy (for early grade literacy instruction), in this case ensuring that

BOX 4.5: *Colombia's Escuela Nueva*

Transforming the practice of Colombia's rural multigrade teachers was the core aim of the Escuela Nueva program, developed in the 1970s. The program promotes "whole school" change by shifting the focus of the learning process from the teacher to students, who use self-paced learning materials, tutor each other (cross-peer tutoring), and draw on an "enriched" classroom learning environment, including different *rincones* (corners) equipped with classroom reading materials, games, and manipulatives to support their learning. The program also empowers students to play a leading role in the governance and maintenance of their schools and to involve parents and community members actively in schools (Fundación Escuela Nueva 2012).

The innovation of Escuela Nueva is to recognize that raising the effectiveness of teachers in multigrade classrooms requires new pedagogical practices, curriculum, and classroom level resources specifically designed to support a multigrade environment. Preparing teachers for the program therefore involves not only intensive training in the new curriculum and the use of the new resources (teacher guides, student self-paced learning materials, and enriched classroom resources) but more fundamentally, a move away from traditional frontal teaching and the development of new skills in facilitating groups of students in their own learning process.

Achieving this transformation of teacher practice requires intensive teacher training and sustained support. From the beginning, the program has combined four core strategies: (a) group training in the aims, concepts, materials, and methods of the Escuela Nueva approach; (b) teacher visits to demonstration schools to see the model in action and learn from experienced teachers; (c) ongoing support to teachers through visits from master teachers in their district; and (d) periodic professional development sessions to reinforce and extend their teaching practice (Fundación Escuela Nueva 2012). In the same way that the model encourages cooperation among students, it does so among teachers, who visit each other and provide advice and encouragement.

Research over several decades has shown that students who attend Escuela Nueva schools perform better on standardized tests than students in traditional rural schools. Even more impressively, thanks to Escuela Nueva, Colombia is the only country in Latin America where rural students outperform urban students (controlling for student background characteristic) on national assessments. (Psacharopoulos, Rojas, and Velez 1993; McEwan 1998). Studies have also demonstrated that Escuela Nueva students have higher self-esteem, stronger democratic values, and civic learning (Chesterfield 1994; de Baessa, Chesterfield, and Ramos 2002) and greater gender equality (Juarez and Associates 2003). Over its 40-year history, the Escuela Nueva has influenced the design of similar programs in other countries, ranging from Vietnam to India, Mexico and Brazil.

teachers understand the core concepts of linguistics. Two of them, each providing two weeks of training in linguistics (and one adding a component on linguistic-specific pedagogy) have led to significant increases in student learning (McCutchen et al. 2009). It is notable that effect sizes are not larger in the study that adds content-specific pedagogy. A third study, by Garet et al. (2008), of a program that provides 48 hours of training on second-grade reading instruction finds increases in teacher knowledge and positive changes in teacher practice in the first year of the program. Changes in practice are larger for teachers who received coaching in addition to the training course. However, the differences in practice between trained and untrained teachers disappear after the first year and there are no impacts of the training on student learning, with or without in-school coaching in addition to the training.

Beyond early grade literacy, a suggestive study of in-service training programs given to 1,027 math and science teachers in the United States finds that a focus on content knowledge is associated with significant, positive effects on teachers' self-reported increases in knowledge and skills and changes in classroom practice (Garet et al. 2001). Another suggestive study of several different teacher training programs in Australia finds significant effects on teachers' self-reported classroom practice and student outcomes (Ingvarson, Meiers, and Beavis 2005). Unfortunately, although low mastery of academic content is a documented issue for LAC's teachers and many countries in the region have implemented training programs aimed at filling these gaps, there is no available evidence on the impact of this type of training in the region. But the evidence from elsewhere supports the intuitive belief that improved teacher content knowledge can raise student learning.

Classroom management

Two experimental studies examine the impact of about 30 hours of training in classroom management focused on positive techniques to reduce disruptive student behavior. Both programs show strong positive effects on both teacher practice and on student behavior and school readiness (Webster-Stratton et al. 2008; Raver et al. 2008).

A less rigorous study in Israel finds that weekly training for math and reading teachers designed to boost their instructional techniques plus the provision of supporting materials (teacher guides) produce improvements in students' reading and math performance (Angrist and Lavy 2001). Another program, which trains teachers in how to read with children in the classroom and provides classroom reading books and books for students to take home, shows significant improvements for student reading fluency (McGill-Franzen et al. 1999).

Unfortunately, there is no rigorous evidence on the current wave of teacher training focused on classroom management with the specific goal of improving student performance (e.g., the Lemov *Teach Like a Champion* techniques or the Teach For All methodology). It will be important to evaluate these techniques rigorously, as they hold promise for helping teachers create a classroom environment where every child can focus and learn.

Aside from the programs mentioned above, much of the teacher training delivered in Latin America has been criticized for short duration, low quality, and lack of reinforcement or support once teachers return to their schools (Vaillant 2005; Verzub 2007). The dominant model has training contracted to university education departments that often deliver courses that are theoretical and disconnected from the reality teachers face in the classroom. More than one education minister in LAC has observed that contracting the same education faculties that produce ill-prepared teachers pre-service to provide their further training in-service is an inherently flawed proposition.

A growing number of education ministries in LAC and secretariats in Brazil are creating their own teacher training institutes to take direct control of the content and delivery of in-service training. There is a visible shift in the region toward professional development programs that directly address identified issues, although it is too early to evaluate their effectiveness. For example, the ministries of education in Mexico and Peru; the Brazilian states of Acre, Ceará, Minas Gerais, and Rio de Janeiro; and the municipal secretariats in Rio de Janeiro and Recife are currently developing training programs focused on improving teachers' classroom practice. In Ceará the state government is planning a rigorous evaluation of the impact of this new approach, with random assignment of teachers to different training options and careful measurement of subsequent classroom practice (through classroom observations) and the impacts on student learning. Solid evidence on a well-designed program of this nature could have wide influence in the region.

Another incipient trend is toward school-based development programs, including efforts to promote peer collaboration at the school level. Ecuador now explicitly links teacher training to school results. Rather than all teachers in the system receiving the same training courses, regardless of need, teachers' needs are identified at the school level and colleagues receive training together (Ecuador, Ministerio de Educación 2012). Under Peru's teacher mentoring program, external coaches work with all of the teachers in a school as a team, providing real-time feedback and advice grounded in the coaches' observation of and understanding of the school's context and specific challenges. Under Rio de Janeiro municipality's new Gente and Ginásio Carioca experimental schools, the school week has been extended to free up time for teacher collaboration and team teaching. All of these represent very new approaches for the LAC region and have yet to be evaluated. But the emphasis they place on looking inside schools and classrooms to identify the issues where teachers most need support is promising.

Grooming teachers through school leadership

Producing effective school leaders is as or more important for LAC education systems as grooming better teachers. Leading a school involves diverse tasks—from managing people, finances and infrastructure to developing outreach to the community and engaging parents in their students' education. As discussed in chapter 5, there is growing global evidence that one of the most crucial roles principals play in raising school performance is in attracting talented teachers and encouraging weaker teachers to leave. This requires a capacity to analyze their teachers' instruction and develop their teachers' potential. High-performing education systems pay close attention to how school principals are selected, trained, and developed, placing special emphasis on their role as instructional leaders (Barber and Mourshed 2007).

Paying close attention to the systems for the selection and development of school leaders is particularly important because of the effects that a single principal has on all students in his or her school. Research from the United States throws some light on this issue. Branch, Hanushek, and Rivkin (2013) measured the quality of different principals in Texas from 1995 to 2001 by comparing the actual math achievement of students in each school with the achievement that would be expected based on the characteristics of students in that school (including prior test scores). By analyzing fluctuations in achievement gains correlated with the arrival of a new school principal, the authors were able to isolate the effect of principals from other school factors (such as the socioeconomic composition of students). They find that principals have a statistically and educationally significant effect on learning: a 1 SD increase in principal quality is associated with a 0.05 SD gain in students' math achievement, or about 2 months of additional learning. While this may be a small impact on an individual student, it is multiplied at the school level by hundreds of different students. The researchers also find that higher levels of principal effectiveness are correlated with higher levels of teacher turnover. A key lever of effective principals' impact on schools is through attracting and retaining better teachers and letting worse ones go (Branch, Hanushek, and Rivkin 2013).

For principals to reshape their schools' teaching team or to serve as an effective instructional leader they need to be aware of the strengths and weaknesses of their teachers. That is why an increasing number of countries involve principals (and other members of the school pedagogical support or management team) in teacher evaluation processes. The nature and degree of this involvement varies widely and may include interviews, classroom observations, or review of other teacher assessment instruments such as the self-evaluation and the peer report. As principals' capacity to learn about the strengths and weaknesses of their teaching staff increases, their role in the coordination of in-service training and whole-school development may increase too. Research by Papay and Kraft (2013) confirms the importance of this dimension of principals' leadership. The authors find that the rate at which teacher effectiveness improves varies systematically across schools. Teachers improve most rapidly at schools where they report that their principals promote peer collaboration, provide professional development, and evaluate teacher performance.

Teacher assessment and development is not the only area in which principals can play a transformational role in schools. Resource allocation and management are a key part of principals' competencies, but one for which they are rarely trained.

It is naïve to expect that all principals will have the aptitude, time, and know-how to align resources and pedagogic priorities to maximize the impact of their budgets on student learning.

Despite increasing awareness of the pivotal role of principals, empirical evidence on how to build their skills and effectiveness is sparse. Establishing an effective system for the selection, training, and coaching of school leaders is not an easy task, particularly when an effective system for teacher evaluation has not been consolidated yet, as is the case in most of the LAC region. However, there are good practices both within and outside the region for the development of school leadership that policy makers can adopt incrementally as they develop their systems for assessment, training, and accountability of teachers.

Chile constitutes an example of an incremental strategy for the selection and training of school leaders. Data from a recent Ministry of Education survey suggests that there has been an increase in the share of principals who consider themselves responsible for instructional leadership and not only school management. Between 2004 and 2005, the government of Chile defined the attributes of good school leaders and established a competitive process for the selection of principals (Concha 2007). In 2005, the Ministry of Education defined a "Framework for Good School Leadership" (Marco para la Buena Dirección), which establishes criteria for the training and assessment of principals in the areas of leadership, curriculum management, resource management, and management of the school environment (MINEDUC 2005). More recently, a 2011 law enhanced the selection process and the accountability of principals in municipal schools. Now principals are selected through Chile's senior civil service selection system (Alta Dirección Pública) and sign a performance agreement with the local government in charge of the school they will lead. In 2011, Chile also introduced the Program for the Training of Excellent Principals (Programa de Formación de Directores de Excelencia), which has now trained more than 2,400 principals (out of about 7,000 in the country) in leadership skills through graduate degrees.

While the Chilean approach to leadership development allows principals to choose among a wide variety of training options, several OECD countries have chosen to develop in-house principal training. Australia in 2010 set up the Australian Institute for Teaching and School Leadership, an independent body supported by the Ministry of Education, to develop standards, accreditation, and training for both teachers and school leaders (OECD 2013). Another example of in-house, proactive principal training is provided by Singapore. In Singapore, young teachers are continuously monitored for leadership potential early in their careers. Those selected for the leadership track are trained in the Management and Leadership in Schools program offered by the National Institute for Education (OECD 2013). Centralized training for principals has recently been adopted by Jamaica, which has established the National Center for Educational Leadership, with the mission of providing training and certification for aspiring and existing principals.

Once principals are selected and trained, support during their early years of work is critical. A recent study analyzes data from New York City schools and finds that, while principals' prior work experience has no effect on their performance, on-the-job experience—particularly during the first few years—has a significant positive effect on school performance, as measured by student exam scores and student absenteeism (Clark, Martorell, and Rockoff 2009). Singapore is a leading example of a system that organizes experienced principals to mentor new ones.

Challenge and promise of information technology

Laptops, tablets, smart phones, digital whiteboards, video-based instruction, and many other technologies are increasingly found in Latin America's classrooms. However, there is a near complete lack of evidence to date that ICTs have improved student learning outcomes in LAC, or are an effective use of budget resources as compared to other potential interventions. A 2012 evaluation of the One Laptop Per Child (OLPC) initiative in Peru finds no effects on student enrollment or student achievement in math or language (Cristia et al. 2012). An evaluation of the Computers for Education program in Colombia similarly finds no student learning improvements despite improved computer access for students and teacher uptake of training on ICT use in the classroom (Barrera-Osorio and Linden 2009). The authors find that teachers tend not to integrate the computers into classroom practice; actual use of computers among students and teachers is only slightly raised by the program; and that, when the computers are used, it is mostly to teach information technology skills and not Spanish, which is the focus of the program.

These studies point to the importance of carefully thought-out implementation strategies for introducing ICTs in the classroom. A randomized control trial with 50 schools and over 2,000 students in western India between 2004 and 2006 found that the introduction of the same computer-assisted learning (CAL) program for math had very different impacts depending on its mode of delivery. In one treatment group, the CAL program supplemented regular classes, with one additional hour of CAL instruction every day after school. In another treatment group, the CAL program was provided as a substitute, with one hour of CAL instruction every day in place of one hour of regular instruction. When compared to the control group, the supplemental CAL program *raised* math scores by 0.28 SD, while in the substitution group it *lowered* scores by an even larger amount, 0.57 SD. The analysis also showed that the biggest impacts of the supplemental CAL program were in raising the learning of the worst performing students, which is consistent with the CAL program design, which aims at reinforcing material presented in regular daily lessons (Linden 2008). A similar program that introduced two hours per week of student work with educational software to reinforce math content presented in class was subject to a randomized experiment, and it found very significant increases in student learning, too: 0.36 SD in the first year and 0.54 SD in the second (Banerjee et al. 2007).

In general, the introduction of ICTs in the classroom is most likely to have a positive impact on student learning when the focus is not on hardware and software but on how these contribute to learning itself. A number of factors appear important for educational ICT programs to improve learning: (a) adequate ICT skills training and hands-on technical and pedagogical support for teachers so that their teaching styles, the curriculum, and the technology can be aligned; (b) sustained support from school leaders; (c) adequate systemwide infrastructure, including ICT hardware, backups, and real-time technical support; and, crucially, (d) a clear strategy defining how ICTs are to be integrated with teaching and put at the service of learning (Barber and Mourshed 2007). These factors are closely aligned with the four forward-looking priorities outlined in a recent report led by Michael Fullan on Uruguay's OLPC program, Plan Ceibal (Fullan, Watson, and Anderson 2013).

Adequate training for teachers in ICTs and their use in the classroom is critical, although as many school systems have observed, teacher proficiency levels rise quickly as younger teachers are hired. In the OECD's 2008 TALIS study, more than one-third of teachers in Brazil report high need for skills training in the use of ICTs (OECD 2013). While teacher training programs in developing countries have tended to focus on basic computer literacy, in high-income countries they focus increasingly on the integration of technology and pedagogy. Along this spectrum, there is a growing body of tested training programs that can be replicated or adapted to local needs. An example is Intel's Teach to the Future program, which has trained more than 10 million teachers in over 70 countries (including 7 in the LAC region) on the integration of technology into the classroom and the promotion of student-centered approaches through a series of flexible modules. Unfortunately, there is no evaluation evidence to date on the effectiveness of this program in raising teachers' skills or its impact on ICT use in classrooms, except for the evaluations in Colombia and Peru, which found no positive impacts (Barrera-Osorio and Linden 2009; Cristia et al. 2012).

Countries in Asia and the Pacific exemplify good practice in raising teachers' tech literacy and putting these skills at the service of learning. In Singapore, both pre-service and in-service teacher training curricula integrate pedagogy and ICT. In-service training for the use of ICT is provided in three levels: basic, for learning to use learning resources on computers; intermediate, for integrating ICT into the curriculum and developing ICT-based learning activities; and advanced, for designing project-based ICT lessons and mastering cutting-edge educational technologies. Training not only teachers but also principals is important to provide the support needed for a successful ICT endeavor and to maximize the impact of technology in the school.

A number of policy lessons emerge from the Asian experience. First, the starting point should be the articulation of ICT policy goals that are linked to education and development goals for the country; these can then be operationalized in standards for ICT competencies for students, teachers, and principals. Second, ICT training must be well-integrated into the rest of teacher training, with the core goal of preparing teachers to support student learning. Training programs should emphasize the rationale for the use of ICTs in the classroom and the role of teachers in this new environment. This motivational aspect is critical for unlocking teachers' interest and potential as users of ICT (UNESCO 2003).

Beyond their role supporting students in the classroom, ICTs are increasingly used as a delivery channel for teacher training. They lower the costs and expand the content available to (a) train teachers across wide geographic areas with large economies of scale; (b) use teachers' time more efficiently at school or at home; (c) provide individualized feedback in a systematic manner through exercises and tests; and (d) promote the emergence of communities of practice and professional support through online forums, which can be especially valuable for teachers in isolated areas.

Initiatives that use ICTs to train teachers are spreading quickly in Latin America and the Caribbean and giving rise to interesting innovations. At the regional level, networks with course offerings include the Inter-American Teacher Education Network, an initiative launched in 2010 by the Organization of American States that provides an interaction-driven platform for teachers in the Americas to share best practices and knowledge and to take online courses on the use of ICTs in the classroom.

Online teacher training platforms have also emerged at the national level, such as Chile's Innovate to Improve program (Innovar para Ser Mejor). This program, developed by the Ministry of Education, supports online learning for teachers in municipal and private subsidized schools. Courses are developed by expert teachers for teachers, and are designed to address weaknesses identified by Chile's teacher evaluation system (e.g., secondary school teachers' math and science content mastery). Each module has three parts: (a) what do I need to know? (b) how do I teach it to my students? and (c) how do I assess students' learning progress? Specific, actionable tools and examples are provided in each module to help teachers apply their new skills and content in the classroom. Participating teachers receive active support from online tutors who facilitate the forums and provide individualized feedback. Tutors are selected from the ministry's Teachers of Teachers Network, which identifies outstanding teachers and provides them with specific training in how to facilitate online courses. Innovar para ser Mejor tries to stimulate the emergence of communities of practice, by encouraging teachers to enroll in courses with other colleagues at the same school. Enrollment is free and those who finish each course receive a certificate. Unlike some other online in-service training models, Innovar para Ser Mejor has fixed periodicity, in that teachers enroll in a given course for 62 to 80 hours in a period of 2 to 3 months, with about 8 to 10 hours of work per week. This helps ensure that online tutoring resources are efficiently deployed.

Another interesting initiative is the State of São Paulo's Escola de Formação e Aperfeiçoamento de Professores Paulo Renato Costa Souza (EFAP). Created in 2009, this school combines virtual and classroom learning. The virtual learning component uses videoconference and teleconference facilities as well as online learning and collaboration tools integrated under a single program called Rede do Saber (Knowledge Network). This network spans 273 dedicated videoconference and online learning rooms in 91 locations across the state. EFAP and the Knowledge Network have supported over 6 million hours of ICT-mediated training and collaboration by teachers. A final innovative example is the online teacher support platform developed by teachers themselves in the Rio de Janeiro municipality, called Educopedia (box 4.6).

There is clearly substantial innovation going on in Latin America and the Caribbean with the application of ICTs to teaching, teacher training, and student

---

BOX 4.6: *Rio de Janeiro's Educopedia*

In 2010, the Rio de Janeiro municipality launched Educopedia, a collaborative online platform of lessons open to students and teachers from all public schools. Educopedia's goals are to support teachers in creating and sharing innovative teaching materials online and to increase students' motivation to learn, by offering stimulating multimedia resources in the classroom.

The lessons available online cover math, Portuguese, science, history, geography, English, music, and physical education, and they are organized by grade and week of the curriculum. Each Educopedia module consists of a lesson plan to help teachers structure the class; supporting content such as PowerPoint presentations on new material and texts, videos, and games; interactive resources such as a chat system, a digital library (Educoteca), quizzes (Educoquiz), summaries (Educosíntese), and sets of test questions (Máquina de Teste). Educopedia materials are projected on digital whiteboards.

Educopedia was initially designed in partnership with a private company and with the Federal University of Rio de Janeiro. When the program was initially piloted low levels of teacher take up encountered in the classroom observations conducted in collaboration with the World Bank was an issue identified in almost all disciplines. The secretariat responded by asking the network of teachers that produces and assesses the adequacy and quality of the online materials (soon nicknamed "Educopedistas") to reach out to colleague teachers and provide hands-on support in the use of the new resources.

Today, Educopedia operates in all 700 Rio de Janeiro municipal schools and serves 680,000 students; 50 percent of teachers report that they use the tool more than once a week. The impact of Educopedia on student learning has not been evaluated yet, but the secretariat believes its effects on the motivation of both teachers and students are positive. In a recent survey, 80 percent of Rio de Janeiro municipal students agree that Educopedia contributes to their learning process, particularly through the interactive exercises and educational games.

learning. It is unfortunate that there is little rigorous evidence on the impact of these creative and sometimes costly investments and programs. Our review found only one study of the impact of ICT-delivered teacher training and, in this case, only indirectly. A randomized study conducted with 78 secondary teachers in the United States included face-to-face workshops and over-the-phone coaching based on digitally uploaded videos of classroom practice. The training focused on interactions between students and teachers and found a significant increase in student test scores following the year of training, although it was not possible to isolate the impacts of the ICT and in-person components of the training (Allen et al. 2011). The classroom-video approach used in the study is coming into wider use. For example, the Measures of Effective Teaching Study conducted by the Bill & Melinda Gates Foundation used classroom video to analyze thousands of hours' worth of teacher practice, and this approach is becoming more common internationally. However, to date there is still little evidence on the relative cost-effectiveness of classroom observations and teacher feedback mediated by different technologies. While there is genuine reason to project large benefits from ICT-supported teacher training and online teacher collaboration in the coming years, particularly as a support for teachers in remote rural areas, expectations are ahead of the evidence at present.

Conclusions

Given the low quality of teachers at entry in Latin America and the Caribbean, policy makers face an important challenge in making teachers as effective as possible throughout their career. Ensuring that teachers are supported and mentored during their first five years on the job is critical to maximize their potential. Systemwide induction programs, which are still rare in the region, are an underutilized tool to improve the quality of teachers when they are at their most malleable. Induction programs are particularly useful when combined with early assessments and probationary periods with consequences. It is a mistake to let the lack of a comprehensive teacher evaluation system result in virtually automatic passage from probation to tenure. Even with a sound teacher evaluation system, it is more costly and complicated to deselect poor performing teachers once they have tenure. There is a high payoff to effective screening and support in the first several years, but it requires the institutional capacity to mentor and assess teachers and to act on the results.

Putting in place a sound system of teacher evaluation is expensive and institutionally challenging, but it is the essential backbone for a high-performing education system. In every area of life, changing adult behavior requires feedback. Individual teachers cannot automatically improve their practice or make the most of training opportunities unless they are guided to do so. From a system standpoint, aggregate information about teachers' strengths and weaknesses is necessary for ministries to identify training priorities and target offerings to teachers who need them most.

If the benefits of more cost-effective training design and delivery are appropriately captured, the net costs of a teacher evaluation system may be low.

Recent research offers valuable guidance on the design of teacher evaluation systems. It indicates that evaluations must be comprehensive. Teacher self-assessments or principal assessments are insufficient on their own. Student learning outcomes should logically be considered, but the reality is that no LAC country has the quantity and quality of classroom-level learning data required to measure learning results for individual teachers. Even systems with high levels of student testing, such as Washington, DC, can generate data on classroom-level test score gains for only 20 percent of its teachers. A more practical strategy is to incorporate school-level learning gains into the performance reviews for all of the teachers in a school, but with a relatively minor weight.

The evidence is now compelling that the most important element in a robust and meaningful teacher evaluation system is direct observation of classroom practice by trained external observers, preferably on unannounced visits and multiple occasions. Research also suggests that student feedback can be valuable. Classroom observation by outside experts is expensive and—probably an even more binding constraint—capacity intensive. It needs to be phased in over a period of years. But Chile's comprehensive teacher evaluation system, Docentemas, has shown that it can be done.

The impact of even a well-designed teacher evaluation depends on its consequences. Teachers who receive a poor evaluation should be supported and offered training, but consistent poor evaluations should trigger dismissal. The experience of Washington, DC, is that a credible threat of dismissal for teachers rated minimally effective stimulates a high share of them to voluntarily leave the system; equally important, it stimulates large improvements in performance for those determined to stay. Research suggests that if school systems consistently are able to remove the lowest-performing 5 percent of teachers, they reap large gains in average student learning over time.

Retaining the highest-performing teachers and leveraging their skills to mentor and train others is even more important. In the next chapter, we focus on the incentives required to keep high-talent teachers adequately rewarded and motivated. From the standpoint of improving overall teacher quality, however, an essential function of teacher evaluation is to identify outstanding teachers, which is the necessary precondition for sharing their practice as widely as possible.

Latin American education systems will not improve unless they find ways to raise dramatically the quality of teacher in-service training. Many LAC teachers need to deepen their content mastery, improve classroom management, and develop more effective teaching practice. While the vast majority of in-service training courses delivered today in the region are not rigorously evaluated, policy makers commonly state they believe these resources are largely wasted. Global evidence suggests that in-service teacher training can be effective if it is delivered by highly qualified trainers, has sufficient duration, and focuses on pedagogy and content directly related to student learning in the subjects the teachers teach. Scripted training approaches that make use of proven teaching strategies and guide teachers to use well-designed materials for the delivery of a daily curriculum have proven effective and are relevant to a number of settings in LAC. Training focused on effective classroom management and student engagement has been almost unheard of in LAC but is beginning to take hold. As chapter 2 documents, there is large scope to increase teachers' classroom effectiveness by equipping them with practical skills missing from their pre-service education.

Designing and delivering capacity-building programs of the caliber and scale required will not be easy. Institutional issues include the weak coupling of ministries of education and university-based pedagogy departments, which means that the latter are ill-prepared to respond to client ministries' needs and the near-complete lack of evaluation evidence on how well existing programs work. Some of the peer-based methods that are most powerful in high-performing school systems such as in Singapore and Japan may be less successful in settings with a lower degree of teacher professionalism. However, efforts to promote teachers' professional interaction, through online platforms such as Chile's Innovar para Ser Mejor and Rio de Janeiro municipality's Educopedia may open more space for peer-led development and teaching support. In the meantime, using teacher evaluation data to determine training priorities, exploiting partnerships with innovative nongovernmental organizations training, such as Brazil's Ayrton Senna and Lemann Foundations, and investing in rigorous evaluation of at least the most important training initiatives will help make investments in this area more cost-effective, which is essential for faster progress in raising the caliber of the current stock of teachers.

Last but not least, full development of teachers' potential requires high-quality principals to assess and groom their capacity, through skilled management of teachers' classroom assignments, rotations, and opportunities for peer collaboration and professional development. Research shows that effective principals can raise school learning results in relatively short periods by reshaping their teaching force. But systems for selecting, evaluating, and developing talented school leaders are only starting to be designed in a comprehensive manner in LAC. Experiences both inside and outside the region suggest some avenues for these programs, but most LAC countries are very far from the capacity of countries such as Singapore to identify potential leaders and systematically prepare them for careers as school directors. There is an important opportunity for countries in the region to learn from each other as they experiment with new standards, selection processes, training models, and evaluation systems for school directors. Effective school directors promote the peer collaboration and professional learning within schools that are the most powerful and cost-effective way to groom teachers to their full potential.

Notes

[1] Countries where the authors did not find an effective probationary period are Argentina, El Salvador, Honduras, Nicaragua, and Uruguay.

[2] Chapter Annexes to the book may be found at http://www.worldbank.org/lac/teachers.

[3] SIMCE test scores have a standard deviation of about 50 points.

[4] Taut and Sun (forthcoming), however, note, "One weakness of the supervisor instrument has always been the inflated scores" with school directors consistently rating all teachers between "competent" and "outstanding."

References

Allen, J., R. Pianta, A. Gregory, A. Mikami Yee, and J. Lun. 2011. "An Interaction-Based Approach to Enhancing Secondary School Instruction and Student Achievement." *Science* 333 (6045): 1034–37.

Angrist, J. D., and V. Lavy. 2001. "Does Teacher Training Affect Pupil Learning? Evicence from Matched Comparisons in Jerusalem Public Schools." *Journal of Labor Economics* 19 (2): 343–69.

Banerjee, A., S. Cole, E. Duflo, and L. Linden. 2007. "Remedying Education: Evidence from Two Randomized Experiments in India." *Quarterly Journal of Economics* 122 (3): 1235–64.

Barber, M., and M. Mourshed. 2007. *How the World's Best-Performing School Systems Come Out on Top*. London: McKinsey.

Barrera-Osorio, F., and L. Linden. 2009. *The Use and Misuse of Computers in Education: Evdence from a Randomized Experiment in Colombia*. Washington, DC: World Bank.

Belize, Ministry of Education. 2009. "Primary School Induction Program for Newly Qualified Teachers." Belize, Ministry of Education, Belize City (accessed March 11, 2013). http://www.moe.gov.bz/~moegov5/images/spdownload/induction-brochure-revised-2009.pdf.

Boyd, D., P. Grossman, H. Lankford, S. Loeb, and J. Wyckoff. 2006. "How Changes in Entry Requirements Alter the Teacher Workforce and Affect Student Achievement." *Education Finance and Policy* 1 (2): 176–216.

Branch, G., E. Hanushek, and S. Rivkin. 2013. "School Leaders Matter." *Education Next* 13 (2): 62–69.

Bruns, B., D. Evans, and J. Luque. 2012. *Achieving World Class Education in Brazil: The Next Agenda*. Washington, DC: World Bank.

Carnoy, M., and L. Costa. 2014. "The Effectiveness of an Early Grades Literacy Intervention on the Cognitive Achievement of Brazilian Students." Paper presented at the Conference of Brazilian Econometric Society Conference, Foz do Iguaçu, Brazil.

Centro de Estudios MINEDUC. 2012a. *Estadísticas de la Educación 2012*. Santiago: Chile, Ministerio de Educación.

———. 2012b. *Evaluación Docente y y resultados de aprendizaje: ¿Qué nos dice la evidencia?* Serie evidencias, 1 (6). Santiago: Chile, Ministerio de Educación.

Chesterfield, R. 1994. "Indicators of Democratic Behavior in Nueva Escuela (NEU) Schools." Project of the Academy for Education Development, Juarez and Associates, IDEAS, and BEST Project of Guatemala for USAID, Guatemala City.

Chesterfield, R., and A. Abreu-Combs. 2011. *Centers for Excellence in Teacher Training (CETT): Two-Year Impact Study Report (2008–2009)*. Washington DC: USAID Bureau for Latin America and the Caribbean. http://pdf.usaid.gov/pdf_docs/PDACS248.pdf.

Chingos, M., and P. E. Peterson. 2010. "Do Schools Districts Get What They Pay For? Predicting Teacher Effectiveness by College Selectivity, Experience, Etc." Harvard University

Program on Education Policy and Governance Working Paper 10-08, Harvard University, Cambridge, MA.
Clark, D., P. Martorell, and J. Rockoff. 2009. "School Principals and School Performance." CALDER Working Paper 38, National Center for Analysis of Longitudinal Data in Education Research, Urban Institute, Washington, DC.
Cohen, D. K., and H. C. Hill. 2001. *Learning Policy: When State Education Reform Works.* New Haven: Yale University Press.
Concha Albornoz, C. 2007. "Claves para la formación de directivos de instituciones escolares." *Revista Electrónica Iberoamericana sobre Calidad, Eficacia y Cambio en Educación* 5 (5): 133–38.
Cortés, F., and M. Lagos. 2011. "Consecuencias de la Evaluación Docente." In *La Evaluación Docente en Chile*, edited by J. Manzi, R. Gonzalez, and Y. Sun, 137–54. Santiago: MINEDUC.
Cristia, J. P., P. Ibarraran, S. Cueto, A. Santiago, and E. Severin. 2012. *Technology and Child Development: Evidence from the One Laptop per Child Program.* Washington, DC: Inter-American Development Bank.
de Baessa, Y., R. Chesterfield, and T. Ramos. 2002. "Active Learning and Democratic Behavior in Guatemalan Rural Primary Schools." *Compare: A Journal of Comparative and International Education* 32 (2): 205–18.
Dee, T., and J. Wyckoff. 2013. "Incentives, Selection, and Teacher Performance: Evidence from IMPACT." Working Paper 19529, National Bureau of Economic Research, Cambridge, MA.
Ecuador, Ministerio de Educación 2012. "Sistema Integral de Desarrollo Profesional Educativo." Ecuador, Ministerio de Educación, Quito. http://sime.educacion.gob.ec/Modulo/SIPROFE/index.php?mp=9_0.
European Commission. 2010. "Developing Coherent and System-Wide Induction Programmes for Beginning Teachers: A Handbook for Policymakers." Commission Staff Working Document SEC 538. European Commission, Brussels.
European Commission/EACEA/Eurydice. 2013. *Key Data on Teachers and School Leaders in Europe.* Eurydice Report. Luxembourg: European Union.
Flotts, M., and A. Abarzúa. 2011. "El modelo de evaluación y los instrumentos." In *La Evaluación Docente en Chile*, edited by J. Manzi, R. Gonzalez, and Y. Sun, 35–61. Santiago: MINEDUC.
Fullan, M., N. Watson, and S. Anderson. 2013. *Ceibal: Next Steps.* Toronto: Michael Fullan Enterprises. http://www.ceibal.org.uy/docs/FULLAN-Ceibal-English.pdf.
Fundación Escuela Nueva. 2012. "Escuela Nueva Model." http://www.escuelanueva.org/portal/en/escuela-nueva-model.html.
Galvis, L. A., and L. Bonilla. 2011. *Profesionalización Docente y la Calidad de la Educación Escolar en Colombia.* Documentos de trabajo sobre economía regional No.154, Cartagena: Banco de la República.
Garet, M. S., S. Cronen, M. Eaton, A. Kurki, M. Ludwig, W. Jones, K. Uekawa, A. Falk, H. Bloom, F. Doolittle, P. Zhu, and L. Sztenjnberg. 2008. *The Impact of Two Professional Development Interventions on Early Reading Instruction and Achievement (NCEE 2008-4030).* Washington, DC: National Center for Education Evaluation and Regional Assistance, Institute of Education Sciences, U.S. Department of Education.
Garet, M. S., A. C. Porter, L. Desimone, B. F. Birman, and K. S. Yoon. 2001. "What Makes Professional Development Effective? Results From A National Sample Of Teachers." *American Educational Research Journal* 38 (4): 915–945.
Glazerman, S., S. Loeb, D. Goldhaber, D. Staiger, S. Raudenbush, and G. Whitehurst. 2010a. "Evaluating Teachers: The Important Role of Value-Added." Brookings Institution, Washington, DC.
Glazerman, S., E. Isenberg, S. Dolfin, M. Bleeker, A. Johnson, M. Grider, and M. Jacobus. 2010b. *Impacts of Comprehensive Teacher Induction: Final Results from a Randomized Controlled Study (NCEE 2010-4027).* Washington, DC: National Center for Education Evaluation and Regional Assistance, Institute of Education Sciences, U.S. Department of Education.

Glewwe, P., E. Hanushek, S. Humpage, and R. Ravina. 2013. "School Resources and Educational Outcomes in Developing Countries: A Review of the Literature from 1990 to 2010." In *Education Policy in Developing Countries*, edited by P. Glewwe, 13–64. Chicago: University of Chicago Press.

Gove, A., and A. Wetterberg, eds. 2011. *Early Grade Reading Assessment: Applications and Interventions to Improve Basic Literacy*. Research Triangle Park, NC: RTI International.

Hanushek, E. A., and S. G. Rivkin. 2010. "Generalizations about Using Value-Added Measures of Teacher Quality." *American Economic Review* 100 (2): 267–71.

Hardman, F., J. Abd-Kadir, C. Agg, J. Migwi, J. Ndambuku, and F. Smith. 2009. "Changing Pedagogical Practice in Kenyan Primary Schools: The Impact of School-Based Training." *Comparative Education* 45 (1): 65–86.

Ingvarson, L., M. Meiers, and A. Beavis. 2005. "Factors Affecting the Impact of Professional Development Programs on Teacher's Knowledge, Practice, Student Outcomes and Efficacy." Education Policy Analysis Archives. http://epaa.asu.edu/ojs/article/view/115.

Juarez and Associates. 2003. "Girls' Education Monitoring System (GEMS): The Effects of Active Learning Programs in Multigrade Schools on Girls' Persistence in and Completion of Primary School in Developing Countries." Report prepared for USAID Bureau of Economic Growth, Agriculture, and Trade, Office of Women in Development, Guatemala City.

Kane, T. J., and D. O. Staiger. 2012. *Gathering Feedback for Teaching: Combining High-Quality Observations with Student Surveys and Achievement Gains*. Seattle: Bill & Melinda Gates Foundation.

Kennedy, M. 1998. "Form and Substance in Inservice Teacher Education." Research monograph., National Institute for Science Education, University of Wisconsin, Madison.

Kirschner, P. A., J. Sweller, and R. E. Clark. 2006. "Why Minimal Guidance during Instruction Does Not Work: An Analysis of the Failure of Constructivist, Discovery, Problem-Based, Experiential, and Inquiry-Based Teaching." *Educational Psychologist* 41 (2): 75–86.

Lemov, D. 2010. *Teach Like a Champion*. San Francisco: Jossey-Bass.

Linden, L. 2008. "Complement or Substitute? The Effect of Technology on Student Achievement in India." Working Paper, Columbia University, New York.

McCutchen, D., D. D. Abbott, L. B. Green, S. N. Beretvas, S. Cox, N. S. Potter, T. Quiroga, and A. L. Gray. 2002. "Beginning Literacy: Links Among Teacher Knowledge, Teacher Practice, and Student Learning." *Journal of Learning Disabilities* 35 (1): 69–86.

McCutchen, D., L. Green, R. D. Abbot, and E. A. Sanders. 2009. "Further Evidence for Teacher Knowledge: Supporting Struggling Readers in Grades Three Through Five." *Reading and Writing: An Interdisciplinary Journal* 22 (4): 401–23.

McEwan, P. J. 1998. "The Effectiveness of Multigrade Schools in Colombia." *International Journal of Educational Development* 18 (6): 435–52.

McEwan, P. J., E. Murphy-Graham, D. Torres Irribarra, C. Aguilar, and R. Rápalo. Forthcoming. "Improving Middle School Quality in Poor Countries: Evidence from the Honduran Sistema de Aprendizaje Tutorial." *Educational Evaluation and Policy Analysis*.

McGill-Franzen, A., R. L. Allington, L. Yokoi, and G. Brooks. 1999. "Putting Books in the Classroom Seems Necessary But Not Sufficient." *Journal of Educational Research* 93 (2): 67–74.

MINEDUC (Ministerio de Educación, Chile). 2005. *Marco para la Buena Dirección*. Santiago: MINEDUC. http://www.mineduc.cl/usuarios/convivencia_escolar/doc/201103070155490.MINEDUC.Marco_para_la_Buena_Direccion.pdf.

———. 2009. *Resultados Nacionales SIMCE 2008*. Santiago: MINEDUC.

———. 2012a. *Docente Más: Sistema de Evaluación Docente de Chile*. Santiago: MINEDUC. http://www.docentemas.cl/.

———. 2012b. *Preguntas Frecuentes: Ley 20.501 de Educación*. Santiago: MINEDUC. http://www.docentemas.cl/dm_faq2.php?id=10.

Mourshed, M., C. Chijioke, and M. Barber. 2011. *How the World's Most Improved School Systems Keep Getting Better*. London: McKinsey.

OECD (Organisation for Economic Co-operation and Development). 2005. *Teachers Matter: Attracting, Developing and Retaining Effective Teachers*. Paris: OECD.
———. 2009. *Creating Effective Teaching and Learning Environments: First Results from TALIS*. Paris: OECD.
———. 2013. *Teachers for the 21st Century: Using Evaluation to Improve Teaching*. Paris: OECD.
Ome, A. 2009. *Meritocracia en la Carrera Docente: Evidencia para Colombia*. Estudios sobre la calidad de la Educación en Colombia. Bogota: ICFES. http://www.icfes.gov.co/investigacion/component/docman/doc_download/145-estudios-sobre-calidad-de-la-educacion-en-colombia.
Papay, J.P., and M.A. Kraft. 2013. "Productivity Returns to Experience in the Teacher Labor Market: Methodological Challenges and New Evidence on Long-term Career Improvement." Working Paper, Harvard University, Cambridge, MA.
Perry, R. R., and C. C. Lewis. 2009. "What Is Successful Adaptation of Lesson Study in the US?" *Journal of Educational Change* 10 (4): 365–91.
Piper, B., and M. Korda. 2010. *Early Grade Reading Assesment (EGRA) Plus: Liberia*. Program evaluation report prepared for USAID/Liberia. Research Triangle Park, NC: RTI International.
Psacharopoulos, G., C. Rojas, and E. Velez. 1993. "Achievement Evaluation of Colombia's Escuela Nueva: Is Multigrade the Answer?" *Comparative Eudcation Review* 37 (3): 263–76.
Raver, C. C., S. M. Jones, C. P. Li-Grining, M. Metzger, K. M. Champion, and L. Sardin. 2008. "Improving Preschool Classroom Processes: Preliminary Findings from a Randomized Trial Implemented in Head Start Settings." *Early Childhood Research Quarterly* 23 (1): 10–26.
Rockoff, J. E. 2004. "The Impact of Individual Teachers on Student Achievement: Evidence from Panel Data." *American Economic Review* 94 (2): 247–52.
Taut, S., M. Santelices, C. Araya, and J. Manzi. 2011. "Perceived Effects and Uses of the National Teacher Evaluation System in Chilean Elementary Schools." *Studies in Educational Evaluation* 37 (4): 218–29.
Taut, S., and Y. Sun. Forthcoming. "The Development and Implementation of a National, Standards-based, Multi-Method Teacher Performance Assessment System in Chile." *Education Policy Analysis Archives* 22 (58).
Taylor, E. S., and J. H. Tyler. 2012. "The Effect of Evaluation on Performance." *American Economic Review* 102 (7): 3628–51.
Turque, Bill. 2010. "Rhee: Election Result 'Devastating' for D.C. Schoolchildren." *Washington Post*, September 16.
UNESCO (United Nations Educational, Scientific, and Cultural Organization). 2003. *Teacher Training on ICT Use in Education in Asia and the Pacific: Overview from Selected Countries*. UNESCO Asia and Pacific Regional Bureau for Education, Bangkok (accessed on May 24, 2013). http://unesdoc.unesco.org/images/0013/001329/132979e.pdf.
Vaillant, D. 2005. "Reformas educativas y el rol de docentes." *Revista PRELAC* 1: 38–51.
Vaillant, D., and C. Rossel. 2006. *Maestros de escuelas básicas en América Latina: Hacia una radiografía de la profesión*. Santiago: Programa de Promoción de la Reforma Educativa en América Latina y el Caribe (PREAL). http://www.oei.es/docentes/publicaciones/maestros_escuela_basicas_en_america_latina_preal.pdf.
Vezub, L. F. 2007. "La formación y el desarrollo profesional docente frente a los nuevos desafíos de la escolaridad." *Profesorado: Revista de currículum y formación del profesorado* 11 (1). http://www.ugr.es/~recfpro/rev111ART2.pdf.
Webster-Stratton, C., M. Jamila Reid, and M. Stoolmiller. 2008. "Preventing Conduct Problems and Improving School Readiness: Evaluation of the Incredible Years Teacher and Child Training Programs in High-Risk Schools." *Journal of Child Psychology and Psychiatry* 49 (5): 471–88.
Wise, A. E., L. Darling-Hammond, M. W., McLaughlin, and H. T. Bernstein. 1985. "Teacher Evaluation: A Study of Effective Practices." *Elementary School Journal* 85 (1): 61–121.

World Bank. 2011. *Project Appraisal Document on a Proposed Grant in the Amount of SDR 43.5 Million (US$70 Million Equivalent) to The Republic of Haiti for the Education for All Project—Phase II.* Washington, DC: World Bank.

———. 2012. *Attracting and Retaining Qualified Teachers in the OECS.* Washington, DC: World Bank. http://siteresources.worldbank.org/EDUCATION/Resources/WB_OECSTeacherReport.pdf.

Yoon, K. S., T. Duncan, S. W.-Y. Lee, B. Scarloss, and K. Shapley. 2007. *Reviewing the Evidence on How Teacher Professional Development Affects Student Achievement.* Washington, DC: National Center for Education Evaluation and Regional Assistance, U.S. Department of Education.

5
Motivating Teachers to Perform

The prior chapters discuss the two critical teacher policy challenges Latin American education systems face: attracting high-talent candidates into teaching and making the existing stock of teachers more effective. Both of these areas pose technical challenges. In recruiting, it is not easy to identify ex ante which candidates have the cognitive and interpersonal skills to become great teachers; therefore, setting recruitment standards and screening processes that can draw in the best candidates is not trivial. In teacher professional development, designing high-quality programs is complicated by the limited evidence on which approaches produce the biggest boost to teacher effectiveness relative to their costs.

But the challenges are not only technical. Both recruitment and teacher development policies interact powerfully with incentives. There is no point in raising the standards for entry into teaching or the rigor of the selection process if compensation, work conditions, and professional gratification are not sufficient to attract a talented pool of individuals to apply. Similarly, there is little reason to expect teachers in service to invest time and effort in developing their skills and applying them to their work if this effort is not rewarded.

This chapter focuses on the incentives surrounding teaching in Latin America. We set out a framework of three broad classes of incentives we see as conceptually distinct yet important to align. With respect to each class of incentive, we analyze the most recent reform experiences in Latin America and the Caribbean (LAC) and compare these with trends and evidence from other parts of the world. The final section summarizes the balance of evidence and its implications for the design of effective policies to motivate teachers.

This chapter was coauthored with Soledad De Gregorio.

What motivates teachers?

Research confirms that individuals are attracted to the teaching profession and inspired to high performance for a variety of reasons. Vegas and Umansky (2005) set out a comprehensive framework of incentives that we suggest can be collapsed into three broad categories: (a) professional rewards, including intrinsic satisfaction, recognition and prestige, professional growth, intellectual mastery, and pleasant working conditions; (b) accountability pressure, encompassing feedback from parents and students, peers, and supervisors, as well as the threat of demotion or dismissal; and (c) financial incentives, such as salary level and differentials, pensions and other benefits, and bonus pay (figure 5.1).

In each area, we focus on the policies and programs that operate most directly on individual teachers. Perhaps especially in the area of accountability policies, there exists a broad range of interventions and policies aimed at making school systems more accountable for results, and it is beyond the scope of this book to review these comprehensively.[1] We focus on the policies that create the most localized

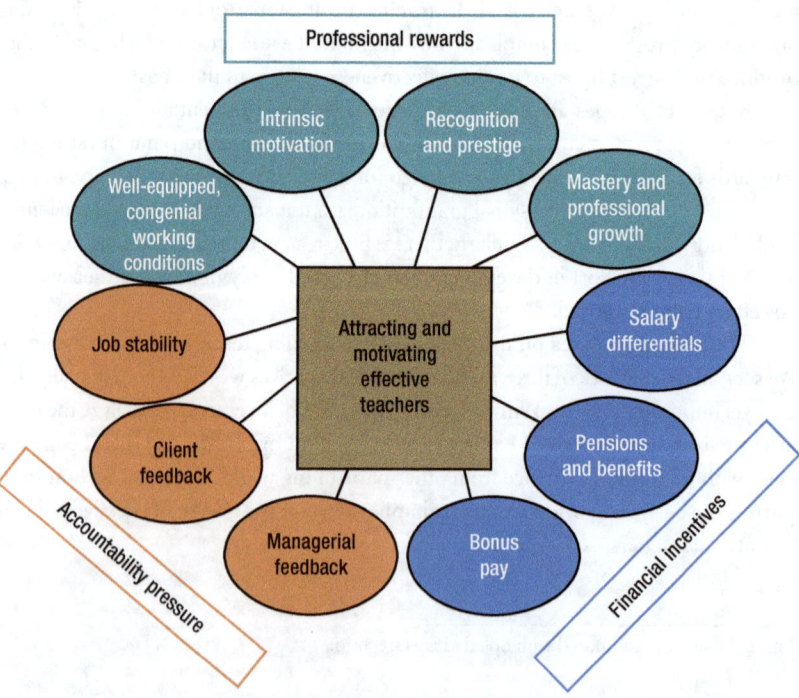

FIGURE 5.1: Three broad classes of incentives motivate teachers

Source: Adapted from Vegas and Umansky 2005.

pressures on teacher performance. For example, a program to train and empower school directors to observe teachers' classroom performance could have a direct impact on teachers' incentives to show up for school and prepare for classes. In contrast, a school system reform that provides for failing schools to be taken over by new managers also creates accountability pressures, but these cascade down to teachers, rather than act on them directly. The impact of the latter policy on teacher performance in the classroom would be part of a longer, multistage process (or results chain), and establishing its causal impact on teachers' motivation is not as straightforward.

This distinction is not crystalline, and ultimately, the relevant question for any school system is the cost-effectiveness of alternative types of reforms in producing better student outcomes. The global research base is currently far short of the evidence needed to support such cost-effectiveness comparisons. This chapter contributes to the broader research agenda by carefully reviewing current evidence on those programs and policies that create professional rewards, accountability pressures, and financial incentives that operate most directly on teachers.

Professional rewards

Chapter 1 documented the eroding prestige and financial rewards of the teaching profession in Latin American countries over the past several decades. Yet as chapter 3 showed, in most countries in the region the supply of new teacher candidates remains robust—even in the face of relatively high rates of teacher unemployment in some countries. These facts suggest that teaching possesses some core attributes of enduring attractiveness: the status of a profession, the fulfillment of helping others in a profound way, opportunities for personal intellectual development and professional mastery, working hours and leave policies that are relatively family friendly, and working conditions that are relatively pleasant.

While these intrinsic and professional rewards may guarantee an adequate *quantity* of teacher candidates in many countries, the evidence marshaled in this book suggests that truly reshaping education in Latin America requires a sharp change in teacher *quality*. It requires attracting more individuals with the talent and ambition to become extraordinary teachers and shifting the overall distribution of teachers in the direction of higher competence and more effective performance. There is evidence that the quality of school infrastructure and materials do impact teachers' choice of schools and can positively affect their motivation, but there is no evidence to suggest that upgrading infrastructure in and of itself is a sufficient strategy for raising the professional rewards to teaching. This section therefore focuses on two of the four sources of professional rewards pictured in figure 5.1 that are attracting growing attention not only in Latin America but also globally, spawned by analyses of some of the world's highest performing school systems: (a) incentives for mastery and professional growth and (b) teacher recognition and prestige.

Mastery and professional growth

One of the sharpest contrasts between the world's highest-performing education systems—such as in Finland, the Republic of Korea, Singapore, and Ontario (Canada)—and those in LAC countries is the emphasis in the former group on professional interaction and exchange of practice among teachers. Teachers in Finland spend only 60 percent as much time in the classroom as the Organisation for Economic Co-operation and Development (OECD) average, but spend substantially more time each week on collaborative work with colleagues: designing lessons, assessing students' work, and developing new teaching strategies (Sahlberg 2012, 17). In Asia, empty seats are stationed at the back of classrooms in the expectation of visitors from other classes, other schools, districts, and even other countries. Teachers in Shanghai, China; Japan; and Singapore observe each other regularly in a culture that allows for candid feedback and rapid exchange of effective strategies, lesson plans, exercises, and examples of student work. Western observers of the Japanese Lesson Study method are struck by the intensity of teacher collaboration in developing and delivering the curriculum and the frankness with which teachers observe and critique each other's work (Fernandez and Yoshida 2004).

Within Latin America, the high-performing Cuban education system is exceptional in its strong emphasis on teamwork and exchange of experience among teachers. Every school has a teacher learning group (*colectivo pedagógico*) for every discipline, and these meet every two weeks to discuss teaching methods, produce materials, and develop common homework exercises and assessment items (*bancos de problemas*). Teachers are observed in the classroom at least once a month by expert teachers, and their professional advancement depends on positive evaluations of their classroom practice as well as their students' learning progress, which is measured frequently and with great transparency in Cuba. All teachers—in every grade and every subject—are expected to conduct independent research on how to improve student learning, and the best proposals from each school compete at the municipal level for the right to be presented at an annual national research conference (Gasperini 2000).

Daniel Pink (2006) has argued that in knowledge professions, the most powerful performance incentives are individual workers' desires for autonomy, mastery, and a sense of contribution. As Barber and Mourshed (2007), Sahlberg (2011), Tucker (2011), and other analysts have noted, these three factors are centrally encouraged and supported in the countries that perform highest on the OECD's Program for International Student Assessment (PISA) test. In Singapore, Korea, and Finland, entry into teacher training is highly selective, and teachers in service are treated as competent and driven professionals. In Finland, teachers enjoy significant latitude over what and how they teach the curriculum, and there is no standardized student testing or external evaluation of school performance. While Singapore places more emphasis on student testing and teachers' performance is evaluated externally, there is a similar ethos of teachers as professionals: teachers receive 100 paid hours of professional development (12 days) annually, and support each other through a teachers' network.

Tucker (2011) notes that as teacher quality has increased in Finland, Japan, and Singapore over the past 20 years, all three countries have moved in the direction of a less directive curriculum and more flexibility for teachers in what they teach and how. Systems such as these create strong performance incentives from the positive encouragement of professional achievement and from peer expectations—what Tucker calls "lateral" accountability, rather than vertical accountability to a superior. The most powerful incentive of all may be the gratification teachers in these countries feel from an ever-growing sense of mastery and increasing power to affect their students' lives. Everyone who works in education has seen the flip side of this: the frustration of teachers who lack the skills or tools they need to help their students learn and the alibis for failure (blaming the students, their families, or poverty) that have corrosive effects on students, schools, and the school system over time.

The power of Japan's Lesson Study, Cuba's *colectivos pedagógicos*, Ontario's whole school development planning, and other forms of school-level professional development is that they provide mechanisms for identifying extraordinary teachers and quickly spreading awareness of their practice. This constitutes a highly cost-effective model of in-service training, as it avoids the logistical expenses of moving large groups of teachers to universities or other training sites and the dispersion of training impact when individual teachers return to their schools and find their new skills are not supported or reinforced. Ontario's experience may have particular relevance for Latin American countries as the province has achieved a significant increase in student learning performance over the past five years through a single core strategy: "finding and sharing outstanding practice" among teachers (Levin 2012, 98). As chapter 2 documented, across Latin America there are many opportunities for low-cost diffusion of better teaching practice from one classroom to another within the same school. What is lacking are systematic and effective efforts by school directors, supervisors, and pedagogical coordinators to identify best-practice teaching within each school, and explicit space in the school calendar for teachers to observe each other and develop lesson plans and strategies together.

There are interesting examples of programs along these lines being implemented by school systems today in Latin America. Rio de Janeiro municipality's Ginasios Experimentais Carioca, (experimental middle schools) introduced in 2011 are a good example. In the *ginásios,* classes are offered in two-hour block sessions rather than the typical 50 minutes to allow for more depth in covering the curriculum as well as interdisciplinary approaches. Classes are taught by two-person teams of teachers who can complement each other's strengths, work together on lesson plans and homework grading, and provide each other with immediate feedback and mentoring. Teachers in these schools also have 40-hour per week contracts, rather than the typical 20-hour per week contract, and have explicit time in the school week blocked for collective work with other teachers in their department and across disciplines for curriculum planning and exchange of experience. While the performance of schools that have become *ginásios experimentais* on annual standardized tests has been improving, schools thus far have self-selected into the program, so it is not clear how the model would work more broadly. Programs this promising deserve rigorous evaluation and costing analysis.

Recognition and prestige

In high-performing East Asian school systems, the incentives for professional mastery are reinforced by an explicit career ladder that promotes extraordinary teachers to the role of master teachers or specialists in curriculum or research. Such promotions can also have significant financial rewards (Mourshed, Chijioke, and Barber 2010). But what drives the incentive is the serious attention these school systems give to differentiating teacher performance and recognizing and rewarding excellence. The definition of excellence is sophisticated; it is not simply the ability to produce high student learning outcomes, but the ability to produce these in challenging contexts. In Shanghai, a teacher cannot be promoted without taking on assignments in difficult schools and demonstrating true mastery by turning around a low-performing school or classroom (Schleicher 2011). In Singapore, high-potential teachers are regularly assigned to low-performing schools, so that the professional incentives for individual teachers are strategically aligned with the systemwide goal of raising performance. In Korea, teachers are randomly reassigned to different schools every three years, on the assumption that teachers' practice will improve with experience teaching all types of students under different school conditions, and that students will benefit from more experienced and versatile teachers.

There are limited rewards for extraordinary teachers in Latin America today. Although many systems are increasing their efforts to identify highly effective teachers and offer them signs of professional recognition—whether it be laptop computers, trips to the capital, or even abroad—the vast majority of teachers in the region doing outstanding work under difficult conditions are unlikely to receive very different treatment than a colleague in an adjacent classroom turning in subpar results. If the school director is not engaged with the teaching team on an ongoing basis in instructional development, there is little chance that regional supervisors, secretaries of education, or ministers will even know where their "irreplaceable" teachers are working. In most Latin American schools, the classroom door is closed; teachers are assumed to have, and want, autonomy; and there is little chance that other teachers, the director, district personnel, or other outsiders will visit to observe.

In contrast to East Asian countries, in school systems in Latin America and the Caribbean the lowest performing or newest teachers are often assigned to the most difficult schools and classrooms—a pattern that has been documented in the United States (Kalogrides and Loeb 2012; Clotfelter, Ladd, and Vigdor 2005; Conger 2005).

In most of Latin America, neither the concept of master teachers nor the incentives for grooming them exist in the same way as in high-performing East Asia. The promotion track for teachers in much of LAC is to move out of the classroom into a district office or pedagogical coordinator position, but these moves are often negotiated through connections rather than experience or competency. Even worse is the relatively common practice of assigning teachers who are ineffective in the classroom but cannot be dismissed to nonclassroom positions, including pedagogical support roles. As a result, pedagogical coordinators and supervisors in Latin America are much less likely to be genuinely respected as master teachers.

There are some notable exceptions to these patterns, and important recent efforts in Peru and elsewhere in the region to develop effective teacher mentoring systems. The two clearest exceptions are the role of Cuba's master teachers and the network of high-quality demonstration teachers that Colombia established as part of the Escuela Nueva program. The high status of Cuban teachers stems to some extent from factors that are not easily replicable elsewhere and may not prove sustainable in Cuba—including salaries on par with doctors, high standards for entry into teacher education, and prominent national priority given to education. But other striking factors include the high degree of practical school experience and demonstrated mastery required for university-level teacher educators (at least six to seven years of demonstrated success teaching at the school level), the expectation that all teachers carry out independent research, and a promotion track for the most expert teachers to the role of pedagogical leader at the school level (*jefe de circulo pedagógico*) and then to methodological leader (*metodologo*) at the municipal level. The *jefes* lead teachers' ongoing teamwork and exchange of practice within the school. The *metodologos* work with each school team in their district on strategies for improved student learning results (Gasperini 2000).

Master teachers also play a central role in the Escuela Nueva model. The core strategy for training teachers and scaling up implementation is the creation of a network of demonstration schools, where carefully selected master teachers may be observed at work. These master teachers are also responsible for regular visits, outreach, and support to the network of schools in their vicinity.

Both Cuba's schools and Colombia's rural multigrade schools have produced impressive learning outcomes. Cuba's students score the highest in LAC by a wide margin on regional tests, and Colombia is the only country in the region where rural school students outperform their urban counterparts. We lack rigorous research on the role that these systems' emphasis on professional rewards has played vis-à-vis other factors in producing these outcomes. But both are distinguished by the explicit recognition, promotion opportunities, and prestige awarded to outstanding teachers.

The broader picture of Latin American education today, however, is one where the ratio of extraordinary teachers to adequate or underperforming ones is low. This means not only that there are relatively few exceptional teachers to observe and learn from but also these "outliers" are more likely to be perceived as a threat to the prevailing school culture than as a stimulus to professional peers. As discussed in chapter 4, Chile, Colombia, Ecuador, Mexico, and Peru have moved or are moving to strengthen the professional rewards for teachers by putting in place formal processes of individual teacher evaluation. With a platform for identifying teachers who demonstrate true mastery, school systems can focus on ensuring that these individuals are recognized, rewarded adequately, and encouraged to train and mentor others. In these and other countries, however, an important second step will be to align classroom assignments, school rotations, and promotion decisions more systematically with the overarching goals of teacher excellence and broad-based school improvement.

Accountability pressure

In most sectors of the economy, powerful performance incentives come from the direct pressures that clients and supervisors exert on workers, backed by the threat of job dismissal. In Latin American education systems, such direct accountability pressure is weak. First, most teachers in the region work in the public sector and enjoy a high level of civil service job security. Second, they face limited managerial oversight; teachers enjoy substantial de facto autonomy behind the closed door of the classroom. Third, while pressure from parents and community members has been enhanced in a number of LAC countries through school-based management (SBM) initiatives, school choice, and other efforts to increase "client power," in most cases the direct accountability pressures on individual teachers are not strong. Under most SBM models, individual teachers cannot be fired from the school system directly by a school, nor are individual salaries determined at the school level.

Job stability

Over 80 percent of all basic education teachers in LAC work in public schools, where civil service protection, as in other parts of the public sector, is a core feature of employment. The extreme degree of status quo job protection for teachers in parts of the region is illustrated by Peru and Mexico. In Peru, until late 2012 the Ministry of Education did not have the legal power to dismiss any civil service teachers—not even those legally convicted of sexual abuse of students or acts of terrorism. In Mexico in 2013, the teachers' union waged successful strikes in several states against government attempts to curb the "right" of retiring teachers to sell their positions or hand them on to family members. High rates of teacher absenteeism are a further indication that school systems across the region face constraints in holding teachers accountable for performance. In Brazil's São Paulo state school system, 15 percent of teachers are formally reported absent each day, and in São Paulo and elsewhere, official absence data are widely believed to be understated. A 2003 global study found 11 percent of Peruvian teachers and 14 percent of teachers in Ecuador were absent on an average day during unannounced school visits (Chaudhury et al. 2006).

The major exceptions in the region are Cuba, where teachers are held accountable for their students' learning progress and are dismissed for poor results, and Chile's publicly funded but privately managed voucher (or publicly subsidized) schools, which follow private sector labor law. The use of temporary contracts, which in theory allow for teachers to be dismissed, is increasing across the region, but there is no clear evidence that this flexibility is exploited. Most teachers initially hired on temporary contracts are eventually converted to permanent positions As discussed in chapter 4, a formal probationary process for new civil service teachers exists in most countries, but it is hard to find cases where teachers' performance is actually monitored closely during the critical early years, let alone examples of weak teachers being counseled out.

There is no good analysis of teacher exits in most LAC countries, whether from temporary contract or permanent positions. In Chile's voucher schools, where the barriers to dismissal are limited, it is estimated that between 7 and 25 percent of teachers are dismissed or counseled out on performance grounds annually. In the United States, where most teachers have contractual job stability, it is estimated that less than 3 percent of the teaching stock annually is dismissed for poor performance, given the high administrative bar for documenting performance issues (Weisberg et al. 2009; Bruns, Filmer, and Patrinos 2011).[2]

There are two channels through which an excessive degree of job stability can undermine education system quality. First, if a school system cannot dismiss poor performers, it loses the chance to replace them with more talented and effective teachers and thereby raise the overall quality of the teaching force. In Singapore, the Enhanced Performance Management System (discussed in chapter 4) is explicitly designed to pinpoint the least effective 5 percent of teachers (and school directors) in each performance cycle, and system managers are not shy about counseling individuals out of the profession if performance does not improve.

Hanushek (2011) estimated the potential effects on education quality from systematic policies to identify and "de-select" the lowest performing teachers in the United States. He projects that if U.S. school systems replaced the bottom 5 to 10 percent of current teachers with teachers of average effectiveness, it would raise learning across all students by roughly 0.04 standard deviation (SD) per year of education, equivalent to 0.5 SD per student learning gains over the course of the K–12 schooling cycle. This increase in learning is worth approximately US$10,000 to US$20,000 annually per classroom in the net present value of earnings generated over each student's lifetime.

Replacing the bottom 5 percent of current teachers could eliminate the gap in student learning achievement between the United States and Canada, which ranked 11 places higher on the 2009 PISA exam. Replacing the bottom 8 percent of teachers would bring the United States up to the level of Finland's PISA performance. Hanushek (2011) notes that it is difficult to identify any other single policy with potential impacts of this size on overall learning results. His estimates assume an unconstrained supply of "average quality" replacement teachers. More recent simulations that factor in the likely need to raise teacher salaries to attract adequate replacement teachers still find that the increase in students' lifetime earnings from replacing the bottom 5 percent of teachers with average quality teachers would be roughly $300,000 in extra earnings per student. This is still roughly 10 times the additional salary costs necessary to attract additional average-quality teachers to replace the lowest performers (Chetty,

Friedman, and Rockoff, forthcoming). The experience in the Washington, DC, public schools, where the introduction of a comprehensive teacher evaluation system triggered a sharp increase in the exit of low-performing teachers, provides one of the clearest examples of how powerfully and quickly this policy can raise school system performance. (See chapter 4 for a detailed discussion.)

The second channel is the more general corrosion of performance incentives that can occur if there are no perceived sanctions for poor performance. Research from the United States suggests that these effects can be large as well (Jacob 2012). A 2004 policy in Chicago's public schools expanded the autonomy of school principals to dismiss probationary teachers with unsatisfactory performance. In the first four years after the reform, roughly 12 percent of all teachers on probation were dismissed. Researchers found that relative to their peers in the same school, dismissed teachers had significantly higher rates of absenteeism (defined as 15 or more absences per school year) and lower job performance ratings, and their students had smaller year-on-year learning gains—seemingly validating the ability of principals to identify the weakest teachers. An unexpected finding was that after the first year of the policy, absenteeism declined sharply not only for probationary teachers but also for tenured teachers (figure 5.2). Across all schools, teacher absences fell by 10 percent and the prevalence of frequent absenteeism fell by 25 percent.

A growing number of LAC countries are adopting reforms to limit job security for poor performing teachers. Colombia's 2002 teacher reform provides that teachers

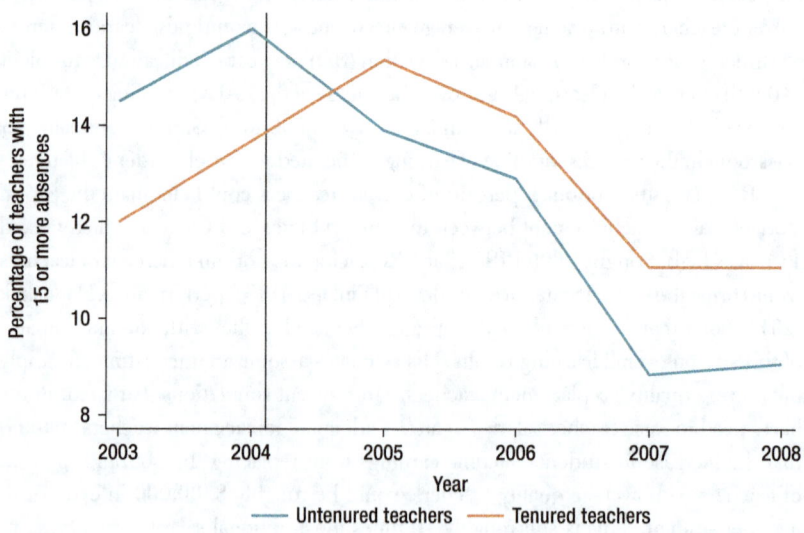

FIGURE 5.2: Teacher absence rates in Chicago public schools after change in probation policy, 2004–08

Source: Jacob 2012.

rated unsatisfactory on two successive annual evaluations will be dismissed. Chile's 2004 teacher evaluation system similarly calls for municipal teachers receiving two successive poor performance evaluations to be separated from the system. Ecuador's 2009 reform of the teacher career path, a teacher reform in the Argentine province of Buenos Aires, and Peru's 2012 teacher reform have similar provisions. While it is difficult to obtain information on the number of teachers actually separated to date, the numbers in all cases appear so far to be relatively small—and far below 5 percent per year.

Legislation passed in 2011 in Chile explicitly allows municipal school directors to dismiss up to 5 percent of teachers each year on performance grounds (defined quite broadly). Coupled with Chile's teacher evaluation system, which generates transparent information on individual teachers' observed classroom practice plus a peer assessment, there is more scope in Chile today than anywhere else in LAC for progressive actions to counsel the lowest performing teachers out of the profession— potentially producing the kind of systemwide impacts on average student learning that Hanushek (2011) has estimated.

While the 2011 Chilean law is a strong reform in the context of Latin America more generally, in the Chilean context it simply brings the powers of public school directors into line with those of publicly subsidized (voucher) schools, which follow private labor law and may dismiss teachers. Giving municipal schools equal autonomy to hire and fire teachers may, in fact, be important for achieving the potential efficiency gains of Chile's voucher system. Until 2011, while students could migrate freely to voucher schools—and government capitation funding transferred with them—civil service job stability left municipal schools in a situation of declining enrollments and falling capitation revenue yet unable to retrench excess teachers. As voucher schools have grown to more than 50 percent of basic education enrollments, many municipalities have been forced to subsidize low-enrollment schools rather than downsize or close them. If schooling supply cannot fully adjust to shifts in demand, the potential efficiency gains of a voucher system are not captured.

Teacher performance evaluation systems adopted in Colombia, Ecuador, Buenos Aires (Argentina), and under development in Peru all allow for teachers identified as consistent low performers to receive remedial training and, if subsequent evaluations do not improve, to be dismissed from the profession. If implemented effectively, these reforms have the potential to strengthen teachers' accountability for performance. Most are quite new, however, and their impact depends on establishing sound systems for individual teacher performance evaluation, as discussed in chapter 4.

Managerial oversight

Performance monitoring and feedback from supervisors is a second major source of accountability pressure in most occupations. All countries in the region have some type of formal system of school supervision. In countries such as Jamaica, where regular visits from district personnel include classroom observations and written feedback, these systems are relatively strong. While these supervisory reports may be useful for schools, however, they have few consequences for individual teachers' careers, either positive or negative.

Most commonly, school supervision is intermittent and perfunctory. Reports of remote rural schools being visited less than once a year are common. Even when visited, supervisors may focus entirely on school infrastructure or issues reported by the director and spend little or no time in observing teachers in the classroom.

Chile launched an initiative to strengthen managerial oversight in 2012 with the creation of an independent institution responsible for monitoring school quality, the Agencia de Calidad de la Educación (Education Quality Assurance Agency). The agency is charged with producing in-depth assessments of individual primary and secondary schools (similar to the role of accreditation agencies in higher education) through school visits and monitoring of student test scores and enrollment data. During visits to schools, the agency assesses the school director's leadership, the classroom learning environment, teacher quality, school climate, resources, and performance. The agency is mandated to provide individual schools with actionable feedback and suggestions on areas to improve. To promote accountability, it will also produce public reports of school performance and rankings. The agency began operations in 2013, and school visits will begin in 2014; it is an interesting model to observe and learn from.

Irrespective of higher-level oversight bodies, the most direct source of accountability pressure on teachers in any school is the director (principal). Research has long pointed to the central importance that school directors have in making schools effective. In Singapore and Ontario (Canada) identifying and grooming talented school directors is one of the school system's highest priorities. Ontario has notably strict requirements to become a director, including classroom experience and a graduate degree (Pervin and Campbell 2011; Schwartz and Mehta 2014). In Singapore, all new teacher candidates are assessed for leadership potential, and the most promising are steered into a specialized track for school directors. In this track, they receive training designed to develop key managerial competencies, including the observation and evaluation of teachers' classroom practice; supervised practice in managerial positions; and internships to shadow experienced principals (Tucker 2011). No country in Latin America at present has such comprehensive measures in place to ensure that teachers are supported and managed by high-quality school leaders.

New research provides insights into the managerial strategies the best directors use. In Latin America and elsewhere, even though teachers cannot easily be dismissed from the school system, directors have managerial authority to shape the teaching team in individual schools through hiring, promotion, and transfer decisions. Research in Florida analyzing low-income schools with impressive improvements in performance concludes that school directors' strategic management of the teaching staff was the key driver. In these school districts, just as in Latin American school systems, teacher rotations must be negotiated with district officials as well as with the teachers involved.

But researchers documented that directors in improving schools were markedly more successful than directors in other schools in encouraging low-performing teachers to transfer out. On average, directors in improving schools achieve a significant turnover in their teaching force within five years of assuming leadership (Boyd et al. 2008; Kalogrides and Loeb 2012).

The researchers also conclude that school directors' ability to identify and remove the lowest performing teachers is linked in an essential way to the attraction of talented teachers. The latter want to work for school leaders who value their work and with colleagues who share their level of performance and commitment (Loeb, Kalogrides, and Béteille 2012).

A third strand of research in the United States, however, has shown that a large share of school directors lack the ability to distinguish between high- and low-performing teachers. As a result, high value-added teachers leave these schools at higher rates, and school performance declines (Jacob, Vidyarthi, and Carroll 2012).

There has been little research attention given to the role of school directors in managing teaching performance in Latin America. An important case is Colombia, where the comprehensive 2002 teacher reform discussed later in this chapter established new entry standards, a probationary process, and a new career path for teachers. The reform also gave school directors explicit responsibility for annual evaluations of their teachers' performance, significant latitude in how to conduct the evaluations (awarding 100 points across a number of dimensions, such as pedagogy, knowledge of the curriculum, communication skills, parent feedback, student feedback, peer feedback, and even student learning progress) and the power to terminate teachers who score below 60 points on two successive performance evaluations. The new regime applies only to teachers hired since 2004 (the first year of implementation), and these teachers as of 2012 still represent only 16 percent of the teaching force. Given the promising design of this reform, it is unfortunate that little research exists on its implementation. The limited evidence available, discussed later in this chapter, is that directors have been reluctant to exercise their power to dismiss teachers.

With the exception of Cuba, managerial oversight of teachers in the region appears notably weak. In Cuba, monitoring teacher performance is a core responsibility of school directors. Carnoy (2007) chronicles the substantial time directors spend observing and working with teachers and the direct manner in which they hold individual teachers accountable for their students' learning progress.

Cuba's managerial model is far from the norm in the rest of LAC. The notion that school directors should be "instructional leaders" responsible for observing teachers in the classroom and guiding their development is uncommon. In Minas Gerais, Brazil, 604 school directors in a statewide representative sample of schools ranked the average amount of time spent observing teachers as eighth priority among eight core tasks, well behind administration and reporting, fundraising, and meeting with parents (Instituto Hartmann Regueira 2011). Indeed, the enormous variation within schools in teachers' use of instructional time is prima facie evidence that school directors are either unaware of these issues or lack the capacity or motivation to address them. (See chapter 2 for a more thorough discussion.)

A number of LAC countries and school systems in Brazil are starting to address this issue. Ecuador in 2009 radically reformed the standards and selection process for school directors, who were previously appointed for life. A large share of the country's school directors was offered early retirement, and a younger, better-trained cohort has now assumed office. Peru's 2012 teacher statute similarly sets higher technical standards for school directors and mandates a formal system for regular evaluation of their performance, currently under development. Minas Gerais, Rio de Janeiro state, and Rio de Janeiro municipality in 2010 and 2011 all adopted new standards and screening procedures for school directors and have invested in specially designed training courses to improve directors' ability to evaluate and manage teacher performance and lead school-improvement strategies.

Client feedback

The third source of accountability pressure in most professions is direct feedback from clients. In education, client power comes through parents' enrollment decisions ("choice" among alternative schools) or voice, the direct expression of complaints or praise to school personnel. These direct feedback mechanisms are sometimes called the "short route" for holding providers of public services locally accountable, in contrast to the "long route" of citizens voting for better service provision through electoral channels (World Bank 2004; Bruns, Filmer, and Patrinos 2011). In private schools and Chile's voucher system, the "choice" lever is powerful, since parent dissatisfaction with school or teacher performance can result in the immediate loss of students and school revenues. As noted earlier, parent demand in Chile has driven a significant shift from municipal to publicly subsidized schools, which now account for about 55 percent of total basic education enrollments (up from 0 percent in 1982 and 30 percent in 1995). However, researchers have documented that parent enrollment decisions in Chile are not strongly influenced by school performance data (Mizala and Urquiola 2007).

In most of the region, parents' scope for choice among alternative schools is limited. In the public system, students are mapped to a specific school in a geographic catchment area, and there are both practical (transport, time) and administrative barriers to switching. Private schools are not an affordable alternative for most parents, although the share of private school enrollments in basic education (currently about 17 percent across the region) is growing, particularly in urban areas. Household surveys confirm that the new demand is coming from middle-income and sometimes quite low-income parents frustrated with the poor quality of public schools.

Across most of LAC, the strongest source of parental "client power" over teacher behavior and school results has come from reforms to increase parental voice in school management. Central American countries such as El Salvador, Nicaragua, Guatemala, and Honduras, as well as several states in Mexico and Brazil, have been global leaders since the early 1990s in adopting SBM reforms designed to empower parents and communities to hold schools accountable for results. SBM decentralizes key areas of decision making from the system to the school level, and typically involves local stakeholders in these decisions through school councils.

The global evidence to date (summarized in Bruns, Patrinos, and Filmer 2011) is that relatively "strong" models of SBM—where school-level councils have the authority to hire and fire school directors and teachers and to control school budgets—can have positive effects on school results. But several studies show this is not guaranteed, if parents and community members involved in school councils lack the information or training necessary to empower them vis-à-vis school authorities (Barrera-Osorio et al. 2009; Duflo, Dupas, and Kremer 2012). Moreover, the majority of school-based management programs today in LAC do not delegate hiring and firing authority to the school level. Even countries that had strong forms of SBM in the 1990s, such as El Salvador and Nicaragua, have subsequently reversed some of these elements. A recent exception is Ecuador, which in 2008 established Gobiernos Escolares Ciudadanos—school-level councils formed by representatives of parents, teachers, and students—and gave them an explicit role in evaluating teacher performance and selecting new teacher applicants.

Looking across the region, however, the attention of reformers in recent years appears to be shifting away from faith in client power as an accountability strategy and toward greater development of the two other levers we have discussed: (a) eliminating job stability for ineffective teachers and (b) strengthening school directors' managerial oversight.

Financial incentives

Chapter 1 documented the weak financial incentives for talented teachers in Latin America: low average salaries relative to teachers' level of formal education; a highly compressed wage scale; and promotion across the career path driven almost entirely by seniority, delinked from performance. In three LAC countries analyzed closely, statutory teachers' wages in the top pay grade (typically accessed after 30 years of service) are only 82 percent higher than entry-level salaries (113 percent higher in the best case; 57 percent higher in the most compressed) (OECD 2012). Representative of the region as a whole are data showing that 90 percent of a teacher's wage anywhere in Brazil is explained by his or her age (a proxy for years of service) and years of education. This compensation structure is strikingly inconsistent with the empirical evidence that identically educated, identically aged teachers in Brazil—and elsewhere—produce very different classroom environments and results, whether observed directly in their use of classroom time and teaching practice, or in the value-added learning outcomes of their students.

These issues are not unique to Latin America. The majority of education systems worldwide are characterized by salary environments where extra effort, innovation, and good results are not rewarded. There is remarkable concurrence in the literature that the widespread pattern of relatively flat salary progression over teachers' careers plus promotion policies rigidly linked to seniority combine to create weak incentives both for ambitious individuals to enter the profession and for teachers in service to perform to the best of their ability (Umansky 2005; Ballou and Podgursky 2002; Delannoy and Sedlacek 2001; Odden and Kelley 2002; Hoxby and Leigh 2004).

Figure 5.1 depicts three policy instruments that can differentiate financial rewards in order to strengthen performance incentives for teachers: (a) salary differentials, (b) bonus pay, and (c) pensions and other benefits.

We do not review pension policy, although it is an important dimension of overall teacher compensation and presents some policy issues in LAC. Countries that began the mass expansion of basic education 30 to 40 years ago are increasingly experiencing the fiscal impact of large numbers of teachers reaching retirement age. In the Brazilian state of São Paulo, for example, almost half of the 500,000 teachers on the state's payroll in 2012 were retirees drawing a pension. Several incentive issues related to pension policy are beginning to get more attention. One is the relative attractiveness of teacher pensions, which tend to be structured as relatively generous defined benefit systems while much of the private sector has moved to less costly defined-contribution systems. A second issue, in countries with decentralized education systems, is that differences in state-, district-, or municipal-level pension policy (and the nonportability of pension contributions across jurisdictions) create differential incentives for teachers— either impeding or stimulating teacher movement across different systems. Pension policy is clearly part of the overall incentives for teachers and of growing concern to policy makers on fiscal grounds. However, we know of no reforms or analysis in the LAC region to date focused on teachers' pensions; most reform efforts and analysis have covered the public sector as a whole.

We also do not attempt to review the considerable experience in LAC countries with salary differentials introduced for ad hoc purposes, such as to attract scarce skills (in science or math) or to top-up salaries or offer in-kind incentives such as housing to compensate for difficult working conditions (remote rural areas or urban at-risk schools). As reviewed in Vegas (2005) for Latin America and Goldhaber (2009) for the United States, there is evidence that this form of incentive pay is generally supported by teachers and can work, but there are common problems. Incentives are often too small to compensate teachers fully for the perceived hardship. Inconsistencies in implementation are also frequent; salary incentives given to rural teachers in Bolivia and Peru are not removed when they transfer to nonhardship schools (Crouch 2005, 411; Urquiola and Vegas 2005). These forms of incentive pay also tend to remain at the margin of the overall salary structure.

Instead, we focus on a new wave of experimentation in LAC with broader financial incentives for teachers. Some of these are at the vanguard of policy globally and could have major impact in the LAC region.

Career path reforms, sometimes called "competency-based promotion and pay" reforms, increase the financial incentives for high-quality teachers through two actions: (a) decompressing the salary scale, with higher compensation for the top pay grades and increased salary increments associated with grade promotion and (b) making promotions contingent on competence, rather than simply seniority. While Mexico's Carrera Magisterial was the only program of competency-based promotion and pay in LAC before 2002, since then four other countries have adopted these: Colombia, Ecuador, Peru, and Brazil (state of São Paulo). Two other systems—in Chile and the Brazilian state of Rio de Janeiro—have developed "hybrid" programs that offer differentiated, competency-based pay increases to teachers for a finite period on top of the traditional seniority-based career path.

School-based bonus pay is the second major reform trend. In 1996, Chile was the first country in the region to launch such a program with the National System of School Performance Assessment (Sistema Nacional de Evaluación del Desempeño de los Establecimientos Educacionales Subvencionados [SNED]) school-based bonus. Since 2008, this approach has been growing rapidly, especially in Brazil where at least 20 different states and municipalities have introduced school-based bonuses linked to performance.

The root aim of both types of reform is stronger financial incentives for teachers, but some key distinctions affect their administrative feasibility and potential impact. First, career path reforms reward individual teachers—and thus require a system for evaluating the performance and competencies of a large number of individuals. In contrast, for most school-based bonus pay schemes, the main administrative requirement is a student assessment system, which is often already in place.

Second, career path reforms typically reward teachers for what they are capable of doing according to some measure of competence (typically, a test of content mastery) that is assumed to be a relatively constant characteristic of the teacher's quality. Bonus pay, however, is typically an ex post reward for results accomplished during a prior period (typically, the prior school year), whether it be an input (teacher attendance), outcome (student test scores, graduation rates), or combined measure of performance.

Third, career path reforms under most models have long-term fiscal implications because they increase teachers' base pay and pensions. Bonus pay, on the one hand, does not add to base salaries and allows for flexible adjustment of the annual fiscal envelope by manipulating either the average size of the award or the share of candidates rewarded. Bonus programs are easier to suspend at short notice; rolling back or substantially adapting a career path reform can be politically and administratively complicated. On the other hand, precisely because career path reforms signal a long-term trajectory of potential performance rewards, they may have more incentive power in attracting more talented individuals into teaching.

Career path reforms

Table 5.1 provides an overview of the major career path reforms in LAC and hybrid programs adopted over the past decade. Career path reforms are almost always

TABLE 5.1: Career path reforms

Country (reform date); evaluator (eval. date)	Type	Design and coverage	Performance measure	Award process	Predictability	Monitoring and support	Salary scale and distribution	Type of increase	Total cost	Evaluation method and period	Results
A. Promotion based on teacher content mastery											
Colombia: Estatuto de Profesionalización Docente, 2002 Orme (2012)	Individual (indiv.)	National, voluntary for teachers in service; mandatory for new entrants	Tests of content mastery, pedagogy, behavioral competencies	Threshold score of 80% required for promotion; promotions contingent on budget available (those with highest scores given priority)	Test implemented yearly since 2010; 45,773 teachers took test in 2011; 19% achieved threshold score for promotion	Tests developed and administered by ICFES, graded by national university. Unsuccessful candidates may retake test following year	Branch 1 (secondary school degree) levels A–D: 127%–204% of base (1A) salary. Branch 2 (bachelor's degree, no specialization), levels A–D: 126%–230% of base salary. Branch 2 (bachelor's degree with specialization) 137%–256% of base salary. Branch 3 (master's degree), levels A–D: 211%–357% of base salary. Branch 3 (doctorate), levels A–D: 279%–475% of base salary	Base pay increase. Must stay 3 years in grade before applying for further promotion	n.a.	Panel regression analysis (2004–11)	Inconsistent effects; positive for some but not all grades and subjects

(continued on next page)

TABLE 5.1: Career path reforms *(continued)*

Country (reform date); evaluator (eval. date)	Type	Design and coverage	Performance measure	Award process	Predictability	Monitoring and support	Salary scale and distribution	Type of increase	Total cost	Evaluation method and period	Results
Peru: Carrera Pública Magisterial, 2008, revised 2012	Indiv.	National, voluntary for teachers in service; mandatory for new entrants	Tests of content mastery and pedagogy	Teachers achieving threshold score passed to second stage evaluation by local committees (for specific school-level CPM positions)	68,000 applicants from 2009–11, of which 24,966 were incorporated into system	Unsuccessful candidates may retake test following year	Level 1: 50% increase over base salary Level 2: 115% base Level 3: 130% base Level 4: 150% base Level 5: 200% base	Base pay increase Must stay 3 years at level 1; 5 years, level 2; 6 years, level 3; 6 years, level 4	S/.38.7 million (US$10.8 million) from 2009–11	n.a.	n.a.
Brazil: SP Prova de Promoção, 2010, revised 2011	Indiv.	State, voluntary for teachers in service	Tests of content mastery, by discipline	Tournament, up to 20% of teachers scoring above threshold test score earn promotion	96,042 teachers took test in 2010; 77,892 achieved threshold score; 43,397 (20% of all teachers) entered level 1 of new career stream	Unsuccessful candidates may retake test following year	Level 1: base teacher salary Level 2: 125% base Level 3: 150% base Level 4: 175% base Level 5: 200% base Revised in 2011 to 8 levels, with 10.5% salary increase with each level	Base pay increase Must stay 3 years in grade	n.a.	n.a.	

(continued on next page)

241

TABLE 5.1: Career path reforms *(continued)*

Country (reform date); evaluator (eval. date)	Type	Design and coverage	Performance measure	Award process	Predictability	Monitoring and support	Salary scale and distribution	Type of increase	Total cost	Evaluation method and period	Results
B. Promotion based on comprehensive teacher evaluation											
Ecuador: Ley de Carrera Docente y Escalafón del Magisterio, 2009	Indiv.	National, initially voluntary; mandatory from 2011	1. Tests of content mastery, by discipline, and pedagogical skills; 2. Teacher self-evaluation; 3. Evaluation by commissions for excellence	Teachers rated excellent (90/100) receive top salary increase; very good (80–89) smaller salary increase; good (61–79) no salary increase and evaluated again within 2 years	In first round (2009), 2% (of 2,570 teachers) rated excellent; 24%, very good; 73%, good; and 3%, poor	Currently Ministry of Education, but plans are to decentralize this to an independent agency. Teachers rated insufficient (60 or below) undergo mandatory training and evaluated again following year. Two successive evaluations below 60 lead to dismissal	In 2009, US$1,200 for teachers rated excellent (5.5% average wage) and US$900 for teachers rated good	Base pay increase for 4 years	n.a.	n.a.	n.a.

(continued on next page)

TABLE 5.1: Career path reforms *(continued)*

Country (reform date); evaluator (eval. date)	Type	Design and coverage	Performance measure	Award process	Predictability	Monitoring and support	Salary scale and distribution	Type of increase	Total cost	Evaluation method and period	Results
Peru: Ley de Reforma Magisterial, 2012	Indiv.	National, mandatory	(Proposed) Tests of content mastery, by discipline; classroom observation; and evaluation by peers, students, parents	Evaluation developed and administered by external agency		Teachers with poor evaluations offered training; teachers with two successive poor evaluations dismissed	Level 1: base salary Level 2: 110% base Level 3: 125% base Level 4: 140% base Level 5: 170% base Level 6: 200% base Level 7: 230% base Level 8: 260% base	Base pay increase Must stay in level 1 three years, levels 2, 3, 4 four years, levels 5, 6, 7 five years	S/.720 million/ year (approx. US$200 million)	n.a.	n.a.

C. Promotion based on comprehensive evaluation including student test results

Country (reform date); evaluator (eval. date)	Type	Design and coverage	Performance measure	Award process	Predictability	Monitoring and support	Salary scale and distribution	Type of increase	Total cost	Evaluation method and period	Results
Mexico-Carrera Magisterial, 1992 Santibáñez et al. (2007)	Indiv.	National, voluntary	Tests of content mastery (28%), student test scores (20%) Other factors such as courses taken, seniority, peer evaluation (52%)	Rank-order within each state	In first years of implementation (1992–94), almost 100% of teachers accessed CM; after 2005, around 1% per year	No	25%–200% of base wage	Base pay increase	n.a.	RDD, 4 years	No impact on learning outcomes for students of teachers facing stronger incentives compared to weaker ones

(continued on next page)

TABLE 5.1: Career path reforms *(continued)*

Country (reform date); evaluator (eval. date)	Type	Design and coverage	Performance measure	Award process	Predictability	Monitoring and support	Salary scale and distribution	Type of increase	Total cost	Evaluation method and period	Results
D. Hybrid career incentives											
Chile: AEP Asignacion de Excelencia Pedagogica, 2002 Eisenberg (2008); Bravo et al. (2008)	Indiv.	National, open to teachers in municipal and voucher schools; voluntary	Tests of content mastery, a videotaped class, and portfolio of work	Teachers scoring above threshold on comprehensive performance measure receive award	Only 20% of applicants achieve award annually, as of 2012, only 4% of all teachers had ever achieved award		Until 2011, flat increase of $1,250 for 10 years From 2012, larger rewards, proportional to salary Avg. reward 8% of annual salary	Base pay increase for 10 years From 2012, pay increase for 4 years		RDD	Higher test scores for students exposed to larger number of AEP teachers
Chile: AVDI Asignacion Variable por Desempeno Individual, 2004 Eisenberg (2008); Bravo et al. (2008)	Indiv.	National, open to teachers in municipal schools only; voluntary	Tests of content mastery and pedagogy (for teachers rated outstanding or competent on comprehensive national teacher evaluation system)	Teachers scoring in top 3 categories (outstanding, competent, or sufficient) receive award	15% of teachers (85% of teachers who take the test earn some bonus, but these represent only 25% of all municipal teachers in 2011)		Maximum award 25% of annual salary; average 7%–11% of annual salary	Base pay increase for four years		RDD	Higher test scores for students exposed to larger number of AVDI teachers

(continued on next page)

TABLE 5.1: Career path reforms *(continued)*

Country (reform date); evaluator (eval. date)	Type	Design and coverage	Performance measure	Award process	Predictability	Monitoring and support	Salary scale and distribution	Type of increase	Total cost	Evaluation method and period	Results
Brazil, State of Rio de Janeiro: teacher certification program, pending, 2014	Indiv.	State (public schools only), voluntary for teachers in service at least one year	Tests of content mastery and pedagogy; classroom observation for level 3	Teachers scoring above threshold receive base pay increase for 5 years	Not yet implemented	Tests developed and applied by external agency. Unsuccessful candidates receive scholarships to finance training	Level 1: additional R$500–1,000 per month (30%–75% increase over base salary) Level 2: additional R$1,000–2,000 per month Level 3: additional R$2,000–4,000 per month	Base pay increase for 5 years May apply for next level after one year Unless promoted or recertified, candidates lose pay increase after 5 years	n.a.	n.a.	n.a.

Notes: Ch$ = Chilean pesos; CPM = Carrera Publica Magisterial; ICFES = Instituto Colombiano para la Evaluación de la Educación; n.a. = not applicable; R$ = Brazilian reais; RDD = regression discontinuity design; S/. = Peruvian nuevos soles.

implemented systemwide, and thus are difficult to evaluate rigorously. There is no experimental evidence—either in LAC or globally—on career path reforms, and there are very few evaluations of any type. Because career path reforms directly tackle some of the most widely diagnosed issues of teacher performance incentives—promotion delinked from performance and flat lifetime salary trajectory—they are the most straightforward policy instrument for attracting higher-caliber candidates into teaching over time. Career path reforms also create incentives for individual teachers, which may have stronger impacts on teacher performance per dollar of expenditure than group incentives, which are subject to free-rider behavior (the tendency of some members of a group to shirk if their effort levels cannot easily be monitored). However, there is no good global evidence currently on any of these important questions.

Looking across the LAC programs, there is no standard design. The programs differ in how teachers' competency is evaluated, what the size of incremental financial rewards is, and who carries out the evaluations. It is also fairly common for programs to be redesigned, sometimes in major ways, within the space of a few years. Finally, in contrast to the United States where the recent trend is for career path reforms to incorporate student learning results into teachers' evaluations, none of the programs in LAC except Mexico's Carrera Magisterial has ever done so.

The one common design feature is that most countries make the new career ladder mandatory for new teacher candidates, but allow existing teachers to opt in on a voluntary basis. Existing teachers may thus remain within a seniority-based promotion system, but to access the new grades and salary inducements, they must submit to new types of evaluation. This condition has resulted in slow uptake of the incentive by the existing teaching stock in several countries, especially if the new standards are perceived to be high. In Colombia, after 10 years, only 14 percent of existing teachers (and 38 percent of all teachers) have entered the new teaching ladder. In Peru, only 10 percent of existing teachers entered the Carrera Pública Magisterial in its first three years of implementation, motivating the ministry to redesign the program in 2012 and make it mandatory.

We review the implementation experience and key features of the major career path reforms in the region, grouped into three broad categories depending upon whether the performance measures used to determine promotion are focused on (a) content mastery and pedagogical skills measured on an examination; (b) comprehensive measures of teachers' skill (for example, including peer feedback and classroom observations); or (c) comprehensive measures that include student learning results. The last dimension is important because generating student test scores for every grade, subject, and classroom—which is necessary if student test score gains are included in individual teacher's performance evaluations—hugely increases the costs and complexity of a student assessment system. The hybrid programs are discussed as a separate group because of their unique implementation features.

Promotion based on knowledge and skills tests

Colombia's Estatuto de Profesionalización Docente (EPD), 2002. Colombia's EPD reform remains one of the most comprehensive and ambitious efforts in the region to improve teacher quality through higher standards, performance evaluation and professional development. Major features include the following:

- *Higher standards for new recruitment*: more flexible entry into teaching of students from different academic disciplines (i.e., not only teacher pre-service training) was allowed and a competitive recruitment process for all teacher candidates managed by the Comisión Nacional de Servicio Civil (rather than the Ministry of Education or local education officials) was introduced. The screening process includes tests of content mastery, skills and aptitudes, and an interview. Only teachers rated 60 out of 100 or higher are hired (about 29 percent of applicants in 2009). Teachers lacking a bachelor's degree in education must subsequently complete one.
- *Annual performance evaluation for all teachers*: school directors formally evaluate the performance of every teacher each year. Teachers rated 60 out of 100 or higher may continue in service. Teachers scoring below 60 in two consecutive years are dismissed from service.
- *Promotion based on competency*: under the EPD, all promotions are based on competence rather than seniority. A rating of 80 out of 100 or higher on a combined assessment of skills and academic qualifications is necessary to move to a higher grade or salary level. Assessments are managed by the national testing agency, Instituto Colombiano para la Evaluación de la Educación (ICFES), and subnational governments under the direction of the Ministry of Education. Actual promotion of those teachers scoring above the threshold, however, is contingent on the availability of budget. Assessments have been held in 2010, 2011, and 2012.

All teachers hired since 2002 are covered by the EPD's competency-based promotion system, but its provisions are voluntary for teachers hired prior to 2002. Voluntary entry into the system by existing teachers has been low; 10 years after its adoption, the EPD covers only 112,000 (38 percent) of Colombia's 295,000 teachers. The career path places teachers and principals in three different grades based on their level of formal education. Each grade consists of four wage levels (A through D) that can be achieved over a teacher's career through demonstrated knowledge, skills, attitudes, performance, and values. As of 2011, 83 percent of all EPD teachers were concentrated in grade 2 (with professional degrees), 15 percent in grade 1, and only 1 percent in grade 3. Within all three grades, 94 percent of teachers are concentrated in the lowest wage level (A). Overall, 69 percent of EPD teachers fall in category 2A.

The bar for promotion is very high. Moving from one salary level to the next requires (a) at least three years in service; (b) scoring at least 60 percent on the compulsory annual performance assessments over the previous 2 years; and (c) scoring 80 percent or higher on the EPD's assessment of competencies, which cover behavioral, pedagogical, and discipline-specific competencies. In 2011, less than 19 percent of candidates passed the threshold for promotion to a higher salary level within their current grade, and less than 22 percent achieved promotion to a higher grade. Almost 60 percent of EDP teachers chose not to take the 2011 competency assessment.

The low pursuit of promotions is striking given that promotions trigger substantial salary increases. In 2012, base salaries for wage level D within grade 2 were 81 percent higher than for level A, and for grade 1 the differential was 104 percent. However, promotions are granted only insofar as the budget for that year allows, with teachers with higher scores given priority.

One factor differentiating the political economy of the Colombia EPD reform from others in the region has been a concern with making the overall wage bill more fiscally sustainable. While the other reforms have been driven by a desire to raise overall teacher remuneration while maximizing performance incentives, the pre-2002 schedule of teacher salaries and pensions in Colombia was unsustainably generous, with the majority of teachers already having attained the highest wage levels through seniority-based promotions.

The reform, however, has not eroded the supply of teacher candidates; in 2009, there were more than nine applicants per opening. As there is no scope for integrating the two regimes, both the ministry and departmental education systems continue to manage their cadres of teachers.

The Colombian reform was comprehensive and coherent in design and incorporated many elements that are considered global best practice, such as a formal probation period for new teacher candidates, regular teacher evaluation, and an explicit route for dismissal of ineffective teachers. Several researchers have tried to evaluate the reform but have been hampered by inconsistent data. Studies show that EPD teachers on average are better educated than non-EPD teachers of the same age (Ome 2012). However, documenting the impact of the reform on student learning outcomes has been difficult. Without access to good prereform trend data, Ome (2012) used regression analysis to correlate school-level test results with the presence of EPD teachers. Schools with higher share of EPD teachers have lower dropout rates and slightly higher test scores in some grades and disciplines, but the correlations are inconsistent (Ome 2012).

A major implementation issue identified in Colombia is a lack of rigor among school directors in conducting teachers' annual performance assessments. Almost all public teachers in the country obtain almost perfect scores in the evaluation. School directors apparently give universally high scores to teachers as a way to avoid conflicts; some are also reported to delegate this task to administrative staff. As a consequence, school-level teacher evaluations are widely believed to be weak indicators of teachers' actual classroom practice and effectiveness. This practice also negates the value of teacher evaluations as providing formative feedback to teachers to improve classroom practice or in motivating them to pursue training.

Although there is little hard research evidence on its impact, a general assessment of the Colombian EPD career path reform is that its impressive design has been undercut by ineffective implementation. Especially relevant for other countries is the observation that relying exclusively on school directors for teacher performance evaluations without objective standards, rubrics, and external evaluators is problematic.

Peru's Carrera Pública Magisterial (CPM), 2008.[3] As part of a major reform effort to raise teacher quality, in 2008 the Peruvian government introduced higher standards for new teachers and a career ladder with significantly higher remuneration. Entry to the new system was voluntary for existing civil service teachers, but mandatory for all new civil service hires and existing contract teachers seeking civil service job stability and pension benefits.

Entry to the new career followed two stages. Under the first stage, CPM applicants take a nationally defined test of content mastery. Those who exceed a threshold score move to the second stage and compete for designated CPM positions at specific schools. Teachers may not receive a CPM salary increase in situ. In the second stage, school-level evaluation committees, including district- and regional-level supervisors, interview and evaluate candidates before making a final selection. Control of the number of CPM positions each year allowed the fiscal impact of the program to be managed.

CPM level 1 offered an annual salary approximately 50 percent higher than the prevailing wage for entering teachers. After three years, teachers achieving level 2 could receive an additional 15 percent salary increment, with salaries at levels 3, 4, and 5, 30 percent, 50 percent, and 100 percent, respectively, above the level 1 salary. The CPM thus represented a very significant decompression of the prior salary scale, where top salaries were only 6 percent higher than entry level.

A striking feature of the implementation experience from 2008–12 was that only 10 percent of the 250,000 existing teachers with civil service status (*nombrados*) opted to enter the system. Even very significant salary increases were not sufficient to induce teachers with job stability to submit to the competency test, which was perceived to be difficult. The vast majority of CPM applicants have been new teacher candidates and those on temporary contracts (*contratados*). Of these, over the first several years only about one-third, on average, achieved the minimum threshold score and only a minority of these actually found school-level positions that incorporated them into the new regime. Interestingly, the classroom observations carried out in Peru in 2011 found CPM teachers to be significantly more effective than regular teachers in using class time and keeping students engaged.

By 2012, only 25 percent of all teachers had entered the CPM and the ministry was concerned by the prospect of managing parallel labor regimes for years to come. Whereas CPM teachers were promoted on competency grounds, were subject to regular evaluation, and could be dismissed from service after successive poor evaluations, the ministry had no such tools for managing the performance of the majority of the teaching force. This was the impetus for a further career path reform in 2012, the Ley de Reforma Magisterial, described in more detail below.

São Paulo State, Brazil, Prova de Promoção, 2009. The state of São Paulo adopted a career path reform that allowed civil service teachers to opt into a higher salary scale by passing a test of content mastery. From an average salary of 1,830 reais (R$)—and top salary of R$3,181—per month in 2009, the fifth and highest salary grade under the Prova de Promoção structure was set at R$6,270 per month, decompressing the ratio of top to bottom teacher salaries from 73 percent to 242 percent. The top salary, at four times per capita gross domestic product annually, also placed these elite teachers in the top 10 percent of professional salaries nationally. Entry to the program was based on tests of content mastery, but the fiscal impact of the reform was also controlled by a tournament rule that only the top 44,000 teachers (equal to 20 percent of all teachers) of those who passed the threshold could access the system each year, in rank order of their performance on the test.

Given the attraction of the higher salaries, 96,000 of the state's 230,000 teachers opted to take the Prova de Promoção in 2010. Of these, 77,000 achieved the threshold score, but only 43,000 (20 percent) were allowed to enter the system. Teachers must wait three years in a new salary grade before they can compete for the next level, with a more demanding threshold score. The goal of the former Brazilian education minister who designed the program was to create radically more attractive incentives for São Paulo's most talented teachers to remain in the profession, for current teachers to continue strengthening their content knowledge, and for new, high-capacity individuals to enter teaching.

However, implementation of the program appears to have been marred by a disconnect between the goal of a highly selective, highly remunerative new career path and a test design that allowed virtually all teachers to exceed the threshold score. The tournament restriction was unpopular. By 2011, the state was forced to revise the reform. In changes aimed at managing the flow and expectations of the large number of teachers already in the new system, the state increased the number of career levels from five to eight and reduced the salary increments between grades. Each promotion now brings only a 10.5 percent salary increase, rather than the previous 25 percent increase, and the additional grades offer the state opportunities to set higher competency thresholds for promotions. Although entry into the program remains voluntary, as of the end of 2012, a significant share of the teaching force was incorporated. As a result, overall salary costs have increased. Unfortunately, there are no evaluations of the impact of the promotion program.

Promotions based on comprehensive performance measures

Ecuador's Ley de Carrera Docente y Escalafón del Magisterio, 2009. After two years of conflict between the teachers' union and the government over the introduction of voluntary teacher performance evaluations, the government in 2009 passed a sweeping reform of the teacher career path that made regular evaluation mandatory and refusal to participate grounds for immediate dismissal.

The evaluation system covers all new teacher applicants, teachers in service, and school directors, and consists of an internal and external evaluation. The internal evaluation includes a teacher self-evaluation, an evaluation by peers, and an evaluation by a commission for excellence. The external evaluation is a test of reading skills, pedagogical skills, and content mastery in a teacher's own discipline.

The Ecuadorian career path builds in incentives for good performers. Teachers and principals evaluated as excellent (90 percent or higher) or very good (80 to 89 percent) receive a salary increase, but it is only for four years, after which they must be evaluated again. The increase is US$1,200 for teachers rated excellent and US$900 for those rated very good. Teachers rated as good (60 to 78 percent) do not receive a salary increase and must be evaluated again within two years. Teachers rated below 60 percent are considered insufficient, must undergo mandatory and comprehensive training, and must be evaluated again the following year. If they score below 60 percent a second time, they are dismissed from the education system.

Evaluation results released by the Ministry of Education to date show that of the 2,570 teachers who took the first round of exams, 2 were rated excellent; 624 (24.3 percent), very good; 1,873 (72.9 percent), good; and 71 (2.8 percent), poor. Unfortunately, there is no evaluation evidence to date on the impact of the reform on school performance.

Peru's Ley de Reforma Magisterial (LRM), 2012. The 2012 LRM in Peru made several key changes to the 2008 CPM. First, and most important, it made the system mandatory, so that all teachers, and not just those seeking promotions, would be subject to performance evaluation on a regular basis. Second, it provides explicit routes for dismissal of teachers with criminal convictions or two successive inadequate performance reviews. Third, it extends the career path to eight levels, with the top salary 260 percent above the entry-level salary. Fourth, it provides for teachers' career progression to be based on comprehensive evaluation of their performance, including classroom observations by trained professionals, and "360-degree" feedback from school directors, peers, students, and community members.

The LRM's design incorporates the latest global evidence on good practice. Especially interesting is its comprehensive approach to teacher evaluation. As discussed in chapter 4, the most rigorous research in this area to date finds that individual teachers' effectiveness in improving their students' learning (value-added learning gains) is well correlated with their ratings on comprehensive evaluation measures that include classroom observations by trained experts and combined feedback from their directors, other teachers, students, and parents (Kane and Staiger 2012). The significant increase in lifetime career incentives represented by the new salary scale in Peru, the explicit processes for targeting support to teachers with poor performance evaluations, the possibility of separating consistent poor performers from service, and the comprehensive approach to teacher evaluation all make the Peruvian reform a promising example for the region that deserves close monitoring and evaluation.

Promotion based on measures including student learning results

Mexico's Carrera Magisterial (CM), 1992. Mexico in 1992 was the first Latin American country to experiment with a higher remuneration career stream within the teaching profession for teachers voluntarily agreeing to performance evaluation. Mexico's CM remains unique in the region for its size and scope.[4] The program awarded permanent pay increases ranging from 25 to 200 percent of base salary to teachers who scored above the evaluation threshold.

The CM used a composite performance measure, in which teacher content knowledge (on a standardized test) represents 28 percent of the total score. The teacher test instrument, which covers subject matter mastery and pedagogy, was considered to present relatively low cognitive demands and teachers took the same test, whether seeking entry in to level A (the lowest level) or promotion to level E (the highest level) (Santibáñez et al. 2007). A further 20 percent of a teacher's score reflects his or her students' learning performance on Mexico's ENLACE (National Assessment of Academic Achievement in Schools). Prior to 1998, student test scores represented 7 percent of the CM total evaluation score.

The CM differs from all of the other programs in LAC in its inclusion of student test scores in the evaluation of teacher performance. The CM has also differed from all other LAC programs in giving a majority weight in the evaluation (52 percent) to factors such as seniority, the highest formal degree earned, and professional development courses taken—criteria for which there is little evidence of impact on student learning outcomes. The final element is a peer review score, but in practice, it has had little variance; almost all teachers received 10 points out of 10 for this element (Santibáñez et al. 2007).

A quasi-experimental evaluation of the CM by McEwan and Santibáñez (2005) used a regression discontinuity design to compare teachers with strong incentives (who needed relatively little extra effort to boost their scores into the qualifying range for promotion) with teachers facing weaker incentives (whose performance levels left them far from the threshold for promotion).[5] The research has found some evidence that students of teachers in the strong incentive group achieved slightly higher test results than teachers in the weak incentive group. However, this effect was been observed only for a very small group of secondary school teachers and was not seen at all among primary school teachers.[6]

More broadly, Santibáñez and McEwan (2005) conclude that inconsistent implementation of the CM affected its power to incentivize change. Although the annual intake into the CM after 2005 was reduced to a very restrictive 1 percent of applicants, during the early years of the program, more than 300,000 teachers (over one-third of all teachers at the time) were incorporated automatically.[7] The rules of the game also changed over time: student test scores increased in weight after 1998.

Resonant of the experience in Colombia with school directors' evaluations and in Chile with teachers' self-evaluations, researchers note that the utility of the CM peer review process was undermined because virtually all teachers received the highest possible score on this dimension.

"Hybrid" career incentive programs

The defining characteristic of a set of career incentive programs in LAC, which we label as "hybrid," is the pursuit of some key goals of a career path reform without the wholesale legislative reform that is often so politically contentious. These programs are typically voluntary, and the salary increases they offer are not permanent. After a fixed four- or five-year period, teachers must be reevaluated and earn the award again. This approach has some advantages. It provides an incentive for teachers to continue to acquire and maintain content mastery. It also allows for more budgetary control, the both the size of the salary increases and the standards for attaining them can be adjusted periodically.

Since the new incentives are simply offered on top of the existing teacher career path, permanent grade promotions and base pay increases continue to be based on seniority. But the "hybrids" introduce the two important changes: (a) a process for transparent assessment of individual teachers' knowledge and skills; and (b) differentiated rewards for the most talented teachers, both in terms of status (certification of excellence) and increases in pay. The cases so far (in Chile and a proposed program in Rio de Janeiro state) are good practice models in terms of their comprehensive measures of teachers' competency, including tests of content knowledge and pedagogy, and provision for direct observation of their classroom practice.

Even though these programs offer teachers a temporary bump in pay, they are conceptually different from bonus pay because they reward individual teachers' knowledge and skills rather than results. More than anything, these programs appear to be an innovative policy response to the political economy challenges of permanent teacher career path reforms. Their disadvantage is that they create a disconnect in career incentives; senior teachers with undistinguished performance may continue to earn more than highly talented younger ones, and teachers with weak knowledge and skills can avoid being evaluated by not opting into the program. For the most part, there is little evidence on the impact of these programs as yet. But their designs will, we hope, attract research attention going forward.

Chile's Asignación de Excelencia Pedagógica (AEP), 2002. Since 2002, Chile's AEP has allowed teachers from voucher and municipal schools to submit to a voluntary evaluation of their content knowledge and classroom practice, including the presentation of a portfolio and a videotaped class. Teachers passing the evaluation receive a salary bonus for the following 10 years. For public school teachers, who are subject to periodic evaluation under the Chile's national teacher evaluation system, the videotaped class can be the same one used for their mandatory evaluations. The municipal teachers may also use their results on the content mastery test to apply for a separate bonus, the Asignación Variable por Desempeño Individual, discussed in the next section (Louzano and Morduchowicz 2011).

The AEP criteria are stringent, and both participation rates and award rates have been low. In a typical year, only about 6 percent of eligible teachers choose to apply and only about one-third of these are successful. As of July 2012, only 4 percent of all teachers in public or publicly subsidized schools have received AEP certification in its entire 10-year history (Libeer 2012). Until 2012, the bonus averaged US$1,250 annually (about 7 percent of an annual salary) and lasted for 10 years (Bravo et al. 2008). Beginning in 2012, the bonus duration was reduced to four years, but the rewards were raised substantially; bonuses for the highest-performing teachers now reach 33 percent of base salary, plus an additional 40 percent of base salary for teachers in the most disadvantaged schools. AEP teachers also are invited to participate in the Red Maestros de Maestros (Teachers of Teachers Network), which supports training activities for other teachers, for which they get additional compensation and public recognition. Teachers may accredit again every four years.

Ministry of Education data show that the AEP is substantially more attractive to younger teachers than more senior ones. In 2010, 61 percent of applicants were in the first (lowest) tier of the teacher career path, and 22 percent were in the second, while only 3 percent of teachers in tier 4 applied. Success rates for the tier 1 and tier 2 applicants are also substantially higher (CPEIP n.d.).

Chile's Asignación Variable por Desempeño Individual (AVDI), 2004. AVDI, the second Chilean program to reward individual teachers for their knowledge and skills, was launched in 2004. It is available only to teachers in the municipal school system. As noted in chapter 4, AVDI builds upon Chile's mandatory teacher evaluation system. It is open to municipal teachers whose performance evaluations place them in the top two tiers: outstanding (approximately 8 percent of teachers annually) or competent (approximately 60 percent of teachers). These teachers may take the AVDI exam to earn a four-year salary increase. The size of the AVDI award (see table 5.2) is scaled to a combination of a teacher's evaluation rating and test performance. The maximum award is 25 percent of base salary (table 5.2).

TABLE 5.2: Financial rewards under Chile's AVDI program, 2013

		AVDI test result		
		Outstanding	Competent	Sufficient
Rating on National Teacher Evaluation System	Outstanding	25% of base salary	15% of base salary	5% of base salary
	Competent	15% of base salary	15% of base salary	5% of base salary

Source: MINEDUC 2014.
Note: AVDI = Asignación Variable por Desempeño Individual.

TABLE 5.3: Teacher results under Chile's AVDI program, 2013

AVDI results	Proportion of teachers tested (percent)
Outstanding	2
Competent	31
Sufficient	59
Do not receive ADVI	8

Source: MINEDUC 2014.
Note: AVDI = Asignación Variable por Desempeño Individual.

After four years teachers must be reevaluated and qualify again for AVDI. Because the AVDI test is considered difficult, only about one-third of eligible teachers opt to take it. Of these, about 85 percent earn a salary increase.[8] But because the test is benchmarked at a high level, only about 33 percent score in the top two performance categories, and 8 percent earn no reward (table 5.3).

It has not been possible to carry out a rigorous evaluation of AEP or AVDI, but a 2008 study has concluded that both programs are successful at identifying the most effective teachers among applicants, and that the students of AEP and AVDI teachers perform better on Chile's standardized tests (Eisenberg 2008; Manzi 2008). Researchers have also found the positive correlation between student test scores and AEP-certified teachers is largest in schools with socioeconomically disadvantaged students (Bravo et al. 2008). These results are useful confirmation that the multidimensional evaluations used for AEP and AVDI have validity as measures of the knowledge and skills that make some teachers more effective than others in the classroom. But the most important objective of a career path—or hybrid—reform is to create incentives that shift the talent pool of entering teachers in a positive direction over time. The research to date has not addressed this question. The small share of eligible teachers applying for these awards—particularly the AEP—suggests that their impact on the overall incentives for teaching in Chile may not be substantial.

Rio de Janeiro state, Brazil's teacher certification program (proposed).[9] The Brazilian state of Rio de Janeiro proposed a teacher career path reform in 2013 that, like the Chilean programs, would complement rather than replace the existing, seniority based, career path. Although the reform has not proceeded, its innovative design merits review. The certification program proposed attractive salary increases for teachers who voluntarily apply. Three grade levels were proposed, with level 1 and 2 certifications raising teachers' annual salaries 25 and 50 percent, respectively, and level 3 certification offering a doubling of annual salaries. Certification at levels 1 and 2 was to be based on teacher performance on competency tests, covering content mastery as well as pedagogical strategies and classroom management. Level 3 certification would additionally require observation and expert evaluation of teachers' classroom practice. The competency tests and classroom evaluation instruments were to be developed and applied by an external agency. Unsuccessful candidates would be eligible for scholarships and training courses to help improve their performance.

Under the certification program, promotions and the associated higher salaries would not be permanent: teachers must either compete for promotion to the subsequent grade or be recertified at their current level within five years. If unsuccessful at both, they would drop back to their previous status and salary. This "up or out" design creates stronger incentives for teachers to pursue continued professional development and avoid coasting. It also raises the risks for teachers who join, and could depress the numbers who enter this voluntary system, as has happened with voluntary programs elsewhere. The credibility of a program with this design, its incentive power, and its long-term sustainability would depend heavily on the perceived legitimacy and rigor of the certification tests and evaluation process.

Balance of evidence with career path reforms

Career path reforms—and hybrid programs—address three central problems with the incentives for teaching in most LAC countries: the lack of rewards for the best teachers, the lack of sanctions for the worst teachers, and a compressed lifetime salary trajectory that is less attractive than in most other professions. Despite their obvious policy relevance, career path reforms are still relatively rare in LAC because they are administratively complex, usually contested by teachers unions, and pose long-term fiscal costs that must be managed carefully. Both the high potential benefits and the relatively high costs argue for serious attention to analyzing how well these reforms work and what design features make them most successful. Given the very limited evaluation evidence that currently exists on this type of reform (except for Mexico's CM and Colombia's EPD), only a few cautious observations may be made to guide future policy.

First, *choosing valid measures of teacher quality and calibrating them* appropriately are crucial steps. Mexico's CM offered strong financial incentives, but based promotion to an important degree on factors that can be manipulated and fail to discriminate teachers who truly are more effective from others. Raising the weight attached to student learning results in the promotion criteria after 2005 attempted to address this problem, but this and other adjustments dramatically reduced new entrants into the system and, thus, the impact of these newer-promoted cohorts within the overall teaching force. While in theory the most important measure of a teacher's individual effectiveness is his or her ability to produce value-added learning gains in students on a consistent basis, no school system in the world has the capacity to measure value-added learning gains in every basic education classroom, grade, and subject. More than 30 U.S. states, incentivized under the Obama administration's Race to the Top program, are currently introducing teacher evaluation systems that include value-added learning gains, but all face challenges in how to handle the large share of teachers whose grades and subjects are not tested annually.

The new wave of career path reforms in LAC do not try to measure teachers' individual contributions to student learning gains, and that seems sensible. Instead, countries are taking the pragmatic approach of anchoring teacher evaluation systems in a combination of teacher competency tests, expert classroom observations, and comprehensive 360-degree feedback from peers, students, parents, and school directors. Peru's new LRM is a good example of this model, and Chile's and Ecuador's teacher evaluation systems are similarly designed. As discussed in chapter 4, conducting periodic, comprehensive teacher evaluations is administratively complex and expensive. But such systems not only create a platform for merit-based promotions and financial incentives but also generate performance feedback for individual teachers and priority topics for in-service training programs. When classroom observations are videotaped, as in Chile, the material has multiple downstream uses.

For school systems introducing competency-based promotion and pay incentives for the first time, relying on a test of subject matter mastery and pedagogical knowledge alone can be a practical first step. Test design is important, so that items are perceived as legitimate measures of what teachers should *know* (in terms of content), *be able to do* (in terms of pedagogical strategies for delivering content at different grade levels), and *understand* about child development and learning styles. A teacher exam in Peru in the early 2000s was widely criticized for esoteric questions. Tests should also be calibrated carefully. In Chile and Colombia, teachers have been reluctant to pursue available incentives because of the perceived difficulty of the test, which to some extent defeats the purpose of offering a new path. The goal is attractive incentives linked to a high performance bar, but there is clearly a challenge in finding the balance.

Second, the *steepness of the salary trajectory* will obviously affect the strength of the incentive on teacher behavior; however, there is a complete lack of evidence on how steeper promotion or salary scales affect student learning and school system performance over time. There is substantial variation across the LAC cases in this dimension, ranging from a top salary band in Peru that is 260 percent of the starting salary to a top band in São Paulo, Brazil (since the 2011 revision), that is now only 180 percent of the starting salary. Current LAC programs also vary substantially in the number of career levels offered. Peru's new career path has eight; Colombia has four. For teachers contemplating a 30-year career, these designs may send significantly different messages about advancement possibilities. As many of these reforms are quite new, there is an important opportunity to research their differential impacts on the recruitment of new teachers over time.

Third, the *long-term fiscal implications* of reforms that increase teachers' base pay are important. LAC cases have used different strategies to build in mitigating controls. In Ecuador and Chile, pay increases are guaranteed for only four years. In São Paulo (Brazil), a tournament approach was adopted (i.e., only the top scoring 20 percent of teachers—in rank order—accessed the promotion) to manage the fiscal impact of the reform while retaining a high-powered financial incentive. These models contrast with the career path reforms in Peru and Colombia that offer teachers permanent promotions and base pay increases. Conditional on their size, permanent pay increases create stronger incentives. But they may also compel fiscal tradeoffs in the size of awards.

Fourth, *who evaluates* is important. Peru, São Paulo (Brazil), and Ecuador have followed Chile's example in contracting external agencies to design and apply the teacher tests and, in the case of Peru, also to carry out proposed classroom observations and gather and analyze comprehensive teacher performance feedback. The Colombian experience indicates that while school directors are a key source of teacher performance feedback, there are political and technical issues in vesting directors with the sole—or even the main—responsibility for teacher performance evaluation. It is hard for directors to have a systemwide perspective on teachers' relative performance, and it is hard for them to deal with the immediate consequences for teacher morale of blocked promotions. Using independent external experts and grounding evaluation standards and feedback in systemwide performance metrics are important.

Fifth, *careful implementation planning* of reforms as complex as these is important. The credibility of several programs—in Mexico, Colombia, São Paulo state (Brazil), and initially in Peru—has been undermined by problems that might have been foreseen and managed differently. In Mexico, the large share of teachers granted immediate access to the promotion when the CM was launched weakened the program's incentive power and eventually required a major adjustment to make it more restrictive. In Colombia, the reliance on school directors for teacher performance evaluations created predictable political issues and perverse incentives. In São Paulo, there was a damaging lack of alignment between a restrictive promotion rule (only 20 percent of teachers could gain the promotion) and a relatively easy competency exam (that the majority of teachers were able to pass). In Peru, the great majority of civil service teachers felt that the risks of performing poorly on the CPM test outweighed the incremental salary gains, which left the Ministry of Education with no instruments for evaluating those teachers' performance. Peru's 2012 reform has an impressive design but the number, complexity, and frequency of individual teacher evaluations it mandates (as many as 50,000 per year from 2015 on) implies a huge implementation challenge, given that neither the ministry nor local universities, think tanks, or consulting firms currently have established capacity in this area.

Finally, *incentive power* hangs on belief that the program will be sustained under consistent rules of the game. Although Peru's 2012 LRM clearly improves on the design of the 2008 CPM, it remains to be seen how the new reform is implemented and how the new career track is integrated with the prior systems. In São Paulo (Brazil), it is not clear what the softer financial incentives of the 2012 revisions to the salary scale have meant for its impact. Whenever teachers perceive that the criteria for entry into a new career track are likely to change, soften, or be disbanded, the incentives to acquire new knowledge or apply to the profession erode. Nevertheless, career path reforms that truly signal substantially higher long-term financial rewards for talented teachers probably offer the clearest direct path to the recruitment of higher-caliber teacher candidates and more effective teaching. Policy makers across the region would gain from careful research on the new wave of career path reforms in LAC.

Bonus pay

A second financial incentive is bonus pay—variable compensation based on performance. Employers in many different sectors use bonus, or merit pay, to stimulate higher productivity and efficiency from workers. In education, in the United States alone there have been hundreds of merit pay programs over more than a century (Murnane and Cohen 1986). Bonus pay or "pay for performance" in education is usually structured as a one-time annual reward for teachers based on a measure of their relative performance or performance against a target. The reward can be for input measures of performance, such as teacher attendance, or outcome measures, such as student learning progress. Bonuses can be awarded to individual teachers or to groups of teachers most typically to a whole school.

There is huge policy innovation and interest in education pay for performance currently in both the LAC region and other parts of the world (table 5.4). In contrast to career path reforms, bonus pay programs typically do not require new legislation. They do not increase the base salary bill, and they maintain the annual "carrot" of an incentive. They are easier to implement, adjust, and disband, if necessary. Countries seeking a quick strategy for injecting performance incentives into dysfunctional teacher pay scales often turn to bonus programs first.

In regions such as LAC, where many countries have student assessment systems in place, bonus pay offers a way to link teacher pay directly to the performance measure they value most—student learning progress. Group bonuses—which reward all staff members in a school for the school's average results—can also create incentives for school members to work as a team.

Despite its logic and implementation appeal, bonus pay remains controversial—particularly where rewards are linked to student test results. Critics argue that bonus pay will be ineffective if teachers lack the capacity to increase desired outcomes, and that it can be unfair if the desired results depend on factors outside of teachers' control (such as students' family background). Some argue that monetary incentives can undermine intrinsic incentives to perform. Bonus pay offered for teachers' individual results can also have perverse impacts on schools' overall results by undermining collaboration among teachers and making teachers unwilling to work with more challenging students (Johnson 1984; Firestone and Pennell 1993).

Two of the deepest critiques have found research corroboration in the United States. First, since bonus pay programs necessarily prioritize a few explicit and measurable objectives—such as increasing student performance in a few tested grades and subjects—they undermine attention to other important goals and subjects, given the "multitasking" nature of teaching (Holmstrom and Milgrom 1991). Second, bonus pay based exclusively or heavily on test student performance can induce perverse

TABLE 5.4: Bonus pay

A. Bonus for student learning outcomes

Individual

Global evidence: Andhra Pradesh, India (Muralidharan 2012)
Chicago Heights, IL (Fryer et al. 2012)
New York City, NY (Fryer 2013)
Nashville, TN (Springer et al. 2010)

Country (eval. date)	Type	Design and coverage	Performance measure	Award process	Predictability	Monitoring and support	Bonus size and distribution	Frequency of bonus	Total cost	Evaluation method	Results
Mexico ALI, 2008–10 Behrman et al. (forthcoming)	Individual	Pilot 20 treatment and 28 control schools Federal upper secondary schools	Math test scores	Payment to math teachers based on math test score improvements of their students	94% of teachers gained some bonus	Test designed and administered by external firm	Up to Mex$25,000/year (10%–15% of annual salary) if students performed as well as under group incentive Actual bonus paid averaged Mex$6,332/teacher	Annual	Cost per student Mex$43.00 (US$ 3.50)	RCT	No impact on test scores

(continued on next page)

TABLE 5.4: Bonus pay *(continued)*

Country (eval. date)	Type	Design and coverage	Performance measure	Award process	Predictability	Monitoring and support	Bonus size and distribution	Frequency of bonus	Total cost	Evaluation method	Results
Group											
Global evidence: Andhra Pradesh, India (Muralidharan 2012) Chicago Heights, IL (Fryer et al. 2012) New York City, NY (Fryer 2013)											
Mexico ALI, 2008–10 Behrman et al. (forthcoming)	Group	Pilot 20 treatment and 28 control schools Federal upper secondary schools	Math test scores	Payment to all teachers, administrators, and students in the school based on overall math test score improvements	100% of teachers and students gained some bonus	Test designed and administered by external firm	Average bonus Mex$19,000 for math teachers; Mex$7,700 for directors; Mex$3,900 for other teachers and administrators; Mex$900–3500 for students (depending on indiv. test performance)	Annual	Cost per student Mex$3,303 (US$ 275) or 15% of annual per student expenditure	RCT	Test scores 0.3–0.6 SD higher than in control schools (adjusted for cheating) Significant student cheating in presence of student incentives

B. Bonus for student learning plus other student outcomes

Individual

Global evidence: no recent cases (see Bruns, Filmer, and Patrinos 2011 for cases before 2011)
No LAC cases

(continued on next page)

TABLE 5.4: Bonus pay *(continued)*

Country (eval. date)	Type	Design and coverage	Performance measure	Award process	Predictability	Monitoring and support	Bonus size and distribution	Frequency of bonus	Total cost	Evaluation method	Results
Group											
Brazil: Pernambuco Bonus de Desempenho Escolar, 2008 Ferraz and Bruns (forthcoming)	Group Performance targets	Statewide (950 schools)	School-level targets for improvement in IDEPE index (student scores on state test and student grade progression) Bonus for individuals within school discounted for individual absence rates and time worked in school	Target-based, piece-wise above threshold of 50% of target attained, up to 100% of target	52% of schools (479/929) in 2009 79% of schools (758/954) in 2010 70% of schools in 2011 56% of schools in 2012 56% of schools in 2013	Impact evaluation of reform, including classroom observations in process	All school personnel eligible (teaching and nonteaching) Bonus paid as % of individual monthly wage (MW) equal to % of school target achieved Average bonus: 2009 = 221% MW 2010 = 168% MW 2011 = 188% MW 2012 = 254% MW	Annual	2009: R$28.8 million (US$15 million) 2010: R$40 million (US$21 million) 2011: R$48 million (US$ 27.5 million) 2012: R$60 million (US$29.5 million) 2013: R$60 million (US$27 million)	DD with 8 neighboring Northeast states	Math and language test scores approx. .12 SDs (across different grades) higher from 2007–11 and significantly larger declines in dropout and repetition rates Weaker impacts after 2011 Impacts larger for small schools and disadvantaged students

(continued on next page)

TABLE 5.4: Bonus pay *(continued)*

Country (eval. date)	Type	Design and coverage	Performance measure	Award process	Predictability	Monitoring and support	Bonus size and distribution	Frequency of bonus	Total cost	Evaluation method	Results
C. Bonus for student learning results plus other (nonstudent) performance measures											
Individual											
Global evidence: no recent cases (see Bruns, Filmer, and Patrinos 2011 for cases before 2011) No LAC cases											
Group											
Chile: SNED 1996 Contreras and Rau (2012)	Group	National (all public and publicly subsidized basic education schools ≈ 90% of schools)	Student test scores (37%), test score gains (28%), equality of opportunity (22%), school initiative (6%), incorporation of parents (5%), improvement of working conditions (2%)	Rank order tournament for schools stratified by region, urbanicity, and SES Carried out every two years	Top schools (accounting for the top 25%–35% of enrollments in each stratum) get award 90% of bonus paid directly to teachers; 10% allocated by school directors	Chile has numerous teacher evaluation, observation, and school support programs not directly related to SNED	40% of MW initially; since 2006, 80% of MW, 7% of annual salary	Quarterly distribution over two years	Annual cost (2012–13) US$108.5 million	DD comparison with private schools not covered by program	Significant effect on standardized math and language test scores 0.16–0.25 SD for math and 0.14–0.26 SD for language

Notes: ALI = Aligning Learning Incentives; DD = difference-in-differences between treatment and control groups; IDEPE = Índice de Desenvolvimento da Educação de Pernambuco; LAC = Latin America and the Caribbean; R$ = Brazilian reais; RCT = randomized controlled trial. SES = socioeconomic status; SNED = National System of School Performance Assessment.

teacher behaviors, notably cheating, as documented in several U.S. school systems (Jacob and Levitt 2003).

Since bonus pay programs, unlike career path reforms, can be implemented through random assignment experiments, there is a growing body of global evidence on their impact. A review of the evidence from developing country experiences through 2010 is found in Bruns, Filmer, and Patrinos (2011), which groups programs on two axes that are relevant for the design and implementation of policies in this area: (a) *what* is rewarded (inputs, such as attendance; outcomes, such as student learning results; or comprehensive measures of school quality and performance)[10] and (b) *who* is rewarded—whether the bonus is a group (school level) or individual teacher reward. This section updates that analysis using the same framework.

The vast majority of bonus pay programs *outside* of Latin America are organized around rewards for a single outcome: student test score improvement. In Latin America, however, most programs to date have avoided reliance on a single outcome measure. Chile's SNED, the first bonus program adopted in the region, launched in 1996, rewards student test scores plus a diverse set of other school quality indicators—ranging from parent feedback to infrastructure improvement to the inclusion of students with disabilities. In Brazil, where more than 20 different states and municipalities have adopted bonus pay schemes over the past eight years, the basis for the bonus is also student results—but using a combined indicator of test score improvements and student flows (reduced dropout and on-time grade promotion) called the Index of Basic Education Quality (IDEB) developed by the federal government. The sole example of a LAC program based on test scores alone is the pilot program in Mexico, Aligning Learning Incentives (ALI), implemented from 2009–12. Given that ALI has been subjected to a rigorous, randomized evaluation, its results are important for the region. But to date there is no sign of other LAC countries considering systemwide implementation of bonus programs based on test scores alone.

Bonuses based on student learning results

One of the biggest policy questions about bonus pay in education is whether rewarding individual teachers for their students' learning progress is more effective than rewarding schools. While individual rewards are presumed to be more powerful as incentives, the administrative costs of measuring student learning gains in every classroom every year are extremely high, and individual incentives may have negative impacts on teacher collaboration and teachers' willingness to teach more difficult students. Three important randomized studies have been designed precisely to address this question: in Andhra Pradesh, India; in Mexico; and in Chicago Heights, Illinois. Several other randomized studies in the United States have tested either individual teacher or group bonuses and contributed evidence as well.

Andhra Pradesh, India's teacher incentive program. In India, Muralidharan and Sundararaman (2011) compare the impact in three randomly assigned groups of schools of individual teacher bonus payments, group bonus payments (to all of the teachers in the school), and control schools. In both sets of incentive schools, the bonus was based on the increase in average student learning results in math and language over the course of a single school year. In the first year of the program, both the group and individual incentives increased student achievement by similar amounts—roughly 0.16 SD more than the control schools. But thereafter performance diverged, with students in the individual teacher bonus schools learning consistently more than those in group bonus schools. For several years, the group bonus schools still registered better results than schools with no teacher incentives, but by the fifth year of the program, these effects faded.

In the schools with individual teacher bonuses, student learning has shown very strong improvement, with test score results 0.54 SD higher in math and 0.35 SD higher in language than in control schools by the fifth year of the program. Learning is also higher in subjects not incentivized by the bonus, such as science (0.52 SD higher) and social studies (0.3 SD). These are large effects for an education intervention, and perhaps especially impressive given the small average size of the bonus (only 3 percent of a monthly wage, on average). Muralidharan (2012) estimates that the individual teacher bonus program is 15 to 20 times more cost-effective at raising test scores in the Indian context than reducing class size from 40 to 30 students per teacher.

In terms of the channel through which the incentives operate, researchers were somewhat surprised to see no impact on teachers' very high absence rates (28 percent), in either individual bonus or group bonus schools. Given the very small average school size (three teachers per school) teachers under the group incentive could presumably monitor each other's performance and avoid the free-rider behavior that typically undercuts group-based incentives. But the very high absence rates suggest that in the Indian context, teachers' professional norms preclude direct monitoring of colleagues' work. On surveys, however, teachers subject to the incentives reported working more intensively, conditional upon being present in school. Incentivized teachers also reported assigning more homework, giving practice tests, focusing on weaker students, and conducting more afterschool tutoring sessions than teachers in control schools. While the research clearly demonstrates that in the Andhra Pradesh context individual teacher bonuses were more powerful than group bonuses, there is still some question about what behaviors led to the superior results. Teachers in both groups reported engaging in extra preparation for end-of-year tests, afterschool classes, and so forth, compared with teachers in the control schools.

Mexico's Aligning Learning Incentives program. From 2008–10, 88 large federal secondary schools across several different states in Mexico implemented a program designed to compare the impacts on student math performance of individual teacher bonus pay, group bonus pay, and bonuses offered directly to students (Behrman et al., forthcoming). The group bonus pay, which rewarded all teachers and administrators, also included bonuses for students. The program was implemented with random assignment of schools to the three different treatments and a control group, and student progress was tracked over three school years, following the initial cohort of ninth-grade students through completion of their secondary schooling.

In contrast to the India program results, the individual teacher bonuses in Mexico produced no improvements in student math scores vis-à-vis the control schools. But including students in the bonus payments raised learning significantly. The largest effects were seen in the group bonus schools where both students and teachers (and other school personnel) were rewarded. Providing incentives to students alone increased math scores by 0.2 to 0.3 SD, depending on the grade and year. Providing the same degree of incentives to students in combination with incentives for their teachers and other school personnel increased test scores by 0.3 to 0.6 SD. The incentive power of the student bonus was so strong as to lead to discernible patterns of student cheating in both sets of schools where students were rewarded. Researchers used statistical screening methods to identify suspect test results and make corresponding adjustments to the estimated program impacts. Even with substantial adjustments, however, the results for the group bonus that included students remain among the largest reported impacts from any form of education bonus pay.

Questionnaires administered to program participants established that offering bonuses directly to students changed their study behavior. In the schools where only teachers were incentivized, students reported no differences in study habits from students in control schools. But in the two sets of schools where students received direct rewards, they reported spending more time studying math and putting "much effort" into their school work. Students also said they were significantly less likely to text or watch TV while doing homework and significantly more likely to give help to classmates.

On measures of teacher effort, the results were less clear-cut. A higher share of the incentivized teachers, under both individual and group incentives, reported spending time both inside and outside of class preparing students for their exams. While these activities were more widespread among teachers offered the group bonus, on most other measures of teacher effort, such as time spent preparing for class, no differences were observed.

Offering bonus payments to students in this case clearly stimulated higher effort, which, combined with higher teacher effort, produced powerful improvements in student learning. Students in the group bonus schools for three years completed secondary school with significantly higher math mastery than students in control schools or in schools where only teachers were offered incentives. However, the costs of the group bonus under this inclusive model were also high. Since the incentive payment for teachers alone yielded negligible learning gains, the per-student costs of that model were low: Mex$43.00 per student (US$3.50 per student). Offering the bonus to individual students produced better results and therefore had costs averaging Mex$2,080 per student (US$173 per student). The group bonus—rewarding all teachers, administrators, and students in a school from students' progress—was most expensive, both because of its inclusiveness and because of the higher results it produced—Mex$3,303 per student (US$275 per student), equivalent to 15 percent of annual per student spending in these secondary schools.

Chicago Heights, Illinois's teacher bonus program. A one-year experimental program involving 150 teachers in 9 low-income primary schools compared individual teacher and group bonuses with an interesting twist: both types of bonus were offered in two formats. In the first format, as under most programs, teachers earned the bonus at the *end* of the school year based on the math score improvements of their students. In the second format, teachers were presented with a US$4,000 payment (the expected average award and roughly equal to 8 percent of the average annual salary) at the beginning of the school year and signed a contract stating that if their students' end-of-the-year math performance was below average they would return the difference between the $4,000 and their final award. The specific performance targets, calibrated on the basis of the prior math performance of the students in each class, and the size of the bonus were identical under both formats; the only difference was the timing and framing of the reward—whether the teachers were presented with a potential end-of-the-year gain or the potential loss of a bonus already received.

Neither the individual bonus nor the group bonus offered as an end-of-the-school-year reward produced improvements in student learning compared with the control schools. But substantial gains were seen in classrooms where teachers were given the reward up front; math scores improved between 0.21 and 0.39 SD on average, similar to the increase in student achievement associated with a 1 SD increase in teacher quality. Impacts were measured on both high-stakes tests that teachers knew were the basis for their bonus payments and a second set of state tests that did not count for the bonus calculation. The results were highly consistent, suggesting that teachers' efforts were not directed narrowly toward teaching to the test that counts for the bonus. Offering group or individual bonuses at the end of the school year had no impact on math performance on either test, whereas presenting teachers with identically sized incentives in the form of a reward up front and the risk of a loss if results did not improve produced large improvements in student results on both tests.

Other experimental evidence. Two other teacher bonus programs in the United States have been carefully evaluated, both for longer periods than the Chicago Heights program. Springer et al. (2010) analyzed an individual teacher bonus program that offered 300 middle school mathematics teachers in Nashville, Tennessee, public schools an individual bonus if their students raised their math scores on the annual state assessment. Teachers volunteering to participate in the program were randomly assigned to bonus and control schools. In the bonus schools, teachers earned US$5,000, US$10,000, or US$15,000 awards if their students reach the 80th, 90th or 95th percentiles on the test, respectively. Relative to an average annual salary of US$40,000, the bonuses were attractive. Over three years, however, Springer et al. (2010) found no difference in student learning results between the bonus and control schools and no significant differences in teaching practices.

In New York City public schools, Fryer (2013) studied a group bonus program involving over 20,000 teachers in more than 200 schools. Schools meeting their annual performance targets set by the New York State Education Department could earn US$3,000 per employee (about 5 percent of the average salary). Schools meeting at least 75 percent of the target gained US$1,500 per employee. Schools could flexibly choose how to allocate the total bonus funds received, such as opting to give more to teachers believed to have contributed most to the results. Findings showed no increase in student learning results vis-à-vis the control schools and no observed changes in teacher behavior. Among schools that gained the bonus, virtually all chose to distribute the rewards evenly, refusing to differentiate their teachers' performance. Goodman and Turner (2013) examined the same program for evidence of a free-rider problem. They confirmed that smaller schools were indeed more likely to achieve the bonus. This is consistent with the expectation that group bonus incentives exert stronger effects in smaller schools because school personnel can more easily monitor the level of effort that their colleagues expend and exert peer pressure on performance.

Bonuses based on student learning results plus other student outcomes

Pernambuco, Brazil's school bonus program, Bonus de Desempenho Escolar (BDE). The Northeast Brazilian state of Pernambuco in 2008 introduced a program to reward its 960 schools for combined improvements in student learning outcomes in math and Portuguese and student grade progression. Under the program, annual targets for each school are developed on the basis of past results. Schools must meet 50 percent of their target to receive any bonus; above that threshold, bonus amounts are proportional to the share of the target met. The state budgets one month of payroll annually for the program; if less than 100 percent of schools achieve their targets, bonus payments for successful schools can exceed one month's salary for every school employee. Over the first four years of the program, average payments have ranged from 168 percent to 221 percent of a monthly salary, which is a significant incentive in the Brazilian context. Over the first four years of the program, the share of schools attaining the bonus (reflecting both variations in the ambitiousness of the targets and changes in school effort) fluctuated between 50 percent and 85 percent, and the average bonus size varied inversely. Schools' performances are calculated at the end of the school year, and schools receive their rewards about five months later. The new round of school targets is also communicated at this point, meaning that schools typically have only about half of the school year to respond to the specific targets.

The Pernambuco program was implemented statewide, so an experimental evaluation was not possible. But Brazil's extensive student testing and administrative data permit a robust quasi-experimental evaluation, comparing trends in Pernambuco both before and after the introduction of the bonus with trends in eight neighboring Northeast states, which do not have bonus pay programs. A unique feature of the Brazilian context is the existence of both a high-stakes Pernambuco state test that determines the bonus results and a low-stakes national assessment that does not count for the bonus and permits direct comparison of Pernambuco's learning progress with that of other states. In a review of design issues in education performance pay programs, Neal (2012) argues that separate no-stakes assessments are critically important for providing reliable information about student achievement under a bonus pay regime, as high-stakes assessments create incentives for educators to take hidden actions that contaminate student test scores. Drawing on the low-stakes assessment data for Pernambuco and eight neighboring Northeast states over a five-year period, Ferraz and Bruns (forthcoming) find several key results.[11]

First, the bonus program has produced significant and sustained improvements in student grade progression, with an especially large decline in dropout and repetition. Second, it produced significant improvements in student learning outcomes for most grades and subjects in the first two years of the program (2008–10) but these tapered off thereafter. This may to some extent be explained by the decline in student dropout, which means that the Pernambuco state schools are educating an increasing number of academically at-risk students, which makes sustained improvements in systemwide learning more difficult.

Third, there was significant heterogeneity in impacts across different-sized schools, with smaller schools (fewer than 10 teachers) showing much stronger improvement in response to the incentive. As in the New York City case, it is more difficult for teachers to monitor each other's behavior in larger schools, giving rise to free riders. Most Pernambuco state schools are large, with 30 teachers on average, making the observed bonus results consistent with what the theory would predict.

Fourth, and perhaps most interestingly, the bonus produced heterogeneous impacts on students as well. Students who are black, who have repeated grades, who work part time, and who have low parental education have shown the strongest improvements.

Fifth, classroom observations conducted in a panel of 220 schools in 2009 and 2010 help explain how successful schools achieved results (Bruns, Evans, and Luque 2012). In 2009, teachers in schools that went on to earn the bonus for that year spent more time on instruction, kept students more engaged, and lost fewer school hours because teachers were absent from the classroom. In 2010, the bonus program also appeared to stimulate a small, systemwide improvement in teachers' use of instructional time. Compared with other Northeast states, Pernambuco's teachers reported conducting more learning activities in Portuguese and math since the bonus was introduced, having lower teacher absence rates, and having fewer schools with teacher vacancies.

Finally, the program has been well accepted by teachers and school directors. A 2009 survey found that 68 percent of school directors believed the bonus program was having a positive impact on their school; in 2010, 90 percent of directors believed this. In 2009, 67 percent of directors believed that the bonus policy was an appropriate policy for improving school quality; in 2010, 85 percent of directors agreed. In 2010,

89 percent of school directors stated that they perceived the bonus program had a positive impact on their teachers' motivation and absence rates.

The Pernambuco BDE is one of the few school bonus programs in the world implemented at scale and evaluated rigorously over a period of years. Chile's SNED is the other. While randomized trial evaluations permit clean and credible estimates of a program's impact, many randomized evaluations are of pilot programs that may not be easily scalable, either on fiscal or administrative grounds. It is also common for such pilot programs and their evaluations to be of short duration, which limits insights into how program impacts might fade out—or intensify—over a longer period. The Pernambuco evaluation, like the five-year Andhra Pradesh, India, evaluation, demonstrates that the impacts of bonus programs may indeed change in important ways over time. The fact that Brazil's unique testing environment makes it possible to analyze the Pernambuco program's impact on student learning outcomes that are not linked to the incentive strengthens confidence in the results. The Pernambuco BDE provides evidence that a well-designed, cleanly implemented, systemwide group bonus can work to stimulate faster improvement in key school results than would have occurred without the bonus, but that there can be important heterogeneity in these effects across different sized schools and declining impacts over time.

Bonuses based on student learning results plus other (nonstudent) performance measures

Chile's school bonus program, Sistema Nacional de Evaluación del Desempeño de los Establecimientos Educacionales. The earliest experience with group bonus pay in Latin America was Chile's SNED, introduced in 1996. SNED is a school-based bonus awarded every two years. The SNED program design incorporated many innovative features. First, it rewarded a particularly broad and comprehensive set of school-level results and input and quality indicators measured through surveys. Student learning counts for 65 percent of the total score, with a combined measure of a school's results on the current year's national assessment (37 percent) plus a value-added measure of the change in the school's average test scores over the past two cycles (28 percent). Other indicators include a school's "equality of opportunities" (22 percent weight, based on retention and pass rates and lack of discriminatory practices, measured through survey data); school initiative (6 percent, based on surveys); integration of parents and guardians into school activities (5 percent, based on a survey of parents and community members); and labor conditions (2 percent, based on the presence of a complete teaching staff, replacement of absent teachers, and other indicators). The diverse factors in the SNED calculation are designed to provide a broad and comprehensive signal of schools' relative quality to both schools and the parents and community. They also reduce the incentives for manipulation of the test score portions of the measure.

Second, SNED is one of the rare bonus programs globally that is conducted as a tournament. After the SNED score is computed for each school, schools are ranked and the bonus payments and the label of "excellence" are awarded to the top 25 percent of schools. Tournament designs avoid the administrative challenges of setting ex ante targets for each school, which pose risks of targets that are either too ambitious or too easy for individual schools or are unfair across schools. Under a tournament design, school system officials do not have to try to predict what degree of improvement is possible; schools may achieve even more than could be expected because they are competing directly against other schools for the highest rankings. As Neal (2012) notes, this also makes tournaments more difficult to manipulate than incentive programs built around performance targets.

Third, the SNED program was carefully designed to make the interschool competition fair. Schools are stratified on a range of geographic, institutional, and socioeconomic factors to ensure that they compete only within "homogenous groups" (see box 5.1). Schools in the top 25 percent of the ranking in each group receive the full bonus, and schools ranked between the 25th and 35th percentile receive 60 percent of the bonus. Ninety percent of the funds are paid to teachers according to their teaching hours. The remaining 10 percent of resources are mandated as a special bonus for outstanding teachers, distributed at the director's discretion. The monthly benefit is paid quarterly during the two years that the results are valid.

Contreras and Rau (2012) use a carefully specified difference-in-differences analysis to estimate the impact that the introduction of the SNED bonus in 1996 had on the quality of Chilean public and publicly subsidized (voucher) schools. They conclude that math scores across the public system improved between 0.16 and 0.25 SD and language scores improved in the range of 0.14–0.25 SD in the first two years after SNED's introduction. They note, however, that these effects are driven by a subset of schools. Despite the ministry's efforts to ensure that the tournament competition is "fair," approximately 60 percent of schools have a consistently high probability of winning the bonus, while one-third of schools are consistently out of the running.

Cabezas, Cuesta, and Gallego (2011) contributed a rare, and welcome, effort to estimate the cost-effectiveness of the SNED bonus in comparison with other education interventions. They conclude that it is highly cost-effective, with an estimated cost of US$2 per 0.1 SD increase in language test scores compared with US$636 per 0.1 SD improvement for Chile's full-day school program.

Balance of evidence on bonus pay

Interest in bonus pay in education continues to grow, among policy makers and researchers. The evaluation evidence base nonetheless remains small in comparison to the wide range of designs different programs employ, in terms of what is rewarded, who is rewarded, and how large rewards are in relation to base salaries. The evidence to date supports relatively few, cautious conclusions.

Bonus pay programs can *work, perhaps especially in developing country contexts.* Different forms of individual and group incentives with a range of designs in a range of low- and middle-income developing country contexts have demonstrated positive impacts on student learning outcomes. Measured impacts across all programs are generally in the range of 0.15 to 0.3 SD improvement in test scores and, in a few cases, are

---

BOX 5.1: *Fair comparisons of school performance: The design of Chile's Sistema Nacional de Evaluación del Desempeño (SNED)*

An important feature of Chile's school bonus program (SNED) is the effort made to ensure that schools in difficult geographic or socioeconomic conditions compete on an equal footing with more advantaged schools. To achieve this, the ministry stratifies all public and publicly subsidized voucher schools into approximately 100 different homogeneous groups, and schools compete within these groups. Schools are classified according to geographic area (urban or rural) and by educational level (e.g., only primary education, only secondary education, all levels). If there are less than 10 schools in a category of geographical area and education level, no further classification is made. If there are more than 10 schools, they are clustered by socioeconomic level according to the following two variables, as depicted in figure B5.1.1:

- Vulnerability Index calculated for each school
- Parents' average educational level and household income

Special education schools are classified in one group per region.

FIGURE B5.1.1: Construction of homogenous school groupings in Chile's SNED

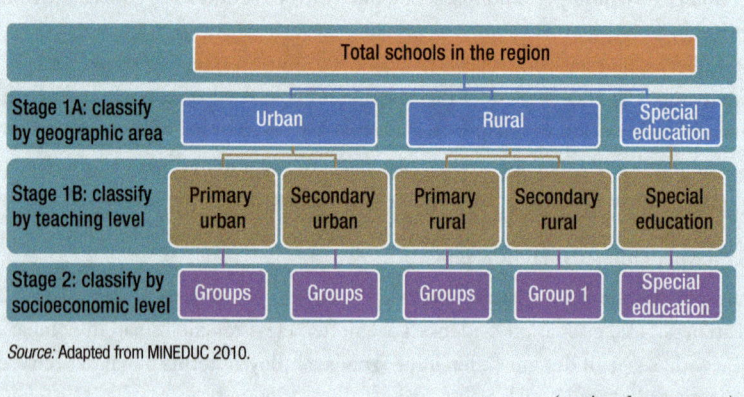

Source: Adapted from MINEDUC 2010.

(continued on next page)

BOX 5.1: *Fair comparisons of school performance: The design of Chile's Sistema Nacional de Evaluación del Desempeño (SNED)*
(*continued*)

Within each group, a SNED index is calculated for each school, and schools are ranked. Each factor is measured using specific indicators and graded on a scale from 0 to 100. Factor scores are weighted and combined into a final SNED score on the same scale from 0 to 100 points (MINEDUC 2010).

TABLE B5.1.1: Six components of the SNED index and their respective weights

SNED factor	Weight (percent)	Indicator and data source
1. Effectiveness (educational results)	37	National student assessment (SIMCE) results: average of all subtests of the most recent test
2. Improvement (change in test scores)	28	Difference between last two SIMCE results
3. Initiative (capacity to innovate and incorporate support from external agents)	6	Pedagogical work in groups Complementary teacher development activities Availability of extracurricular and interscholastic activities School management team meets periodically Existence of a school board Students with disabilities integrated in regular classes and supported clear educational and management goals Preschool education curriculum offered (Marco de Bases Curriculares de Educación Parvularia) Vocational and technical internships offered for high school students
4. School working conditions	2	School complies with all admissions, teacher eligibility, qualification, and promotion processes
5. Equality of opportunity: accessibility, retention, and integration of the school population	22	Rate of retention of students Rate of promotion of students Students with disabilities as a percentage of total enrollment Incorporation of students with multiple and/or severe deficits Existence and development of a school integration program Absence of discriminatory practices Absence of undue student sanctions
6. Integration of teachers, parents, and guardians in school's educational plan	5	Existence and functioning of a teachers' council Existence and functioning of a parents' council Existence and functioning of a representative student council Incorporation of the community in educational agreements Public disseminations of school learning (SIMCE) results Public dissemination of school SNED results Outreach to parents and guardians

Source: MINEDUC 2010.
Note: SNED = Sistema Nacional de Evaluación del Desempeño.

much higher. These are significant-sized effects for education interventions. Although the number of cases remains small, bonus pay programs in developing country settings have produced more consistently positive results than in developed country settings to date. Encouragingly, the only two rigorously evaluated cases of bonus pay programs operating at scale are both from Latin America, and both have demonstrated positive results on student learning and grade attainment. A reasonable hypothesis is that financial incentives for school results will be most productive where other mechanisms (e.g., management oversight, school supervision, peer interaction among teachers) for performance monitoring, accountability, and teacher professionalism are weak.

Matching incentive design to context is crucial. Much of the global experimental evidence is from studies testing multiple bonus formats—group versus individual incentives; teacher versus student incentives; gain versus loss bonus awards—and the impact these design factors have on results, even within a single context, is striking. Individual teacher bonuses produced strong test score improvements in rural Andhra Pradesh, but group bonuses produced none. Group bonuses for teachers and students in Mexico produced strong results but individual bonuses produced none. Both group and individual bonuses granted up front and framed as a loss produced large impacts in Chicago Heights, but the same size bonuses offered at the end of the year, in the typical format of a performance award, had no impact on student learning.

Bonus size is another design issue on which there is as yet little practice guidance from research. While it is intuitively logical that larger bonuses will stimulate stronger impacts, there is no research yet that permits an apples-to-apples comparison of the power of larger bonuses controlling for other design features. Looking across evaluated programs, Bruns, Filmer, and Patrinos (2011) found average bonus size to range from 36 to 300 percent of monthly salary, with the largest reported impacts in the literature from the smallest reported bonus size (for India). The research base today is far short of a providing a guide to the most productive bonus pay designs for a given context. But it serves as a caution that if a given program's impact appears to be weak, there may well be a more effective alternative design.

Designing the performance measure(s) to be rewarded is a key challenge. Basing bonus pay on test scores alone has been problematic in several U.S. settings because of documented cheating and broader concerns that it focuses teachers too narrowly on specific subjects. No LAC country to date has introduced bonus pay for test scores alone, and this strategy appears wise. Chile's SNED program defines one end of the spectrum in its use of an extremely comprehensive set of performance indicators that includes test scores (65 percent weighting) and student retention and promotion rates (22 percent) but also a large number of other qualitative, process, and feedback indicators the Ministry of Education generates through institutional evaluations and special surveys. Given these costs and complexity, the SNED is one of the few programs where the bonus is offered only every two years. It is difficult to say whether this dampens its strength as an incentive compared to annual bonuses. The evidence that SNED has had some positive impact on learning outcomes

confirms that the weighting given to test scores in the composite indicator has been sufficient to incentivize this result.

The composite indicator used in Pernambuco is an interesting model for countries to consider. There is little question that the rapid spread of bonus pay programs in Brazil over the past five years is related to the federal Ministry of Education's development of a composite basic education quality index, called Indice de Desenvolvimento da Educacao Basica. Every state and municipal program to date in Brazil uses increases in schools' IDEB scores as the basis for the bonus. Because the index is the product of both test scores and pass rates, it discourages both automatic promotion of children who are not learning and the reverse strategy of holding children back or encouraging dropout in order to boost test scores. While the ministry calculates an IDEB index score every two years for every school, municipality, and state in Brazil based on national assessment results, school systems introducing bonus pay have developed state- or municipal-level assessments scaled to the national test that are applied in the intervening year. The widely perceived validity of the IDEB indicator has made it a useful platform for bonus pay in Brazil.

Programs are likely to have heterogeneous impacts on different types of schools. In both of the (only) two evaluated cases of bonus programs operating at scale, significant heterogeneity has been observed. In Chile's SNED program, about one-third of schools appear consistently "out of the money" in the tournaments, despite the serious efforts made to ensure that schools compete only against similar schools (Mizala and Urquiola 2007). In Pernambuco's case, the bonus produces stronger impacts in small schools, where teachers can collaborate and monitor each other more easily than in larger schools. Research evidence of this type can provide useful guidance for tweaking a program's design and raising its impact.

Students are key partners in the production of learning results. The innovative design of the ALI experiment in Mexico generated powerful evidence of this. This result is also consistent with cross-country studies of PISA results, for example, which show stronger student learning outcomes for countries whose students face high-stakes examinations at the end of secondary school (Fuchs and Woessmann 2007). While the sustaining costs of offering bonuses linked to learning for all students and teachers in a school may be prohibitive, the Mexico ALI results suggest that school systems can gain by finding ways to make students feel more invested in their own learning progress.

Finally, despite growing evidence that school bonus programs can stimulate improved results, our understanding of "how" is still weak. The logic of incentive pay is to stimulate teacher behaviors that help raise student learning—either increased teacher effort or more effective effort. However, relatively few evaluations have documented changes in teachers' classroom practice that plausibly explain increases in student learning, such as increased time spent on instruction, higher levels of student engagement, or less time lost because teachers are absent from the classroom. Research on teachers' classroom practice is becoming more feasible with the declining costs of installing video cameras in samples of classrooms or use of standardized methods for coding and analyzing teacher-student interaction. Systematic inclusion of such analysis in impact evaluations of pay for performance programs can not only illuminate the channels through which such programs produce results but also generate evidence and examples of effective teaching that can more broadly benefit these school systems.

Conclusions

Major progress in raising the quality of teachers in Latin America will require attracting high-caliber applicants, continuously and systematically weeding out the lowest performers, and motivating individuals to keep refining their skills and working their hardest over a long career. These three processes characterize the labor market for high-status professions in all countries. In countries with high-performing education systems, these processes operate in teaching as well. Previous chapters analyzed the importance of effective systems for preparing, screening, and training teachers. This chapter focused on the way those systems interact with three broad classes of incentives that shape the relative attractiveness and status of teaching: professional rewards, accountability pressures, and financial rewards.

While it seems intuitively obvious that all three types of incentives are important, there is a deep asymmetry in the research base. Very little research exists on specific policies or programs to raise the professional rewards for teachers, and there is no rigorous impact or cost-effectiveness evidence on these that can be directly compared with the impacts of programs in the other two areas. There is more research on reforms to strengthen accountability pressures on teachers—especially through school-based management—but very little evidence on some key questions such as the impact of policies that reduce teachers' job stability or improve school directors' capacity to evaluate and manage teacher performance. The greatest research attention, by far, has been focused on financial incentives, especially bonus pay. But this research bias should not be taken to mean that financial incentives are the most important. If anything, cross-country studies suggest that professional incentives are a very powerful element in high-performing education systems. In Finland, for example, the professional rewards for teachers are very strong, and accountability pressures and financial rewards are relatively weak.

It is also likely that these three types of incentives are complementary; they have extra impact when they are well aligned and undercut each other if they are not. While there is no rigorous research on this, case studies of high-performing school systems show positive incentives in all three areas, although their relative strength can vary. In this section, we try to pull together what is known about all three types of incentives, their relative importance, and their interaction.

Professional rewards. While there is virtually no experimental evidence on the impact of alternative strategies for raising the professional rewards to teaching, cross-country studies show that high-performing school systems offer teachers abundant opportunities for continued *mastery and professional growth* and that outstanding teachers receive substantial *recognition and prestige*. Compared with most of Latin America, countries with high-performing education systems invest more resources in teacher professional development—Singapore's 100 hours annually of paid professional development for every teacher is a leading example—but most important is the quality of those investments. Courses are developed by university practitioners in close collaboration with ministries of education, grounded in research evidence, and focus on specific issues in effective delivery of the curriculum, the classroom practice of highly effective teachers, and lessons from education systems elsewhere in the world.

In most of Latin America, except for Cuba, teacher professional development is outsourced to providers that do not carry out classroom-based research and that produce courses with little practical relevance for teachers. High-performing systems also support teachers' professional growth by promoting constant interaction and peer collaboration among teachers. Finland's teachers spend only 60 percent as much time as the OECD average in the classroom teaching; the rest of their time they work jointly on new curriculum content, learning materials, and ways of assessing students' progress. Peru's teacher mentoring program, Rio de Janeiro municipality's Ginasio Experimental Carioca, and Teach For All's approach to teacher development are promising new examples in the LAC region of efforts to promote teachers' professional mastery through peer collaboration. Colombia's escuela nueva was one of the first programs in the region to put peer learning at the core of its teacher development model.

High-performing education systems also give substantial *recognition and prestige* to excellent teachers. They have systems in place to evaluate individual teachers' potential and performance and promote the best teachers into special status as master teachers or leaders in specific curriculum areas, such as math. In contrast, teachers in Latin America are rarely observed or evaluated closely and whether their performance is outstanding or deeply deficient, in most systems teachers advance equally through the ranks on the basis of seniority.

Accountability pressure. High teacher absence rates across the LAC region and classroom observations showing that teachers are often poorly prepared to use class time effectively are evidence that the pressures teachers feel to perform accountably are generally weak. Strategies for strengthening accountability include actions to *reduce or eliminate teachers' job stability*, *increase managerial oversight*, and *empower clients* (parents and students) to monitor or evaluate teachers. There is little research evidence to date on any of these strategies except client empowerment; "strong" forms of school-based management, in which parents and community members have a voice in the hiring and firing of school personnel, has been shown to reduce teacher absence and raise student learning results (Bruns, Filmer, and Patrinos 2011).

In terms of job stability, new reforms in Chile, Peru, and Ecuador and an earlier reform in Colombia have created a path out of the profession for teachers with unsatisfactory performance. While potentially very important, the number of teachers dismissed to date has been tiny. This contrasts with the practice in Singapore, where all teachers are evaluated regularly and actions are regularly taken to counsel the lowest 5 percent of performers out of the profession, and in Washington, DC, where 33 percent of the teaching force was dismissed or voluntarily left in the first four years after its teacher evaluation system was introduced. Radical upgrading of the teaching profession in Latin America will require much more aggressive action to weed out the lowest performing teachers on a continuous basis.

In terms of managerial oversight, the role of school directors in managing teacher performance has generally been weak. School directors in Latin America are rarely trained to be instructional leaders, observing their teachers in the classroom and giving them regular formative feedback. Recent efforts in Chile, Jamaica, Brazil, Peru, and Ecuador to raise the standards for school directors and to train and empower them to be accountable for instructional quality and teacher development are important initiatives. But Colombia's experience—where directors have found it difficult to give teachers critical feedback—suggests that relying only on school directors for teacher performance evaluation can be problematic. Instead, teacher evaluation needs to be a systemwide function guided by common standards and evaluation processes and rubrics—both for fairness and for systemwide learning. The key goals are fair, actionable, and formative feedback to all teachers and the ability to weed out the lowest performers on a continuous basis, so that the average quality of the teaching force keeps rising over time.

Financial incentives. Cross-country research suggests that the financial rewards for teaching must meet a threshold level of parity with other professions to attract high talent. As chapter 1 showed, average salaries in some countries and the pay trajectory in most LAC countries are currently below this threshold.

Across-the-board salary increases—which are politically popular and easy to implement—have the potential to shift the overall teacher supply curve outward. But these are inefficient. For the same fiscal expenditure, school systems can achieve higher quality by raising average salaries through a pay scale differentiated by performance. This avoids overcompensating weak performers, can keep overall pension liabilities lower, and creates stronger incentives for the most talented individuals.

The two main strategies for differentiated financial rewards are *career path reforms* and *bonus pay*. Career path reforms typically make permanent promotions contingent on performance rather than seniority and expand salary differentials across different grades. The number of LAC countries that have implemented career path reforms is small but growing. Although there is no direct research on this, by analogy with other occupations it is likely that career path reforms have more powerful selection effects than bonus pay toward who goes into teaching. Career path reforms signal a permanent and cumulative structure of rewards for high performance, have attractive pension implications, and are reaped by individual teachers.

These are some key lessons that can be drawn from the experience with *career path reforms* in LAC to date:

- *Choosing a valid measure of teacher quality and calibrating it appropriately are crucial steps.* Global research suggests that comprehensive measures of teacher performance are the soundest basis for promotion decisions. Peru's new teacher law, which proposes promotions based on a combination of tests of teachers' knowledge and skills; expert observations of teachers' practice in the classroom; and 360-degree feedback from peers, students, parents, and school directors, is an example consistent with global best practice. Although comprehensive evaluation is administratively complex and costly, both global research and the experience of schools systems such as Washington, D.C., and Cincinnati, Ohio, show that the payoffs can be large.

  For school systems introducing competency-based promotion and pay for the first time, relying on a well-designed test of subject matter mastery and pedagogical knowledge alone may be the most practical first step. To be legitimate, tests should measure what teachers *know* in terms of content, what they *understand* about child development and learning styles, and what they are *able to do* to tailor pedagogical strategies for the delivery of content at different grade levels. Tests must also be benchmarked appropriately; if promotions are gained too easily, as in the early years of Mexico's CPM, or are too inaccessible, incentive strength erodes. Finally, the new wave of career path reforms in LAC do not try to measure teachers' individual contributions to student learning gains, and that seems sensible. First, the testing requirements to establish value-added learning measures are enormous and expensive; second, attaching high stakes to student test scores can create overwhelming pressures for cheating that undermine the integrity and value of the entire assessment system.

- *Who evaluates* is important. Although ministries of education should closely control the design and implementation of teacher promotion policies, contracting external agencies to design and administer competency tests can increase their legitimacy. For classroom observations, using independent external experts and grounding evaluation standards and feedback in system-wide performance metrics are important.

- The *steepness of the salary trajectory* affects incentive strength, but there is little evidence as yet to guide reform design. All of the recent reforms expand the number of promotion levels and decompress the band between top and initial salaries. But across the new programs, these dimensions vary: there are three different promotion levels in Colombia, five in São Paulo (Brazil), and eight in Peru. Top-level salaries are 100 percent higher than starting level in some systems and almost 300 percent higher in others. Since most of these reforms are quite new, there is an important opportunity to research their differential impacts on the attractiveness of the profession to high-talent new teachers over time.

- *Strategies for managing the long-term fiscal implications of career path reforms are important.* Although the permanence of promotions and base pay increases is central to its strength as an incentive, it runs the risk of locking in high compensation for teachers who are promoted but subsequently fail to keep up their skills. Ecuador, Chile, and the proposed system in the state of Rio de Janeiro safeguard against this by requiring that teachers recertify every four years and can face downgrades as well. Building an "up or out" strategy into career path reform is an ingenious approach that appears to be a Latin American innovation and merits impact evaluation.

- *Careful implementation planning* of reforms as complex as these is important. The credibility of several programs—in Mexico, Colombia, São Paulo state (Brazil), and Peru's initial, 2008 reform—was undermined by problems that might have been foreseen and managed differently.

- *Incentive power hangs on belief that programs will be sustained* under consistent rules of the game. Whenever teachers perceive that the criteria for entry into a new career track are likely to change, soften, or be disbanded, the incentives to acquire new knowledge or apply to the profession erode. In contrast, career path reforms that truly signal substantially higher long-term financial rewards for talented teachers probably offer the clearest direct path to the recruitment of higher-caliber teacher candidates and more effective teaching. Policy makers across the region would gain from careful research on the new wave of career path reforms in LAC.

Bonus pay is the other major instrument for raising the financial rewards for teaching. Bonus pay programs are proliferating in LAC, especially in Brazil. They are both politically and technically easier to implement than career path reforms and do not have long-term fiscal or pension implications. Bonus programs typically offer a one-time reward for teachers (or schools) for specific results achieved during the prior school year. There is no evidence yet on the impact of bonus pay programs on the critical long-term question of teacher selection: Are bonus pay programs a sufficiently strong financial incentive to attract higher-caliber candidates into teaching? But the experience in LAC and other regions provides evidence of short-term impacts on teacher and school performance and some lessons for program design:

- *Bonus pay programs can work, perhaps especially in developing country contexts.* Although the number of cases remains small, bonus pay programs in developing country settings have produced more consistently positive results than in developed countries to date. Encouragingly, the only two rigorously evaluated cases of bonus pay programs operating at scale (Chile's SNED and the school bonus in Pernambuco, Brazil) are both from Latin America, and both have demonstrated positive results on student learning and grade attainment. Measured impacts across programs evaluated in the global research literature are generally in the range of 0.15 to 0.3 SD improvement in test scores, which are significant-sized effects for education interventions. A reasonable hypothesis is that financial incentives for school results are most productive where existing systems for performance monitoring, accountability, and teacher professionalism are weak.

- *Matching incentive design to context is crucial.* Much of the experimental evidence is from studies that tested alternative bonus designs—school-level versus individual teacher incentives; teacher versus student incentives; gain versus loss bonus awards—and it is striking how much the impact of alternatively designed bonuses can vary within a single context. Bonus size is another design issue on which there is as yet little practical guidance from research; some of the largest reported impacts in the literature are from bonuses that represent a very small increment of teachers' average pay. The research base today is far short of providing a guide to the most productive bonus pay designs for a given context. But it suggests that if a given program's impact appears to be weak, there probably exists a productive alternative design.

- *Designing the performance measure(s) to be rewarded is a key challenge.* Basing bonus pay on test scores alone has been problematic in several U.S. settings because of documented cheating and broader concerns that it focuses teachers too narrowly on specific subjects. No LAC country to date has introduced bonus pay for test scores alone, and this strategy appears wise. The composite indicator used in Brazil, which is a product of both test scores and pass rates, is an interesting model for countries to consider, as it discourages both automatic promotion of children who are not learning and the reverse strategy of holding children back or encouraging dropout in order to boost test scores.

- *Programs are likely to have heterogeneous impacts on different types of schools.* In both of the bonus programs operating at scale, significant heterogeneity has been observed. In Chile's SNED program, about one-third of schools appear consistently "out of the money" in the tournaments, despite the serious efforts made to ensure that schools only compete against similar schools. In Pernambuco, Brazil, the bonus produces stronger impacts in small schools, where teachers can collaborate and monitor each other more easily than in larger schools. Research evidence of this type can provide useful guidance for program design.

- *Students are key partners in the production of learning results.* The innovative design of the ALI experiment in Mexico has generated powerful evidence that school systems can gain by finding ways to make students feel more invested in their learning progress.

- *Our understanding of the mechanisms through which bonus pay improves student outcomes is still weak.* The logic of incentive pay is to stimulate teacher behaviors that help raise student learning—either increased teacher effort or more effective effort. However, few evaluations have documented changes in teachers' classroom practice that can plausibly explain increases in student learning. Research on teachers' classroom practice is becoming more feasible with the declining costs of installing video cameras in samples of classrooms and increasing use of standardized methods for coding and analyzing teacher-student interaction. Systematic inclusion of such analysis in impact evaluations of pay for performance programs will not only illuminate how such programs work but also generate evidence and examples of effective teaching that can more broadly benefit these school systems.

Finally, cross-country studies suggest that no education system achieves high teacher quality without aligning all three types of incentives: professional rewards, accountability pressures, and financial rewards. But these studies also suggest that the particular combinations that are most efficient are highly context-specific. Finland, Singapore, and Ontario (Canada) for example, have all built strong professional rewards for teaching, but accountability pressures are much stronger in Singapore than in Finland or Ontario. And none follows a textbook approach on financial incentives. Finland achieved a sharp upgrading of teacher quality over several decades with little increase in teachers' relative salaries. Singapore keeps entering salaries for teachers on par with other professions and offers bonuses for high performance but has an overall career ladder that is much flatter than other professions. Ontario pays competitive salaries, but the core of its strategy is team-based professional development at the school level that is supported by outside experts but not otherwise incentivized. These examples suggest that there are multiple roads to the goal: a balanced set of incentives sufficient to attract talented applicants, establish accountability for results, and motivate continued professional growth and pursuit of excellence.

Notes

[1] Bruns, Filmer, and Patrinos (2011) provide an overview of the developing country evidence on a broad range of accountability-based school reforms, including school-based management, information for accountability, and teacher incentives linked to school accountability.

[2] Overall churning in U.S. school systems is much higher: close to 33 percent of all teachers hired are gone within three years, and close to half are gone in less than five years. These teachers are widely believed to be the more talented members of the profession, who find more attractive career options outside of teaching.

[3] The CPM was created by Law 29062 in July 2007.

[4] Hundreds of thousands of teachers and millions of students have been tested every year as part of its yearly evaluations.

[5] Teachers must obtain a minimum of 70 out of a 100 total points to be promoted. Up to 80 of these points can be thought of as exogenous, because they either increase automatically every year or remain the same (e.g., the points given for seniority and highest degree earned); have virtually no

variation (the case of the peer review component); or are within the control of the teacher (points given for obtaining professional development or the teacher test). Teachers with exogenous point scores below 50 or above 70 are in the weak incentive group. Teachers with exogenous point scores between 50 and 70 have a high incentive to improve student achievement, which is worth 20 points and could get them above the minimum cutoff for incorporation (McEwan and Santibáñez 2005).

[6] See McEwan and Santibáñez (2005) and Santibáñez et al. (2007).

[7] This was done to accommodate teachers who, prior to the CM, were on a differentiated pay scale called "Esquema Básico de Educación." Because this pay scale was eliminated with the introduction of the CM, these teachers automatically entered CM's first level (level A) and received a bump in salary.

[8] All teachers who take the AVDI test obtain a small reward of US$100 (MINEDUC 2010), irrespective of their results.

[9] In early 2014, the proposed program was on hold.

[10] Programs in India (Duflo and Hanna 2005) and Kenya (Kremer et al. 2001) that award bonus pay based on teacher attendance have been rigorously evaluated, with contrasting results. Since no bonus program in LAC to date has been based on teacher attendance alone, and we consider this also unlikely in the future, this research is not included here. Results may be found in Bruns, Filmer, and Patrinos (2011).

[11] National assessment data show virtually identical student demographic characteristics and school characteristics (average size, average class size) for the approximately 57,000 students and 750 schools tested in each cycle in Pernambuco and approximately 225,000 students and 3,500 schools tested in the other eight Northeast states.

References

Ballou, D., and M. Podgursky. 2002. "Returns to Seniority among Public School Teachers." *Journal of Human Resources* 37 (4): 892–912.

Barber, M., and M. Mourshed. 2007. *How the World's Best-Performing School Systems Come Out on Top.* London: McKinsey.

Barrera-Osorio, F., T. Fasih, H. A. Patrinos, and L. Santibáñez. 2009. *Decentralized Decision-Making in Schools: The Theory and Evidence on School-Based Management.* Washington, DC: World Bank.

Behrman, J., S. Parker, P. Todd, and K. Wolpin. Forthcoming. "Aligning Learning Incentives of Students and Teachers: Results from a Social Experiment in Mexican High Schools." *Journal of Political Economy.*

Boyd, D., P. Grossman, H. Lankford, S. Loeb, and J. Wyckoff. 2008. "Who Leaves? Teacher Attrition and Student Achievement." NBER Working Paper 14022, National Bureau of Economic Research, Cambridge, MA.

Bravo, D., D. Falck, R. González, P. Manzi, and C. Peirano. 2008. *La Relación entre la Evaluación Docente y el Rendimiento de los Alumnos: Evidencia para el Caso de Chile.* Santiago: Centro de Medición de la Universidad Católica, MIDE UC. http://microdatos.cl/docto_publicaciones/Evaluacion%20docentes_rendimiento%20escolar.pdf.

Bruns, B., D. Filmer, and H. A. Patrinos. 2011. *Making Schools Work: New Evidence on Accountability Reforms.* Washington, DC: World Bank.

Bruns, B., D. Evans, and J. Luque. 2012. *Achieving World Class Education in Brazil: The Next Agenda.* Washington, DC: World Bank.

Cabezas, V., J. Cuesta, and F. Gallego. 2011. "Education Outcomes in Low-Income Sectors: Evidence from Two Randomized Evaluations in Chile." Unpublished manuscript, Pontificia Universidad Católica de Chile, Santiago, Chile.

Carnoy, M. 2007. *Cuba's Academic Advantage: Why Students in Cuba Do Better in School*. Palo Alto, CA: Stanford University Press.
Chaudhury, N., J. Hammer, M. Kremer, K. Muralidharan, and F. H. Rogers. 2006. "Missing in Action: Teacher and Health Worker Absence in Developing Countries." *Journal of Economic Perspectives* 20 (1): 91–116.
Chetty, R., J. N. Friedman, and J. E. Rockoff. Forthcoming. "Measuring the Impacts of Teachers II: Teacher Value-Added and Student Outcomes in Adulthood." *American Economic Review*.
Clotfelter, C. T., H. F. Ladd, and J. Vigdor. 2005. "Who Teaches Whom? Race and the Distribution of Novice Teachers." *Economics of Education Review* 24: 377–92.
Conger, D. 2005. "Within-School Segregation in an Urban School District." *Educational Evaluation and Policy Analysis* 27 (3): 225–44.
Contreras, D., and T. Rau. 2012. "Tournament Incentives for Teachers: Evidence from a Scaled-up Intervention in Chile." *Economic Development and Cultural Change* 91 (1): 219–46.
CPEIP (Centro de Perfeccionamiento, Experimentación e Investigaciones Pedagógicas). n.d. *Asignación de Excelencia Pedagógica*. Santiago: Chile, Ministerio de Educación. http://aep.mineduc.cl.
Crouch, L. 2005. "Political Economy, Incentives, and Teachers' Unions: Case Studies in Chile and Peru." In *Incentives to Improve Teaching: Lessons from Latin America*, edited by E. Vegas, 389–424. Washington, DC: World Bank.
Delannoy, F., and G. Sedlacek. 2001. *Brazil: Teachers Development and Incentives: A Strategic Framework*. Washington, DC: World Bank.
Duflo, E., P. Dupas, and M. Kremer. 2012. "School Governance, Teacher Incentives and Pupil-Teacher Ratios: Experimental Evidence from Kenyan Primary Schools." NBER Working Paper 17939, National Bureau of Economic Research, Cambridge, MA.
Duflo, E., and R. Hanna. 2005. "Monitoring Works: Getting Teachers to Come to School." NBER Working Paper 11880, National Bureau of Economic Research, Cambridge, MA.
Eisenberg, N. V. 2008. "The Performance of Teachers in Chilean Public Elementary Schools: Exploring Its Relationship with Teacher Backgrounds and Student Achievement, and Its Distribution across Schools and Municipalities." PhD thesis, University of California, Los Angeles.
Fernandez, C., and M. Yoshida. 2004. *Lesson Study: A Japanese Approach to Improving Mathematics Teaching and Learning*. London: Lawrence Earlbaum Associates.
Ferraz, C., and B. Bruns. Forthcoming. "Paying Teachers to Perform: The Impact of Bonus Pay in Pernambuco, Brazil." Manuscript, World Bank, Washington, DC.
Firestone, W. A., and J. R. Pennell. 1993. "Teacher Commitment, Working Conditions, and Differential Incentive Policies." *Review of Educational Research* 63 (4): 489–525.
Fryer, R. 2013. "Teacher Incentives and Student Achievement: Evidence from New York City Public Schools." *Journal of Labor Economics* 31 (2): 373–407.
Fryer, R., S. Levitt, J. List, and S. Sadoff. 2012. "Enhancing the Efficacy of Teachers Incentives through Loss Aversion: A Field Experiment." NBER Working Paper 18237, National Bureau of Economic Research, Cambridge, MA.
Fuchs, T., and L. Woessmann. 2007. "What Accounts for International Differences in Student Performance? A Re-Examination Using PISA Data." *Empirical Economics* 32 (2): 433–64.
Gasperini, L. 2000. *The Cuban Education System: Lessons and Dilemmas*. Education Reform and Management Publication Series, Vol. 5. Washington, DC: World Bank.
Goldhaber, D. 2009. *Teacher Pay Reforms: The Political Implications of Recent Research*. Washington, DC: Center for American Progress.
Goodman, S. F., and L. J. Turner. 2013. "The Design of Teacher Incentive Pay and Educational Outcomes: Evidence from the New York City Bonus Program." *Journal of Labor Economics* 31 (2): 409–20.
Hanushek, E. A. 2011. "The Economic Value of Higher Teacher Quality." *Economics of Education Review* 30 (3): 466–79.

Holmstrom, B., and P. Milgrom. 1991. "Multitask Principal-Agent Analyses: Incentive Contracts, Asset Ownership, and Job Design." *Journal of Law Economics and Organization* 7 (special issue): 24–52.

Hoxby, C., and A. Leigh. 2004. "Pulled Away or Pushed out? Explaining the Decline of Teacher Aptitude in the United States." *American Economic Review* 94 (2): 236–40.

Instituto Hartmann Regueira. 2011. *Pesquisa sobre a qualidade do ensino nas escolas do Estado de Minas Gerais*. Belo Horizonte, Brazil: IHR.

Jacob, B. 2012. "Teacher Labor Markets: Current Evidence and Continuing Questions." Presentation at Latin American Economics Association Meetings, November 2012, Lima.

Jacob, B., and S. Levitt. 2003. "Rotten Apples: An Investigation of the Prevalence and Predictors of Teacher Cheating." *Quarterly Journal of Economics* 118 (3): 843–77.

Jacob, A., E. Vidyarthi, and K. Carroll. 2012. "The Irreplaceables: Understanding the Real Retention Crisis in America's Urban Schools." TNTP, New York. http://files.eric.ed.gov/fulltext/ED533959.pdf.

Johnson, S. M. 1984. "Merit Pay for Teachers: A Poor Prescription for Reform." *Harvard Educational Review* 54 (2): 175–86.

Kalogrides, D., and S. Loeb. 2012. *Different Teachers, Different Peers: The Magnitude of Student Sorting Within Schools*. Palo Alto, CA: Center for Education Policy Analysis, Stanford University.

Kane, T. J., and D. O. Staiger. 2012. *Gathering Feedback for Teaching: Combining High-Quality Observations with Student Surveys and Achievement Gains*. Seattle: Measures of Effective Teaching Project, Bill & Melinda Gates Foundation.

Kremer, M., D. Chen, P. Glewwe, and S. Moulin. 2001. "Interim Report on a Teacher Incentive Program in Kenya." Unpublished paper, Harvard University, Cambridge, MA.

Levin, B. 2012. "Building Capacity for Sustained School Improvement." In *Teacher Education around the World: Changing Policies and Practices*, edited by L. D. Hammond and A. Lieberman. New York: Routledge.

Libeer, C. 2012. *Área de Acreditación y Evaluación Docente*. Santiago: Centro de Perfeccionamiento, Experimentación e Investigaciones Pedagógicas, Chile, Ministerio de Educación.

Loeb, S., D. Kalogrides, and T. Béteille. 2012. "Effective Schools: Teacher Hiring, Assignment, Development, and Retention." *Education Finance and Policy* 7 (3): 269–304.

Louzano, P., and A. Morduchowicz. 2011. *Formación Docente en Chile*. Santiago: PREAL. http://www.preal.org/Archivos/Preal%20Publicaciones/PREAL%20Documentos/PREALDOC57V.pdf.

Manzi, J. 2008. "Individual Incentives and Teacher Evaluation: The Chilean Case." Paper prepared for the International OECD and Mexico Joint Conference, Teacher Incentives and Stimuli Session, "Quality of Education," Mexico City.

McEwan, P. J., and L. Santibáñez. 2005. "Teacher and Principal Incentives in Mexico." In *Incentives to Improve Teaching: Lessons from Latin America*, edited by E. Vegas, 213–54. Washington, DC: World Bank.

MINEDUC (Ministerio de Educación, Chile). 2010. *SNED Hacia la Excelencia Academica*. Santiago: MINEDUC. http://www.mineduc.cl/usuarios/sned/doc/201108031652330.Documento_SNED.pdf.

———. 2014. *Resultados AVDI 2013*. Santiago: MINEDUC. http://www.avdi.mineduc.cl/.

Mizala, A., and M. Urquiola. 2007. "School Markets: The Impact of Information Approximating Schools' Effectiveness." NBER Working Paper 13676, National Bureau of Economic Research, Cambridge, MA.

Mourshed, M., C. Chijioke, and M. Barber. 2010. *How the World's Most Improved School Systems Keep Getting Better*. London: McKinsey. http://mckinseyonsociety.com/downloads/reports/Education/How-the-Worlds-Most-Improved-School-Systems-Keep-Getting-Better_Download-version_Final.pdf.

Muralidharan, K. 2012. "Long-Term Effects of Teacher Performance Pay: Experimental Evidence from India." Working Paper, University of San Diego, San Diego.

Muralidharan, K., and V. Sundararaman. 2011. "Teacher Performance Pay: Experimental Evidence from India." *Journal of Political Economy* 199 (1): 39–77.

Murnane, R. J., and D. K. Cohen. 1986. "Merit Pay and the Evaluation Problem: Why Most Merit Pay Plans Fail and a Few Survive." *Harvard Educational Review* 56 (1): 1–18.

Neal, D. 2012. "The Design of Performance Pay in Education." In *Handbook of the Economics of Education*, edited by E. A. Hanushek, S. Machin, and L. Woessmann, vol. 4, ch. 6. Amsterdam: North-Holland.

Odden, A., and C. Kelley. 2002. *Paying Teachers for What They Know and Do: New and Smarter Compensation Strategies to Improve Schools.* Thousand Oaks, CA: Corwin Press.

OECD (Organisation for Economic Co-operation and Development). 2012. *Education at a Glance 2012: OECD Indicators.* Paris: OECD Publishing. http://dx.doi.org/10.1787/eag-2012-en.

Ome, A. 2012. "The Effects of Meritocracy for Teachers in Colombia." Manuscript, Centro de Investigación Económica y Social Fedesarrollo, Bogota.

Pervin, B., and C. Campbell. 2011. "Systems for Teacher and Leader Effectiveness and Quality: Ontario, Canada." In *Teacher and Leader Effectiveness in High-Performing Education Systems*, edited by L. D. Hammond and R. Rothman, 23–32. Washington, DC: Alliance for Excellent Education, and Stanford, CA: Stanford Center for Opportunity Policy in Education.

Pink, D. H. 2006. *A Whole New Mind: Moving from the Information Age to the Conceptual Age.* New York: Riverhead Books.

Sahlberg, P. 2011. *Finnish Lessons: What Can the World Learn from Educational Change in Finland?* New York: Teachers College Press.

———. 2012. "The Most Wanted: Teacher and Teacher Education in Finland." In *Teacher Education around the World: Changing Policies and Practices*, edited by L. D. Hammond and A. Lieberman, 1–21. New York: Routledge.

Santibáñez, L., J. Martinez, A. Datar, P. McEwan, C. Setodji, and R. Basurto-Davila. 2007. *Breaking Ground Analysis of the Assessment System and Impact of Mexico's Teacher Incentive Program "Carrera Magisterial,"* RAND Technical report, RAND Corporation, Santa Monica, CA.

Schleicher, A. 2011. *Building a High-Quality Teaching Profession: Lessons from around the World.* Paris: OECD Publishing. http://dx.doi.org/10.1787/9789264113046-en.

Schwartz, J., and J. Mehta. 2014. "Ontario: Harnessing the Skills of Tomorrow." In *Lessons from PISA for Korea, Strong Performers and Successful Reformers in Education*, edited by OECD. Paris: OECD Publishing. http://dx.doi.org/10.1787/9789264190672-en.

Springer, M. G., D. Ballou, L. Hamilton, L., Le, VN. J. R. Lockwood, D. F. McCaffrey, M. Pepper, and B. M. Stecher. 2010. *Teacher Pay for Performance: Experimental Evidence from the Project on Incentives in Teaching.* Nashville: National Center on Performance Incentives. http://www.performanceincentives.org/data/files/pages/Point%20REPORT.9.21.10.pdf.

Tucker, M., ed. 2011. *Surpassing Shanghai: An Agenda for American Education Built on the World's Leading Systems.* Cambridge, MA: Harvard Education Press.

Umansky, I. 2005. "A Literature Review of Teacher Quality and Incentives." In *Incentives to Improve Teaching: Lessons from Latin America*, edited by E. Vegas, 1–20. Washington, DC: World Bank.

Urquiola, M., and E. Vegas. 2005. "Arbitrary Variation in Teacher Salaries." In *Incentives to Improve Teaching: Lessons from Latin America*, edited by E. Vegas, 187–212. Washington, DC: World Bank.

Vegas, E., ed. 2005. *Incentives to Improve Teaching: Lessons from Latin America.* Washington, DC: World Bank.

Vegas, E., and I. Umansky. 2005. "Improving Teaching and Learning through Effective Incentives." In *Incentives to Improve Teaching: Lessons from Latin America*, edited by E. Vegas, 21–62. Washington, DC: World Bank.

Weisberg, D., S. Sexton, J. Mulhern, and D. Keeling. 2009. *The Widget Effect: Our National Failure to Acknowledge and Act on Differences in Teacher Effectiveness.* Brooklyn, NY: New Teacher Project.

World Bank. 2004. *World Development Report 2004: Making Services Work for Poor People.* Washington, DC: World Bank.

6
Managing the Politics of Teacher Reform

Teachers are not only key actors in the production of education results; they are also the most powerful stakeholder in the process of education reform. No other education actor is as highly organized, visible, and politically influential (Grindle 2004). Because of their unique autonomy behind the closed door of the classroom, teachers also have profound power over the extent to which new policies can be implemented successfully. By global standards, teachers' unions in Latin America and the Caribbean (LAC) have been considered especially strong, with a history of effective use of direct electoral influence as well as disruptive actions in the streets to block reforms perceived as a threat to their interests. Yet the traditional political dynamics appear to be shifting. A growing number of countries are adopting previously unthinkable teacher policy reforms. This chapter explores that evolution.

The political dynamics of education reform are shaped by three factors:

- How a reform affects key stakeholders' interests
- The relative power of key stakeholders
- The effectiveness of their political strategies

The first section of this chapter looks at the most important types of education reform being pursued in LAC countries through the lens of teachers' interests. Like all organized workers, teachers' unions exist to defend the rights they legitimately earn through negotiations and to oppose policy changes that threaten those rights. Teachers and their representatives are entirely justified in pursuing these goals, and teachers' unions throughout history have been a progressive force in achieving equal pay and fair treatment for women and minority members. But it is also true that the

---

This chapter was coauthored with Marco Fernández.

goals of teachers' organizations are not congruent with the goals of education policy makers or the interests of education beneficiaries—including students, parents, and employers who need skilled workers. The first section lays out some of the areas in which these interests collide and a few in which they are aligned.

The second section documents the structure and power base of the major teachers' unions in LAC countries today. It analyzes the capacity for collective action that is one of the key sources of union power and its converse, union fragmentation. It also reviews five core strategies that unions employ to advance their interests.

The third section analyzes the political dynamics of four recent cases of major teacher policy reform in Chile, Mexico, Peru, and Ecuador. The policies are similar, but the specific reform strategies pursued and the relative strength of union power and government political leadership in each context produced different political dynamics. We look for lessons from these cases with wider relevance for countries in the region.

Education policies through the lens of teachers' interests

LAC countries—like those in other regions—pursue a wide variety of strategies for raising education quality and improving efficiency. Teachers' unions resist a number of these, either by blocking them from adoption or undermining them during implementation. Unions' resistance to reforms can generally be traced to threats these pose to members' benefits (salaries, pensions, and job stability); their working conditions and challenges (curriculum changes, student testing, performance evaluation, and accountability pressure); or the union's own survival. Teachers' unions perceive clearly that policies that impact their size or structure—ranging from decentralization proposals to career path reforms that differentiate salaries based on competency—can fragment union membership and undermine the capacity for collective action, which is a fundamental source of union power.

In contrast, teachers' unions commonly lobby in favor of higher salaries and benefits for their members and policies that create more pleasant working conditions. One of the most important of these is smaller class size, which also resonates with parents as a quality-enhancing education strategy. Unions are often an organized and influential proponent of increased public spending on education and class size reductions.

We review key types of education reforms being introduced by LAC countries and their alignment with teachers' interests.

Reforms perceived as threats to teachers' benefits

Loss of job tenure. Teaching positions in the public sector have long offered a high degree of job stability, and teachers' unions typically resist proposals that endanger it. Nevertheless, over the past decade several governments in the region, including Colombia, Chile, Ecuador, and Peru, have passed new legislation that allows authorities to strip poor-performing teachers of their civil service job protection. In most cases, some type of political compromise was necessary for the legislation to be adopted, whether accompanying the new reform with salary increases or exempting existing teachers from the provisions and applying them only to new hires. Progressive union leaders may calculate strategically that their long-term survival prospects are higher if they avoid expending political capital on weaker members and allow the gradual substitution of these by more competent teachers. Such movement does not threaten the unions' size or structure and over the long term can raise its profile.

Reduction or loss of other benefits. Teachers in most of LAC retire at a relatively early age, and most governments have not saved sufficient funds to guarantee teachers' pensions. Several governments have attempted to increase the retirement age and reduce teachers' pension benefits. Unions in all cases have fought proposals, often under the argument that the policy prescriptions are imposed by international organizations as part of a neoliberal canon with negative consequences for society. However, teachers can also be divided over pension issues, with younger teachers much more willing to trade off pension benefits for wage increases. Recent research in the United States (Koedel, Podgurksy, and Shi 2013) has concluded that pension enhancements are not an efficient strategy for raising teacher quality, as they create a rent that is captured by senior teachers and burden future teachers and employers moving forward, which undermines school systems' ability to recruit the best into the profession.

Reforms perceived as threats to teachers' working conditions

Curriculum reform. Teachers often oppose reforms to the curriculum, especially if they believe they have not been consulted adequately by education authorities. In 2001, the teachers' union in Colombia fought a Ministry of Education effort to standardize curriculum guidelines and to establish common criteria to evaluate students' performance.[1] A 2004 Currículo Nacional Básico in Honduras similarly was resisted. Programs introducing new technologies in the classroom are also often viewed by teachers as an imposition and to some extent a threat. However, information and communications technology (ICT) programs tend to face less organized union resistance, perhaps because they are so popular with parents and students. The adoption of new technologies in the classroom is nonetheless often undermined in practice—whether in protest or simply lack of competence—by the unique power teachers have to control what is implemented in schools.

Uruguay is a reminder of the dangers of not adequately consulting the teachers' union before changing the curriculum. A 1995 reform at the secondary school level radically changed the curriculum from one based on discrete subjects (e.g., history, geography, and sociology) to one based on broader areas (e.g., social sciences). The change forced teachers to incorporate elements from areas outside of their expertise into courses (history teachers needed to incorporate geography and sociology, for example) and caused profound discontent in the teacher's union (FENAPES). The reform also included an effort to reform pre-service teacher training and eliminate subject-based teaching there. This triggered a bitter confrontation between the government and the teachers' union from 1997 to 1998. The area-based curriculum for secondary education was eventually eliminated in a 2008 education law, which reestablished a subject-based curriculum.

Student testing. Standardized testing has grown enormously in Latin America over the last decade as government and civil society interest in "benchmarking" education systems, both internally and internationally, has increased. Unions have opposed standardized tests on numerous grounds, many of which are supported by global evidence: the tests are not valid measures of student knowledge; they do not take students' socioeconomic differences into account; they encourage a narrowing of the curriculum and teaching to the test; they can undermine teachers' incentives to teach challenging students or work in teams with other teachers if individual teacher performance will be judged by students' results. But also underlying these arguments is a rational perception by teachers that student test scores expose teacher and school performance and increase accountability pressure in their work environment.

Nonetheless, many governments across the region have prevailed in establishing both national testing systems and participating in high-visibility international tests, such as the Organisation for Economic Co-operation and Development's (OECD) Program for International Student Assessment (PISA). There are signs of political compromise in the way standardized testing has been introduced in the region, though. Unlike the United States, LAC countries have by and large avoided attaching high-stakes accountability to student test scores, either for individual teachers or individual schools. Even countries with national student testing systems already in place, such as Chile, have not tried to include student learning results among the performance indicators in their teacher evaluation systems.[2] The only incentives linked to student test scores in the LAC region currently are group based and positive: bonuses for whole schools based on their average performance. No program in the region to date imposes sanctions on schools with poor test performance. In the case of Uruguay, a unique compromise was reached: there is a system of standardized testing, but the results are not made public and are known only by the teachers themselves.

The growth of student testing has been a powerful factor in education reform politics in LAC, however. Standardized test results—and especially international results such as PISA—have been widely reported in the media and influenced public perceptions of education quality and the need for reform. Over the ten-plus years since LAC countries joined PISA and participated in regional assessments of student learning sponsored by the United Nations Educational, Scientific, and Cultural Organization (UNESCO), there has been a perceptible increase in both the number and visibility of civil society groups pressing governments for actions to reform education. A number of presidents and other political leaders have used international test data prominently in communications strategies to build public support for reforms. Having data on student learning outcomes has been a game changer in reform politics in LAC, greatly strengthening the relative power of government authorities vis-à-vis teachers' unions in reform dynamics.

Teacher evaluation systems. Some of the deepest conflicts with teachers' unions, not only in LAC, are over teacher performance evaluation. While proposals typically establish attractive incentives for good performers and promise support for teachers needing improvement, the sanctions proposed for teachers who consistently underperform (including dismissal) incite controversy. Teacher performance evaluation systems in Colombia, Mexico, Ecuador, and Peru have been resisted in all cases, and triggered protracted, violent strikes in Ecuador and Peru. Proposals for similar reforms in Honduras and Jamaica in 2013 were embroiled in controversy.

Chile is the only country in the region where teacher performance evaluation (covering municipal school teachers) was adopted without major conflict, although it was initially introduced on a voluntary basis and only later—after uptake was deemed too slow—made mandatory. In the Chilean context, however, less than half of all teachers work in municipal schools and are subject to the evaluations. In contrast, an agreement was reached with the Mexican teachers' union on mandatory teacher evaluation in 2011, but only 35 percent of teachers presented themselves for the tests implemented in July 2012, and the ministry found itself without an effective enforcement mechanism. The low participation attracted intense criticism in the press, however, and augmented public debate on the need to enforce teacher evaluation, as discussed later in this chapter.

Reforms perceived as threats to union structure and power

Decentralization. Over the past several decades a number of countries in Latin America and the Caribbean have pursued strategies to decentralize public service delivery, including education. Goals have included the desire to improve the efficiency of public service provision by bringing political and managerial responsibility for programs closer to the clients and in some cases to strengthen democratization processes (Di Gropello 1999).

Decentralization is seen as a threat by teachers' unions since it can fragment their organizations—reducing their numbers if smaller unions form at the subnational levels and making it harder to coordinate efforts, which undermines bargaining power. Decentralization also poses the danger of responsibility for education being transferred to levels of government with inadequate fiscal resources to fulfill budgetary commitments for teachers' salaries and long-term benefits. Three examples illustrate how unions have opposed decentralization policies and in several cases influenced its implementation.

In Colombia, when the government attempted to transfer education management from the departmental authorities to municipalities in 1989, the union, Federación Colombiana de Educadores (FECODE), effectively opposed the implementation of this policy by forming a strategic coalition with municipalities (Lowden 2004; López 2008). FECODE also played a major role in blocking a 1991 municipalization initiative, which in consequence has been implemented only partially.

The confusing institutional framework that resulted created incentives for subnational governments to hire additional teachers without necessarily increasing education coverage (Lowden 2004). Departmental governments racked up large debt and the national government, although obligated to cover education expenditures, was unable to do so (López 2008). Although education spending increased under the decentralization bill, funding was insufficient to cover the growth in teacher numbers and their pay increases—and there were no incentives for subnational governments to be fiscally responsible. The financial crisis in education spilled over to threaten national economic stability and eventually paved the way for a comprehensive decentralization reform in the 2000s.

In Peru, after a series of unsuccessful decentralization attempts, the government of President Alan García in 2007 launched a pilot program to give municipalities control over the budget for teachers' salaries and basic services such as water and electricity. The teachers' union opposed this move, arguing that it was a veiled attempt to privatize education. During the 2010 presidential campaign, the opposition candidate Ollanta Humala successfully mobilized union support by promising to reverse the decentralization. After he was elected in 2011, President Humala did reverse the program, citing concerns that municipal mayors lacked the fiscal and managerial capacity to handle education responsibilities.[3]

In Mexico, education decentralization attempts over several decades provoked conflict between the federal government and the teachers' union. After successfully resisting several government attempts to decentralize education, the union accepted it in the early 1990s, after obtaining institutional guarantees that the union would retain monopoly of representation of education workers. The union was also able to extract large salary and benefit concessions, including control of implementation of the merit pay program, Carrera Magisterial (CM). Ultimately, decentralization blurred the division of state responsibilities in education between federal and subnational authorities, while the teachers' union was able to retain monopoly of representation. Given the concessions granted, the union ended up benefitting from the decentralization, expanding its control over education management positions at both the federal and state levels—control that has elicited administrators' loyalty to the union rather than to the ministry or to subnational authorities (Street 1992; Cook 1996; Fernández 2012a).

School choice. Proposals to open public education to competition, by channeling some public funding to privately managed schools are also perceived by teachers' unions as threats to union size and structure. Teachers in voucher, charter, and concession schools are typically covered by private labor law, rather than public sector regulations. Chile is unique in the size of its publicly subsidized voucher school sector, which has grown from 30 percent to 56 percent of total enrollments since 1990. The long-term growth of this sector likely has contributed to a softening of union power. But, as discussed later in this chapter, the relatively low levels of conflict around major teacher policy reforms in Chile also owe much to the consistent support of post-1990 democratic governments for teacher professionalism and steadily rising teacher compensation.

Colombia has established a much smaller system of concession schools in which successful private schools are contracted to manage public schools under clear performance standards.[4] These schools are also perceived by union leadership as a threat to its power and have been resisted. Finally, under Honduras' PROHECO (Programa Hondureño de Educación Comunitaria) school-based management program, parents and civil society participate in school-level hiring and firing decisions and teachers in these schools are not affiliated with unions. Under Honduras' SAT (Sistema de Aprendizaje Tutorial) program (discussed in chapter 3), teachers are also hired by community-level associations and not affiliated with unions. Teachers' associations have opposed PROHECO, arguing that it is inequitable that teachers working in PROHECO schools do not benefit from the labor conditions established in the teachers' statute (Barahona Mejía 2008).

Higher teacher standards. A key challenge in the LAC region is to make teaching a more selective profession. Even though this transition would mean higher prestige and higher salaries for teachers eventually, teachers' organizations in the region have generally opposed the imposition of higher standards for teacher recruitment, whether through the requirement of higher formal credentials or more stringent competency tests. Such policies can threaten the expansion of teacher numbers, which unions perceive as a fundamental source of power. In cases where higher degree requirements have been imposed, such as Brazil's 1997 FUNDEF (Fundo Nacional Para o Desenvolvimento do Ensino Fundamental)reform requiring a higher education degree for all teachers, political compromises have typically involved extensive funding for teacher upgrading programs to give existing teachers the same level of qualification.

Alternative certification. Unions consistently maintain that the teaching profession should be exclusively in hands of individuals graduated from teacher education program and oppose the idea of professionals from other fields competing for teaching positions. While alternatively certified teachers may be eligible for union membership and do not necessarily threaten union size, they can and often do introduce fragmentation of members' background, culture, and interests. Unions' official position is generally that "alternatively certified" individuals lack the skills and training to be effective teachers. However, research in the U.S. context reported in chapter 3 has generally found no systematic differences in effectiveness between traditional and alternatively certified teachers, and some cases where alternatively certified teachers perform better (Kane, Rockoff, and Staiger 2008). Several U.S. urban school systems such as New York City's have made strategic use of alternative certification programs to raise teacher quality; today about half of the city's teachers are alternatively certified, mainly through Teach For America and the New York Teaching Fellows program.

The Teach For America model of alternative recruitment has been spreading in Latin America since 2007, under the umbrella name of Teach For All (TFA). Programs launched in Argentina, Brazil, Chile, Colombia, Mexico, and Peru have demonstrated a "proof of concept": talented young graduates from top universities who were not otherwise considering a teaching career have been willing to commit to two years teaching in disadvantaged schools. In every Latin American country to date, the number of applicants has been hugely larger than the number of teaching positions the program can fund.

But teachers' unions have resisted the introduction of Teach For All in public schools. In Chile, Peru, and Colombia, the TFA teachers work in voucher, religious (Fe y Alegría), or concession schools. In Brazil, where such private alternatives are limited, the Rio de Janerio municipal teachers' union was able to block the assignment of TFA teachers into regular classroom teaching positions, constraining them to work after school as tutors. This not only reduced their potential impact but it evaded the possibility for head-to-head performance comparisons with regular teachers. After two years of such limited operation, the program in Brazil was suspended.

Individual pay based on skills or performance. Although a core goal of teachers' organizations is higher salaries for their members, unions typically oppose payment systems that create differentiated rewards for individual teachers. Whether based on measures of teachers' individual competency (skills and knowledge) or evaluations of their individual performance, unions perceive these measures to reduce cohesion. Unions' preferred political strategy is to argue that all teachers are badly paid and to seek higher wages across the board. Researchers have noted that "it is much easier to call a strike for a uniform percentage increase than it is if members are all getting different raises and when better paid teachers may defect" (Mizala and Schneider 2014). Unions also argue that differentiated pay undermines incentives for teachers within a school community to work cooperatively. They defend career ladders based on seniority and academic credentials, which are transparent, widely attainable, and within members' power. In contrast, salary scales based on skills measures or performance evaluation are less controllable, have the potential for subjectivity and unfairness, and can make members more heterogenous, resulting in a fragmentation of their interests.

Despite this resistance, differentiated pay scales based on skills and performance are being adopted across the region, including Chile, Colombia, Ecuador, Mexico, Peru, and Brazil's São Paulo state. Governments appear to perceive that the fragmentation of interests that threatens union power can also mean potential allies for proposed reforms within the teaching force. This split has been clearly visible in career path reforms in the U.S. context. In the final vote by Washington, DC, teachers on the 2009 teacher evaluation system, which offered a doubling of salaries for teachers willing to give up tenure and submit to annual performance evaluations, the vast majority of young teachers opted for the change, splitting the union vote and allowing the reform to proceed. Similar dynamics are beginning to be observed in Latin American cases.

Reforms aligned with union interests

Although many key education reforms are typically resisted by teachers' unions, there are three important education policies that unions strongly support, with major consequences for education systems.

Higher spending. Teachers' unions are politically vocal proponents of higher education spending, especially in the form of across-the-board salary increases and increases in nonsalary spending. From a political perspective, having large numbers of low paid teachers creates a strong base from which to lobby for spending increases. There is no major country in LAC that has not succumbed to this pressure over the past 20 years: the share of gross domestic product (GDP) spent on public education has risen in every country, in some cases dramatically so (figure 6.1). To some extent, the interests of teachers' unions are aligned with those of students and the public over higher education spending—increases are necessary to expand coverage and raise quality. But these interests are not necessarily aligned when it comes to how incremental spending is used. For increases in salary spending to have impact on teacher quality, they must be linked to the types of reforms discussed in chapters 3, 4, and 5, which unions often resist.

With respect to nonsalary spending, teachers' interests converge with those of students and parents. Teachers' unions pressure governments to increase not only salaries but also budgets for teaching supplies, school infrastructure upgrading, school maintenance, and extracurricular support for children (such as sports, arts, tutoring, and counseling programs). During negotiation of the Alliance for Education reform implemented in Mexico during the Calderón administration, the teachers' union produced television ads spotlighting poor education infrastructure across the country. The ads also underscored how union demands have pushed the government to improve school conditions. The campaign resonated with the public and ratified the importance of increased spending on school infrastructure and supplies as part of the Alliance.

Bonus pay for school results. While performance pay for individual teachers is resisted by unions, the politics around school-based bonus programs are

FIGURE 6.1: Total public spending on education as percentage of GDP in selected Latin America and the Caribbean countries, 1990–2010

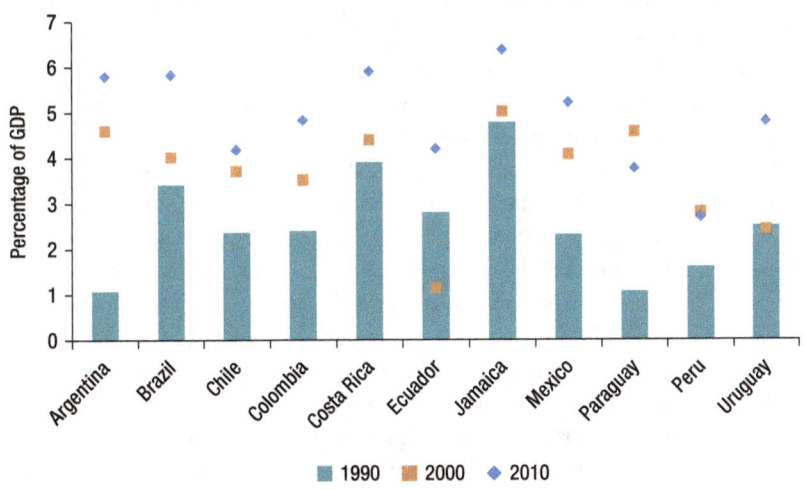

Source: World Bank and UN Economic Commission for Latin America and the Caribbean data.
Note: GDP = gross domestic product.

slightly different. School-based bonuses also link results to financial rewards, but they are perceived by unions as less divisive and threatening than individual bonuses. This was very clear in the case of São Paulo state, where a school-based bonus program introduced in 2008 saw no opposition from the teachers' union, but a career path reform the following year, which offered large salary increases for individual teachers based on competency tests, was bitterly resisted. As discussed in chapter 5, this asymmetry—and the research evidence that well-designed school-based bonus programs *can* stimulate improvements in school performance—offers governments the opportunity for a quality-enhancing reform that is aligned with teachers' interest.

Lower pupil-teacher ratio. The most politically consequential reform aligned with teachers' union interests is class-size reduction. Teachers' organizations have overwhelming incentives to exert political pressure in this area. First, smaller class size is popular with members because it facilitates their work. Second, it directly contributes to union power because it implies the hiring of more teachers and expansion of union numbers. Teachers' organizations are vociferous in insisting that a lower pupil-teacher ratio is a necessary condition for higher-quality schools and better attention to the learning needs of individual students.[5]

The convergence of these arguments with parents' and students' own perceptions that lower class size enhances school quality creates one of the most powerful of all drivers of education policy—a strong tendency in every education system for average class size to decline. Unless governments take conscious and politically unpopular actions to maintain or raise average class size, it almost inevitably begins to decline once universal coverage has been reached, simply because of demographic trends. As seen in chapter 3, this phenomenon has already taken hold in a number of LAC countries, particularly in the southern cone, where class size has declined steadily over the past two decades. Nine countries in the LAC region (Argentina, Brazil, Chile, Costa Rica, Cuba, Ecuador, Panama, Paraguay, and Uruguay) now have a pupil-teacher ratio less than 20 to 1—lower than in some high-performing OECD countries.

The benefits of smaller class size are perceived immediately by both stakeholder groups allied in their support—teachers and parents. But the policy's profound long-term costs are rarely apparent to either group. As discussed in chapter 3, there is no consistent research evidence that class size reductions in the range from 30 to as low as 15 have positive impacts on student learning outcomes, despite their very high costs (Hanushek 2002). A declining pupil-teacher ratio is implicitly financed by trading off alternative investments in education quality, which research shows can be more cost-effective. The most obvious alternative is to prioritize a smaller, better trained, and higher-paid teaching force. But while this long-term outcome may be in the interests of all education stakeholders—future teachers; parents and students; and the broader public and private sector interest in a high-quality education system—it cannot be achieved in most countries with serious challenge to the status quo.

In education policy debates in LAC, this tradeoff is almost never made explicit. To do so risks the political juggernaut of teachers' unions and parent and civil society stakeholders united in opposition. Yet the failure to confront this issue—and explicitly consider the alternative investments that could be financed under a policy of a higher, or even constant, pupil-teacher ratio—locks education systems into an inertial pattern of higher spending per student with little impact on quality. Teacher numbers (and the number of schools) do not decline, because the political path of least resistance is to avoid retrenching teachers or consolidating schools. But under these scenarios, even with increased education spending as a share of GDP, it becomes impossible in most countries to finance the higher and more differentiated teacher compensation scale needed to attract highly talented individuals into teaching.

Sources of union power

In a seminal work, Olson (1965) identified the power over government decisions that organized interests within the public sector can achieve through collective action. Unionized public sector workers have the organizational capacity to process information affecting the policy arena under their influence and are better equipped to monitor government activities than the general public (Grossman and Helpman 2001; Lohmann 2003). In contrast to many private sector unions, unionized public sector workers are typically protected from global competition so neither they nor the government employer face the pressure of market forces during wage negotiations. Through mandatory fees from their members, unions often have access to large financial resources. Through their political outreach, unions can also directly influence elections and thus operate "on both sides of the negotiating table" (Hannaway and Rotherham 2006). Unions with large membership can also use politically damaging strikes and protests in the streets to advance their demands (Corrales 2003; Kaufman and Nelson 2004; Palamidessi and Legarralde 2006).

In most countries, not only in Latin America, teachers form the most powerful union in the public sector because their numbers are large and there is relatively little internal differentiation in members' interests. When teachers' unions have a monopoly of representation at the national level, their strength and influence over education policy increases. Monopoly of representation reduces coordination problems and facilitates bargaining by reducing interunion competition (Golden 1993). All else equal, a single national teachers' union can more successfully advance shared demands for higher salaries and benefits and defend job stability and tenure.

Table 6.1 provides an overview of the major teachers' unions in Latin America and the Caribbean. Although fragmentation can result from leadership competition within unions (Corrales 1999; Murillo 2001), the two most systematic sources of fragmentation are geographic separation and separate organization across different levels of service delivery. In countries such as Brazil and Argentina, where education service delivery is decentralized, unions are geographically organized at the state, provincial, or municipal levels. Geographic fragmentation can spawn significant regional variation in union power and political dynamics; within Brazil, some states and municipalities

TABLE 6.1: Characteristics of teachers' unions in Latin America and the Caribbean

Country	Teachers' union(s)	Union density	Fragmentation	Relation with political parties	Disruptive behavior	Capture of education ministry
Argentina	Confederación de Trabajadores de la Educación de la República Argentina (CTERA) is the most important, but there are several other state organizations that do not belong to CTERA	50.8% (234,000)	High fragmentation (but effective coordination through CTERA)	Diverse strategies and alliances	High (but varies by province)	Not at the national level, but some state unions have participated in disciplinary boards and school councils
Brazil	Confederação Nacional dos Trabalhadores em Educação (CNTE) is the most important, but several municipal and state unions do not belong to CNTE	44.2% (925,229)	High fragmentation (with only partial coordination through CNTE)	Closer to the Workers Party (PT)	Intermediate (varies by municipality and by state)	Intermediate (some positions by former leaders of CNTE)
Chile	Colegio de Profesores	53.3% (71,982)	Monopoly of representation	Not formally but supported the presidential candidates of the left coalition, Concertación de Partidos por la Democracia	Low levels of disruptive behavior	No
Colombia	Federación Colombiana de Educadores (FECODE)	81.6% (membership numbers are not available)	Monopoly of representation	Although not formally linked to any major political parties, FECODE has recently allied with Polo Democrático	Intermediate (disruptive behavior has weakened in recent years)	No

(continued on next page)

TABLE 6.1: Characteristics of teachers' unions in Latin America and the Caribbean *(continued)*

Country	Teachers' union(s)	Union density	Fragmentation	Relation with political parties	Disruptive behavior	Capture of education ministry
Costa Rica	Asociación Nacional de Educadores (ANDE); Asociación de Profesores de Segunda Enseñanza (APSE); Colegio de Licenciados y Profesores en Letras, Ciencias y Artes (COLYPRO); and Sindicato de Trabajadores de la Educación Costarricense (SEC); ANDE and APSE are the main unions, for primary and secondary education, respectively	100% (membership est. 140,000–200,000)	Fragmentation by education level	Relationship with political parties reflects short-term common issues, and there is no formal systematic alliance across issues or time with any political party	Low levels	Some high-ranking union and association members are recruited by the national legislative and executive branches to perform legislative or bureaucratic activities
Ecuador	Unión Nacional de Educadores (UNE); minor competition from Frente Unionista de los Trabajadores de Educación del Ecuador (FUTE); regional organizations orbit around UNE	79%–90% for UNE during 1990s, 79% after 2000; since 2010, membership numbers are not available	Monopoly of representation	Union leadership is not organically part of the government, but identifies publicly with the left-wing Movimiento Popular Democrático (MPD)	Intermediate to high (protests, strikes; 62 during 1998–2007; protests occur at least once a year according to some observers)	Traditionally held influence over teachers' careers; tense relationship with President Correa because of policies to curb UNE's influence on education system

(continued on next page)

TABLE 6.1: Characteristics of teachers' unions in Latin America and the Caribbean *(continued)*

Country	Teachers' union(s)	Union density	Fragmentation	Relation with political parties	Disruptive behavior	Capture of education ministry
Honduras	Colegio Profesional para la Superación Magisterial de Honduras (COLPROSUMAH), Primer Colegio Profesional Hondureño de Maestros (PRICPHMA), Colegio de Profesores de Educación Media de Honduras (COPEMH); the Federación de Organizaciones Magisteriales de Honduras (FOMH) is an effort to unify teachers' unions in the country, but it is not a formal teachers' union; COLPROSUMAH is the largest union	Mandatory affiliation (membership numbers are unavailable) (Arcia and Garguilo 2010)	Fragmented	—	High	No
Jamaica	Jamaica Teachers' Association (JTA)	76%–89% (22,000)	Monopoly of representation	Not formally allies with a political party, but closer to the People's National Party (PNP)	Low	No
Mexico	Sindicato de Trabajadores de la Educación (SNTE)	100% (membership est. between 1.2 million and 1.5 million)	Monopoly of representation	Diverse alliances (has traditionally demonstrated ability to form alliances with different ruling parties)	Intermediate (disruptive behavior varies by state: Guerrero, Michoacan, and Oaxaca with high levels of protests)	Yes (several positions, both at the federal and state levels, including state secretaries and undersecretaries of education)

(continued on next page)

TABLE 6.1: Characteristics of teachers' unions in Latin America and the Caribbean *(continued)*

Country	Teachers' union(s)	Union density	Fragmentation	Relation with political parties	Disruptive behavior	Capture of education ministry
Paraguay	Federación de Educadores de Paraguay (FEP), Organización de Trabajadores de la Educación del Paraguay (OTEP), Agremiación de Docentes y Funcionarios de la Educación Paraguaya (ADOFEP), and Federación de Educadores de Capital e Interior (FECI)	55% for FEP and OTEP (membership numbers for ADOFEP and FECI are not available)	Fragmented	Diverse strategies and alliances	Low	No
Peru	Sindicato Único de Trabajadores en la Educación del Perú (SUTEP) and Sindicato de Docentes de Educación Superior del Perú (SIDESP); SUTEP is most important teachers' union	41.9% (membership est. between 145,000 and 200,000)	Monopoly of representation	Close historical relationship between the union and Patria Roja	High; approximately 88 protests between 1998 and 2007	No (tense relationship with Ministry of Education under García and Humala administrations)
Uruguay	Federación Uruguaya de Magisterio-Trabajadores de la Enseñanza (FUM-TEP) for primary education and Federación Nacional de Profesores de Enseñanza Secundaria (FENAPES) for secondary education	77% primary (16,000) and 34% secondary (5,500)	Fragmented by education level	Alliance with Frente Amplio	Low	No (teachers are members of school-level evaluation committees, but not as union representatives)

Source: Fernández 2012b.
Note: — = not available; est. = estimated.

have relatively smooth relations with teachers, while others are frequently threatened by unions' disruptive actions.

In other countries, such as Costa Rica, Honduras, or Uruguay, there is fragmentation by level of education. Fragmentation by education level weakens collective capacity because competition for members and coordination problems increase. For example, in Paraguay, according to data from the Ministry of Justice and Labor, there were 22 registered teachers' unions in 2007. The three main organizations (Federación de Educadores de Paraguay [FEP], Organización de Trabajadores de la Educación del Paraguay [OTEP], and Unión Nacional de Educadores [UNE]) have been unable to coordinate successfully to block proposals such as new retirement conditions approved in 2003 (Becker and Aquino Benitez 2008). In Costa Rica, a third union since 1969 has competed for representation with the older unions representing primary and secondary school teachers, Asociación Nacional de Educadores (ANDE) and Asociación de Profesores de Segunda Enseñanza (APSE).

In Uruguay, the Federación Uruguaya de Magisterio-Trabajadores de la Enseñanza (FUM-TEP) represents preprimary and primary school teachers, with 16,000 members (77 percent of the teachers in these education levels). The union representing secondary school teachers, FENAPES, has a lower density of approximately 34 percent of the teachers in public secondary schools. An interesting feature in Uruguay is that these unions are key participants in the education sector and participate formally on the national education council, Consejo Directivo Central de la Administración Nacional de Educación Pública (CODICEN).[6]

When fragmented unions are capable of working through umbrella organizations to articulate their interests and demands, they enhance their influence over education policy. Argentina's multiple provincial unions have been able to coordinate through a national confederation, the Confederación de Trabajadores de la Educación de la República Argentina (CTERA). The CTERA represents approximately 35 percent of teachers (Rivas 2004) by grouping together unions from 23 provinces and the federal capital. Union de Docentes Argentinos (UDA) is the second-largest teachers' union at the national level in Argentina. Similar to the CTERA, the UDA has branches at the provincial level. The UDA has around 50,000 affiliates, or 6 percent of teachers in Argentina (UDA data for 2005; National Teachers Census data for 2004).[7]

In Honduras, teachers' organizations fragmented by educational level have also attempted to unite over the past several years through the Federation of Teachers' Organizations.[8]

In contrast, unions in Mexico, Jamaica, Colombia, Ecuador, and Peru have maintained or built a near monopoly of national representation. Mexico's Sindicato de Trabajadores de la Educación (SNTE) has traditionally been the strongest teachers' union in the region with approximately 1.4 million members (100 percent) of preprimary, primary, and lower secondary public education teachers.[9] The SNTE emerged as a centralized union from the merger of four education unions in 1943 (Murillo 2001, 122) and played a key role in the expansion of the education system in Mexico. A mandatory quota of 1 percent of members' salaries generates substantial union income, which has historically been used to help mobilize electoral support for the ruling party (Solis Sanchez 2011). The SNTE's powerful political alliances have helped to achieve expanded benefits for teachers as well as formal positions in the governing structure of the education system, at both the federal and subnational levels.

The union adapted successfully to the democratization process in Mexico over the last two decades, playing to the electoral needs of all major political parties to advance its political influence over education policy. The SNTE has for decades enjoyed virtual veto power over the education reform agenda in Mexico, and reforms such as decentralization, the Carrera Magisterial teacher career path reform, and the new teacher evaluation process proposed in 2008 were either blocked from adoption or undermined during implementation. However, as we discuss later in this chapter, 2013 saw a major realignment of political forces in Mexico, with a splintering of SNTE's power and reform opposition now concentrated among dissident teachers' groups in a small number of states, notably Oaxaca, Guerrero, and Michoacán.

In Jamaica, the Jamaica Teachers' Association (JTA) also has near-monopoly representation of teachers at the primary and secondary level, with a union density between 76 and 89 percent. The JTA has demonstrated strong capacity to influence government education policy. For example, the Jamaican government is still in the process of reforming the teacher pay scale to include the quality of teaching as an evaluation criterion, although this has been on the bargaining table for some years. The JTA has rejected the government proposal of performance-based pay since it was recommended by a government-appointed task force in 2004 (Petrina 2004). In December 2010, Education Minister Andrew Holness announced a three-year plan to increase literacy in the country and declared that the ministry was prepared to reward and, if necessary, separate teachers on the basis of students' performance on the Grade Four Literacy Test (Hill 2011). However, after Holness's party lost the general election in 2011, the proposed change in the teacher salary scale remained an unfinished task, and a move to merit pay has not been agreed upon.

Ecuador's UNE until 2008 represented 80 percent of teachers (Gindin 2009; Vaillant 2005), which gave it significant influence over policy. When the central government signed agreements with local governments in 2006 to increase parents' participation in the evaluation of teachers, the UNE carried out multiple protests and six months later, a presidential decree reversed the proposal. Nevertheless, as we analyze later in this chapter, the political dynamics of education reform in Ecuador have also shifted in recent years. Major reforms of teacher policy, including new mechanisms for selecting teachers and evaluating their performance in the classroom, have advanced despite UNE opposition, protests, and strikes.

Colombia's FECODE, formed during the nationalization of the education system in the 1960s, has consolidated power as a centralized participant (López 2008; Lowden 2004). FECODE officially represents teachers at the primary, lower secondary, and upper secondary levels from all 32 Colombian departments and the

Bogotá district. Almost every teacher in the public sector in Colombia is affiliated with FECODE.[10] Nevertheless, while the union in the early 1990s successfully opposed decentralization of education, FECODE's influence over education policy has weakened during the last decade. Since 2000, important decentralization actions and a major teacher policy reform have been implemented.

The most important teachers' union in Peru is Sindicato Único de Trabajadores en la Educación del Perú (SUTEP). Founded in the 1970s, SUTEP includes teachers across all educational levels and has an estimated membership of 200,000 (Grindle 2004; Zegarra and Ravina 2003).[11] SUTEP has traditionally had substantial influence over education policy in Peru; as recently as 2012, the government could not dismiss teachers from their civil service positions even if they had been legally convicted of sexual abuse or acts of terrorism. Since 2007, however, successive presidents have battled with the union over two major reforms of the teacher career ladder that were analyzed in chapter 5. The first, the Carrera Pública Magisterial, raised standards for new teachers in exchange for higher pay, but was voluntary for teachers in service. In 2012, an even deeper reform, the Ley de Reforma Magisterial (LRM), was adopted. The LRM makes regular performance evaluations mandatory for all teachers and eliminates job security for teachers with successive poor evaluations. The political dynamics of this reform process and its eventual results are examined later in this chapter.

Chile's Colegio de Profesores has monopoly of representation for public sector teachers, and has been a powerful player since Chile's transition to democracy in 1990 (Vaillant 2005). The Chilean context has unique political features, however, which have shaped its reform dynamics. First, Chile is the only country in Latin America where the fully public schools face competition from publicly financed, privately managed voucher schools. The voucher sector has expanded greatly since 1990, eroding the monopoly power of the Colegio, which represents only public (municipal) teachers. However, government policy has also played an important role in building a relationship with the union that created political space for major reforms (Mizala and Schneider 2014). Successive democratic governments after 1990 explicitly sought to rebuild political trust with teachers after the conflictive relationships of the dictatorship and for more than 20 years have pursued a strategy of continuous and respectful negotiations over education policy. The government also steadily raised teacher salaries throughout this period. These strategies and other factors are explored in the final section of this chapter, which analyzes the political dynamics of major teacher policy reforms in Chile.

Union political strategies

Strikes and protests. Teachers' unions use a portfolio of strategies to advance their members' interests. The most visible and frequent strategy is demonstrations of collective action, whether through strikes or large public demonstrations. Strikes and threats of strikes are highly disruptive in the case of teachers. Parents immediately face the challenge of finding alternative childcare. According to the Observatory for Adult

Education in Latin America and the Caribbean, during the first months of 2006 (the most recent data available), out of 18 countries in the region, 16 had conflicts between the teachers' unions and the governments.

Most of the disruptive actions were aimed at improving teachers' economic conditions (60 percent of the protests). Another 23 percent were related to other education policy issues (Gentili and Suárez 2004; Gindin 2007). Argentina, Brazil, and Mexico had the largest number of protests between 1998 and 2003. Most actions were against national governments, although nearly a third of the protests carried out in this period targeted state and local authorities. Union actions lasted on average 11 days. Mexico had the highest number of days per year engaged in conflicts (21), followed by Argentina, Ecuador and Brazil, with 14 days each. None of the protests observed during this period in Latin America lasted less than three days.

Disruptive strategies to defend demands are an entrenched practice in the region, and in many cases succeed. An analysis of the distribution of education transfers in Mexico from 1996–2008 found that states with higher levels of protests received larger federal education grants (Fernández 2012a). Fernández also documented an empirical correlation between subnational authorities' higher spending on primary and lower secondary education and the higher incidence of disruptive union behavior at those education levels.

Linkages with political parties. A second core strategy is the development of strategic alliances with political parties. Teachers' unions' mobilization capacity is highly attractive to political parties, and unions in many LAC countries have contributed to the electoral gains of allied parties in exchange for favorable education policies (for Colombia, Duarte 1997; for Brazil, Plank 1996; Oxford Research 2006, 2008).

Historically, many unions in the region have allied with leftist parties, but increasingly in recent years these alliances appear to be neither a permanent guarantee of union support nor an airtight government commitment to union-favored education policies. Mexico's union was historically the handmaiden of the ruling party Partido Revolucionario Institucional (PRI), but it cultivated electoral relationships with other major parties after the PRI lost national power. In an historic twist, although union support contributed to the return of a PRI candidate to the presidency in 2012, the government immediately launched the most ambitious education reform program in Mexico's history, directly threatening the union's interests and inciting powerful opposition, particularly from its extremist wing. Argentina's CTERA federation of provincial unions was aligned with the reformist Frente por un País Solidario (FREPASO) party in the 1990s, but the Peronist party today. The Peruvian teachers' union, SUTEP, contributed to the election of President Humala in 2011 but has since bitterly fought his teacher policy reforms. Brazil's national umbrella organization of teachers, the Confederação Nacional dos Trabalhadores em Educação (CNTE), has a close relationship with the Workers Party of Presidents Luiz Lula and Dilma Rouesseff and has successfully lobbied for major increases in federal education spending. But it opposes the federal proposal for a national examination for new teacher candidates.

Costa Rica's union, ANDE, has effectively negotiated benefits irrespective of the party in government. More unusually in the region, the Jamaica Teachers' Association JTA keeps a distance from both government and opposition parties.

Government capture. A third strategy is to exercise direct pressure in defense of union interests by capturing key government positions in the education structure. Mexico is the most extreme example, with major lines of education authority at both the federal and state levels at times controlled by the union (Fernández 2012a). Eight of Mexico's education ministers through 2012 had been state level union heads. In 2012, more than half of the 32 local coordinators of the Carrera Magisterial program, which evaluates teacher performance and awards pay increases, were union officials (Fernández 2012a). Control over key government positions has allowed the union to maintain high levels of discipline among its members. Teachers who disagreed with the union leadership could be fired, denied access to favorable benefits, or sent to remote locations far from where they live as a punishment. All of these long-entrenched rights, however, were directly challenged by the constitutional reform of education that the government elected in 2012 pushed through congress within six months of assuming power.

Ecuador's union also historically enjoyed the right to name high-level officials within the ministry and at times to a say in the selection of ministers. But several of the Correa administration's teacher policy reforms have acted to curb the union's influence in system governance. In Costa Rica, ANDE has had a say in the lists of candidates to fill teaching posts and in the selection of the teachers' national pension board members (Loyo, Ibarrola, and Blanco 1999, 8). In Paraguay, the union has increased the level of teacher participation in committees that evaluate and select teaching, technical, and administrative staff of the Ministry of Education (Becker and Aquino Benitez 2008). In Uruguay, the teachers' unions have strong influence over the operation of the education sector, with two representatives on the national education board (CODICEN) and active participation in teacher technical assemblies, which have authority over technical and pedagogical issues (Vaillant 2008).

In Argentina, three out of the five members on provincial level Juntas de Calificaciones (Qualifications Committees) are elected by teachers using secret and compulsory voting. These committees are in charge of clearing the lists of potential candidates for teaching posts (Murillo et al. 2002). When the province of Buenos Aires proposed eliminating the Qualifications Committees, the union organized massive strikes to defend its influence over the governance of the education system. Eventually the government abandoned its proposal.

Finally, beyond the capacity of teachers' unions for formal capture of education ministries, union leaders frequently have more leverage over their counterparts due to more accumulated experience. Corrales (1999) documented the high rate of turnover among education ministers in Latin America, in contrast to the much longer average tenure of teachers' union leaders.

Legal strategies. A fourth strategy is the use of the judicial system to challenge the legality of reforms advanced by governments. For example, in 2007 Colombia's

FECODE launched legal action to reverse a constitutional reform that reduced federal transfers to subnational governments. In Uruguay, FENAPES challenged the constitutionality of the 2008 General Education Law before the Supreme Court, which eventually, however, confirmed the legality of the reform. Ecuador's UNE has challenged provisions of the teacher evaluation system, particularly the article that allows teacher dismissal after two consecutive poor evaluations. In 2009, the union mobilized enough signatures from its members to challenge the constitutionality of this provision, on the grounds that it abrogated teachers' guaranteed right to work stability.

Union-sponsored research and policy analysis. Finally, unions have created think tanks and established strategic relationships with public universities to conduct research and analysis, in order to equip themselves for more informed and effective negotiations with authorities. In many cases, unions have developed proposals or alternative proposals for education reform. The Peruvian union, SUTEP, has a long-standing relationship with the Universidad Nacional de San Marcos; the Argentine union CTERA created the Instituto de Investigaciones Marina Vilte; Colombia's FECODE has established the Center for Studies and Teachers' Research (Centro de Estudios e Investigaciones Docentes [CEID]); and Mexico's SNTE finances the SNTE Foundation, an education think tank.

Political dynamics of education reform: Four recent cases

Negotiated reform with sequencing: Chile

Of all the countries in the region, Chile experienced the most radical assault on the traditional interests of the teachers' union and the traditional structure of education when the Pinochet dictatorship in 1982 decentralized school management to municipalities, stripped teachers of their status as civil servants, and introduced a nationwide voucher program to subsidize private schools in competition with municipal schools. The reform profoundly changed the education landscape in Chile and deeply depleted the political power of the teachers' union in education policy.

This context created strong incentives for the democratic government that returned to power in 1990 to engage with teachers, who had been in the forefront of the political struggle to oust Pinochet, as a legitimate political partner (Núñez and Cox 2003). Although Chile's history is unique, Mizala and Schneider (2014) argue that the political strategy of negotiated reform pursued by successive democratic governments since 1990 has led not only to the progressive adoption of major teacher policy reforms that are often blocked by teachers' unions elsewhere but also, significantly, to the successful implementation and sustainability of those reforms.

Among these reforms are (a) standardized student testing, (b) school-based bonus pay (Sistema Nacional de Evaluación de Desempeño [SNED]), (c) higher standards for teachers (Marco de la Buen Enseñanza), (d) individual teacher performance evaluations, (e) individual teacher bonus pay (Asignacion de Excelencia Pedagogica

[AEP] and Asignacion Variable por Desempenho individual [AVDI], (f) an exit exam for graduates of teacher education programs (Inicia), and (g) the elimination of job stability for poor-performing teachers. No other country in Latin America has achieved an equally comprehensive set of policies aimed at rewarding teacher excellence and enforcing accountability for performance. Many other important, quality-promoting policies have also been adopted by the Chilean government since 1990, including a longer school day, ICT investments, and targeted support to low-performing schools. It is impossible to untangle the relative contribution of Chile's teacher reforms vis-à-vis other policies in Chile's education outcomes. But there is no question the country is seeing results in education: since 2000, Chile has registered the largest sustained improvement in PISA scores of any of the 65 participating countries.

Mizala and Schneider (2014) identify two major elements of government political strategy in Chile: negotiation and sequencing. They note that all of the major changes in teacher policy have been developed in consultation with the teachers' union, and hammered out in often-protracted, multiyear negotiations. They also note that the entire 20-year reform process was prefaced by what appeared to be a step backward by the government in 1990—the passage of a new Teacher Statute that was demanded by the union and resisted within the cabinet at the time and adopted only after several brief teachers' strikes. The Teacher Statute restored teachers' civil service status and the union's right to collective wage bargaining. It also established parameters for gradually increasing teacher salaries, which had fallen sharply in real terms during the 1980s. However, a third key union demand, for the elimination of voucher schools, was not met.

The 1990 Teacher Statute increased the political power of the union to challenge government policy, but Mizala and Schneider believe it was also a crucial first step in paving the way for future reforms. The negotiations and important government compromises over the Teachers Statute sent a strong signal to teachers that the new democratic government could be trusted. The reestablishment of centralized wage negotiations also created a regular forum for negotiating not only salaries but also teacher career issues and incentives more generally. Finally, restoration of civil service status required teachers, like other public sector workers, to have performance reviews at regular intervals. Agreement over the Teacher Statute, plus the significant annual increases in real teacher salaries triggered from 1991 onward, has created a political platform of collaboration between the government and the teachers' union upon which further reforms can build.[12]

It is significant that the first major reform introduced was a national student assessment system, Sistema de Medición de la Calidad de la Educación (SIMCE), in 1994. Chile also quickly joined all of the major international and regional assessments, including Trends in International Mathematics and Science Study (TIMMS), Latin American Laboratory for Assessment of the Quality of Education (LLECE), Second Regional Comparative and Explanatory Study (SERCE), and PISA to benchmark its education performance internationally. The Chilean government has consistently used data on student and school performance and international comparisons to make the case for reform.

Another political strategy that the Chilean government has used consistently and effectively is the establishment of high-level national commissions for the development of reform proposals. The first of these, the 1995 Commission on the Modernization of Chilean Education (known as the Brunner Commission, after its chair, Jose-Joaquin Brunner), was able to unite all key stakeholders behind a strong call for education reform and a number of specific recommendations, including performance incentives. Similarly, in the early 2000s, in order to develop Chile's standards for teachers (eventually called the Marco de la Buena Enseñanza), the ministry established a joint commission with the teachers' union, which worked for four years on the proposal.

The second important sequence Mizala and Schneider (2014) identify in the Chilean reform process is that the government moved gradually from teacher policy reforms that are relatively easier for unions to accept toward those that are more challenging. For example, the first step in the direction of pay for performance was the 1995 school-based bonus program, SNED. Although it required substantial negotiation with the union at the time, school-level bonus pay typically attracts less union resistance than individual performance pay. In comparison with school bonus programs in other countries, SNED is also noteworthy for the comprehensive way that school performance is measured, including survey feedback from parents on a wide range of issues. The design signaled sensitivity to teachers' belief that school quality encompasses more than simply student test scores.

Mizala and Schneider (2014) believe that the SNED school-based bonus first institutionalized the concept of pay linked to performance and made it possible for the government later to broach the topic of individual performance evaluations—a much more controversial policy with unions.

In that reform as well, both sequencing and negotiation played an important role in the strategy. First, the ministry established a voluntary teacher evaluation program, the AEP, which offered the prospect of 10-year bonuses to teachers who agreed to comprehensive performance evaluations. Although uptake of this program was limited because of the perceived difficulty of the evaluations, AEP established a precedent and model for a teacher evaluation process. The government then pushed a step further, working with the Colegio on the design of a teacher performance evaluation that would be mandatory for all municipal teachers. This system, adopted in 2004, is notably more holistic than teacher evaluation programs in other countries, which typically are paper-based assessments of teachers' subject knowledge and pedagogical skills. Chile's evaluation tests teachers' competency, but also includes rich, qualitative information from a teaching portfolio (including videos of teachers' classroom practice), teachers' self-assessment, and evaluations from principals and teachers' peers. Another important feature is that the design and implementation of both the test and the portfolio parts of the evaluation are handled by a respected third-party research agency, rather than the ministry or the union. The union and government agreed on performance evaluations for every municipal teacher every four years. Those ranked as "outstanding" or "competent" qualify for an individual performance bonus, called AVDI. Those rated as "basic" gain no benefits, and those deemed "unsatisfactory" must have annual follow-up evaluations annually and may be dismissed after consecutive poor evaluations.

Making individual performance evaluations mandatory for municipal teachers triggered resistance and conflict within the union, even with the gradual introduction, and led to a change in union leadership in 2007. The leftist challenger who won election to the Colegio's presidency openly opposed compulsory teacher evaluation. Nonetheless, the gradual and negotiated process that led to the adoption of the teacher evaluation law and previous policies had established an irreversible base of support. Somewhat ironically, the Colegio's influence has declined under more radical leadership, and surveys show that a majority of teachers, school directors, and civil society stakeholders support Chile's teacher evaluation and bonus pay policies (Mizala and Schneider 2014).

In 2012, the government proposed a new Ley de Carrera Profesional Docente, a comprehensive reform of the teacher career path. It aimed to eliminate the disconnect discussed in chapter 5—the fact that Chile's system of individual teacher performance evaluations and bonus incentives currently is overlaid on top of a traditional teacher career path that still awards permanent promotions and pay increases to teachers based on seniority and formal qualifications alone. The 2012 reform proposed eliminating seniority-based promotion and establishing a career path solely based on performance, with high salary rewards for top performers, support for teachers at all levels, and dismissal for teachers whose performance does not progress. It also proposed higher standards for new teacher candidates and entrance into teacher training schools, a mandatory teacher exit exam (based on the Inicia), and attractive starting bonuses to incentivize high-talent individuals to enter teaching. Finally, it proposed granting substantial autonomy to directors of municipal schools to grant annual bonuses to individual teachers and (as already legislated in 2011) continuing to allow them to dismiss directly up to 5 percent of their teachers annually on performance grounds.

In a complicated and politicized environment marked by ongoing student protests over tuition fees in higher education and a change of government, the 2012 Carrera reform proved too ambitious to command adequate political support. The outgoing government made a tactical decision to break up the draft legislation and focus on adoption of the elements related to initial teacher standards and recruitment, still pending in the legislature in mid-2014.

The 2012 proposal set out what would have been the most comprehensive and coherent teacher policy reform in the LAC region to date. Within its provisions, one can delineate building blocks of teacher policy that had been developed, experimented with, refined, and institutionalized over the past 24 years in Chile, through gradually sequenced and carefully negotiated individual reforms. While major elements of the proposed reform remain pending, the Chilean story has several lessons for other countries. First, it shows consistent use by the government of two key political strategies to bolster its leverage in the reform process: (a) the use of student testing and internationally benchmarked education results to support the case for reform and (b) the use of high-level commissions to build broad stakeholder consensus on reform proposals.

Second, Chile's experience shows the importance of political pragmatism in the service of a broader vision. Chile's strength is technical capacity in education—both in and out of government—that supports the design of innovative education policies. No other country in LAC has as consistently pushed the envelope of education policy over the past 25 years. But, by and large, Chile's record since 1990 has been of gradual experimentation and implementation rather than sweeping reform. Individual programs and policies are adopted as a political base of support for them evolves. This piecemeal approach has produced some inconsistencies in the overlay of different policies over time, but it has also produced steady progress in education results.

Negotiated reform, giving way to confrontation: Mexico

The political dynamics of education reform processes in Mexico have been dominated by the exceptional power of the SNTE, the largest teachers' union in Latin America, with approximately 1.4 million members.[13] Although many aspects of education service delivery were decentralized to states in 1992, the union was able to maintain a monopoly of representation at the national level, which makes it unique among teachers' organizations in large, federalized countries.

SNTE's influence over the education system has been consolidated over a 70-year history through effective use of all of the major political strategies at unions' disposal: strategic and effective disruptive actions; effective mobilization of electoral support for major political parties; and an unequalled degree of government capture, both at the federal and subnational levels. These instruments and SNTE's sheer size have endowed it with a virtual veto capacity over education reforms. In consequence, the only political strategy left to successive governments at both the federal and state level has been continuous negotiations.

Institutional features of the Mexican political system, however, have undermined the power of the government side in these negotiations. First, given the existence of term limits with no immediate reelection, Mexican politicians typically have shorter-term time horizons than the SNTE, which enjoys more stable leadership. Second, the juxtaposition of a decentralized framework for education service delivery and financing with a single national union creates information asymmetries that the union has been able to exploit. Teachers' salaries and benefits are set through two rounds of negotiation: first at the national level between the federal government and the SNTE executive committee and in a second round between state authorities and local SNTE leaders. While local union leaders receive the advice of the union's executive committee, federal and state authorities—especially when they belong to different political parties—do not always have equally complete information on agreements reached. Finally, to a far greater extent than in any other LAC country, the union has directly controlled key government appointments in the education sector. In 2012, 8 of 31 state-level education ministers were union appointees, as were 38 other key figures, such as undersecretaries of education and coordinators of the teacher bonus program Carrera Magisterial. Capture of the CM program by the union has been an important tool for extending its control. Undisciplined members suffer negative consequences by being excluded from this program.[14] The union has also secured substantial control over the entire education system hierarchy by requiring that all school principals, school supervisors, school superintendents, and several of the general directors for primary and lower secondary schools be members of SNTE (Fernández 2012a).

In this context, the Calderón administration in 2007 launched negotiations with SNTE over education reform. The government's main political strategy was to capitalize on growing public outcry over corrupt practices in the education system documented by the press and civil society organizations such as Mexicanos Primero. News reports highlighted egregious cases of union members selling their teaching posts or transferring them to relatives. Administration of the Carrera Magisterial was also exposed, with the SNTE accused of corruption and clientelistic practices in controlling which teachers received CM promotions and inflating teacher evaluations carried out by school principals to ensure maximum salary increases for loyalist union members (McEwan and Santibañez 2005).

The government's goals were to agree with the union on actions to ensure meritocratic hiring of new teachers; clean up the administration of the Carrera Magisterial; and institute a new system of mandatory, periodic evaluation of all teachers (public and private). In exchange, it promised increased education spending on infrastructure and school-level working conditions. In May 2008, President Calderón and the SNTE signed the "Alliance for the Quality of Education."

Under the new agreement, the government launched a key reform, to replace discretionary hiring of new teachers by union-dominated state level committes with a transparent process based on competency tests. As discussed in chapter 3, the reform implementation was not uniform across the country. At the federal level, while over 600,000 candidates applied for 140,000 teaching positions between 2008 and 2012, a large majority of applicants scored below the minimum threshold, and the ministry was forced to lower standards in many places to fill available openings. Because the new process applied only to teaching positions financed by federal funds, it also did not eliminate discretionary hiring of new teachers at the state level. In the state of Nayarit, the governor agreed with the SNTE that 50 percent of state-financed positions would continue to be allocated by the union according to its "internal procedures," and the remaining 50 percent distributed to teachers loyal to the governor's party (PRI). In Guerrero, after a series of union protests and highway blockades, the governor agreed to exempt all state-financed teaching positions from competitive hiring and to uphold teachers' right to inherited positions. In Michoacan and Oaxaca, SNTE sections sabotaged not only competency-based teacher hiring but also the implementation of the ENLACE student learning assessment.[15]

After three years of intensive negotiations, the Alliance reached agreement on new criteria for the award of teacher incentive pay and promotions under the Carrera Magisterial. Since it was agreed that teachers' contribution to students' learning would factor more prominently in the evaluation, the National Assessment of Academic Achievement in Schools (ENLACE) student assessment was transformed into a test with high stakes for teachers. The weight attached to teacher seniority in the CM was eliminated and the weight of teachers' formal academic credentials also reduced. Teachers' participation in training courses was rewarded according to a point system. The reformed system required teachers to take competency tests every three years and to have their performance evaluated through an additional comprehensive process to be defined. Finally, the government established individual and collective bonuses for teachers and schools based on standardized test results.

In 2012, the government announced plans for the new teacher evaluation system, making it mandatory for all basic education teachers, whether public or private. Implementation would be over three years, with primary teachers evaluated in July 2012; secondary school teachers in 2013; and special education, arts, and physical education teachers in 2014. The evaluation would be a competency test of teachers' pedagogical skills and content knowledge.

Almost immediately, the Alliance agreement began to unravel; several SNTE state sections protested the launch, and the union's left wing mobilized in Chiapas, Guerrero, Michoacan, and Oaxaca. Even central SNTE representatives spoke out against the mandatory evaluations that their leadership had signed onto. State leaders of SNTE sections argued that the ministry had not provided full information about the evaluation instruments and procedures. The national leader finally joined the criticism, suggesting that the evaluation should be postponed because of the impending presidential elections.[16] Ultimately, the education minister, interior minister, and union leader agreed that the universal evaluation for all teachers would be carried out after the elections. But the ministry also backtracked significantly, emphasizing that the sole purpose of the tests was to identify strengths and weaknesses in teachers' skills and knowledge in order to improve their training.

In June 2012, teachers in the Carrera Magisterial took standardized tests as part of their evaluation; however, many CM teachers did not participate yet continued to receive merit bonuses. The proposed new criteria for evaluating teachers' professionalism were not defined. In July 2012, the first round of mandatory universal evaluations was implemented, with low participation of teachers from both public and private schools. Teachers in Chiapas, Oaxaca, and Michoacan refused to take the exams, and across the rest of the country, only 53 percent of teachers mandated to take the exam did so.[17] The press documented cases of exams sold online. Authorities launched an investigation but no sanctions resulted.

Beyond these issues, the market for selling and inheriting teachers' posts continued at the state level, and state authorities continued paying the salaries of teachers working as full-time union employees, despite legislation that made it illegal to use federal transfers for this purpose. No subnational authority was sanctioned in connection with irregularities documented by the federal audit entity and the press.

The asymmetry in power between organized teachers' interests and the national government in Mexico has been one of the most striking in the world. Given institutional and legal features that consolidated union strength and undermined government power, negotiation with the union has been the only political strategy open to the government. Several Mexican presidents have launched high-profile efforts to reform education through negotiations with the SNTE. But negotiated agreements have rarely proven enforceable or sustainable. The original Carrera Magisterial of 1992 was progressively amended to eliminate hard performance measures and increase discretionary union power over promotions and bonuses. The Alliance for Quality established a comprehensive and progressive reform agenda focused on key issues and the government negotiated changes in good faith. However, the union proved an unreliable partner, with an apparent agenda of dragging out reform negotiations until the government partner was voted out of power.

The Calderón government's strategy may have have been instrumental in shifting the political landscape in Mexico, however. Through the Alliance, the government simultaneously signaled a strong and unwavering commitment to working with individual teachers in pursuit of education quality while lifting the veil on corrupt union practices and its leadership. The government's calls for deep educational change in response to stagnant PISA results (Mexico has improved less than Chile and Brazil) have been increasingly matched by business leaders and well-organized civil society groups such as Mexicanos Primero, expressing open frustration with the status quo. The Mexican media has also grown more aggressive, documenting egregious examples of corruption and nepotism within the education system, both in the union and with allied government agencies.

A tipping point appeared to be reached in 2012, when the SNTE's long-time political ally, the PRI, regained the presidency. Rather than return to business as usual, the new administration launched the boldest teacher policy reforms in Mexico's history, directly attacking key union powers—eliminating job stability and union voice in government appointments—and succeeded in enshrining these in a constitutional amendment that would be much harder to reverse. In 2013 the government arrested SNTE's long-time leader, one of the country's most powerful political figures, on embezzlement charges. Visible elements of President Enrique Peña Nieto's political strategy include (a) moving quickly to launch big reforms at his highest point of leverage in the political cycle; (b) mobilizing public support for reform through communications; (c) using student test results, international comparisons, and the business community to connect education reform with competitiveness and growth; (d) attacking the legitimacy of the union; and (e) seeking to institutionalize reforms through constitutional change, to be followed by legislation.

The sweeping reform program has included policies proposed under the Alliance, but has also gone further. All new teacher hiring is to be through transparent, competitive processes; teachers will have a mandatory six-month probationary period and performance evaluation before being confirmed to permanent positions; an independent agency, the National Institute for Educational Evaluation (INEE) has been established to manage all student testing and teacher performance evaluations; individual teacher performance evaluations for all teachers every four years are mandatory; and job stability is eliminated for poor-performing teachers.

The contrast with Chile's reform process is striking. In Chile, Mizala and Schneider (2014) argue, respect for the union as a partner in both the design and implementation of reforms has contributed to the sustainability, or "resoluteness," of the reform process. In Mexico's climate of confrontation with the teachers' union, resoluteness has had to come from other sources, such as embedding key reform provisions in a constitutional change.

Nonetheless, the impact of education policies hangs on their implementation, and no policy can be effectively implemented down to the classroom level, where education results happen, without teachers' buy-in. Among teachers' unions in LAC, the SNTE still has unequalled power to control teachers' compliance with new reforms and reform implementation by the education administrators under its political control. From the vantage point of 2014, there has been a sea change in the political dynamics of education reform in Mexico. How quickly and effectively the radically new policies will filter through a contested education bureaucracy to schools and classrooms, however, are major questions.

Reform in the face of union opposition: Peru

Peru's experience in reforming the teacher career path since 2007 illustrates several important issues in the politics of reform.

First, it is an interesting example of how the political dynamics between a strong teachers' union and the government can shift when confident political leaders effectively mobilize public support to challenge union power. As in other countries, teacher quality has been at the center of national debate on education for some time in Peru. The 1984 Ley del Profesorado guaranteed teachers' civil service status and job stability and established seniority-based promotions and salary increases. Practically all of the 260,000 teachers working in the public sector were regulated by the teachers' law and affiliated with the most powerful union in Peru, SUTEP. Successive education ministers had conducted studies pointing to the need for a new teachers' law, to establish meritocratic teaching hiring as well as a system for evaluating the performance of teachers in service. However, reform proposals were consistently blocked by SUTEP. Through massive protests and painful strikes, the union not only blocked reform but extracted economic benefits, with a 45 percent real increase in salaries under the Toledo government between 2001 and 2005 (Chiroque 2005). The higher salaries were not linked to any change in teacher performance expectations or education outcomes, however.

When Alan García was elected in 2006 on a growth-oriented economic agenda, he moved almost immediately to put his political capital on the line with a set of sweeping teacher policy reforms. The Ley de Carrera Pública Magisterial (CPM), approved by Congress in July 2007 in the middle of a national strike by SUTEP, established mandatory competency exams for new teacher candidates, mandatory evaluations for teachers in service, and dismissal for teachers failing consecutive evaluations. As discussed in chapter 3, in 2008 the government also set higher standards for admission into teacher training colleges, which resulted in sharp enrollment declines for many of these Institutos Superiores Pedagógicos (ISPs) and the threat of closure. In 2010, the government also challenged SUTEP's monopoly by allowing the hiring of qualified professionals from other sectors into teaching.

When faced with a teacher career path reform that directly threatened its core interests and job protections, SUTEP resorted to traditional political strategies of public demonstrations, strikes, and legal challenges. Large teachers' protests occupied the streets in Lima and different regions around the country, with sometimes violent actions.

Nonetheless, President García ably used an active communication campaign and compelling data on the low performance of the education system and the low quality of teachers to build public support for major reforms. The government accused union leaders of attempting to kidnap the education of Peruvian students and of defending a status quo inimical to education quality. It cancelled the salaries of all teachers commissioned to work for SUTEP, including its leader. To persuade the public of the need for better teachers, the government released the 2006 evaluation (see chapter 1) that exposed the shocking share of sixth-grade teachers who were unable to read and do math at the sixth-grade level (Cisneros 2008). The education minister drove home the message: "the results show that there hasn't been adequate training for teachers, nor a correct selection of teachers into the profession. We must implement radical changes." President García took on the union directly: "We are in a process of transformation which hurts some interests ... but I govern for 28 million Peruvians, not for a group. You can keep your union, but let us change education" (Peru 21 2007).

The business community supported the government position. The Business Association for Education (Empresarios para la Educación) funded a campaign on the importance of quality education for stronger economic growth in Peru. Public opinion aligned with the government: a 2007 national poll revealed that 43 percent of Peruvians believed the main problem in the education system was the poor quality of teachers (Montero and Cuenca 2008). Parents began to protest the SUTEP-organized strikes that had disrupted the school year and led to violence in some parts of the country. The National Parents Association (Central Nacional de Asociaciones de Padres de Familia [CENAPAFAS]) called on authorities to fire teachers who continued protesting (Andina 2007). García consolidated his strategy of public assault on the union's position. In a rally in favor of public education he said, "the true left is concerned with improving society and not only with improving salaries" (El Comercio 2007).

The image of the union deteriorated: 46 percent of respondents believed the SUTEP's behavior was negative for education. A poll conducted by Ipsos-Apoyo showed that 74 percent of people in Lima thought the government's CPM would be beneficial for students and for good teachers (Andina 2007). The government had successfully persuaded the general public to support its teacher reform agenda.

A second lesson of Peru's experience, however, is that even when beaten in the court of public opinion, unions retain substantial ability to undermine reform implementation. In the face of its political erosion and the economic losses of continuous strikes, SUTEP's leadership shifted to a legal strategy: challenging the constitutionality of the new law. The court process succeeded in delaying implementation of the first round of teacher evaluations. However, the Supreme Court eventually confirmed the legality of the CPM.

But the accumulated legal and political considerations persuaded authorities to provide a major concession to the union: the new law would be mandatory for all newly hired teachers, but voluntary for those already in service. The government calculated that CPM's higher salaries would be attractive enough to persuade existing teachers to enter the new regime. But this was not the case. Over the final three years of the García administration, only 10 percent of existing civil service teachers submitted to the competency tests required to access the CPM. Higher potential salary increases were insufficient to compensate for the risk that low performance on the test would trigger annual performance reviews and possible dismissal. By the end of the administration, the ministry was managing a dual career structure, with one set of performance evaluations, promotions, and sanctions for 25 percent of teachers (new hires plus those existing teachers who opted in) alongside a traditional career path for the remaining 75 percent of teachers, with no performance evaluation, complete job stability, and automatic, seniority-based promotion.

Beyond the risk of union efforts to undermine them, major reforms adopted through confrontation rather than negotiated reform processes may pose broader implementation challenges. In contentious processes, reformers are forced to devote time and energy to political and communications strategies, with likely tradeoffs for implementation planning. Indeed, high uncertainty about reform outcomes or final design makes it difficult to plan implementation. Above all, the conflict with the other party to the reforms—teachers—makes it impossible to engage with them in the type of extended dialogue and joint planning that went into the design of Chile's teacher evaluation system. In Peru's case, the ambitious scale of the reforms combined with relatively weak technical capacity in the Ministry of Education already created a challenge to implementation; a lack of time for careful planning exacerbated it.

A first implementation issue was the competency test for the selection of new teachers. Test design was contracted out to an institution without previous experience in education testing, and the resulting instrument was criticized as having numerous flaws (CNE 2012). Even more damaging was the first round of implementation, marred by accusations of stolen exams being sold to applicants.

Political issues also arose. The central government had designed the Carrera Pública Magisterial, and some regional presidents complained that they had not been consulted even though the law had economic consequences for their governments. The autonomous human rights ombudsman, Defensoría del Pueblo, warned that several regional and municipal governments lacked the technical capacity and the resources to handle new responsibilities the CPM transferred to them. Some regional authorities complained that their federal education transfers were not sufficient to cover the CPM's higher salaries. Some teachers who had already entered the CPM did not receive the higher salaries promised by the law.

Although the García administration eventually conducted eight rounds of evaluation for the selection of new teachers under the CPM, it never completed a protocol for the mandated performance evaluations of teachers in service. Most of the school committees, which include parents, and which are in charge of the second-stage selection of new teachers, did not receive the envisaged training. These issues in the implementation of the CPM strengthened skepticism among teachers.

A third lesson from Peru's experience is that political lines can shift over time as public opinion stabilizes. After its bitter fights with the García government over the teacher career path, SUTEP used its mobilization capacity to campaign for the opposition party in 2011 and helped it win the election. But rather than accede to union calls to roll back the reform, the Humala administration opted to continue the reform and in fact deepen it. Rather than maintain dual salary scales for teachers with the same training and experience, the government presented a law to make the new regime mandatory for existing teachers, while further extending the number of career levels and salary incentives. Despite more strikes and demonstrations from SUTEP and violence from the union's far left wing, the government retained provisions for automatic dismissal of teachers with consecutive poor evaluations, exclusion of union members from school evaluation committees, and introduced a new provision for immediate dismissal of any teacher convicted of a terrorist act or sexual abuse. The only concession made to the union was a general salary increase in exchange for incorporation of all teachers into the new Ley de Reforma Magisterial (LRM), adopted by Congress in late 2012.

The accumulated evidence that public opinion strongly favored the reforms and disapproved of the union's disruptive methods had changed the political calculus in Peru. A national poll in August 2012 showed that 71 percent of the public considered the new teachers' law beneficial for education and an even higher segment of the general public than previously (62 percent) believed that teachers were among the main threats to education quality in Peru. A majority of citizens agree that teachers failing three consecutive evaluations should be fired (65 percent), and 51 percent of Peruvians consider SUTEP to be harmful to the education system (El Comercio 2012).

The government's success in achieving universal incorporation of teachers into a career path that rewards skills and performance instead of seniority is a major political achievement unthinkable in Peru even a decade ago. But it implies a fivefold increase in the number of teacher performance evaluations to be conducted at regular intervals. The ministry's goal of assessing teacher performance in a comprehensive way, with observations of classroom practice and 360-degree feedback, in addition to tests of teacher knowledge and skills, represents global best practice. But it also presents a complex implementation challenge. Intensive work on the design of new assessment instruments and processes is underway with respected academic partners in Peru, and the ministry is also tapping into Chile's accumulated experience with teacher evaluation through technical cooperation agreements. The government appears to have learned from both the political dynamics of prior teacher reform efforts and the lessons of implementation experience.

Reform in the face of union opposition: Ecuador

The teacher reform process in Ecuador has parallels with neighboring Peru. After his election in 2007, President Rafael Correa made education reform a top priority and was willing to tolerate open conflict with a strong union in pursuit of his goals. The most controversial reform proposals—as in Peru—were changes to the teacher career path: to eliminate seniority-based promotion in favor of salaries linked to teachers' performance on competency tests, to introduce mandatory performance evaluations for all teachers at regular intervals, and to eliminate job stability for teachers with two consecutive poor evaluations.

Correa's political playbook paralleled García's: (a) launching big reforms early, (b) relentless communications to mobilize public opinion on the side of reform, (c) use of student testing to expose school system results, (d) testing teachers' competency and exposing the results, (e) introducing new teacher policies initially for new hires and on a voluntary basis for teachers in service, and (f) using increases in real teacher salaries (financed through oil wealth in Ecuador's case, other mineral wealth in Peru's) as the main strategy for mollifying teachers' opposition over time.

As in Peru, education results in Ecuador were abysmal. Little national data existed on student learning outcomes because the country had suspended efforts to develop a student assessment system. Ecuador had participated only in one international education test, which revealed it as the worst performer among 13 countries tested in the 1999 UNESCO regional assessment, Prueba del Laboratorio Latinoamericano de Evaluación de la Calidad de la Educación (LLECE) (Froemel 1999). Teacher absenteeism was endemic: a 2004 World Bank study showed that, on average, teachers were present in schools only 62 percent of their contractual hours (Chaudhury et al. 2004).

Ecuador's teachers' union, UNE, was the most powerful actor in the sector, with a history of disruptive behavior. Between 1998 and 2006, the country suffered almost constant teachers' protests and strikes. The UNE had consolidated its political influence through an alliance with the left-wing party Movimiento Popular Democrático (MPD), one of the supporters of Correa's presidential candidacy in 2006.

A former economics professor, President Correa made education a central priority immediately upon assuming office. He signaled to the union that he was prepared for conflict by naming an education minister with a history of outspoken criticisms of teacher absenteeism and union resistance to reform.

Taking advantage of strong oil prices, he coupled the launch of major reforms with a large increase in education spending, investing massively in school infrastructure and announcing the hiring of 12,000 new teachers. The new recruitment, however, would follow new rules: a November 2007 decree (decree 708-07) modified the teacher career path that had been in place since 1990 (Ley de Carrera Docente y Escalafón del Magisterio Nacional). The new decree created commissions of excellence to oversee the selection of new teachers through a meritocratic process. In a first move, the government removed the seats traditionally held by the UNE in teacher selection committees. The union reacted immediately with a series of protests, but was unable to derail the new process.

For new teacher candidates, the hiring bar was raised substantially. In addition to formal credentials, applicants were for the first time required to take a test of language and logical reasoning capacities, pedagogical skills, and the specific subject areas they intend to teach. In a final step, teacher candidates had to teach a demonstration class and were observed and evaluated by a school-level commission for excellence.

The rules also changed for school principals. Previously granted lifetime tenure with no performance evaluation, school principals now must undergo public contests every four years with the possibility of being reelected for one additional period. Defying protests from teachers and school directors over these measures, the government also introduced standardized tests for students. The UNE also fought these bitterly, but they went forward in 2008.

In 2008, the government pushed a step further: to evaluate the competency of existing teachers. It announced a voluntary test of teachers' reading proficiency and logic. Only 1,569 of Ecuador's 200,000 teachers took the exam, and of those who took it, just 4 percent passed. Correa blasted teachers publicly for their resistance to being evaluated and—citing the poor results as proof of the teacher quality problem—instructed the education minister to make teacher evaluations compulsory.

After his reelection with 52 percent of the vote in April 2009—the first time in 30 years that the country had reelected a president—Correa redoubled his education reform effort. The following month, the ministry launched mandatory performance evaluations for teachers in service, as part of the National System of Evaluation and Accountability (Sistema Nacional de Evaluación y Rendición de Cuentas [SER]), with the goal of evaluating 25 percent of the teachers every year so that all teachers are evaluated every four years. The system involves a school-level assessment by an evaluation committee that includes parents, the school principal, and one teacher chosen by all teachers in the school, plus tests of pedagogical skills, reading comprehension, and specific content in the teacher's area of specialization. Similar to regulations in Chile and Peru, those who perform poorly are offered a year's training and then required to be reevaluated. Those who fail a second time forfeit their careers as educators.

The UNE boycotted the mandatory evaluations, and in May 2009 only 4,855 teachers took the exams. Correa responded with a rally in Guayaquil to protest the UNE's intransigence, winning the support of organizations such as the Catholic University of Guayaquil, one of the most prestigious universities in the country. The government upped the stakes again, initiating administrative procedures to fire all teachers who refused to take the exams. Decree 1740 established that teachers who refused to submit to evaluation would be fired for demonstrating "professional incompetence" (*Diariocrítico* 2009). This regulation was subsequently incorporated into the new Teacher Law and Teacher Salary Scale (Ley de Carrera Docente y Escalafón del Magisterio).

The Ministry of Education publicly released results for the first 2,570 teachers tested: only 2 teachers had an excellent performance, 624 (24.3 percent) had a very good performance, 1,873 (72.9 percent) had a good performance, and 71 (2.8 percent) had a poor performance. As per the regulation, the 71 teachers had to attend special training sessions and be evaluated the following year.

These measures infuriated the UNE, which expanded its protests across the country. There were violent actions in Guayaquil. The UNE launched administrative procedures to defend its members against the decree's provisions and the Movimiento Político Democrático in Congress broke its legislative alliance with the president's party and assumed the legal defense of teachers being sanctioned.

The government increased its pressure further, adding a provision to the reform law prohibiting teachers (and consequently the union) from paralyzing education services as a form of protest. It introduced sanctions for individuals who disrupted classes. In August 2009, it published its decision to stop collecting the voluntary quotas teachers paid to the UNE, stating that the UNE would have to collect them directly from its members.

The government also pursued a strategy of counterbalancing the influence of the union by strengthening the role of parents and civil society in the education system. The new teachers' law established school-level "citizens' governing bodies" (Gobiernos Escolares Ciudadanos [GEC]) formed by representatives of parents, teachers, and students. Two main responsibilities of the GECs are to form the evaluation committees in charge of assessing the classroom practice of new teacher candidates and to monitor schools' activities, as a form of accountability pressure.

Accountability for performance has been an explicit theme of the government. A ministerial agreement in 2009 extended mandatory evaluations to school principals, the school curriculum, and the performance of the education system as a whole. Inspired by the Chilean AVDI model, the ministry also introduced individual bonus pay. Teachers and principals who rated "excellent" (90 points or higher out of 100) receive a salary increase equal to US$1,200 per year for the next four years; those rated "very good" (80 to 89) receive a salary increase of US$900. All are evaluated again after this period. Teachers rated "good" (61 to 88) do not receive any increase and are evaluated in two years. Teachers rated "insufficient" undergo mandatory training courses and are evaluated again the following year. If they score below 60 percent a second time, they are removed from service.

In the face of the government's resolve, the union shifted some of its positions. Teachers were not opposed to evaluation but wanted fair evaluations that did not imply the loss of job stability; teachers' tenure was a protected right. They also argued that the tests of teacher competency were unfair because they made no allowance for the different socioeconomic environments in which teachers worked.

President Correa continued his public excoriation of the union's resistance to teacher evaluation, stating that in his vision for the country there could be no tolerance of mediocrity, especially at the school level where human capital is formed. Defying his threat to fire teachers participating in disruptive actions, however, the UNE called for an indefinite strike. It blocked streets and occupied school buildings, particularly in Quito. Student organizations with linkages to the UNE supported the teachers' protests. Other unions joined teachers in the streets to oppose education reform. In September, the powerful Confederation of Indigenous Nationalities of Ecuador (Confederación de Nacionalidades Indígenas del Ecuador [CONAIE]) increased the tension in Ecuadorean streets by adding to the mobilization, also protesting water resources and mining laws. The mobilizations turned violent, with one teacher killed and several protesters injured.

In the face of escalating violence, the government decided to open negotiations first with the indigenous organization, and then with the UNE. The union continued its disruptive strategy, with UNE protests in major cities across the country in October 2009. The most important mobilization, known as the *marcha de cacerolas vacías y toma de Quito* ("March of the empty pots and occupation of Quito") reached the presidential palace, forcing the vice president to enter into a dialogue with the union. The authorities and union finally reached an agreement: the UNE suspended the 22-day strike in exchange for a guarantee that (a) all teachers under administrative procedures would be exonerated and their salaries restored, (b) teachers who failed their evaluations a second consecutive time but were of retirement age would not be fired and would receive their pensions, and (c) teachers who fail two evaluations and are not of retirement age would still have the opportunity to participate in teacher selection contests to reenter the teaching career and receive compensation according to the law.

Since November 2009, implementation of the new teacher career path, plus broader accountability-promoting reforms have continued. Conflict with the UNE has abated. The government has consolidated its position further by exploiting internal divisions among teachers. In April 2010, a new teachers' organization called "Red de Maestros por la Revolución Educativa" (teacher network for the revolution in education) emerged in Ciudad Alfaro. Although this union is much smaller than the UNE, it has created competition with the UNE's former monopoly.

The development, piloting, and progressive implementation of Ecuador's teacher career reform occurred against a backdrop of high political conflict. The UNE pursued a single strategy—disruptive action. The government focused on mobilizing public support for the reform program by exposing the weak performance of students, the school system, and, above all, teachers, and by drawing parents into the school system with a voice in teacher hiring and teacher evaluation. It is unquestionable that Ecuador's education system was in deep need of reform when Correa took office. Specific reforms introduced are also consistent with global best practice: student assessment, meritocratic teacher hiring, regular teacher and principal performance evaluation, bonus pay, and dismissal of persistent poor performers. It is unfortunate that there is relatively little public information available on how these policies have been implemented and what impacts they are having.

Basic information has not been publicly divulged—how many teachers have been evaluated to date; how many have failed their evaluations; how many have been dismissed from the education system. There is also little information on student learning results; Ecuador recently joined PISA, but its students will be tested for the first time in 2015. This is an important step that will allow transparent benchmarking of its educational progress. Ecuador's experience does, however, provide a further example of how political leaders in Latin America can build popular political support to challenge the power of an established teachers' union and push through major changes in teacher policy.

Conclusions

Recent reform experiences in Mexico, Peru, and Ecuador suggest the balance of power between governments and some of Latin America's traditionally powerful teachers' unions has shifted. In an age where mass media afford political candidates a direct channel of communication with even the most remote and rural of their citizens, one of the long-time sources of union power—the ability to mobilize their members for large-scale grassroots political campaigning—may be of diminishing utility. In a region where democracy has taken hold in most countries, mass media have also become increasingly vociferous in exposing government failure and political corruption. This, in turn, feeds public demand for more accountable and effective government and resonates particularly strongly in education, which touches every family's hopes and aspirations for their children. Increasingly, Latin American political leaders appear to be making the calculation that popular support for education reform is a stronger bet for their political future than the traditional quid pro quo of electoral support from teachers' unions in exchange for education policies that do not threaten unions' interests.

This chapter reviewed how the interests of unions and governments diverge over key education reforms; the political strategies that unions use to advance their interests; and the dynamics of recent reform processes in Chile, Mexico, Peru, and Ecuador. While there is substantial heterogeneity across the region in union power, government reform priorities, and the dynamics of recent interactions, several observations may have broad relevance for policy makers in the region:

- *Political leaders can build effective pro-reform alliances of business leaders and civil society through communications campaigns* that paint a compelling picture of the current failures of the education system and the importance of better education for economic competitiveness. Uniting two sides of the stakeholder triangle (civil society and government) against the third (organized teachers) can create political space for the adoption of reforms, including the three that most directly threaten the interests of teachers as an organized group: individual performance evaluation, differentiated pay, and loss of job stability.

- *Reform momentum is greatest if launched at the start of an administration.* In most cases, the reform process is contentious, and unions have a strong interest in dragging it out. If leaders move quickly, they capitalize on their point of maximum political leverage and establish education as a top priority. As they begin to govern, administrations are inevitably forced to spend time on a wide range of other issues and suffer some political reversals; this diffuses their messages and erodes their leverage.

- *Hard data on education system results are a crucial political tool.* Especially powerful are data on student learning outcomes, results that are internationally benchmarked (such as PISA, TIMMS, and SERCE), and data on teachers' performance on competency tests. Political leaders' use of these to build the case for reform has been a factor in all successful strategies to date. Of all international tests, the OECD's PISA seems to resonate most strongly with the business community and civil society groups, likely because the comparator countries are those that LAC countries aspire to join and because it is easy to interpret the results for 15-year-old youths as a direct barometer of labor force quality and economic competitiveness.

- *Reform strategies based on confrontation with unions may succeed in securing the legislative adoption of major reforms, but not necessarily their implementation.* In many countries the political space for negotiating major reforms with teachers' unions may not exist. In Mexico, Peru and Ecuador, confrontation politics were required to produce the legislative and constitutional adoption of teacher policy reforms that global evidence suggests are needed for education quality—student testing, teacher performance evaluation, teacher hiring and promotions based on skills and performance rather than seniority, and dismissal of teachers with consistently poor performance. However, in all three cases it is too early to evaluate the success of these reforms in actually raising education quality—in no case is implementation very advanced.

- *Confrontation reform strategies create issues for implementation.* Confrontation strategies virtually demand one-time reforms; if a president is going to stake political capital on contentious change, it seems to make political sense to push for something sweeping—both to move as quickly as possible in one fell swoop and to maximize the potential for big and visible results before the next election.

Chile's experience stands in sharp contrast to other countries in the region in that all of its major teacher policy reforms have been designed through negotiated, collaborative processes with the teachers' union. This has resulted in reforms that look quite different—less sweeping, more piecemeal, and more nuanced than the reforms adopted in Peru, Ecuador, and Mexico. The teacher career law proposed in Chile in 2012 is substantively similar to the career path reforms passed in Peru and Ecuador. But the Chilean proposal integrated different building blocks that had been adopted, implemented, and fine-tuned over more than 15 years, while the laws adopted in Peru and Ecuador have to be designed from the top-down, with many key elements still to be defined.

It is not clear that there is a political alternative to confrontation strategies in many contexts. But it is important for policy makers to realize that these strategies imply a major trade-off: confrontation makes it impossible to gain input from teachers that could genuinely improve a reform's design and smooth its implementation.

- *Sequencing reforms can ease adoption and improve implementation.* Chile's experience suggests a political logic to a certain sequence of education reforms. The first step is *student testing*, with transparent dissemination of results, both nationally and to individual schools; this is the anchor that makes it possible to introduce performance-based reforms. A second step can be the adoption of *school-based bonus pay*, which establishes the concept of pay for performance and focuses schools on student learning progress but is more palatable to unions than individual bonus pay. A third step is *individual teacher evaluation on a voluntary basis*, with the incentive of individual bonuses for teachers who demonstrate excellence. Unions typically oppose this, but making the program voluntary can avoid all-out confrontation. The Brazilian states of São Paulo in 2011 and Rio de Janeiro (pending in 2014) are interesting examples of school systems following something close to Chile's sequence, first introducing annual student testing, then school-based bonus programs, and finally programs for individual teacher evaluation on a voluntary basis. Almost all of the LAC cases of voluntary teacher evaluation so far (with the exception of São Paulo state), have experienced low teacher uptake, motivating governments eventually to make evaluations mandatory. In Chile's case at least, this sequencing allowed the ministry time to develop evaluation instruments and procedures and gain experience with the implementation challenge of performing thousands of teacher evaluations per year.

- *Incorporating parent and student feedback into teacher evaluation poses political challenges.* The new system of teacher and school director performance evaluation introduced in Ecuador and being considered in Peru includes feedback from parents and students, which is consistent with global best practice.[18] This can pose challenges, however, in the asymmetrical power of school stakeholders, particularly in rural communities and low-income urban areas. Research on school-based management experiences in settings as diverse as Nicaragua, Kenya, and India has shown that parents may not feel empowered to monitor or challenge the decisions of school personnel, who are often better educated and perceived as authority figures (Edgerton 2005; Duflo, Dupas, and Kremer 2012; Banerjee and Duflo 2007). Interviews suggest that parents also fear teachers may retaliate against their children if given a poor evaluation. It is important that ministries provide parents and students with clear guidelines, training, and survey instruments that protect confidentiality, to enable them to play this role effectively.

Notes

[1] Letter from the Colombian teacher's union to President Juan Manuel Santos, November 11, 2010. http://www.aducesar.com/media/CARTA%20DE%20FECODE%20AL%20PRESIDENTE%20SANTOS.pdf.

[2] Mexico's Carrera Magisterial, adopted in the early 1990s, has been the only exception. However, this is currently under review in the design of a new teacher evaluation system, in part because of concerns about incentivizing cheating.

[3] The Defensoría del Pueblo, an autonomous constitutional entity in Peru, conducted a report on the decentralization experience. The report concluded that there were problems with the design and implementation of the pilot municipalization program. The shared responsibilities between the national and municipal authorities undermined accountability in the adequate provision of education services. Resources were also insufficient for municipalities to carry out their new education attributions.

[4] According to the Education Ministry, there are 56 concession schools that benefit 82,029 students. See http://www.semana.com/nacion/cancelan-clases-colegios-oficiales-bogota/177967-3.aspx.

[5] In Colombia, in a recent general strike called by FECODE, the union argued that classrooms were overcrowded and that a lower student-teacher ratio demanded the hiring of more teachers. Education authorities pointed out that 3,700 new teachers had been hired from 2009–11. The authorities also argued that 48 percent of classrooms have between and 1 and 15 students and only 2 percent of classrooms in public schools have more than 45 students. See http://www.semana.com/nacion/cancelan-clases-colegios-oficiales-bogota/177967-3.aspx.

[6] The CODICEN has five members: the president of the council, two political members, and two members representing teachers. The former three members are designated by Uruguay's president and must be approved by the Senate. The latter two members are elected by the teachers in the preprimary, primary, secondary, and technical education levels during elections held regularly and supervised by the Electoral Court, the national independent body in charge of organizing and supervising every election in Uruguay. In 2012 there was a reform to CODICEN giving the council's president two votes. More information available at http://www.anep.edu.uy/anep/index.php/codicen/codicen.

[7] The other three teacher unions—SADOP, AMET, and CEA—account for around 4 percent of total teachers (Gajardo and Gomez 2005). The Sindicato Argentino de Docentes Privados (SADOP) is a union of teachers of private institutions. The Asociación del Magisterio de Enseñanza Técnica (AMET) is the union of technical education workers. Finally, the Confederación de Educadores Argentinos (CEA) was founded in 2004 by the SEDEBA (Sindicato de Educadores de Buenos Aires) and CAMYP (Unión Argentina de Maestros y Profesores).

[8] The three main teachers' unions are the Professional Association for the Advancement of Teaching (Colegio Profesional para la Superación Magisterial de Honduras); the Primer Colegio Profesional Hondureño de Maestros, which represents mainly the teachers at the primary education level; and the Honduran Secondary Teachers' Association (Colegio de Profesores de Educación Media de Honduras), which represents the teachers of secondary schools. The Federación de Organizaciones Magisteriales de Honduras (FOMH) has tried to coordinate the efforts of the different teachers' unions and has contested education reforms with limited success. For example, it has resisted the proposal to establish a teacher evaluation system.

[9] The SNTE also represents teachers from the Teacher Training Colleges and some workers of the National Institute of Arts. Although there are some states with local unions, such as in the State of Mexico, Quintana Roo, Tabasco, and Veracruz, SNTE is by far the strongest teacher union in Mexico (Fernández 2012a; Muñoz 2008; Ornelas 2010).

[10] See http://www.fecode.edu.co/index.php?option=com_content&view=article&id=5&Itemid=102.

[11] A minor union is the Sindicato de Docentes de Educación Superior del Perú (SIDESP), founded in 1984. This union organizes teachers from higher education, technological institutes, and art schools, but its influence over education policy is limited.

[12] Between 1990 and 2010, average teachers' salaries increased 200 percent in real terms, compared with a 50 percent increase in economywide average real wages. However, given the very low starting level, average wages for teachers as a percentage of per capita GDP in Chile, even by 2009, did not exceed the OECD average.

[13] It was not until July 2012 that the Ministry of Education was able to establish a national database of public sector teachers (1.46 million), and the ministry reported that only seven states provided all of the information required by Congress. The ministry has been unable to impose consequences on states that refuse to comply.

[14] Given SNTE representation in the evaluation committees of Carrera Magisterial, union leadership has the institutional capacity to retaliate against those members who behave against their leaders. Confidential interviews with teachers have pointed out this behavior (Fernández 2012a).

[15] See for example Hallack and Poisson (2007), Del Valle (2011), Martinez (2008), and Flores (2012).

[16] The school year would officially end on July 6.

[17] Authorities had calculated that approximately 270,000 teachers from public and private elementary schools would take the exam. Among states where less than 10 percent of teachers to be evaluated actually took the exam, in Colima only 1 percent participated; in Veracruz, only 2 percent; Hidalgo, 4 percent; Aguascalientes, 5 percent; and Tlaxcala, 9 percent. Finally, only 6 percent of private school teachers participated. See www.evaluacionuniversal.sep.gob.mx.

[18] As described in chapter 4, box 4.2, the large-scale Measures of Effective Teaching (MET) study in the United States has confirmed that teachers' ratings on comprehensive evaluations that combine parent feedback, student feedback, school directors' and peers' feedback, plus expert observations of teachers' classroom practice are highly correlated with teachers' ability to generate increases in student learning.

References

Andina (Peru News Agency). 2007. "Padres de familia instan a maestros a dejar de lado las medidas de fuerza." Lima, Peru. http://www.andina.com.pe/Espanol/Noticia.aspx?id=Tkc12qB50BY=.
Arcia, G., and C. Gargiulo. 2010. *Análisis de la fuerza laboral en educación en Honduras*. Washington, DC: Banco Interamericano de Desarrollo.
Banerjee, A. V., and E. Duflo, E. 2007. "The Economic Lives of the Poor." *Journal of Economic Perspectives: A Journal of the American Economic Association* 21 (1): 141.
Barahona Mejía, B. E. 2008. "Impacto de las reformas educativas en el movimiento magisterial hondureño." Graduate thesis, FLACSO Andes, http://hdl.handle.net/10469/1979.
Becker, G., and M. A. Aquino Benitez. 2008. *Sindicatos docentes y reformas educativas en América Latina: Paraguay*. Fundacion Konrad Adenauer, Asuncion. http://www.kas.de/wf/doc/6796-1442-4-30.pdf (accessed May 24, 2013).
Chaudhury, N., J. Hammer, M. Kremer, K. Muralidharan, and F. Rogers. 2004. *Teacher and Health Care Provider Absence: A Multi-Country Study*. Washington, DC: World Bank.
Chiroque Chunga, S. 2005. "Estudio de los conflictos en los sistemas educativos de la región: Agendas, actores, evolución, manejo y desenlaces. Estudio de caso: El conflicto educativo en Perú (1998–2003)." Laboratorio de Políticas Públicas (LPP), Buenos Aires.
Cisneros, L. J. 2008. "La prueba bajo examen." *La República*, March 30. http://www.larepublica.pe/30-03-2008/aula-precaria-la-prueba-bajo-examen.
CNE (Consejo Nacional de Educación). 2012. "Proyecto educativo nacional: Balance y recomendaciones." Lima. http://www.cne.gob.pe/images/stories/cne-publicaciones/Balance2012alta.pdf.
Cook, M. L. 1996. *Organizing Dissent: Unions, the State, and the Democratic Teachers' Movement in Mexico*. University Park, PA: Pennsylvania State University Press.
Corrales, J. 1999. "The Politics of Education Reform: Bolstering the Supply and Demand; Overcoming Institutional Blocks." Education Reform and Management Series II (1), World Bank, Washington, DC.
———. 2003. "The Conflict between Technocracy and Participation in Education Reforms in Latin America." Paper presented at the XXIV International Congress of Latin American Studies Association (LASA), Dallas, March.
Del Valle, S. 2011. "Exhibe maestros transa del SNTE." *Reforma* (México D.F.), December 12. http://ntrzacatecas.com/2011/12/12/exhibe-maestro-transa-del-snte/.
Diariocrítico. 2009. "Sancionarán a los docentes ecuatorianos que no acepten evaluaciones." May 27. http://ecuador.diariocritico.com/2009/Mayo/noticias/152290/se-evaluaran-a-profesores-ecuatoranos.html.
Di Gropello, E. 1999. "Los modelos de descentralización educativa en América Latina." *Revista de la CEPAL* 68: 153–70.
Duarte, J. 1997. "Clientelismo e implementación de programas sociales. El caso de un proyecto del Banco Mundial para Educación Primaria en Colombia." Bogotá: Seminario Internacional Nuevas Tendencias en Política Social, Pontificia Universidad Javeriana.
Duflo, E., P. Dupas, and M. Kremer. 2012. "School Governance, Teacher Incentives, and Pupil-Teacher Ratios: Experimental Evidence from Kenyan Primary Schools." NBER Working Paper 17939, National Bureau of Economic Research, Cambridge, MA.
Edgerton, D. C. 2005. *Schools, Communities, and Democracy: The Nicaragua BASE Project*. Academy for Educational Development, Washington, DC.
El Comercio. 2007. "Reemplazo de docentes en huelga empieza este miércoles." July 9. http://elcomercio.pe/edicionimpresa/html/2007-07-09/ImEcPolitica0751383.html.
———. 2012. "Santos es prejudicial para el 53%: Encuesta nacional urbana." August 8.
Fernández, M. A. 2012a. "From the Streets to the Classrooms: The Politics of Education Spending in Mexico." PhD thesis, Duke University, Durham, NC.

———. 2012b. "The Political Challenges in Pursuing an Agenda for Quality of Education in Latin America." Backgound paper for Latin America Regional Study on Teacher Quality, World Bank, Washington, DC.

Flores, J. C. 2012. "Defiende herencia de plazas magisteriales." La Jornada, México D.F.

Froemel, J. E. 1999. "Evaluación de la Calidad de la Educación con Equidad. El modelo de valor agregado." UNESCO-ORLEALC, Santiago.

Gajardo, M., and F. Gómez. 2005. "Social Dialogue in Education in Latin America: A Regional Survey." Backgound document for the Joint ILO/UNESCO Committee of Experts on the Application of the Recommendations Concerning Teaching Personnel (CEART), Geneva.

Gentili, P., and D. Suárez. 2004. "La conflictividad educativa en América Latina." Paper presented at the Online Latinamerican Forum on Educational Policies, Buenos Aires, July–December.

Gindin, J. 2007. *La Conflictividad Docente en América Latina: Un Balance del año 2004*. Buenos Aires: Laboratorio de Políticas Públicas.

———. 2009. "Sur, neoliberalismo… ¿y después? Los sindicatos docentes en Venezuela, Argentina, Bolivia, Brasil, Uruguay y Ecuador." NUPET/IUPERJ, Rio de Janeiro.

Golden, M. 1993. "The Dynamics of Trade Unionism and National Economic Performance." *American Political Science Review* 87 (2): 437–54.

Grindle, M. S. 2004. *Despite the Odds: The Contentious Politics of Education Reform*. Princeton, NJ: Princeton University Press.

Grossman, G. M., and E. Helpman. 1996. "Electoral Competition and Special Interest Politics." *Review of Economic Studies* 63 (2): 265–86.

———. 2001. *Special Interest Politics*. Cambridge, MA: MIT Press.

Hallak, J., and M. Poisson. 2007. *Corrupt Schools, Corrupt Universities: What Can Be Done?* Paris: UNESCO.

Hannaway, J., and A. J. Rotherham. 2006. *Collective Bargaining in Education: Negotiating Change in Today's Schools*. Cambridge, MA: Harvard Education Press.

Hanushek, E. 2002. "Evidence, Politics, and the Class Size Debate." In *The Class Size Debate*, edited by L. Mishel, and R. Rothstein. Washington, DC: Economic Policy Institute.

Hill, Keisha. 2011. "Performance-Based Pay Still Being Rejected By Teachers." *The Gleaner*, January 31. http://jamaica-gleaner.com/gleaner/20110131/lead/lead8.html.

Kane, T. J., J. E. Rockoff, and D. O. Staiger. 2008. "What Does Certification Tell Us about Teacher Effectiveness? Evidence from New York City." *Economics of Education Review* 27 (6): 615–31.

Kaufman, R. R., and J. M. Nelson. 2004. *Crucial Needs, Weak Incentives: Social Sector Reform, Democratization, and Globalization in Latin America*. Washington, DC: Woodrow Wilson Center Press.

Koedel, C., M. Podgursky, and S. Shi. 2013. "Teacher Pension Systems, the Composition of the Teaching Workforce, and Teacher Quality." *Journal of Policy Analysis and Management* 32 (3): 574–96.

Lohmann, S. 2003. "Representative Government and Special Interest Politics (We Have Met the Enemy and He Is Us)." *Journal of Theoretical Politics* 15 (3): 299–319.

López, M. M. 2008. "Sindicatos docentes y reformas educativas en América Latina: Colombia." Fundación Konrad Adenauer, Bogota.

Lowden, P. S. 2004. "Education Reform in Colombia: The Elusive Quest for Effectiveness." In *Crucial Needs, Weak Incentives: Social Sector Reform, Democratization, and Globalization in Latin America*, edited by R. Kaufman and J. M. Nelson, 350–74. Baltimore, MD: Johns Hopkins University Press.

Loyo, A., M. D. Ibarrola, and A. Blanco. 1999. "Estructura del sindicalismo docente en América Latina en." *Propuesta Educativa* 21: 4–15.

Martínez, N. 2008. *Maestros Reprobados y de "Panazo."* Mexico City: El Universal.

McEwan, P., and L. Santibáñez. 2005. "Teacher and Principal Incentives in Mexico." In *Incentives to Improve Teaching*, edited by E. Vegas, 213–53. Washington, DC: World Bank.

Mexico, Gobierno de la Republica. n.d. "Sobre la Reforma Constitucional en Materia Educativa." http://www.presidencia.gob.mx/reformaeducativa/#sobre-la-reforma.

Mizala, A., and B. R. Schneider. 2014. "Negotiating Education Reform: Teacher Evaluations and Incentives in Chile (1990–2010)." *Governance: An International Journal of Policy, Administration and Institutions* 27 (1): 87–109.

Montero, C., and R. Cuenca. 2008. "Sobre notas y aprendizajes escolares: Opiniones y demandas de la población del Perú." Segunda Encuesta Nacional de Educación-ENAED 2007. Foro Educativo, Lima.

Muñoz Armenta, A. 2008. "Escenarios e Identidades del SNTE: Entre el sistema educativo y el sistema político." *Revista Mexicana de Investigación Educativa* 13 (37): 377–417.

Murillo, M. V. 2001. *Labor Unions, Partisan Coalitions, and Market Reforms in Latin America.* Cambridge, U.K.: Cambridge University Press.

Murillo, M., M. Tommasi, L. Ronconi, and J. Sanguinetti. 2002. "The Economic Effects of Unions in Latin America: Teachers' Unions and Education in Argentina." IDB Working Paper 171, Inter-American Development Bank, Washington, DC.

Núñez, I., and C. Cox. 2003. "El profesorado, su gremio y la reforma de los años noventa: Presiones de cambio y evolución en la cultura docente." In *Políticas Educacionales en el Cambio de Siglo: La Reforma del Sistema Escolar en Chile*, edited by C. Cox, 455–518. Santiago: Editorial Universitaria.

Olson, M. 1965. *The Logic of Collective Action: Public Goods and the Theory of Groups.* Cambridge, MA: Harvard University Press.

Ornelas, C. 2010. "Aterrizaje forzado." *Revista Mexicana de Investigación Educativa* 15 (45): 627–31.

Oxford Research. 2006. "BRAZIL: PT Faces Challenge of Education Reform." Oxford Analytica, Oxford, U.K.

———. 2008. "BRAZIL: Public Education Lags Despite Reform Efforts." Oxford Analytica, Oxford, U.K.

Palamidessi, M., and M. Legarralde. 2006. "Teacher's Unions, Governments and Education Reforms in Latin America and the Caribbean: Conditions to Dialogue." IDB Working Paper 14978, Inter-American Development Bank, Washington, DC.

Peru 21. 2007. "Presidente confirma que habrá despidos." February 24. http://peru21.pe/noticia/16355/presidente-confirma-que-habra-despidos.

Petrina, F. 2004. "JTA Stands Firm: Warns of Protest Action against Pay-By-Performance Proposal." *Jamaica Gleaner,* August 19. http://jamaica-gleaner.com/gleaner/20040817/lead/lead1.html.

Plank, D. N. 1996. *The Means of Our Salvation: Public Education in Brazil, 1930–1995.* Boulder, CO: Westview Press.

Rivas, A. 2004. *Gobernar la Educación: Estudio Comparado Sobre el Poder y la Educación en Las Provincias Argentinas.* Buenos Aires: Ediciones Granica SA.

Rojas, H. 2012. "Falla evaluación universal, asiste 30% de docentes." *Educación a Debate.* http://educacionadebate.org/37995/falla-evaluacion-universal-de-docentes-asiste-30-de-docentes/.

Solis Sánchez, I. 2011. "Transparencia, acceso a la información y rendición de cuentas en el SNTE." Instituto de Acceso a la Información Pública del Distrito Federal, Mexico City, Mexico.

Street, S. 1992. "El SNTE y la política educativa, 1970–1990." *Revista Mexicana de Sociología* 54 (2): 45–72.

United Nations. 2011.

Vaillant, D. 2005. *Education Reforms and Teachers' Unions: Avenues for Action.* Paris: International Institute for Educational Planning, UNESCO.

———. 2008. "Sindicatos y la educación pública en América Latina: El caso Uruguay." Fundación Konrad Adenauer, Política Social en América Latina-SOPLA, Montevideo.

Zegarra, E., and R. Ravina. 2003. "Teacher Unionization and the Quality of Education in Peru: An Empirical Evaluation Using Survey Data." IDB Working Paper 182, Inter-American Development Bank, Washington, DC.

Index

Boxes, figures, tables, and notes are indicated by *b, f, t,* and *n* following the page number.

A

absenteeism of teachers, 230, 232, 232*f*
accountability, 230–37
    client feedback, 236–37
    job stability, 230–33
    managerial oversight, 233–36
    overview, 42–43, 224
active instructional methods, 105, 114
AEP (Asignación de Excelencia Pedagógica, Chile), 253–54
Agencia de Calidad de la Educación (Chile), 233–34
Alfonso, M., 165
Aligning Learning Incentives (ALI), 46, 264, 265–66
alternative certification, 31, 163, 293–94
AMET (Asociación del Magisterio de Enseñanza Técnica), 327*n*7
ANDE (Asociación Nacional de Educadores), 302, 306
Appraisal for Professional Development (Korea), 190
APSE (Asociación de Profesores de Segunda Enseñanza), 302
Araujo, M. C., 71
Argentina
    job stability in, 233
    PISA scores in, 65
    pupil-teacher ratio in, 171, 296
    strikes and protests in, 305
    teacher demographics in, 75
    teachers' unions in, 297, 298*t*, 302, 305, 306, 327*n*7
Teach For All program in, 31, 165, 293
Asignación de Excelencia Pedagógica (AEP, Chile), 253–54
Asignación Variable por Desempeño Individual (AVDI, Chile), 191, 195, 254–55, 254–55*t*, 308, 310
Asociación del Magisterio de Enseñanza Técnica (AMET), 327*n*7
Asociación de Profesores de Segunda Enseñanza (APSE), 302
Asociación Nacional de Educadores (ANDE), 302, 306
Australia, school leadership training in, 39, 210
autonomy, 230, 232
AVDI (Asignación Variable por Desempeño Individual, Chile), 191, 195, 254–55, 254–55*t*, 308, 310

B

Barber, M., 37, 139, 200, 226
Barón, J., 75
Bassi, M., 165
BDE (Bonus de Desempenho Escolar, Brazil), 268
Beca Vocación de Profesor (BVP, Chile), 26, 147–48, 175
Behrman, J. R., 90
Belize, teacher induction in, 34, 181
benchmarking, 1, 105, 106*t*

331

Bill & Melinda Gates Foundation, 98, 185*b*,
    198*b*, 214
Bolivia
    economic growth and education
        performance in, 4
    PISA scores in, 63
Bonus de Desemphenho Escolar (BDE, Brazil),
    268
bonus pay, 258–75, 260–63*t*
    lessons learned, 280–82
    as motivation, 237
    nonstudent performance measures as basis
        for, 270–73, 271–72*b*
    other student outcomes as basis for,
        268–70
    overview, 45–47
    politics of teacher reform and, 295–96
    student learning results as basis for, 264–73
    union support for, 295–96
Botswana, teacher demographics in, 8
Boyd, D., 162
Branch, G., 209
Brazil. *See also specific city and state school
    systems*
    accountability pressure in, 42
    bonus pay in, 45, 46, 264, 268–70, 281
    classroom management in, 130
    classroom observation in, 99, 104
    compensation in, 84, 85
    demographic shift in, 33
    economic growth and education
        performance in, 5
    financial incentives in, 238
    ICT use in, 212
    in-service training in, 37, 196, 200, 204,
        208
    instructional time use in, 12, 13–14*f*, 18,
        18*f*, 22, 108
    managerial oversight in, 235, 277
    PISA scores in, 60, 64, 65
    pre-service teacher practice in, 153, 154
    probationary periods in, 183
    pupil-teacher ratio in, 171, 172, 296
    school choice in, 236
    standards for teachers in, 293
    strikes and protests in, 305
    teacher demographics in, 7, 74, 75, 76
    teacher salaries in, 8
    teacher standards in, 31, 161–62
    teachers' unions in, 297, 298*t*, 305
    Teach For All program in, 31, 165, 293, 294
    working hours in, 84

Brunner Commission (Chile), 309
Bruns, B., 259, 268, 274, 282*n*1
Business Association for Education (Peru), 316
BVP (Beca Vocación de Profesor, Chile), 26,
    147–48, 175

C

Cabezas, V., 273
CAL (computer-assisted learning), 211
Calderón, Felipe, 312
Canada
    job stability in, 231
    peer collaboration in, 38
    professional rewards in, 40
    school leadership training in, 39
    teacher education quality in, 11
career development, 190–94, 192*b*, 193*f*.
    See also in-service training
career path reforms, 239–46, 240–45*t*
    hybrid career incentive programs, 252–56
    implementation challenges, 256–57
    lessons learned, 278–79
    overview, 43, 238
    promotions based on comprehensive
        performance measures, 250–51
    promotions based on knowledge and skills
        tests, 246–50
    promotions based on student learning
        results, 251–52
Carnoy, M., 38, 204, 235
Carrera Magisterial (Mexico), 44, 73, 183, 238,
    246, 251–52, 292, 312, 326*n*2
Carrera Pública Magisterial (CPM, Peru), 124,
    246, 248–49, 304, 316
cascade training, 203
Catholic University of Guayaquil, 321
CEA (Confederación de Educadores
    Argentinos), 327*n*7
Ceará, Brazil
    classroom management in, 135
    in-service training in, 37, 204, 208
Center for Studies and Teachers' Research,
    307
Centers of Excellence for Teacher Training,
    203
Central Nacional de Asociaciones de Padres de
    Familia (CENAPAFAS, Peru), 316
certification exams, 30, 31, 156–57, 255
character skills, 66, 67
charter schools, 292–93
Chetty, R., 69, 72

Chicago, Illinois
  bonus pay in, 264, 266–67
  job stability in, 232
  probationary periods in, 181
Chijioke, C., 37, 200
Chile
  accountability pressure in, 42
  accreditation standards in, 149–50, 150*f*
  alternative certification in, 31
  bonus pay in, 45, 46, 264, 269, 270–73,
    274, 275, 281, 307
  career incentive programs in, 253–55, 256
  career path reforms in, 257
  cognitive skill development in, 66
  compensation in, 84, 85, 294
  compressed wage scale in, 90
  content knowledge in, 78
  economic growth and education
    performance in, 5
  entry standards for teacher education in,
    26
  evaluation of teachers in, 35–36, 183–84,
    186, 188, 188–90*f*, 191, 193*f*, 194,
    216, 291
  excess supply of teachers in, 11
  financial incentives in, 238, 279
  ICT use in, 213, 217
  innovation awards in, 155
  job stability in, 230, 232, 233, 277, 288
  managerial oversight in, 233, 277
  PISA scores in, 60, 64, 65
  politics of teacher reforms in, 50, 307–11,
    325
  professional rewards in, 229
  pupil-teacher ratio in, 172, 296
  quality of teacher education in, 28
  recruitment of teachers in, 141–42, 147–48,
    175
  school choice in, 292
  school leadership training in, 39, 210
  selectivity of teacher education in, 24
  student testing in, 290, 307
  teacher demographics in, 7–8, 75, 76, 77
  teacher effectiveness in, 74
  teacher salaries in, 8
  teacher standards in, 29, 29*f*, 31, 156,
    160–61, 161*f*
  teachers' unions in, 298*t*, 304
  Teach For All program in, 31, 165, 293,
    294
  voucher schools in, 236
  working hours in, 84

China. *See also specific city and state school
    systems*
  evaluation of teachers in, 35
  pupil-teacher ratio in, 32, 170
  teacher effectiveness in, 74
Cincinnati, Ohio, career path reforms in, 278
civil society organizations, 324
Classroom Assessment Scoring System
    (CLASS), 100, 185*b*
classroom management, 97–137
  good practice benchmarks, 106*t*
  ICT use, 15–17, 114–19, 118–19*f*
  in-service training for, 37, 207–8
  instructional time, 12–15, 13–14*f*, 14*t*,
    16*f*, 17–23, 18*f*, 20–22*f*, 107–14, 107*f*,
    109–11*b*, 109*f*, 112*t*, 113–17*f*
  interschool variances in, 17–19, 18*f*,
    122–26, 123–25*f*
  intraschool variances in, 19–23, 20–22*f*,
    126–32, 127*t*, 128–29*f*, 131*f*
  lessons learned, 105–32
  observation methodology, 100–105,
    101–3*b*
  observation sample, 99, 100*t*
  overview, 11–23
  unengaged students, 17, 17*f*, 119–22,
    120–21*f*
client feedback, 236–37
CNTE (Confederação Nacional dos
    Trabalhadores em Educação, Brazil),
    305
CODICEN (Consejo Directivo Central de la
    Administración Nacional de Educación
    Pública), 302, 326*n*6
cognitive skills of teachers, 7–8, 8–9*f*
Colegio de Profesores de Educación Media de
    Honduras, 327*n*8
Colegio Profesional para la Superación
    Magisterial de Honduras, 327*n*8
Colombia
  accountability pressure in, 42, 43
  alternative certification in, 31
  career path reforms in, 246, 257, 258, 280
  classroom management in, 128*f*, 130, 131
  classroom observation in, 99
  cognitive skill development in, 66
  compensation in, 294
  curriculum reform in, 289
  decentralization in, 291
  demographic shift in, 167
  entry standards for teacher education in, 26
  evaluation of teachers in, 36, 194, 291

financial incentives in, 44, 238, 279
ICT use in, 211
in-service training in, 205, 206*b*
instructional time use in, 12, 13, 13–14*f*, 18*f*, 19, 20, 21*f*, 22, 22*f*, 108, 124
job stability in, 232, 233, 277, 288
managerial oversight in, 235
PISA scores in, 60, 64
probationary periods in, 182–83
professional rewards in, 229
promotions based on knowledge and skills tests in, 246–48
promotions based on student learning results in, 252
pupil-teacher ratio in, 172
recruitment of teachers in, 148–49, 176*n*3
school choice in, 292–93
selectivity of teaching education in, 144
strikes and protests in, 326*n*5
teacher demographics in, 7, 75
teacher induction in, 35
teacher standards in, 30, 159–60
teachers' unions in, 298*t*, 302, 303, 306–7
Teach For All program in, 31, 165, 293, 294
unengaged students in, 120
Commission on the Modernization of Chilean Education, 309
compensation, 78–91
competency-based, 44, 238, 257
compressed wage scale, 9–11, 88–91, 88–91*f*, 237
politics of teacher reform and, 294
salaries relative to other professionals, 8, 10*f*, 84–88, 85–87*f*
trends in, 79–83, 81–83*f*
competency-based promotion and pay, 44, 238, 247, 257
computer-assisted learning (CAL), 211
Computers for Education program (Colombia), 211
concession schools, 292–93, 294
Confederação Nacional dos Trabalhadores em Educação (CNTE, Brazil), 305
Confederación de Educadores Argentinos (CEA), 327*n*7
Confederación de Nacionalidades Indígenas del Ecuador (CONAIE), 322
Confederación de Trabajadores de la Educación de la República Argentina (CTERA), 302, 305, 307

Consejo de Evaluación, Acreditación y Certificación de la Calidad de la Educación Superior No Universitaria (CONEACES, Peru), 150
Consejo de Evaluación, Acreditación y Certificación de la Calidad de la Educación Superior Universitaria (CONEAU, Peru), 151
Consejo de Rectores de las Universidades de Chile, 155
Consejo Directivo Central de la Administración Nacional de Educación Pública (CODICEN), 302, 326*n*6
content mastery
as constraint on education progress, 2
in-service training for, 205–7
as professional reward, 37, 200, 225–27
Contreras, D., 273
Corrales, J., 306
Correa, Rafael, 319, 320, 322
Costa, L., 204
Costa Rica
compensation in, 84, 85, 87, 88
compressed wage scale in, 90
excess supply of teachers in, 11
PISA scores in, 60, 63, 65
pupil-teacher ratio in, 171, 296
recruitment of teachers in, 141
selectivity of teacher education in, 24
teacher demographics in, 74, 76
teacher salaries in, 8
teachers' unions in, 299*t*, 302, 306
unemployment among teaching graduates in, 83
value of teachers measured in, 68
working hours in, 84
CPM (Carrera Pública Magisterial, Peru), 124, 246, 248–49, 304, 316
crèche care, 67
CTERA (Confederación de Trabajadores de la Educación de la República Argentina), 302, 305, 307
Cuba
early childhood development programs in, 67
entry standards for teacher education in, 26
job stability in, 230
managerial oversight in, 235
pre-service teacher practice in, 153, 154
professional rewards in, 226, 227, 229, 276
pupil-teacher ratio in, 171
quality of teacher education in, 28
value of teachers measured in, 68

Cuesta, J., 273
Currículo Nacional Básico (Honduras), 289
curriculum reform, 289–90

D

Danielson Framework for Teaching, 185*b*
decentralization, 291–92
Dee, T., 198*b*
Defensoría del Pueblo (Peru), 326*n*3
democratization processes, 291, 303
demographic shift, 2–3, 167–74, 168*f*, 169*t*, 172*f*
deployment and management of teachers, 39–40
deskilling of teachers, 82
developmental deficits, 66
Docentemas (Sistema de Evaluación del Desempeño Profesional Docente, Chile), 186, 189
Dominican Republic
  classroom observation in, 99
  demographic shift in, 167
  probationary periods in, 182–83
  pupil-teacher ratio in, 172
  quality of teacher education in, 151
  selectivity of teacher education in, 31–32
  teacher induction in, 35
dropouts, 248

E

early childhood development programs, 67
East Asia and Pacific
  classroom management in, 132, 135
  economic growth and education performance in, 4, 4*f*
  educational attainment in, 56, 57*t*, 59
  ICT use in, 212
  PISA scores in, 65
  professional rewards in, 226, 228
  pupil-teacher ratio in, 32, 170
ECAP (Evaluación de las Competencias Académicas y Pedagógicas, El Salvador), 159
economic growth, 3–5, 4*f*
Ecuador
  accountability pressure in, 42
  career incentive programs in, 256
  career path reforms in, 257
  client feedback in, 237
  cognitive skill development in, 66
  compensation in, 294
  early childhood education in, 99
  entry standards for teacher education in, 25
  evaluation of teachers in, 35, 36, 183, 291
  financial incentives in, 44, 238, 279
  in-service training in, 38, 208
  job stability in, 230, 232, 233, 277, 288
  managerial oversight in, 235, 278
  national teacher education university in, 147, 175
  politics of teacher reforms in, 325
  professional rewards in, 229
  promotions based on comprehensive performance measures in, 250–51
  pupil-teacher ratio in, 171, 296
  strikes and protests in, 305
  teacher demographics in, 7
  teacher standards in, 184
  teachers' unions in, 48, 49, 299*t*, 302, 303, 306
  value of teachers measured in, 71, 72
education performance, 3–5, 4–5*f*
Educopédia (Brazil), 118, 213, 214*b*, 217
EFAP (Escola de Formação e Aperfeiçoamento de Professores Paulo Renato Costa Souza, Brazil), 213
El Salvador
  client feedback in, 237
  compensation in, 84, 85, 86
  pupil-teacher ratio in, 172
  school choice in, 236
  teacher demographics in, 76
  teacher salaries in, 8
  teacher standards in, 30, 30*f*, 159, 160*f*
  unemployment among teaching graduates in, 84
Empresarios para la Educación (Peru), 316
Enhanced Performance Management System (EPMS), 192*b*, 231
ENLACE (National Assessment of Academic Achievement in Schools), 158, 252, 313
Enseña Chile, 31, 165–66
Enseña Peru, 165
entry standards for teacher education, 25–27, 26*f*
EPD (Estatuto de Profesionalización Docente, Colombia), 194, 246–48
EPMS (Enhanced Performance Management System), 192*b*, 231
Escola de Formação e Aperfeiçoamento de Professores Paulo Renato Costa Souza (EFAP, Brazil), 213

Escuela Nueva (Colombia), 37, 124, 205, 206*b*, 229
Estatuto de Profesionalización Docente (EPD, Colombia), 194, 246–48
Estrada, Ricardo, 158, 159
Evaluación de las Competencias Académicas y Pedagógicos (ECAP, El Salvador), 159
evaluation of teachers, 183–96, 183*t*, 197–99*b*
    career development linked to, 190–94, 192*b*, 193*f*
    defining good teaching, 184–85
    defining levels of teacher quality, 188–89, 188–90*f*
    implementation challenges, 194–96
    measurement instruments, 185–88, 185–86*b*
    overview, 35–37
    politics of teacher reform and, 291
exam cheating, 159, 259, 266

F

Federación Colombiana de Educadores (FECODE), 291, 303–4, 307, 326*n*5
Federación de Educadores de Paraguay (FEP), 302
Federación de Organizaciones Magisteriales de Honduras (FOMH), 327*n*8
Federación Uruguaya de Magisterio-Trabajadores de la Enseñanza (FUM-TEP), 302
Federation of Teachers' Organizations, 302
FEP (Federación de Educadores de Paraguay), 302
Fernandes, M., 121
Fernández, M. A., 305
Ferraz, C., 121, 268
Filmer, D., 259, 274, 282*n*1
financial incentives, 43–45, 224
Finland
    bonus pay in, 47
    compensation in, 84
    entry standards for teacher education in, 26
    evaluation of teachers in, 191
    peer collaboration in, 38
    PISA scores in, 62*b*
    professional rewards in, 40, 41, 225–26, 276, 277, 282
    recruitment of teachers in, 139, 143*b*, 147

    selectivity of teacher education in, 24, 25, 140, 143, 143*b*
    teacher education quality in, 11
    teacher effectiveness in, 74
    teacher standards in, 156
Florida, managerial oversight in, 234
FOMH (Federación de Organizaciones Magisteriales de Honduras), 327*n*8
Fredriksson, P., 80
free-rider behavior, 239, 265, 269
Frente por un País Solidario (FREPASO, Argentina), 305
Friedman, J. N., 69
Fryer, R., 267
Fullan, Michael, 212
FUM-TEP (Federación Uruguaya de Magisterio-Trabajadores de la Enseñanza), 302
Fundo Nacional Para o Desenvolvimento do Ensino Fundamental (FUNDEF, Brazil), 293

G

Gallego, F., 273
García, Alan, 292, 316
gender equality, 206*b*
Germany, evaluation of teachers in, 191
Ginásio Experimental Carioca (Rio de Janeiro), 41, 135, 227, 277
Gobiernos Escolares Ciudadanos (Ecuador), 237, 321
Goldhaber, D., 238
Goodman, S. F., 268
grooming of teachers, 179–221
    deployment and management, 39–40
    evaluation, 35–37, 183–96, 183*t*, 197–99*b*
    ICT and, 211–15, 214*b*
    induction, 34–35, 179–83, 180*t*, 182*b*
    in-service training, 196–208, 201–2*t*
    overview, 34–40
    probationary periods, 179–83
    professional development, 37–38
    school leadership's role, 208–10
group bonuses, 259, 274, 296
Guatemala
    expansion of education coverage in, 3, 55
    pupil-teacher ratio in, 172
    quality of teacher education in, 151
    recruitment of teachers in, 176*n*4
    school choice in, 236
    teacher effectiveness in, 73

H

Haiti
    expansion of education coverage in, 3, 55
    in-service training in, 200, 205
    quality of teacher education in, 151
Hanushek, E. A., 56, 58, 59, 60, 63, 92n4, 171b, 209, 231, 233
Hawthorne effects, 104
Heckman, J. J., 67
Hernani-Limarino, W., 9, 89
high-stakes assessments, 268, 290
high value-added teachers, 69
hiring standards, 156–66
    alternative certification, 164–66
    overview, 28–31, 28–30f
    teacher standards, 156
    tests of skills and competencies, 156–63, 158t, 160–61f, 163f
Hoddinott, J., 66
Holness, Andrew, 303
home visit programs, 67
homework, 121–22
Honduras
    alternative certification in, 164
    classroom management in, 129f, 130
    classroom observation in, 99
    compensation in, 84, 85
    curriculum reform in, 289
    demographic shift in, 167
    economic growth and education performance in, 4
    evaluation of teachers in, 291
    expansion of education coverage in, 55
    ICT use in, 16, 116, 118
    in-service training in, 37, 204
    instructional time use in, 12, 13–14f, 15, 18, 18f, 22, 22f, 108, 112, 114, 123–24
    PISA scores in, 63
    pupil-teacher ratio in, 172
    quality of teacher education in, 151
    recruitment of teachers in, 176n4
    school choice in, 236, 293
    teacher demographics in, 7, 75, 77
    teacher salaries in, 8
    teachers' unions in, 300t, 302, 327n8
    unengaged students in, 120
Hong Kong SAR, China
    entry standards for teacher education in, 26
    recruitment of teachers in, 147
Hoxby, C. M., 9, 89

Humala, Ollanta, 292, 305, 318
hybrid career incentive programs, 252–56

I

ICETEX (Instituto Colombiano de Crédito Educativo y Estudios Técnicos en el Exterior), 149
ICFES (Instituto Colombiano para la Evaluación de la Educación), 159, 247
ICT. *See* information and communication technologies
IMPACT (Washington, DC), 197b, 199b
India
    bonus pay in, 264–65, 269, 274, 283n10
    evaluation of teachers in, 326
    ICT use in, 211
Indice de Desenvolvimento da Educacao Basica (IDEB), 13, 264, 274
Indonesia, teacher certification in, 141
induction of teachers, 34–35
INEE (National Institute for Educational Evaluation, Mexico), 315
INEP (Instituto Nacional de Estudos e Pesquisas Educacionais, Brazil), 161
information and communication technologies (ICT)
    curriculum reform and, 289
    grooming of teachers and, 211–15, 214b
    One Laptop Per Child (OLPC) initiatives, 16, 116, 211
    use of, 15–17, 114–19, 118–19f
Innovar para Ser Mejor (Chile), 213, 217
in-service training, 196–208, 201–2t
    classroom management, 207–8
    content mastery, 205–7
    evaluation of teachers and, 35, 37
    scripted training, 203–5
Institute for Teaching and School Leadership (Australia), 39, 210
Instituto Colombiano de Crédito Educativo y Estudios Técnicos en el Exterior (ICETEX), 149
Instituto Colombiano para la Evaluación de la Educación (ICFES), 159, 247
Instituto de Investigaciones Marina Vilte, 307
Instituto Nacional de Estudos e Pesquisas Educacionais (INEP, Brazil), 161
Institutos Superiores Pedagógicos (ISPs, Peru), 145, 146f, 151, 316
instructional leaders, 235

instructional time
　classroom observations, 107–14, 107*f*, 109–11*b*, 109*f*, 112*t*, 113–17*f*
　interschool variances in, 17–19, 18*f*, 122–26, 123–25*f*
　intraschool variances in, 19–23, 20–22*f*, 126–32, 127*t*, 128–29*f*, 131*f*
　overview, 12–15, 13–14*f*, 14*t*, 16*f*
Intel's Teach to the Future program, 212
interactive instructional methods, 114
Inter-American Teacher Education Network, 213
ISPs. *See* Institutos Superiores Pedagógicos
Israel
　cash incentives for students in, 97
　classroom management in, 207

J

Jamaica
　accountability pressure in, 42
　classroom management in, 126, 129*f*, 130
　classroom observation in, 99
　evaluation of teachers in, 291
　instructional time use in, 12, 13*f*, 18*f*, 19, 20*f*, 22
　managerial oversight in, 233, 277
　school leadership training in, 39, 210
　teachers' unions in, 300*t*, 302, 303
Jamaica Teachers' Association (JTA), 303
Jamaica Teaching Council, 157
Japan
　classroom management in, 132
　compensation in, 84
　evaluation of teachers in, 35, 183, 191
　in-service training in, 203
　peer collaboration in, 38
　professional rewards in, 226, 227
　pupil-teacher ratio in, 32, 170, 171*b*
　recruitment of teachers in, 139
　teacher effectiveness in, 74
　teacher standards in, 156
job stability, 11, 42, 83–84, 84*f*
job tenure loss, 288–89
JTA (Jamaica Teachers' Association), 303

K

Kain, J. F., 92*n*4
Kautz, T., 67
Kenya
　bonus pay in, 283*n*10
　cash incentives for students in, 97
　evaluation of teachers in, 326
　in-service training in, 203
Knight, S., 12, 105
Korda, M., 200
Korea
　compensation in, 84
　evaluation of teachers in, 35, 183, 190, 191
　PISA scores in, 60
　professional rewards in, 225–26, 228
　pupil-teacher ratio in, 32, 170, 171*b*
　recruitment of teachers in, 139
　teacher education quality in, 11
　teacher effectiveness in, 74
　teacher standards in, 156
Kraft, M. A., 209

L

LAST (Liberal Arts and Sciences Teacher) certification, 162, 163*f*
lateral accountability, 227
Latin American Laboratory for Assessment of the Quality of Education (LLECE), 49, 63, 308
Leigh, A., 9, 89
Lemov, Douglas, 182*b*, 207
Lesson Study method (Japan), 38, 132, 203, 226, 227
Ley de Carrera Docente y Escalafón del Magisterio (Ecuador), 250–51
Ley de Carrera Profesional Docente (Chile), 310
Ley del Profesorado (Peru), 315
Ley de Reforma Magisterial (LRM, Peru), 251, 304, 318
Liberal Arts and Sciences Teacher (LAST) certification, 162, 163*f*
Liberia, in-service training in, 200, 203, 204
LLECE. *See* Latin American Laboratory for Assessment of the Quality of Education
low value-added teachers, 69
LRM. *See* Ley de Reforma Magisterial
Lula, Luiz, 305

M

malnutrition, 66
Maluccio, J. A., 66
Marco para la Buena Enseñanza (MBE, Chile), 156, 186, 188, 309
Marshall, J. S., 73

master teachers, 192*b*, 206*b*, 228, 229
Mathematical Quality of Instruction, 185*b*
McEwan, P. J., 252
Measures of Effective Teaching (MET) program, 97, 185*b*, 214, 327*n*18
Mejoramiento de la Calidad y la Equidad en la Educación Superior (Chile), 155
mentoring, 181, 229, 277
Metzler, J., 73, 77
Mexicanos Primero, 314
Mexico
   accountability pressure in, 42
   alternative certification in, 31
   bonus pay in, 46, 264, 265–66, 275, 281
   career path reforms in, 246, 256, 258, 280
   cash incentives for students in, 97
   classroom management in, 126, 128*f*, 131, 133, 133–34*b*
   classroom observation in, 99
   compensation in, 84, 85, 294
   decentralization in, 292
   early childhood education in, 176*n*6
   education spending in, 295
   evaluation of teachers in, 36, 183, 291
   financial incentives in, 44, 238
   ICT use in, 114
   in-service training in, 37, 196, 208, 313
   instructional time use in, 13, 13–14*f*, 15, 18*f*, 19, 20*f*, 22, 108, 109–11*b*, 112, 122
   job stability in, 230
   PISA scores in, 60, 64, 65
   politics of teacher reforms in, 325
   pre-service teacher practice in, 153
   professional rewards in, 229
   promotions based on student learning results in, 251–52
   pupil-teacher ratio in, 172
   school choice in, 236
   strikes and protests in, 305
   teacher effectiveness in, 73
   teacher salaries in, 8
   teacher standards in, 29, 157–59
   teachers' unions in, 48, 49, 300*t*, 302, 303, 305, 306, 311–15
   Teach For All program in, 31, 165, 293
   working hours in, 84
Michigan, probationary periods in, 181
Minas Gerais, Brazil
   classroom management in, 129*f*, 130, 132
   classroom observation in, 99
   in-service training in, 37, 208

   instructional time use in, 20, 21*f*
   managerial oversight in, 235
Mizala, A., 11, 85, 86, 87, 307, 308, 309, 315
motivating teachers, 223–86
   accountability pressure, 42–43, 230–37
   bonus pay, 45–47, 258–75
   career path reforms, 239–46, 240–45*t*
   financial incentives, 43–45, 237–39
   hybrid career incentive programs, 252–56
   incentives, 224*f*
   overview, 2, 40–47, 41*f*
   professional rewards, 40–42, 225–29
   promotions
      based on comprehensive performance measures, 250–51
      based on knowledge and skills tests, 246–50
      based on student learning results, 251–52
Mourshed, M., 37, 139, 200, 226
Movimiento Popular Democrático (MPD), Ecuador), 319, 321
Muralidharan, K., 264, 265

N

National Assessment of Academic Achievement in Schools (ENLACE), 158, 252, 313
National Center for Educational Leadership (Jamaica), 39, 210
National Institute for Education (Singapore), 25, 144*b*, 210
National Institute for Educational Evaluation (INEE, Mexico), 315
Neal, D., 268, 270
Netherlands
   recruitment of teachers in, 139
   teacher education quality in, 11
   teacher effectiveness in, 74
New York City
   alternative certification in, 166, 293
   bonus pay in, 267–68
   pre-service teacher practice in, 152–53
   school leadership training in, 39–40
   teacher standards in, 31, 162–63, 163*f*
   temporary license teachers in, 30, 162, 163*f*
New Zealand, probationary periods in, 181
Nicaragua
   client feedback in, 237
   cognitive skill development in, 66
   compensation in, 84, 85, 86

evaluation of teachers in, 326
expansion of education coverage in, 55
pupil-teacher ratio in, 172
quality of teacher education in, 151
school choice in, 236
teacher demographics in, 7, 75, 77
teacher salaries in, 8
value of teachers measured in, 68
noncognitive skills, 66
Ñopo, H., 11, 85, 86, 87
Norway, compensation in, 84
no-stakes assessments, 268
nutrition, 5, 66

O

Observatory for Adult Education in Latin America and the Caribbean, 304–5
Ockert, B., 80
OECD countries. *See also* Program for International Student Assessment (PISA)
    alternative certification in, 164
    compensation in, 79
    economic growth and education performance in, 4, 4*f*
    educational attainment in, 58–59
    evaluation of teachers in, 36
    expansion of education coverage in, 3, 55
    instructional time use in, 12
    PISA scores in, 65, 92*n*3
    politics of teacher reforms in, 50
    professional rewards in, 226
    pupil-teacher ratio in, 171*b*
    school leadership training in, 39, 210
    teacher induction in, 34, 180, 181
    teacher standards in, 29, 156, 184
OECS (Organization of Eastern Caribbean States), 180
off-task teacher time, 12–13, 14*f*, 112
Olson, M., 297
One Laptop Per Child (OLPC) initiatives, 16, 116, 211
Ontario, Canada
    bonus pay in, 47
    in-service training in, 203
    managerial oversight in, 234
    peer collaboration in, 38
    professional rewards in, 226, 227, 282
    school leadership training in, 39
Organización de Trabajadores de la Educación del Paraguay (OTEP), 302

Organization of American States, 213
Organization of Eastern Caribbean States (OECS), 180

P

PAIC (Programa de Alfabetização na Idade Certa, Brazil), 204
Panama
    compensation in, 85, 86, 87, 88
    compressed wage scale in, 89, 89*f*
    excess supply of teachers in, 11
    pupil-teacher ratio in, 296
    teacher demographics in, 7, 74, 76, 77
    teacher salaries in, 8
    unemployment among teaching graduates in, 84
    working hours in, 84
Papay, J. P., 209
Paraguay
    demographic shift in, 167
    expansion of education coverage in, 55
    pupil-teacher ratio in, 172, 296
    teachers' unions in, 301*t*, 302, 306
parental education programs, 67
parent feedback, 43, 236–37, 326
parent-teacher associations, 203
Partido Revolucionario Institucional (PRI, Mexico), 305, 312, 314
passive instructional methods, 105
Patrinos, H. A., 259, 274, 282*n*1
pay for performance. *See* bonus pay
peer collaboration, 37, 38, 41, 200, 203, 208, 226
peer review, 187
Peña Nieto, Enrique, 314
pensions, 237–38
performance-based pay, 294. *See also* competency-based promotion and pay
performance measurement, 55–74
    drivers of student learning, 66–72, 68–69*t*, 70–71*f*
    LAC education systems, 55–66, 56–61*f*, 57*t*, 62*b*, 63*t*, 64–65*f*
    teacher effectiveness, 72–74
Pernambuco, Brazil
    bonus pay in, 46, 268–70, 274, 275, 281
    classroom management in, 125
    classroom observation in, 99
    ICT use in, 118
Peru
    accountability pressure in, 42
    accreditation standards in, 149, 150–51

career path reforms in, 124, 246, 257, 258, 280
classroom management in, 128f, 132, 133
classroom observation in, 99
cognitive skill development in, 66
compensation in, 82, 84, 85, 86, 87, 88, 294
decentralization in, 292, 326n3
economic growth and education performance in, 5
entry standards for teacher education in, 25
evaluation of teachers in, 35, 36, 183, 291
excess supply of teachers in, 11
financial incentives in, 43, 44, 238, 279
ICT use in, 16, 116, 118, 211
innovation awards in, 155–56
in-service training in, 208
instructional time use in, 12, 13–14f, 18f, 108, 124
job stability in, 230, 232, 233, 277, 288, 315
managerial oversight in, 277
nonuniversity teacher education programs closed in, 145–46
peer collaboration in, 38
PISA scores in, 60, 62b, 64, 65
politics of teacher reforms in, 325
pre-service teacher practice in, 153
professional rewards in, 41, 229, 277
promotions based on comprehensive performance measures in, 251
promotions based on knowledge and skills tests in, 248–49
quality of teacher education in, 28
recruitment of teachers in, 140, 141, 145–46, 146f, 175
selectivity of teacher education in, 24
teacher demographics in, 7, 74, 76, 77
teacher effectiveness in, 73
teacher salaries in, 8
teachers' unions in, 48, 49, 301t, 302, 304, 305, 315–19
Teach For All program in, 31, 165, 293, 294
unemployment among teaching graduates in, 83–84
unengaged students in, 120
working hours in, 84
Philippines, teacher demographics in, 8
PIBID (Programa Institucional de Bolsa de Iniciação à Docência, Brazil), 154
Pink, Daniel, 226

Piper, B., 200
PISA. *See* Program for International Student Assessment
Plan Ceibal (Uruguay), 212
Planes de Superación Profesional (PSPs), 191, 195
political parties, 305–6
politics of teacher reform, 287–330
  alternative certification, 293–94
  benefits threatened by reforms, 48, 288–89
  bonus pay, 295–96
  case studies, 307–23
  curriculum reform, 289–90
  decentralization and, 291–92
  job tenure loss, 288–89
  lessons learned, 323–26
  overview, 2, 47–51
  performance-based pay, 294
  pupil-teacher ratio, 296–97
  school choice and, 292–93
  sequencing of reforms, 325–26
  sources of union power, 297–307
  student testing, 290
  teacher evaluation systems, 291
  teachers' unions and, 288–97
  union structure and power threatened by reforms, 48, 291–94
  working conditions threatened by reforms, 48, 289–91
prestige as professional reward, 228–29
PRI. *See* Partido Revolucionario Institucional
Primer Colegio Profesional Hondureño de Maestros, 327n8
principals. *See* school leadership
private schools, 67, 90, 236
production function, 97, 98f
professional development, 37–38. *See also* in-service training
professional improvement plans, 191
professional rewards, 40–42, 224, 225–29
Programa de Alfabetização na Idade Certa (PAIC, Brazil), 204
Programa de Formación de Directores de Excelencia (Chile), 210
Programa de Fortalecimiento de la Formación Inicial Docente (Chile), 155
Programa Hondureño de Educación Comunitaria (PROHECO, Honduras), 293
Programa Institucional de Bolsa de Iniciação à Docência (PIBID, Brazil), 154

Program for International Student Assessment (PISA)
  content knowledge and, 78
  economic growth correlated to results of, 3, 58, 59
  math and reading skills as measured on, 62b
  as political tool, 49
  professional rewards and, 226
PROHECO (Programa Hondureño de Educación Comunitaria, Honduras), 293
promotions
  based on comprehensive performance measures, 250–51
  based on knowledge and skills tests, 246–50
  based on student learning results, 251–52
  competency-based, 44, 238, 247, 257
  as professional reward, 228
protests by teachers' unions, 304–5
Protocol for Language Arts Teaching Observations, 185b
Prova de Promoção (Brazil), 73, 121, 249–50
Prova Nacional de Concurso para o Ingresso na Carreira Docente (Brazil), 161
Prueba del Laboratorio Latinoamericano de Evaluación de la Calidad de la Educación (LLECE), 319
Prueba de Selección Universitaria (PSU, Chile), 148, 176n2
Prueba Inicia (Chile), 29, 160–61, 161f
PSPs (Planes de Superación Profesional), 191, 195
pupil-teacher ratio
  politics of teacher reform and, 296–97
  recruitment and, 32, 170–74, 171b, 173t

Q

quality of teacher education, 151–56, 153t, 154f
quality of teachers
  as constraint on education progress, 2
  as driver of learning outcomes, 2, 5–6, 6f
  evaluation of, 188–89, 188–90f

R

Race to the Top grants (U.S.), 197b, 256
Rau, T., 273
recognition as professional reward, 228–29

recruitment, 139–78
  demographic shift and, 167–74, 168f, 169t, 172f
  entry standards for teacher education, 25–27, 26f
  hiring standards, 28–31, 28–30f, 156–66
  key steps in, 139–40, 140f
  overview, 2, 23–34
  pupil-teacher ratios and, 170–74, 171b, 173t
  quality of teacher education, 27–28, 27f, 151–56, 152f, 153t, 154f
  selectivity of teacher education, 23–25, 24f, 31–34, 33f, 144–51, 146f, 150–51f
Red de Maestros pro la Revolución Educativa (Ecuador), 322
Red Maestros de Maestros (Chile), 254
resource teachers, 119
results chain, 97, 98f
Rio de Janeiro, Brazil
  career path reforms in, 255–56
  classroom management in, 133, 135
  classroom observation in, 99
  financial incentives in, 238
  ICT use in, 118, 213, 214b
  in-service training in, 208
  instructional time use in, 13, 14t, 112
  managerial oversight in, 235
  peer collaboration in, 38
  politics of teacher reforms in, 50, 325
  professional rewards in, 41, 227, 277
  teacher induction in, 35, 182b, 183
Rivkin, S. G., 92n4, 209
Roberto Marinho Foundation, 205
Rockoff, J. E., 69
Rothstein, J., 92n4
Rouesseff, Dilma, 305
roving resource teachers, 119

S

SABER Pro examination, 144, 149, 159–60, 183
SADOP (Sindicato Argentino de Docentes Privados), 327n7
Sahlberg, P., 226
salaries. *See* compensation
salary differentials, 237, 238
San Marcos University, 76
Santiago, A., 165
Santibáñez, L., 252

São Paulo, Brazil
  bonus pay in, 296
  career path reforms in, 257, 258, 280
  compensation in, 294
  financial incentives in, 238, 279
  ICT use in, 213
  job stability in, 230
  politics of teacher reforms in, 50, 325
  promotions based on knowledge and skills tests in, 249–50
  teacher effectiveness in, 73
  unengaged students in, 121
SAT. *See* Sistema de Aprendizaje Tutorial
Schady, N., 66
Schneider, B. R., 307, 308, 309, 315
scholarships, 25
school-based management (SBM), 230, 236–37
school choice, 230, 236, 292–93
school infrastructure, 225, 295
school leadership
  accountability pressure, 233–36
  grooming of teachers and, 39–40, 208–10
Scotland
  entry standards for teacher education in, 26
  recruitment of teachers in, 147
  teacher induction in, 181
scripted training, 37, 200, 203–5
Second Regional Comparative and Explanatory Study (SERCE), 49, 63, 152, 308
SEDEBA (Sindicato de Educadores de Buenos Aires), 327*n*7
selectivity of teacher education
  accreditation standards, 149–51, 150–51*f*
  incentives for top students, 147–49
  national teacher education universities, 147
  nonuniversity programs, 145–46, 146*f*
  overview, 23–25, 24*f*, 31–34, 33*f*
self-assessment, 186, 195, 215, 250, 252
self-efficacy, 31
self-esteem, 31, 206*b*
SER (Sistema Nacional de Evaluación y Rendición de Cuentas, Ecuador), 320
SERCE. *See* Second Regional Comparative and Explanatory Study
Shanghai, China
  classroom management in, 132
  evaluation of teachers in, 35, 183
  PISA scores in, 59, 60, 62*b*
  professional rewards in, 226, 228
  teacher education quality in, 11
  teacher standards in, 156

SIDESP (Sindicato de Docentes de Educación Superior del Perú), 327*n*11
SIMCE (Sistema de Medición de la Calidad de la Educación, Chile), 194, 308
Sindicato Argentino de Docentes Privados (SADOP), 327*n*7
Sindicato de Docentes de Educación Superior del Perú (SIDESP), 327*n*11
Sindicato de Educadores de Buenos Aires (SEDEBA), 327*n*7
Sindicato de Trabajadores de la Educación (SNTE), 302, 307, 311–15, 327*n*9
Sindicato Único de Trabajadores en la Educación del Perú (SUTEP), 304, 307, 315–19
SINEACE (Sistema Nacional de Evaluación, Acreditación y Certificación de la Calidad Educativa, Peru), 150
Singapore
  accountability pressures in, 282
  bonus pay in, 47
  content knowledge in, 78
  entry standards for teacher education in, 26
  evaluation of teachers in, 35, 183, 191, 192*b*
  ICT use in, 212
  job stability in, 231, 277
  managerial oversight in, 234
  National Institute for Education in, 25
  PISA scores in, 60, 62*b*
  professional rewards in, 41, 226, 228, 276
  pupil-teacher ratio in, 32, 170
  recruitment of teachers in, 139, 141*f*, 143–44*b*, 147
  school leadership training in, 39, 40, 210
  selectivity of teacher education in, 24, 140
  teacher education quality in, 11
  teacher effectiveness in, 74
  teacher standards in, 156
Sistema de Aprendizaje Tutorial (SAT, Honduras), 37, 164, 204, 293
Sistema de Evaluación del Desempeño Profesional Docente (Docentemas, Chile), 186, 189
Sistema de Medición de la Calidad de la Educación (SIMCE, Chile), 194, 308
Sistema Nacional de Evaluación, Acreditación y Certificación de la Calidad Educativa (SINEACE, Peru), 150

Sistema Nacional de Evaluación de Desempeño (SNED, Chile), 45, 46, 239, 264, 270–73, 271–72*b*, 275, 309
Sistema Nacional de Evaluación y Rendición de Cuentas (SER, Ecuador), 320
SNED. *See* Sistema Nacional de Evaluación de Desempeño
SNTE. *See* Sindicato de Trabajadores de la Educación
socioeconomic background, 5, 97
socioemotional competencies, 66
Sorto, M. A., 73
Springer, M. G., 267
Stallings, J., 12, 100, 105
Stallings Classroom Snapshot, 12, 100–105, 101–3*b*, 133–34*b*
strikes by teachers' unions, 304–5
Sun, Y., 217*n*4
Sundararaman, V., 264, 265
supply of teachers, 11
Suriname, quality of teacher education in, 151
SUTEP. *See* Sindicato Único de Trabajadores en la Educación del Perú
Sweden
　compensation in, 80, 82, 88
　compressed wage scale in, 11, 89
　recruitment of teachers in, 147
Switzerland, teacher education quality in, 11

T

Taiwan, China, content knowledge in, 78
TALIS (Teaching and Learning International Survey), 181
Taut, S., 217*n*4
teacher absenteeism, 230, 232, 232*f*
teacher demographics, 7–11, 74–91, 75–80*f*, 84*f*
teacher education
　entry standards for, 25–27, 26*f*
　proliferation of, 11
　quality of, 27–28, 27*f*, 151–56, 153*t*, 154*f*
　selectivity of, 23–25, 24*f*, 31–34, 33*f*
teacher learning groups, 226
Teachers of Teachers Network, 213, 254
teachers' unions
　legal strategies, 306–7
　linkages to political parties, 305–6
　political strategies of, 304–7
　politics of teacher reform and, 2, 3, 288–97
　research and analysis sponsored by, 307
　sources of power, 297–307, 298–301*t*
　strikes and protests by, 304–5

Teacher Training Institute (Brazil), 182*b*
Teach For All (TFA), 31, 74, 108, 164–65, 166, 277, 293–94
Teach For America, 31, 163, 166, 293
Teaching and Learning International Survey (TALIS), 181
Teach Like a Champion (Lemov), 182*b*, 207
Teach to the Future program (Intel), 212
TEDS-Math (Teacher Education and Development Study in Mathematics), 77–78
temporary contracts, 249
temporary license teachers, 30, 162
TFA. *See* Teach For All
think tanks, 307
360-degree feedback, 43, 251, 278
Trends in International Mathematics and Science Study (TIMMS), 49, 78, 308
Tucker, M., 226, 227
Turner, L. J., 268

U

Umansky, I., 40, 224
UNAE (Universidad Nacional de Educación, Ecuador), 25, 147
unengaged students, 17, 17*f*, 119–22, 120–21*f*
UNESCO (United Nations Educational, Scientific, and Cultural Organization), 32, 167, 176*n*6, 290
Union de Docentes Argentinos (UDA), 302
Unión Nacional de Educadores (UNE), 302, 303, 319–23
unions. *See* teachers' unions
United Kingdom
　alternative certification in, 164
　compensation in, 84
　evaluation of teachers in, 191
　probationary periods in, 181
　recruitment of teachers in, 147
United States
　accountability pressure in, 42
　alternative certification in, 164, 293
　bonus pay in, 46, 258, 259, 264, 267–68, 281
　career path reforms in, 246, 256
　cash incentives for students in, 97
　classroom management in, 105
　compensation in, 79, 84, 294
　evaluation of teachers in, 35, 191, 327*n*18
　financial incentives in, 238
　in-service training in, 203
　job stability in, 231, 282*n*2

managerial oversight in, 235
pension benefits in, 289
pre-service teacher practice in, 154
probationary periods in, 181
pupil-teacher ratio in, 170
school leadership training in, 209
teacher induction in, 34–35, 180
value of teachers measured in, 6, 68, 69, 74
Universidad Nacional de Educación (UNAE, Ecuador), 25, 147
Universidad Nacional de San Marcos, 307
university entrance exams, 26
University of São Paulo, 76
"up or out" strategy, 279
Uruguay
  compensation in, 84, 85, 86, 87
  curriculum reform in, 289
  excess supply of teachers in, 11
  ICT use in, 212
  PISA scores in, 60, 63, 65
  pupil-teacher ratio in, 171, 172, 296
  student testing in, 290
  teacher demographics in, 7, 75, 76, 77
  teacher salaries in, 8
  teachers' unions in, 301t, 302, 306, 307
  unemployment among teaching graduates in, 83
  working hours in, 84
U.S. Agency for International Development, 203
UTeach Teacher Observation Protocol, 185b

V

Vegas, E., 40, 224, 238
Venezuela, República Bolivariana de
  economic growth and education performance in, 4
  PISA scores in, 63
voucher schools, 90, 230–31, 233, 253, 271–72b, 292–94, 304

W

Washington, DC public schools
  accountability pressure in, 42
  career path reforms in, 278
  compensation in, 294
  evaluation of teachers in, 36, 184, 197–99b, 215
  job stability in, 231, 277
  teacher evaluation in, 197–99b
Woessmann, L., 56, 58, 59, 60, 63, 73, 77
women
  compressed wage scale and, 89
  job stability of teaching and, 83
  as teachers, 7
Wyckoff, J., 198b

Y

Young Lives Longitudinal Survey, 140

ECO-AUDIT
Environmental Benefits Statement

The World Bank is committed to preserving endangered forests and natural resources. ***Great Teachers: How to Raise Student Learning in Latin America and the Caribbean*** was printed on recycled paper with 50 percent postconsumer fiber in accordance with the recommended standards for paper usage set by the Green Press Initiative, a nonprofit program supporting publishers in using fiber that is not sourced from endangered forests. For more information, visit www.greenpressinitiative.org.

Saved:
- 22 trees
- 10 million British thermal units of total energy
- 1,886 pounds of net greenhouse gases (CO_2 equivalent)
- 10,226 gallons of waste water
- 685 pounds of solid waste

www.ingramcontent.com/pod-product-compliance
Lightning Source LLC
Chambersburg PA
CBHW071757300426
44116CB00009B/1114